THE FIRM

PENNY JUNOR

The Firm

The Troubled Life of the House of Windsor

Thomas Dunne Books
St. Martin's Press ✖ New York

FOR LUPUS

THOMAS DUNNE BOOKS.
An imprint of St. Martin's Press.

www.stmartins.com

Library of Congress Cataloging-in-Publication Data (TK)

ISBN 0-312-35274-3 3364 5416 11/05
EAN 978-0-312-35274-5

First published in Great Britain by HarperCollins*Publishers*

First Edition: July 2005

10 9 8 7 6 5 4 3 2 1

List of Illustrations

The King, Queen and Princess on the balcony (Rex)

Lady Diana Spencer in see-through skirt (Rex)

The Royal Family on the balcony with Diana and young Princes at Trooping the Colour (Tim Graham)

The Family on the balcony during the Golden Jubilee (Tim Graham)

The Party at the Palace (Tim Graham)

The Prince of Wales shooting with Michael Fawcett (Eddie Boldizsar/Rex)

Paul Burrell carrying a corgi (Tim Graham)

The Queen arriving in Saudi Arabia on Concorde (Tim Graham)

The Queen and Prince Philip in the Gold State Coach (Tim Graham)

Prince Philip in bearskin (Les Wilson/Rex)

Queen Elizabeth the Queen Mother with Irish Guards and wolfhound (Tim Graham)

The Queen at the Windsor Horse Show (Les Wilson/Rex)

The Kiss on the balcony (Tim Graham)

Charles and Diana in Korea (Tim Graham)

The Princess of Wales with children in her arms (Tim Graham)

Princess Anne standing by a cot (Tim Graham)

Diana crouching to talk to hospice patient (Tim Graham)

Diana in surgical mask (Rex)

The Firm

Prince William with hand to mouth for 18th birthday (Rex)

Queen Elizabeth II's coronation (Rex)

Queen Mother's funeral (Tim Graham)

Prince William over a hot stove (Rex)

Prince William in school uniform with Union Jack waistcoat (Rex)

Prince Edward with Sir Cliff Richard at *It's a Royal Knockout* (Rex)

Princes William and Harry playing polo on bicycles (Les Wilson/Rex)

The Queen wrapped up against the weather with a labrador and spaniel (Greaves/Rex)

The Queen with Princess Anne and Zara Philips, all on horseback (Tim Graham)

A tearful Queen leaving the 9/11 memorial service (Tim Graham)

The Prince of Wales and Camilla Parker Bowles on the evening their engagement was announced (Rex)

Prince Charles with Lady Diana Spencer after their engagement (Tim Graham)

Prince Charles and Prince William on the 50th anniversary of VJ Day (Tim Graham)

Prince Charles and Prince William with cows on the Home Farm (Les Wilson/Rex)

Prince Harry being restrained outside a London nightclub (David Abiaw/Rex)

The Princess of Wales during the *Panorama* interview (Rex)

The Queen at the Derby – both glum and jubilant (Les Wilson/Rex)

The Queen and Duke of Edinburgh meeting flag-waving children (Tim Graham)

The Queen arriving at Bristol on the Royal Train (Tim Graham)

Princes William and Harry sharing a joke on the balcony at Buckingham Palace (Les Wilson/Rex)

Acknowledgements

Books like this are only ever as good as the people one talks to, and these days, in the wake of so many damaging memoirs and betrayals, it is so much easier for people close to the Royal Family, in whatever capacity, to play safe and say they don't want to be involved. I understand their position entirely. Fortunately, however, there are some who are prepared to take a risk – and I would like to thank those people most sincerely for their generosity in giving up their time to talk to me (sometimes, when my tape recorder failed me, on more than one occasion!) and to pass on their knowledge and expertise about the business of monarchy. I hope that I have faithfully represented them – any errors are down to me (and possibly my tape recorder). Many of them spoke to me anonymously; those who were prepared to be named appear throughout the text so I will simply say a blanket thank you. I am very much indebted to you all and have very much enjoyed meeting you.

I have also had a lot of help from the Press Offices at Buckingham Palace and Clarence House, and would particularly like to thank Penny Russell-Smith, Samantha Cohen, Colette Saunders, Ailsa Anderson, David Pogson, Meryl Keeling, Emma Copper and Elizabeth Plant – and from across the Mall,

The Firm

Paddy Harverson, Patrick Harrison, Rebecca Packham and Alexandra Birney.

My publisher Trevor Dolby has been inspirational and I have thoroughly enjoyed working with him. Likewise, Monica Chakraverty, Commissioning Editor at HarperCollins, who helped pull everything together in break-neck time without ever losing her good humour or patience. My thanks to them both – and to everyone else at HarperCollins, particularly Terence Caven, Louise Edwards, Lucy Vanderbilt, Jennifer Callaghan and Rhiannon James.

My thanks also to photographer Les Wilson for having found such perfect photographs for this book and taken the one of me for the jacket.

Then there is Jane Turnbull, my friend and agent who is just the very best.

Contents

Introduction

Once upon a time kings and queens ruled the land. There was nothing mysterious about it; some of them invaded to take up the throne, others inherited via one route or another, but once installed they governed, they were the executive, they were all-powerful, they had their own armies and they chopped off the heads of anyone who thwarted them. People may not have liked their monarch, they may have grumbled about taxes or the extravagance of the court, or been tired of endless skirmishes with France, but no one was ever in any doubt about what their monarch was for.

Twelve hundred years later, after many changes (and a brief period in the seventeenth century when there was no monarch at all), we have a Queen who has no executive power, who acts entirely on the advice of ministers, who reads speeches that others have written, and who relies upon government for her keep. Four years after she came to the throne, a poll suggested that 34 per cent of the population believed that Elizabeth II had been chosen by God. Today you'd be hard pushed to find anyone who believed that God was involved in the process – it's becoming enough of a challenge to find people who believe in God, full stop. Under these circumstances, in an age when our social order is based upon merit rather than inheritance, it is not surprising that we should ask what monarchy is for. Most children haven't a clue, wouldn't recognize members of the Royal Family and probably couldn't care less. Their local football team or the latest contestants in *I'm A Celebrity . . . Get Me Out Of Here!* are more relevant to their lives. There is indifference among the younger generation that must make the future of the monarchy highly questionable.

Republicanism is nothing new. There has always been a minority chipping away at the credibility of the monarchy, and although they seem to be increasingly vocal, they are still very much in the minority. But today even monarchists are beginning to question whether the institution, steeped as it is in history and tradition, can survive in the current climate of indifference and disrespect towards institutions and author-ity. And perhaps more importantly, as the newest member, the controversial figure of Camilla Parker Bowles is finally welcomed into the fold, as HRH the Duchess of Cornwall, whether the Royal Family, as individuals, can survive the ever more intrusive and destructive demands of the modern media.

The world has changed during the course of the present Queen's reign, arguably more radically in the time span than at any period in history. Television was in its infancy when the Queen came to the throne in 1952. Many families, my own included, bought their first television set to watch the coronation – tiny little black and white sets that had to warm up before you saw a picture which then shrunk to a white dot when you turned them off. Fifty-two years later even the most modest mobile home has a colour television with a satellite dish on the roof, and in most households people would sell their granny before parting with the TV. It sits in pride of place, chattering away every waking hour, and defines our view of the world. News rolls seamlessly into drama, fact into fiction and all that is remembered is the sound bite.

And what television has created is the cult of the celebrity.

People whose faces we recognize from the screen are the new idols, no matter whether they have talent, wit or wisdom. If their face has been on the box often enough for it to become familiar, they have instant status and national fame. And the public is greedy to know everything about its celebrities – which is where newspapers come into their own.

Newspapers have also changed since the fifties. When the Queen first came to the throne the newspapers, reflecting the age, were deferential towards the monarch. Proprietors could be relied upon to keep any whiff of royal scandal out of the papers. There were two court correspondents employed by the Press Association who went to Buckingham Palace for briefings – dressed in morning dress and top hat – and meekly lapped up official notices and announcements.

Today's equivalent is a tabloid 'rat pack' charged by their editors with finding exclusives – gossip, scandal and as much personal detail as possible, and, in some cases, by whatever means possible. And the Royal Family is considered to be fair game, as the Countess of Wessex discovered to her cost when a reporter posing as a Middle Eastern sheik tried to employ her PR company. Actors, footballers, pop stars, politicians – many have suffered similar stings or found themselves unwillingly making headline news. And for a family that is dependent upon an army of staff to run their lives, it was only a matter of time before some of them became disgruntled or found irresistible the opportunity to make money by speaking to the press.

This is the environment in which today's monarchy has to operate. It needs the oxygen of publicity no less than actors, entertainers and politicians, or anyone else with something to sell. The Queen understands this only too well, from history as well as her own experience. Never has the monarchy been so unpopular in modern times as when Queen Victoria vanished from sight after Prince Albert's death in 1861. In her grief, she hid herself away at Balmoral and, although she carried on the affairs of state perfectly well, she did not make a public appearance in London for three years. The people were furious and when they did finally catch sight of her they pelted her carriage with stones. It was apparently not enough that she saw to her constitutional duties. The present Queen stayed away from London after the death of the Princess of Wales – she was also at Balmoral – and the public was again furious. They wanted to see their Queen. The newspaper headlines during the week before the funeral were the most critical of her reign and it was not until she returned to London and spoke to the nation on television, both as a grandmother and as Head of State, that the crisis, possibly the most serious of her reign, was averted.

The question is why? Why did so many thousands of people flock to Buckingham Palace in their grief rather than to Kensington Palace, which was where Diana had lived after all? Why did the nation want to see the Queen so badly? Strictly speaking, at the time of her death Diana was no longer a member of the Royal Family, and anyway, ought it not to have been her former husband to whom they should have looked?

The reason, I suspect, goes to the very heart of what monarchy is all about. It goes far beyond the constitutional. The Queen provides the focus for the nation's emotion. When the nation is in mourning, it looks to the monarch to lead the process. In every major disaster, from Aberfan in 1966, where schoolchildren were buried beneath tons of coal slag, to 9/11, in 2001, when al-Qaeda suicide bombers flew passenger aircraft into the World Trade Center in New York and the Pentagon in Washington, or the Asian tsunami that killed over

120,000 people on Boxing Day in 2004 and left millions homeless, the Queen or another close member of the Royal Family has been there to express the nation's grief. When the nation is jubilant at having won the World Cup or gold medals at the Olympics, the Queen congratulates and honours the winning teams on our behalf. When the East End of London and other cities were bombed during the Second World War the Queen's parents, George VI and Queen Elizabeth, went to visit the devastation and much of the warmth that attached to the Queen Mother throughout her life came as a result of the solidarity and concern she and the King showed to the people of London.

The magic of monarchy is in the seeing. And it *is* magic – despite what cynics might say. Many of the people who work for the Queen and accompany her on away days and foreign tours describe their jobs as being the 'Feel-Good Business'. And there is no doubt that people do feel good when they meet her. It doesn't seem to matter that the papers have been filled with tawdry details of her children's domestic disasters – the day she comes to town they stand for hours in all weathers clutching Union Jacks. They cheer when her gleaming Bentley with its royal flag on the roof appears with its police motor-cycle outriders down the car-free high street. They cheer again when she steps out, smiling and waving; they reach forward at perilous angles to offer flowers and posies, proffer their children, and click frantically at their pocket Pentaxes when she comes within range. Everyone is smiling, everyone is elated and everyone takes away with them a memory to treasure for the rest of their lives. And for those who strike lucky and are the ones the Queen stops and talks to, they will probably never have an experience to match it.

Of course, the people who want to see the Queen on these visits already like her and probably approve of the institution.

If they didn't they wouldn't bother standing and waiting in all weathers. But there are other occasions on which the Queen meets people when that is not the case. Not every worker in a factory, hospital or school is a monarchist; not everyone who is invited to a garden party or a reception at Buckingham Palace is a devoted fan, but there are not many who fail to be impressed when they meet the Queen, or who are indifferent to the recognition of their work and worth that such a meeting implies.

Recognizing, thanking, praising and rewarding citizens for their bravery, dedication, charity or work is another part of the monarch's job. At one end of the scale outstanding service is rewarded to an individual with a peerage or a knighthood – although most of that is on the Prime Minister's say-so and overtly political – but at the other end a visit to a factory is no less significant, and for the people on the production line to be asked to explain what they do by the Queen or the Prince of Wales, her heir, or even another member of the Royal Family, is a real fillip. It's like as a schoolchild being singled out for praise by the headmistress when you didn't even think she knew your name. People feel that their effort has been noticed and is appreciated, and in the lower-paid jobs that tend to be vocational, such as nursing or care work, that matters.

During the nineteenth century the family became an important part of monarchy, as Benjamin Disraeli, Prime Minister in 1868 and again from 1874 to 1880, acknowledged: 'The influence of the Crown is not confined merely to political affairs. England is a domestic country. Here the home is revered and the hearth sacred. The nation is represented by a family – the Royal Family; and if that family is educated with a sense of responsibility and a sentiment of public duty, it is difficult to exaggerate the salutary influence they may exercise over a nation.'

Introduction

Walter Bagehot was the first to note this. A Victorian economist and political analyst, Bagehot is often quoted from his book *The English Constitution*, first published in 1867 and which still provides the most enduring analysis of monarchy to date. 'A family on the throne is an interesting idea,' he wrote. 'It brings down the pride of sovereignty to the level of petty life. No feeling could seem more childish than the enthusiasm of the English at the marriage of the Prince of Wales. They treated as a great political event, what, looked at as a matter of pure business, was very small indeed. But no feeling could be more like common human nature as it is, and as it is likely to be.'

The Prince of Wales he was referring to was the future Edward VII and the marriage that of Edward to the Danish Princess Alexandra in 1863, but he could just as easily have been writing about the first marriage of the present Prince of Wales to Lady Diana Spencer in 1981, 112 years later. There was a great display of childish enthusiasm for the event: the newspapers talked about little else for weeks beforehand, London's Oxford Street hosted the biggest street party in the world in the couple's honour, there was a massive fireworks display in Hyde Park and celebratory beacons were lit up and down the country. On the day of the wedding – declared a public holiday – millions lined the route between Buckingham Palace and St Paul's Cathedral; the first arrivals had staked their claim to a piece of pavement three days before the wedding and an estimated seven hundred million more watched it on television. The Royal Wedding, as it was referred to for many years, notwithstanding the fact it had not been the only one, was a major landmark in most people's memories, and until the cracks began to show it was an event that reaffirmed the monarchy's place in people's hearts.

Those were halcyon days. For the first thirty-five years of

the Queen's reign the Royal Family had been everything the nation could have wished for, a model for us all. But since then three of her four children have been through a divorce, with all the tawdry details paraded by the press, and the influence they exercise over the nation today is perhaps less than salutary. The troubled private life of the Prince of Wales, who finally, in February 2005, announced his intention to marry Camilla Parker Bowles, has made international news on and off for nearly twenty years. The breakdown of his marriage to Diana – according to her because of his obsession with Camilla – her revelations about their life together, his admission of adultery on prime-time television, their divorce and her subsequent death, split the nation's loyalty. Some people recognized it to be an ill-starred match from the start and felt nothing but sympathy for everyone involved. Others, for whom Diana was an icon, roundly blamed the Prince, as Diana had done, for having destroyed her happiness. And the question of whether he should marry Camilla Parker Bowles, the figure at the centre of it, caused even greater division in the country.

But their private lives are a distraction. What the Royal Family does do, divorced or not, is work tirelessly for the people of Britain. First and foremost they give an inestimable boost to charity. The Queen, the Duke of Edinburgh and each of their children, as well as several more distant relations, are all attached to charities – hundreds of them – to which they give time and support, and those charities benefit demonstrably from their royal connection. The profile goes up and so too do the donations; and there are many areas of national life, including education and health, that rely heavily upon the charitable sector.

Then there is tourism. Again, it is demonstrable that having a real live Royal Family who walk the corridors of Buckingham Palace, the Palace of Holyroodhouse and Windsor Castle is much more of a draw to visitors than empty buildings steeped in history; in Britain visitors get the best of both worlds. Hotels, shops, restaurants, pubs, trains, planes, taxis, car hire firms, not to mention galleries, museums and the regular tourist attractions and street stalls, all reap the rewards of having a town full of tourists.

But there are other functions of monarchy. Representing the nation to itself is another important one. The fact that the Royal Family has been a fixture in the life of everyone born and bred in either Britain or one of her dominions means that we associate the Royal Family with our roots, with home. They are familiar, just as red telephone boxes and double-decker buses are familiar, or driving on the left-hand side of the road, and for many people those familiars are comforting and define who we are and what we stand for. You may dislike buses, think phone boxes old-fashioned and think we would be better off driving on the right, but those fixtures still denote home and form part of our identity.

And because they are a fixture and change only imperceptibly, their very presence creates stability and continuity. The Queen has appeared in our living rooms on Christmas afternoon for more than fifty years; she has been Trooping the Colour on her official birthday on Horse Guards Parade for as long, and laying a wreath at the Cenotaph every 11 November. She and the Royal Family spend August in Scotland, Christmas at Sandringham, Easter at Windsor Castle and the Queen hasn't missed Royal Ascot since 1945. It takes a birth, a death or a disaster to alter the routine of the Royal Family, and when so much else in life is turning upside down, that permanence and predictability provides an anchor, a national reference point, which makes people feel secure.

But her most obvious role is Head of State; she is also

Supreme Governor of the Church of England, Colonel-in-Chief of the Armed Forces and Head of the Commonwealth. As a constitutional monarch, the Queen has no executive power – everything is done on advice from her ministers – and she reigns rather than rules, but she has great capacity for influence. She keeps her ministers in check and the system keeps the monarch in check. She undertakes ceremonial duties such as opening Parliament – and has the prerogative, among other things, to close it too should the need arise – she receives visiting heads of state, goes on state visits to other countries, receives diplomats, holds investitures and keeps abreast of affairs of state by weekly audiences with her prime minister and 'doing the boxes', her daily digest of Cabinet papers, Foreign and Commonwealth telegrams and ministerial papers. And having spent more than fifty years steeped in state papers, travelling the world, visiting cities, towns and villages, meeting everyone from presidents to farm and factory workers, she has more experience than anyone else in government. She has worked with eleven prime ministers and was discussing affairs of state with Winston Churchill before Tony Blair was even born.

That, in a nutshell, is what monarchy is for. Its critics say the system is outdated, that the hierarchical and hereditary nature of the institution is unacceptable in modern society, that the Royal Family lives a life of privilege and luxury at public expense and does nothing to earn it; individuals have been accused of abusing their position. All points that need to be addressed in assessing whether the monarchy is relevant in twenty-first-century Britain and whether it is likely to have a future beyond the reign of Queen Elizabeth II.

What follows is highly subjective. Having written about the Royal Family on and off for more than twenty years I have seen a lot of change, met a lot of people who have worked with and for members of the Royal Family, and seen the effect that they and their work and activity have had on individuals and society as a whole. I was not a dedicated monarchist when I started twenty years ago, and I am certainly not without criticism now. Nor am I without fears for the future. But I am convinced that this system that has stood the test of time, hierarchical and hereditary though it is, enriches our community beyond measure and Britain would be a poorer place without a monarch at the helm. And this is why . . .

ONE

An Extraordinary Way to Live

My first encounter with Buckingham Palace was in 1981. The Prince of Wales had just married Lady Diana Spencer in a spectacular ceremony at St Paul's Cathedral; the country had been in a fever of excitement for months and I had been commissioned to write a biography of the bride. I approached the Palace and was instantly rebuffed. A letter on thick cream paper with Buckingham Palace at the top of the page, embossed in red, but with no address, informed me that they would not be able to help in any way. It was signed by Michael Shea, Press Secretary to HM The Queen – a very nice man, I subsequently discovered, an ex-diplomat, who is now an author himself, although not of royal books.

Four months later I wrote again and Michael Shea invited me in to see him. I will never forget the sensation of scrunching across the pink gravel at the front of Buckingham Palace, watched by dozens of Japanese tourists and busloads from Burnley, and stepping through the Privy Purse door at the extreme right of the building, into a world where time seemed to have stopped. Outside were guards standing stock-still in scarlet coats and black bearskins, with rifles beside their right ears, which immediately brought to mind A. A. Milne's refrain about changing guard at Buckingham Palace. Inside were footmen in red waistcoats and tails and I was invited to wait in a room beautifully furnished with antiques. A copy of *The Times* – I am tempted to say, crisply ironed, but that would be a lie – lay on a table.

Michael Shea appeared, friendly palm outstretched, and took me down wide red-carpeted corridors into his office, another room beautifully furnished with antiques; not as one might have expected the communications centre of the British monarchy to have looked in 1981. But then there was no great tradition of helping the media at the Palace. Up until just thirteen years before, the man in Shea's shoes was known as 'The Abominable No Man'. Commander Richard Colville hated the press and for the twenty years he held the job he made no secret of his contempt. Newspapers didn't even bother ringing the Palace when a royal story cropped up because they knew there would be no comment. Every other organization I had dealt with took public relations seriously; press officers went out of their way to help journalists and writers get the material they needed, aware that a good relationship could be extremely useful all round. Michael Shea was charm itself, but I wasn't convinced that the Palace had come far from the days when the colour and fabric of the Queen's outfit was their stock in trade. And in the absence of reliable guidance, journalists were apt to make mistakes, and *in extremis* to make things up.

These days they are more inventive. On 20 November 2003 the Royal Family awoke to the news that for the last two months they had had an impostor in their midst. Ryan Parry, a *Daily Mirror* reporter, had applied for a job as a trainee footman at Buckingham Palace, and, despite giving dodgy references, had been given a job which brought him into direct contact with members of the Royal Family. He was given a security pass that allowed him access to all areas and within days he had been shown the hiding place for skeleton keys to open every door in the Palace. He was still *in situ* when President Bush arrived on his state visit, amidst one of the tightest and most expensive security operations ever mounted in Britain. Not once was Parry questioned and not once were bags that he brought into the Palace checked. For two months he carried a camera in his pocket and the photographs he took of private areas, including bedrooms, were spread across the pages of the *Daily Mirror* for two days until the Palace sought an injunction to stop any more material being published.

It was a terrifying breach of security. Parry repeatedly pointed out that, had he been a terrorist, he could have killed the Queen or any member of the Royal Family. He could even have killed the President of the United States.

But as Edward Griffiths, the Deputy Master of the Household who employed the man, points out, he wasn't. 'He was neither a criminal nor had links with terrorists. In that sense he passed all the security checks.' What the system doesn't allow for is journalists posing as would-be terrorists.

Parry's stunt was dressed up as a security alert. And, post 9/11, terrorism is a very real threat, although I'd have thought today's suicide bombers are unlikely to go through the charade of applying for a post as an under-footman at Buckingham Palace. There must be quicker and more spectacular methods of blowing up the Queen or annihilating the British Royal Family. This was simply the most audacious assault yet on the Queen's privacy and the privacy of other members of her family. And that was what had copies of the *Daily Mirror* flying off the shelves and newspapers and television channels all over the world reproducing the pictures. It was nothing more noble than the desire to see how the most famous family in Britain, notoriously secretive about its private life, actually lives. And the surprise was that the Queen, who lives in such grand palaces and castles, wears priceless diamonds and jewels and is reputed to be one of the richest women in the world, keeps her breakfast cornflakes in plastic Tupperware boxes, and when she's not hosting state banquets for 160 she has supper in front of the television watching serials and soaps.

The word dysfunctional has often been used to describe the House of Windsor and it's hard to find a better word. It's equally hard to know why they behave so strangely. It is not that there is a lack of affection. The Prince of Wales has a tricky relationship with his father but that aside, the family are all very fond of one another, and in private there are great displays of affection when they meet and a lot of jokes and laughter. But they don't talk to one another in the way that most families who enjoy one another's company do. They don't pick up the phone when they have something to say, and would never dream of saying 'What a brilliant speech you gave last Wednesday' – praise for each other's achievements is not something they go in for – or 'I've got a free evening, what are you up to?' They write memos to each other or liaise through private secretaries.

And yet it seems to be only contact within the family that they find so difficult. They all make phone calls perfectly happily to courtiers, friends, government ministers and the people running their charities. Indeed, the Prince of Wales is seldom off the phone, as his private secretaries, and more particularly their wives, know all too well. He often makes calls himself – although ever since he announced who was calling and the voice at the other end said, 'Yes, and I'm the Queen of Sheba', he has said it is his Private Secretary calling until he is certain he has the person he wants.

The inter-family formality is perhaps a result of there being no clear distinction between their business and personal lives. They are on duty so much of the time and live so much on top of the job that they see more of their private secretaries than they do of their spouses or children. Yet although the relationship with their private secretaries is close, it is almost never a personal one. While the private secretaries are in post they are indispensable, not just in running their principals' lives but also as sounding boards and occasionally confidants. They know everything that goes on, everything that passes through their bosses' heads. But they are never friends, and as soon as they have gone, and someone else is in post, with very few exceptions they are lucky if they get a Christmas card.

The time of my first meeting with Michael Shea in 1981 were heady days for the House of Windsor. The wedding had been a triumph – 'the stuff of which fairy tales are made' as the Archbishop of Canterbury had said in his address. Diana, who was tall, leggy and gloriously photogenic, was on her way to becoming a superstar, and after months of recession, depression and inner-city riots, extravagant though it was, a full-blown state wedding with grand coaches and all the paraphernalia was just what the country needed. For most people it was a welcome distraction, a wonderful opportunity to celebrate; it was a boost to the nation's morale, to tourism and to the security and popularity of the monarchy.

Diana had very exceptional qualities. I remember watching her during her first visit to Wales with the Prince, immediately after the honeymoon. As she climbed out of the car at their first stop, she looked briefly to her husband for reassurance and then set off into the crowds with a big smile on her face and arms outstretched to shake as many hands as she could reach. She was a natural; there wasn't an elderly person in a wheelchair or a babe in arms that she didn't notice and single out for attention. A thirty-second conversation is going to be banal at the best of times, but she seemed to find just the right words. 'What nice shiny medals,' she said to one hunchbacked

5

old soldier, and then to his beaming wife, 'Did you polish them for him?' And when a seven-year-old boy called out from a couple of rows back, 'My dad says give us a kiss', she smiled and responded, 'Well then, you'd better have one', and leaning right forward gave the boy a kiss on the cheek.

The crowds were contained behind barriers on either side of the street, as with all such visits, leaving the middle clear for the royal party. Diana and Charles took one side each and there were audible groans of disappointment when people realized that they would get Charles rather than Diana. It was no secret that the enthusiasm and the flowers were all for Diana. 'Do you want me to give those to her?' Charles said time and time again as people held posies aloft and looked longingly in her direction. 'I seem to do nothing but collect flowers these days. I know my role.' He was laughing, and I have no doubt at all that at that time he was terribly proud of his wife and pleased that people liked her, but as time went by and the pattern repeated itself endlessly, his laughter began to ring hollow.

He was not used to sharing the limelight. He had been the centre of attention wherever he went for thirty-two years – and he was being eclipsed by his wife. His work, his speeches, his visits, everything was being overshadowed by Diana; and through no fault of her own. Later it became a deliberate ploy but at that time she was as surprised as anyone by the mania which gripped the nation. Every day some trivial story provided an excuse to have her on the front page of the newspapers. Charles began to lose heart – and who can blame him? There were so many serious and important issues that needed airing but no one seemed to be listening. All they seemed to care about was Diana's wardrobe. Diana wore pearl chokers that had scarcely been seen since the nineteenth century and suddenly the shops were full of them. She wore culottes on honeymoon and culottes returned to fashion; high necks and they too flooded the market; and her hairstyle was copied in every high-street salon.

Diana's popularity was phenomenal but it was not the first time that the nation, or indeed the world, had fallen in love with a beautiful royal princess. The Queen is good-looking now in her seventies – as the young Princess Elizabeth she was breathtakingly pretty. She was not tall and rangy like Diana, and her style was quite different, but she had flawless skin, a good figure and the most radiant smile that won hearts as surely as Diana's did thirty years later. When the mania over Diana was at its height, one of the Queen's courtiers said, 'Ma'am, you will never have seen anything like the publicity Charles and Diana are having.' 'You were not around,' she said witheringly, 'when Margaret and I were having our future husbands talent-spotted for us. In comparison with the width and breadth and depth of the media in those days, it was just as great if not greater. Daily we were being lined up with some new suitor.' 'I couldn't argue,' he says. People turned out in their thousands not just in Britain but in the countries she visited all over the world to see Princess Elizabeth and cheer her. Monarchy at that time was revered in a way that the youth of today would find incomprehensible.

Her marriage in November 1947 to the Greek Prince Philip, a tall, blond, handsome naval officer, riveted a nation still in the grip of post-war austerity. It was broadcast on the radio in forty-two countries, millions of people sat glued to their sets, thousands lined the route to Westminster Abbey, dozens camped out in the Mall overnight to be sure of their place, and all over the country there were parties, fireworks and celebrations.

At her coronation six years later the traffic jams in London, into which people had begun flooding ten days before the ceremony, were so bad that the police had to ban all but priority and public service vehicles from entering an area within a two-mile radius of Westminster. 'Never has there been such excitement,' wrote Jock Colville, her Private Secretary, 'never has a monarch received such adulation.' Sir Charles Petrie, the monarchist historian, concurred. 'For the first few years of her reign,' he wrote in 1961, 'she was the subject of adulation unparalleled since the days of Louis XIV.'

The excitement of the coronation went on for weeks, and the adulation for perhaps the first ten years of her reign, but as the Queen's biographer Ben Pimlott observed, 'Popularity is not normally seen as a reason for self-appraisal – it is more likely to encourage a belief that the existing formula is a successful one ... Hence in the mid-1950s, on the back of the fragile post-war recovery, and cosseted by governments that were happy to bask in the reflected glory, the monarchy wasted its most bountiful years – taking what it was given in mindless admiration as its due.'

Elizabeth II was never going to be a radical monarch in any event. Her personality didn't allow it. She was too shy and introverted, too conservative, too responsible to risk rocking the boat. She stepped into King George VI's shoes when she was just twenty-five, a young mother with two small children and a passive acceptance of her destiny but no burning ambition to change either the world or the monarchy. She hero-worshipped her father and he was her role model; he was not the most charismatic of men, he was shy and had struggled with a stammer all his life, but he cared about people, about the less privileged, and with Queen Elizabeth beside him he had been an exemplary monarch, and perfect for restoring confidence in the monarchy after the trauma of his brother's abdication. He was also perfect for the period when Britons pulled together against a common enemy; and in identifying himself so completely with their difficulties helped to stimulate a spirit of social solidarity which his daughter inherited. In the immediate aftermath of her coronation, there was no obvious need for change; and so along with his quiet, dutiful manner, she also inherited his courtiers, his palace and his way of working.

The young Elizabeth's personality was both her handicap and her saviour. It may have prevented her from moving monarchy forward in those early years, but it also prevented her from believing her own publicity. It would have been very easy to let the adulation go to her head; to take it personally, as Diana, thirty years later did. The Queen never fell into that trap. She has always managed to differentiate between the public persona and the private one. In public she is Queen, Head of State, Supreme Governor of the Church of England, an office that she has the privilege to hold by virtue of her birth. And when people cheer and shout and proffer gifts and flowers, she knows they are only doing that because of the office she holds. If she were plain Mrs Windsor no one would turn a hair as she walked down the street. The face she presents to the outside world is the public face. Privately she is a wife, mother and rather doting grandmother, with a passion for dogs, horses, the countryside and traditional country sports.

With Diana there was no such demarcation; there had been no long preparation for a public role in life. Since the age of ten the Queen had been aware of the future that lay ahead and her education was tailored to that end. Diana started seeing the Prince of Wales in the summer of 1980; she was young and unsophisticated. She had come away from school with few qualifications, she had been briefly to finishing school in Switzerland, she had danced a bit, been a nanny for a while and was working as an assistant in a nursery school when she was suddenly, and unceremoniously thrust into the limelight.

Less than a year later, on 29 July, just a month after her twentieth birthday, she had become the Princess of Wales, one of the most famous faces in the world. The Queen was used to the cameras, used to the publicity, used to being the centre of attention. She was a steady character from a secure and loving background. Diana was not. Aristocratic blood may have coursed through her veins but she was vulnerable and needy; she came from a broken home, with all the resultant insecurities. She had been parted from her mother when she was six years old and was desperate to be loved.

The media idolized Diana and public affection and adulation became a substitute for real-life emotions and personal relationships; but the public are fickle in their affections and the media brutal in its treatment of heroes who prove to have feet of clay.

It was not long before the great wave of popularity on which the Waleses and the monarchy rode at the time of the wedding collapsed into a deep trough and the media began to criticize the Princess it had once proclaimed so perfect. There were a hundred and one reasons why the fairy-tale match didn't work but the Diana years, both good and bad, had a major effect on the monarchy and more change has probably come about since Diana married into the Family Firm – and quite a few since her death – than in all the years of the Queen's reign put together.

TWO

Keeping House

The old-fashioned names haven't changed – visitors are still met by a footman in red waistcoat at the Privy Purse door when they arrive at Buckingham Palace – and the protocol and ceremonial are just as they have been for centuries, but everything else behind that famous façade has undergone a major revolution and what was once an overstaffed, anachronistic and expensive rest home for landed peers and retired brigadiers in the heart of London has been quietly turned into a lean, mean, monarchy machine.

The monarchy is never going to be run exactly like any other business; it is obviously unique. It has to deal with everything from counting swans on the River Thames to making arrangements for visiting foreign potentates, but it is a business. The modern family regards itself as a working outfit, and Buckingham Palace is first and foremost the company's head office. It is no cosy home and anyone who would like to evict the Royal Family and install the homeless, or whatever other change of use has been suggested for Buckingham Palace over the years, would also be evicting more than a hundred employees who live in the Palace, several hundred more who come in daily to work there, and yet more who come in on a casual basis when there are ceremonial events to marshal or big dos to cater. Buckingham Palace is not just a luxury home for the Queen and her family, where they are waited on hand and foot by flunkies with absurd-sounding names like Silver-Stick-in-Waiting and Ladies of the Bedchamber. Several members of the family have apartments there, where they stay during the week when they are in London, but it is not a home in any real sense and the Queen certainly doesn't regard it as such.

The Palace is like a small village; it even has its own post office, doctor's surgery and travel agent. Accommodation takes up a high percentage of the building: there are 52 royal and guest bedrooms, 188 staff bedrooms, and 78 bathrooms and lavatories; also 19 glorious state rooms and 92 offices. There are rooms for courtiers to sleep in if they are kept at the Palace late at night, and rooms for ladies-in-waiting and other members of the Queen's household to stay in when they are on duty; there are suites for visiting heads of state and their entourages, and, of course, apartments for immediate members of the family. Prince Charles no longer has one – he moved out soon after his marriage and has always had a base in London since, but his sister and two brothers all have their own quarters on the second floor, quite separate from their parents. The rest of the Palace is given over to all the paraphernalia that goes with running a huge catering and hospitality operation: giant kitchens, store rooms, cellars, boiler rooms and a labyrinth of underground passages with great pipes and heating ducts, not unlike the lower decks on an ocean-going liner.

During the Middle Ages, the Norman and Plantagenet kings and their successors lived at the Palace of Westminster, which was rebuilt and now forms part of the Houses of Parliament. For two centuries, from the reign of Henry VIII to that of William III, Whitehall took its place but that was destroyed by fire and in the eighteenth century the Hanoverian kings used St James's Palace, which Henry VIII had built as a hunting lodge. And although George III bought – in 1761 – and lived in the house that became Buckingham Palace, the ceremonial centre of the court remained at St James's, which is why foreign ambassadors are still accredited to the Court of St James two centuries later. It was George IV who decided to convert Buckingham House (where his father had lived) into a palace and employed the architect John Nash for the job. George IV died before the work was completed – and Nash was sacked for financial incompetence – and the palace completed by William IV and the architect Edward Blore. But William never lived there. Queen Victoria was the first monarch to use Buckingham Palace when she came to the throne in 1837, and soon decided to extend it. None of the rooms was big enough for a court ball and after her marriage to Prince Albert she needed nursery space and so a new wing was built, on the eastern side of the building in the space where Nash had erected a decorative marble arch at the entrance to the forecourt. The arch was subsequently moved to the top of Park Lane and is the Marble Arch of fame from which distances to London are still measured.

So although it is not as old as the Queen's other official residences, Buckingham Palace has been home to six monarchs and the focal point of the nation for more than 160 years. It is where visiting kings, queens and presidents are made royally welcome, where sumptuous state banquets are held, the tables adorned with antique glass, gilt, silver and priceless porcelain. It is where ambassadors and diplomats come to present their credentials, where the Prime Minister comes for his weekly audience, and where investitures are held, garden parties, informal lunches and lavish receptions. It has high ceilings, wide corridors and sweeping staircases, marble columns, miles of red carpet, and sumptuous furnishings. Fabulous paintings and etchings hang on the walls, giant crystal chandeliers dangle precariously from the ceilings; even the corridors are furnished with intricate inlaid cabinets, ornate clocks, sparkling mirrors, elegant tables, gilt-framed banquettes, delicate statues and tapestries centuries old.

It is probably one of the busiest buildings in London and one of the most versatile. And the reason it is only open to the public for six weeks of the year is because that is when the Queen is away and the only time of the year when the state rooms are not in constant use. Fifty thousand people are entertained in Buckingham Palace every year and the state rooms have a fast turnaround. It requires a small army to service those kinds of numbers and exceptional organization. There can be no off-days, no slip-ups. Everyone invited to the Palace, whether it is for a meal, a glass of wine or a cup of tea and a bun in the garden, will remember the experience and it has to be perfect.

The guards are largely ceremonial these days. It's the armed policemen on the gate who form the first line of defence and, since 9/11, security has been stepped up. Visitors now need to have photographic proof of identity when they arrive, and their appointments must be known to the footmen at the Privy Purse entrance, but otherwise it is surprisingly relaxed. The Queen is not prepared to turn her home into a fortress. She accepts security as a necessary evil of the modern world, but she doesn't like it, any more than the rest of the family; and she takes a pragmatic view of the matter – the only sensible thing to do in her situation. If someone wanted to kill her I have no doubt they could. One former minister says he would scrap security altogether. 'I'm very fatalistic about these things,' he says. 'It's part of being royal; you are at risk. No security is absolute.'

The Prince and Princess of Wales lived in an apartment in Kensington Palace, where they were neighbours of Princess Margaret, Prince and Princess Michael of Kent, Princess Alice, Duchess of Gloucester, and the Duke and Duchess of Gloucester. After their divorce Diana stayed at KP, as it is known, and Charles moved into York House, a part of St James's Palace, where he and the Princess had their offices. And after the Queen Mother's death in 2002 he took over Clarence House, across the courtyard from St James's and a four-minute walk from Buckingham Palace. Clarence House was a sentimental return for him to a house filled with good memories. He lived there until the age of three when his mother became Queen and the family had to move to Buckingham Palace. None of them wanted to go. They loved Clarence House; it was a family home but Winston Churchill, who was then Prime Minister, insisted upon it and according to Michael Parker, the Duke of Edinburgh's Private Secretary at the time, who travelled with the family as they left for Buckingham Palace, 'there was not a dry eye in that car'. It then became Queen Elizabeth The Queen Mother's home and Charles, who adored his grandmother, was a constant visitor both as a child and adult.

The Queen has five residences in all – Buckingham Palace is head office, and where over half of all the 650 or so people who work for her in these various residences are based. Windsor Castle, in Berkshire, is where she goes at weekends and the Palace of Holyroodhouse in Edinburgh, where she spends a week in the summer. If she is at either of those in her official capacity, the court travels with her. If it is informal, she takes minimal staff but always a Private Secretary. These three residences are all official and effectively owned by the state. Sandringham House in Norfolk and Balmoral Castle in Deeside are privately owned and the Royal Family traditionally spends several weeks after Christmas at Sandringham and two months in the summer at Balmoral.

The most senior member of the Queen's household is the Lord Chamberlain, currently Lord Luce, a former Conservative minister, a charming, popular and clever man with perfect credentials for the job; but arguably the more powerful individual in Buckingham Palace at any one time is the Queen's Principal Private Secretary. In an ordinary company he would be the equivalent of managing director or chief executive, and the Lord Chamberlain chairman. The Private Secretary is the one who advises the Queen, who structures her programme, who writes her speeches and who is the interface between her and 10 Downing Street; also with her governments in the seventeen Commonwealth countries in which she is sovereign. And the current incumbent, Sir Robin Janvrin, is generally agreed to be a very good thing.

The Queen has worked with eleven prime ministers in Britain and since devolution now meets the Scottish First Minister for regular audiences too, and after more than fifty years there is very little to surprise her in politics. John Major met her almost every week for the six and a half years of his premiership and spent a weekend at Balmoral each summer with his wife Norma, as prime ministers traditionally do. Insiders say she liked Major. Margaret Thatcher never seemed to relax; Tony Blair she finds easier.

'The monarch's power is not raw power but influence,' says Major; 'influence and access.'

Politicians have taken the power away from the monarchy for the last three hundred years. Charles II came back post-Cromwell with few of the powers of Charles I. It has lessened ever since. There are residual powers; if the country was deadlocked after a general election the Queen would have to decide who to send for; but that's not to say the Queen doesn't express opinions to the Prime Minister, delicately. She wouldn't say 'x is good and y is bad, you ought not to appoint them', but she does ask questions about policy. The Queen would pose questions that other people might not necessarily ask the PM and he would not be able to say to the Queen, 'I'm sorry I can't tell you that', because there is nothing barred in those conversations. They talk freely, no one records the meeting, nor is any note taken. It is entirely private; on both sides there is a total block on the detail of what is discussed. Because of that, there can be, and in my experience is, total freedom of expression between the Monarch and her Prime Minister about what is happening, what it means and what might follow from it. There is humour too, and in privacy, personal vignettes. I found my discussions with the Queen immensely valuable. First, because one could talk to the Queen in a way you could talk to no one else. I can't tell you how useful that is. A sounding board, partly, yes, but what she gave was a completely dispassionate point of view. Whenever a PM talks to his ministers, unless he has a very close relationship, of the sort I had, say, with Douglas Hurd or Ian Lang, you don't have the total certainty that you have an absolutely unbiased answer coming back. The more self-opinionated the PM is the less you are likely to get a proper answer, but I don't think the Queen would be unwilling to give a proper answer or express a view. She wouldn't charge in and say 'I think you're making a complete mess of this policy', she would ask about it, how it affected people, how it would work, what its implications would be. She would have a sense of value too: 'Isn't that going to be very expensive?' And that's extremely valuable because in my case – although this might vary with other PMs – I would talk about the principles of the policy sometimes even before I put it to the Cabinet or anywhere else. My Audiences with the Queen were a breath of fresh air.

During the difficult and unpredictable days when the royal marriage was unravelling, Sir Robert Fellowes held the post of Private Secretary. It was a tough call since he was also Diana's brother-in-law, married to Diana's eldest sister, Jane. He was the son of the Queen's land agent at Sandringham, and very much of the aristocratic, Old Etonian, ex-Army, ex-City, hunting, shooting, fishing brigade and therefore someone with whom the Queen was entirely comfortable. He looked 'the part' as John Major would say, 'but he was never a stuffed shirt'. Others describe him as Bertie Wooster-ish, after the P. G. Wodehouse character, and to outsiders he seemed to embody so much of the stuffiness that the Princess of Wales complained about in the royal household. But as everyone who knows Sir Robert says, his looks are deceptive: he was actually a modernizer and greatly behind the move for change. He is very able, sensitive, shrewd and hugely underestimated. 'He's got a lot of realism, an ability to get things done, to embrace ideas even if they are not his own, and be open to suggestion,' says a former colleague. 'When you went into battle with him on your side you knew you might be shot on the field of battle but by the enemy, not your own team. That's a nice feeling.'

However, for much of the time during the 1990s the Prince of Wales didn't share the same warm feeling about his mother's Private Secretary, and by no means always felt he was on his side. He felt that Fellowes was out to scupper him and there were times of virtual warfare between his office in St James's Palace and Buckingham Palace, particularly over the matter of Camilla Parker Bowles. Fellowes disapproved of the Prince's relationship with Camilla. It was his conviction that all the difficulties that had befallen the House of Windsor in recent times had been because of the Prince's determination to hang on to Camilla, and there was a lot of truth in that.

THREE

Winds of Change

When Robert Fellowes retired in January 1999 after twenty-two years with the Queen, some of the most difficult of her reign, for a lucrative life in the City, his deputy, Sir Robin Janvrin, stepped into his shoes. Janvrin, now in his late fifties, is a departure from his predecessors, and relations with the Prince of Wales's office have improved since his appointment. He has no landowning background, no country pile. The son of a vice admiral, he was educated at Marlborough and Brasenose College, Oxford, where he studied, fortuitously given his current job, under the constitutional historian Dr Vernon Bogdanor, who is still a good friend and useful ally. He then followed his father into the Navy for a ten-year stint before joining the Foreign Office, and in 1987, at the age of forty-one, began work in the Buckingham Palace Press Office. He is another clever man, but wears it lightly. He is cautious; he likes to think things through before making a decision, but his style is relaxed, he doesn't panic, his colleagues love him and he has an air of normality which so many courtiers of yore never had. One could imagine him running for a bus, hanging from a strap on the underground, or washing the family car – all everyday Middle England things that if the Queen herself can't do, then those around her certainly should.

In the late 1950s Lord Altrincham (later John Grigg, the historian and biographer) had attacked the Queen for surrounding herself by hunting, shooting and fishing types – many of whom wouldn't have known where to find a bus. He wrote a stinging critique of the monarchy in a journal he edited called *National and English Review*, and, coming at a time when no one said or wrote anything derogatory about the monarchy, it caused outrage. He said it had become complacent and hidebound, that the Queen had failed to take the opportunity in this 'New Elizabethan Age' to make changes. His ideal was a 'truly classless and Commonwealth Court'; George V had shaped the modern institution and borne a 'classless stamp', the Queen and her sister, by contrast, largely because of their conventional aristocratic education, bore 'the debutante stamp' and, by favouring 'the "tweedy" sort', bolstered the court's 'social lopsidedness'. He went on to attack the Queen's speaking style, 'which is frankly "a pain in the neck"', and said that 'The personality conveyed by the utterances which are put into her mouth is that of a priggish schoolgirl, captain of the hockey team, a prefect, and a recent candidate for Confirmation.'

The utterances, of course, were put into her mouth by her Private Secretary, at that time Sir Michael Adeane, who was fiercely clever but ultra-conservative and a courtier to his boot straps. He had been Assistant Private Secretary to George VI from 1937 and stayed in post with the Queen for nineteen years. However, the whole episode provided ample proof of how very influential the Private Secretary was, and still is. He determines how the sovereign's reign is viewed by the public and ultimately posterity. He sees the Queen almost as much as her husband; they meet every morning to go through correspondence and paperwork, he briefs her on the day's programme and the people she will meet, and they discuss anything that is relevant in the news or of constitutional or political interest. She relies upon him to be her eyes and ears and to give her sound advice and guidance.

Today the Principal Private Secretary has two deputies and one of the three of them will always be with the Queen. He will travel with her on major engagements away from the Palace and will be on duty wherever she is in residence, even during holiday periods like Christmas and Easter in case anything unforeseen happens. Robin Janvrin was on duty the night of Diana's fatal accident in Paris. He was asleep in a cottage in the grounds at Balmoral when a call came through from the British Ambassador in Paris. It was Janvrin who had the unenviable task of breaking the news to the Queen and to the Prince of Wales, both of whom were also asleep in the castle. And it was he during the following week – which so very nearly brought about disaster – who tried to persuade the Queen to let a flag fly over Buckingham Palace. Robert Fellowes has been blamed for the failures of that week but it was the Queen, backed up by the Duke of Edinburgh, who was refusing to listen to advice. Fellowes was in London and could see at first hand what was going on outside the gates of Buckingham Palace and the damage being done by the Queen remaining silent and stoic in the Highlands.

The Queen is said to regret her delay in visiting Aberfan in 1966, recognizing with hindsight that it was a mistake not to be there immediately to comfort the grieving and express her sorrow; I suspect she regrets her instincts during that week after Diana's death, too. Her first thoughts were for her grandsons, and for once she put family before duty. It was a mistake, however, to let the nation believe that neither she nor any other member of the Royal Family cared about the tragedy that had pole-axed the nation. She misjudged it. Shut away in Balmoral she was insulated from the real world; she couldn't feel the raw emotion that those in the streets could feel, particularly in London around the palaces where tributes, flowers and teddy bears were being piled high. She thought that the answer to the mass hysteria was to stay calm and to keep on doing what the family had always done, safe in tradition. A flag had never flown at half mast over Buckingham Palace, not even for the death of a sovereign; it would be wrong to do it for Diana. The Queen only ever broadcast to the nation in times of national emergency and on Christmas afternoon; why speak now when Diana was no longer even a member of the Royal Family? What they all learned that week was that doing things in a certain way, because it was the way they had been done in the past, was not the safe formula they had hoped. They wisely changed, just as they had wisely changed a decade earlier.

In the mid-1980s the monarchy had hit a low patch. The honeymoon was over, both for the royal marriage and the revived fortunes of the institution. The media were becoming critical of the younger members of the family and the Labour Party was becoming ever more critical of the cost. The flashpoint was *It's A Royal Knockout*, a television programme aired in June 1987, which marked the Royal Family's descent to celebrity showbiz status. It was a one-off special of the then hugely popular but very silly BBC game show *It's A Knockout*. It was Edward's idea for raising money for the Duke of Edinburgh's Award's 30th anniversary. The show parodied royal ceremonial and he persuaded Princess Anne, Prince Andrew and his new wife Sarah Ferguson, the Duchess of York, to join him in dressing up in mock Tudor costume and making complete fools of themselves alongside celebrities like Barbara Windsor, Les Dawson and Rowan Atkinson. The ratings soared through the roof and the event raised over £1 million, which was divided between the Award, Save the Children, the

World Wildlife Fund and the International Year of Shelter for the Homeless. But it came at a terrible price for the dignity of the monarchy. To make matters worse, at a press conference afterwards, as embarrassed journalists tried to find some way of being polite when asked what they had thought of it, twenty-three-year-old Edward, at that time very arrogant, lost his temper and stormed petulantly out of the tent. The following day's newspapers led with the inevitable headline 'It's A Royal Walkout'.

It is incidents like this that have cemented attitudes over the years. Prince Edward has never been allowed to forget his mistake and understandably he resents the press as a result which simply reinforces the impression that he is arrogant, and it becomes a vicious circle.

Princess Margaret was always perceived as spoilt because of her behaviour when she was young and that label stuck, yet the people who knew her say while she could be imperious, she was actually very kind and caring. Prince Philip is thought of as a reactionary old fool who always puts his foot in it. He has made some howlers in his time, there is no escaping it, but he is about as foolish as a fox. History will show him to have made a very serious contribution to the success of the Queen's reign – as well having been a prime mover in the field of conservation. Yet whenever he makes a joke that falls flat – usually done in an attempt to put some stranger at their ease – out comes the catalogue of blunders from the past and suggestions from some nonentity of an MP that he should stay out of public life. The Prince of Wales once admitted to talking to his plants and has been ridiculed as the loony Prince by his detractors ever since. Princess Anne is about the only one who has managed to turn round her early image and having once been one of the most unpopular members of the Royal Family is now seen as one of the hardest working and best liked.

It will be interesting to see whether Prince Harry will be able to shake off the labels that have already been attached to him. Of all his misdemeanours, choosing a Nazi outfit to wear to a friend's fancy dress party in January 2005 was the most idiotic. The underage drinking, the partying, the marijuana, the girls, even taking a punch at a photographer outside a London nightclub were forgivable. He was young, not thinking, he's had an unsettled childhood; any or all of these could have happened to any teenager or twenty-year-old. As could the Nazi episode. Today's young are blissfully unaware of history (some of them aren't even taught it in our schools). None of his contemporaries at the party noticed anything wrong, and the person who sent the photos to the *Sun* hadn't even realized the significance. They thought the interesting picture was the one of Prince William dressed as a lion.

The problem is that Harry isn't just any twenty-year-old. He may not feel any different from his mates but he can't afford to behave like them. He is third in line to the throne and, like it or not, he is living in a goldfish bowl. Wherever he goes – even to the most private of parties – where there is a mobile phone, there is a camera. And after this the tabloids will be sitting with cheque books open waiting for the next cracking picture. They have had Harry tailed in the past and they can do it again; it may not be fair but it sells newspapers and some of those are always happy to have a pop at the monarchy.

During the eighties there were two key people in the household who realized that if there was to be a secure future change was imperative. Both were newly in post. In December 1984, David, the thirteenth Earl of Airlie, had become Lord Chamberlain in place of Lord 'Chips' Maclean, twenty-seventh chief of Clan Maclean, the last in a long tradition of well-bred amateurs. David Airlie may have been aristocratic, and with a family castle and sixty-nine thousand acres in Scotland he was undoubtedly 'tweedy', and he may have been a Scots Guard for five years, but he was no amateur. He was a highly successful merchant banker with thirty-five years' experience – he had just stepped down as chairman of Schroders when he came to the Palace – and, according to one colleague, was 'marvellous, canny, and a wise businessman'. Better still, he was an old friend of the Queen – they are less than four weeks apart in age and have known each other all their lives. His family home was five miles from Glamis Castle, where the Queen Mother grew up, his wife, Virginia, was and still is one of the Queen's ladies-in-waiting, and his younger brother was Sir Angus Ogilvy, who sadly died recently but who was married to the Queen's cousin, Princess Alexandra. He was just what the House of Windsor needed: a delightful, wise and down-to-earth man who could gently steer the monarchy away from the treacherous rocks towards which it was surely headed.

Two years later Sir Philip Moore retired as Private Secretary – the last of the ancien régime – and was replaced by Bill Heseltine, who had been patiently waiting in the wings. He was the Australian who had succeeded Commander Richard Colville as Press Officer at the end of the 1960s and revolutionized the Palace's relationship with the media. The two men were of one mind: the growing criticism had to be addressed; the world had moved on – just about every other major company and business in the Western world had reorganized itself; streamlined, modernized and introduced best practices. The Firm needed to be firmly nudged into the twentieth century.

It was George VI who first referred to the House of Windsor as The Firm and the name stuck – although some have called it Monarchy plc – and when David Airlie was appointed it was still run along lines that George VI and probably even

Queen Victoria a century earlier, would have recognized and felt comfortable with.

When Michael Colborne, a naval chief petty officer, arrived to look after the Prince of Wales's office in 1979, he was the only person at his level in the Palace who had not been to a major public school. 'If you didn't go to the right school you didn't fit; you didn't speak the language. It could be very uncomfortable for people like me. They called me the "Rough Diamond". I lived there for six months and I felt so lonely in the Palace.'

'It was all rather stuck in the mud, in a time warp,' remembers someone else. 'The Palace was still recruiting from certain sections of society and the Queen hadn't been particularly well served. There was a country house atmosphere; things were being done in the same way they'd been done for twenty, thirty or nearer a hundred years – since Prince Albert's time probably. There were some excellent individuals there, who had no doubt wanted to move things forward a bit, but there had never been the concerted pressure to do it.'

David Airlie provided that pressure. He already had experience of modernizing companies and had learned lessons in the process which were invaluable in the mammoth task before him at Buckingham Palace. He had done it at General Accident and Schroders, in both cases bringing in outside consultants to report on whether best practices were being followed; he recommended to the Queen that they go down the same route. And so in February 1986, by which time he had a good idea of what needed to be done – and it included first and foremost getting rid of excessive government interference – he called in the City accountancy firm Peat Marwick McLintock, who were already the Palace auditors, to overhaul the finances and look at the workings of the household from top to bottom. He was anxious that the Treasury should take the findings seriously and Peat Marwick had the necessary clout to impress them. It was vital, he felt, for the report to be paid for and carried out internally and not financed by government money; the Treasury could see the report but they were not to be involved. The man who conducted the study was Michael Peat, a partner in the family firm then in his mid-thirties. His father, Sir Gerrard Peat, had been auditor and assistant auditor to the Queen's Privy Purse since 1969 and Michael had frequently worked alongside him in the past so was already familiar with the Palace's finances, and, crucially, already knew David Airlie.

It was a major undertaking which took a full year, but in 1987 Peat came up with a report that ran to 1383 pages, with no fewer than 188 recommendations for change. They were wide-ranging but fundamentally changed the working practices of every department in the Palace, from the dining arrangements to the way in which the private secretaries operated.

Michael Peat gives all the credit to David Airlie, on the grounds that identifying what was wrong was the easy bit; persuading the Queen and everyone else in the Royal Family and the household to accept it and to agree to change, was quite another matter. And, to his lasting credit, David Airlie achieved it, although he is equally modest and says that Michael Peat was the mastermind. In truth they were a formidable double act who both became extremely unpopular in the process. It was an unhappy time in the Palace with everyone uncertain about their future. One of Airlie's stipulations was that there would be no job losses – natural wastage yes, but no one would find themselves out of a job. That was paramount because he could not put the Queen in a position where she had to sack people – they couldn't afford bad publicity during this process – but there was a lot of uncertainty and edginess nevertheless and a feeling that each department was the next for change. But between them they achieved what many thought was the impossible.

FOUR

188 Recommendations

I can't help thinking about A. A. Milne again and his wonderful poem, 'The King's Breakfast' in which the King laments the lack of butter on his breakfast table. He isn't a fussy man but he knows what he likes. And so he tells the Queen and the Queen tells the dairymaid who goes to tell the cow. But the cow wants to go to sleep and suggests he try marmalade on his bread instead of butter. So back goes the suggestion from the cow to the dairymaid and the dairymaid to the Queen and from the Queen to the King. But the King is forlorn and sobs and whimpers and when the news reaches the cow, via the Queen and the dairymaid, the cow relents and gives him milk as well as butter. And the King is so delighted he does a little jig.

I am not sure that the dairymaid actually attended the royal breakfast before Lord Airlie called in Peat Marwick McLintock to see how Buckingham Palace might be modernized, but the royal household was certainly overrun with flunkies – 'Why have I got so many footmen?' the Queen was said to have asked when she saw the report. And whether A. A. Milne knew it or not, milk and butter for the royal breakfast does come from a royal herd of Jersey cows in Windsor Great Park, delivered to the Palace each morning before dawn.

The Palace dining arrangements were definitely in need of

an overhaul and Peat and Airlie discussed them but decided this was one change too far for the immediate future. In the grand scheme of things, five tiers of dining and waiting staff in tailcoats was a mere detail compared with the other 188 problems they had earmarked for change, and they feared that coming between their colleagues and their comestibles might be the straw that broke the camel's back.

It was a very quaint system nonetheless and one which was only changed a couple of years ago. The most senior members of the household ate in the grandest dining room; that included the Lord Chamberlain, the private secretaries, the Master of the Household, ladies-in-waiting, press secretaries, and chaplains, senior Women of the Bedchamber, the Mistress of the Robes and the Keeper of the Privy Purse. A second dining room was the province of senior officials such as the assistants to the Master of the Household, the Chief Housekeeper and the Paymaster. Then there was one for the officials – secretaries and assistants, clerks, press officers, typists and administrative personnel. Next rung down were the stewards: pages, yeomen, the Queen's dressers and her chauffeur. And below stairs – in the basement – was the fifth and final dining room for the most junior members of the domestic staff: under-butlers, footmen, chefs, maids, porters, postmen, plumbers, gardeners, grooms and chauffeurs.

The first summer the Palace was opened to the public, the most senior of the dining rooms was given over to the summer opening administrative staff which involved some very unpopular rearrangements. The occupants of that room took over the room belonging to the next tier down, and they in turn were forced to double up with the junior staff in the basement. Some of them had never ventured into the basement and so many got lost en route that they had to put up signs to direct them. August was not a happy month.

When change finally came, in June 2003, the four dining rooms were reduced to two. The household continues to eat separately, except during the summer opening and on a few other occasions, and everyone else has a snazzy new self-service restaurant. There is also a separate room with comfortable chairs for coffee and tea which is also open to every grade of employee. Since so many work shifts and odd hours it was the only sensible solution, and in a stroke attacked the rigid hierarchy that most enlightened companies abandoned years ago.

The organizational structure Lord Airlie discovered inside Buckingham Palace when he arrived there as Lord Chamberlain in 1984 was unique. And although he implemented well over 160 of 188 recommendations for change to make it more efficient and businesslike – including the role of the Lord Chamberlain – it remains unique to this day. Nothing compares, and yet the monarchy is more of a business today than it ever was in previous reigns. In a typical company you have a chairman, a chief executive who reports to the chairman, and four or five departmental heads who report to the chief executive. All of these posts exist in the royal household, by one name or another, but in the final analysis the Queen is the one who makes the decisions about the day-to-day affairs and so the departmental heads have direct access to the Queen over the head of the Lord Chamberlain. 'The Lord Chamberlain is a sort of hands-on chairman of a company with one shareholder' is the way it was described to me. The departmental heads do report to him and he chairs regular meetings with them all, but he does not get involved in the detail of whether the Queen goes to New Zealand or Birmingham, who she invites to lunch or which state coach she uses for a state visit. Before Lord Airlie took up the post there was no cohesion at the top of the household, no communication and no reporting structure, and although it is still not set in stone because of the Queen's role in the decision-making process, it is a lot more efficient than it was before.

The names of the posts, however, are still from another era. The Lord Chamberlain is not, as the name might suggest, in charge of the Lord Chamberlain's Office. That is the Comptroller's job – currently held by Lieutenant Colonel Sir Malcolm Ross, a thoroughly charming old Etonian of sixty plus, who spent twenty-three years in the Scots Guards and the remainder of his career in the royal household. He is a wonderful product of the two and perfect for the job of running the ceremonial side of the monarchy, which he does except when there are 'issues of import' such as the Princess of Wales's funeral to be arranged. In that event, the Lord Chamberlain swings into action and takes charge of the Lord Chamberlain's Office, which is where you would have expected him to be in the first place.

Once he had completed the report, Lord Airlie arranged for Michael Peat to stay on at the Palace for the next three years to help him develop and implement the recommendations Peat had made. The two men had worked very closely together during the writing of the report and got on well together; Airlie's past experience at Schroders and General Accident had taught him that it was vital for the chairman to work closely with the consultant. Airlie knew that many of Peat's ideas would never fly and he was able to say so right away and eliminate unnecessary work. The entire thing was the art of the possible and some reforms had to be sacrificed in the interests of progressing more important ones.

Among the most important was sorting out the Civil List. This is the sum voted by Parliament to pay for the sovereign in carrying out her duties as Head of State, and for the running of the royal household. It is much misunderstood and has

33

caused more grief over the years to the monarchy than anything else. It is worth putting the cost into perspective. The
monarchy costs £36.8 million a year to run; the Atomic Physics
Particle Research Laboratory, by comparison, costs about
£100 million, the Welsh fourth television channel (S4C) about
£74 million a year, the British Museum about £40 million.
But where the comparison falls down is that the last three are
paid for by the taxpayer, and the taxpayer doesn't actually
pay for the monarchy at all. It is paid for by the revenue that
comes from the Crown Estates. The taxpayer doesn't pay a
penny. After the Norman Conquest in 1066 all the lands of
England belonged to William the Conqueror and he and his
successors received the rent and profits from the land, which
they used to finance the government. Over the years monarchs
sold bits of land or gave away large estates to nobles and
barons in return for military service until, by 1702 (historians
must forgive me for simplifying the story), there wasn't enough
income from what remained to pay for the cost of the government (which had grown in the intervening seven hundred years)
and the royal household. Parliament therefore introduced an
Act to stop the Crown selling off more of its land, and took over
management of the estates. When George III came to the throne
in 1760 he relinquished his right to the revenue in return for a
fixed annual sum of money from Parliament, which became
known as the Civil List. The Crown Estate still belongs to the
sovereign 'in the right of the Crown', which means it is not
her private property, but at the beginning of each reign the
new sovereign traditionally hands over the revenue from the
Crown Estate to the Exchequer for his or her lifetime.

It is a huge business. The Estate owns more than 250,000
acres of agricultural land throughout England and Scotland:
7500 acres of forestry at Windsor, another 7500 at Glenlivet,
more in Somerset and smaller amounts elsewhere; and it owns

Windsor Great Park – a further 5313 acres which includes Ascot Racecourse. It also has urban estates, mostly in central London – residential property in Regent's Park, Kensington and Millbank; and commercial property in Regent Street, Victoria Street and in the City, including the site of the Royal Mint. It also owns more than half of the United Kingdom's foreshore and almost all the seabed to a limit of twelve miles from the shore, which is used for everything from marine industries to leisure activities.

All of this is run by a Board of Commissioners which employs experts in various fields of estate management, and under the Crown Estate Act of 1961 has a duty to maintain and enhance the value of the Estate. Management fees are taken out of the revenue, but the remainder – about £150 million – goes to the Treasury. Thirty-six million pounds from that sum is paid to the Queen, and the government pockets the rest to meet general government expenditure.

Even with my limited grasp of mathematics, the Queen is not the leech we have been led to believe. She does not cost the country a brass farthing, but is actually saving the taxpayer something like £114 million. If that money wasn't coming from the Crown Estate you can bet your boots it would come from the taxpayer, and, indeed, if the Queen went mad and splashed out on a new aircraft, or a flashy new coach and spent too much the taxpayer would have to pay more for the shortfall. Parliament decides how much money the sovereign should have, and in that respect acts like a trustee of an old family trust, which in a constitutional monarchy is just as it should be. Parliament needs to make sure the Queen isn't more of a financial burden than she has to be, not because it has to pay for her if she is, but because the more money there is left over after paying the Civil List, the more there is for general expenditure.

When Airlie arrived the Civil List was paid and reviewed annually, and this had been the arrangement since the 1970s when inflation had started running rampant. Some years it was running in double figures and each year there were increases in the Civil List, announced in Parliament, in line with inflation. From the public relations point of view this was bad news. It looked as though the Queen was being voted a 10 or 15 per cent pay rise, which, of course, was nonsense but made a very provocative headline. In practical terms it was disastrous too; government was so heavily involved in the detail and the every-day running of the organization, checking and rechecking expenditure to the point where it was impossible to make any long-term decisions and impossible to do what they wanted to do with the money. Airlie and Peat wanted the Treasury off their backs and were determined that the royal household should be master of its own destiny.

Their plan was to get the Civil List agreed for a ten-year period and be allowed to manage the money themselves, free from government interference. The Treasury agreed in principle; the difficulty was agreeing a figure, which, even if inflation continued to rise, would not leave the household short of funds. The Treasury's refusal to acknowledge the existence of inflation made life difficult, but they found another way. They calculated the average rate of inflation during the past ten years, which was 7.5 per cent – acceptable to the Treasury – and settled on a figure for the ten-year period from 1 January 1991 of £7.9 million. If they had taken too much money, there was a deal that the surplus would roll over into the next ten years' allowance. The Earl of Airlie took a punt. At the time, inflation was running at 9 per cent. If it had continued to rise the household would have run out of funds before the ten years were up and caused untold damage to the monarchy. As it was, inflation went down during the nineties and David Airlie was roundly praised for having struck such a good deal. Little did anyone know how very concerned he was that it might so easily have gone the other way.

Having stayed at the Palace on secondment from his own family firm for three years to implement the first round of changes and to work on the Civil List negotiations, Peat was persuaded to join the household for another three years to see in those changes which were announced by Margaret Thatcher in the House of Commons in 1990. For the first three years he had been called Administrative Adviser; but for the next three years, as a member of the household, he was called director of Finances and Property Services, a new title Airlie created to oversee a whole new business that was another calculated gamble.

Having established that the household had a ten-year Civil List to manage, it seemed sensible to bring the maintenance of the occupied palaces, run by yet another government department, under Palace control. And so they created a department called Property Services which covered not just the maintenance but everything involved in running the occupied royal palaces, from heating and cleaning them to mowing the lawns, training personnel and meeting fire, health and safety regulations. All of this had been farmed out many years before to the Department of the Environment (which became and is now the Department for Culture, Media and Sport) and they were spending over £20 million on the palaces. Peat and Airlie reckoned they could do it more cost-effectively themselves. It was yet another cry to be masters of their own destiny. They knew the buildings, knew what they wanted and knew whether a tap worked or not; why not take it over? And so once again they stuck their necks out. It was a mammoth undertaking, and, as they are the first to acknowledge in retrospect, quite brave. They had no expertise and, apart from the odd plumber on the books, no manpower; and there are a lot of occupied palaces – Buckingham Palace, St James's Palace, Clarence House and Marlborough House Mews, the residential and office areas of Kensington Palace, the Royal Mews and Royal Paddocks at Hampton Court and Windsor Castle and buildings in the Home and Great Parks at Windsor. But they pulled it off. They effectively started up a brand-new business, contracted out some of the services such as cleaning, took on staff for other jobs, employed specialists and, while reducing the amount that was spent on the palaces, nevertheless carried out a huge number of improvements and came in well under budget. It was, and still is, paid for by the Department for Culture, Media and Sport by way of Grant-in-Aid, but the savings and improved efficiency have continued. For the last five years funding has remained at £15 million – savings of around £50 million since Peat took it over in March 1991.

By the time Michael Peat was due to return to Peat Marwick McLintock (by now renamed KPMG), in 1993, there was a great deal going on in which he was heavily involved. Fire had devastated Windsor Castle; another new department – Royal Enterprises, the trading arm of the Royal Collection – was just coming on-stream; there were plans for Royal Travel, Communications and the Historic Royal Palaces – all changes that he had recommended in his report – and he was far too busy to leave. KPMG, who had been paying him a very generous partnership share all the while, began to get restless and Peat had to make a choice: to stay at the Palace and see through what he had begun, or go back to a very lucrative number in the City and amass a fortune for his declining years. To his family's chagrin he opted to stay, becoming Keeper of the Privy Purse, and has so far resisted all enticements to return. Indeed, in 2003 he took on the ultimate challenge and became

Private Secretary to the Prince of Wales, just in time to field the fallout from the Burrell trial.

Peat is not universally liked; he is frequently described as lacking charisma, being a faceless accountant, a cold fish; but new brooms are seldom liked and it's too easy to attach damning labels. He was effecting radical change in a cosy, hierarchical environment and interfering with working practices that no one has questioned for decades. He disturbed some well-feathered nests. No wonder he upset a few people along the way. As he has been heard to say, 'We changed a huge amount in terms of the head; whether we changed the heart I don't know.' The heart was easier to change in those areas where staff were better educated, among those who come into the Palace in administrative posts – finance, press, property, private secretaries – but it was more difficult to change the heart in the domestic areas, the Mews, the Master of the Household's department, areas where there was a very strong military background.

Educated at Eton and Oxford, Peat is tall and slim, a year younger than the Prince of Wales and two years younger than Robin Janvrin. I first met him in April 2003, shortly after his move to St James's Palace. He was impeccably mannered, charm itself and as cool as a glacier; I was happy then to believe what people said about him. But I have changed my view; I had known and liked Mark Bolland – and Peat was making a break with the past and the methods of the past. I was probably seen as part of that and I think he was expecting hostility. He was in a new job, he had the reputation of being a ruthless accountant, and the Prince's staff, members of which had always enjoyed a more luxurious life than their counterparts across the Mall, were extremely wary. First impressions were misleading. Peat is far from glacial and far from grand; he makes his own calls and answers his own telephone (as opposed to routing calls through his secretary, as many at his level do); he gets around London on a bicycle; and he has a real life outside the Palace with a wife, three children and a farm in Berkshire. Given what he has achieved over nearly twenty years, he is remarkably self-effacing.

During the period of his secondment, in 1991, Peat began working on new tax arrangements for the Queen. He had decided not to mention tax in his report, but, having looked at her finances from top to bottom during its preparation, he felt strongly that the Queen could and should be paying income tax. He knew it was a matter that needed careful handling; the Queen had never paid tax, but that was not a tradition that went back generations. Queen Victoria and Edward VII had both paid tax, George V and George VI had paid tax on investment revenue, and complete exemption only began at the start of the present Queen's reign in 1952. However, the feeling in the household had always been that the Queen could not afford to pay tax and maintain her current lifestyle, given her outgoings: she was paying for her children and other members of the Royal Family, paying for the upkeep of Balmoral and there was the small matter of horseracing. There was also a fear that any change would involve time-consuming legislation.

But the tax issue was inflicting grave damage and David Airlie was in full agreement with Peat. The monarchy was coming under heavy fire from the media on a number of counts, but the underlying malaise was its expense. The Waleses were at war with one another, Prince Andrew had married Sarah Ferguson, who was proving to be too much the girl next door and had an appetite for parties and holidays, and Prince Edward had shown himself to be arrogant and petulant. People were beginning to question why the taxpayer should be paying for the Royal Family to live the life of Reilly when they were patently no better than anyone else. The Palace had always been very coy about how much the Queen was worth, and in the absence of hard information journalists speculated. She was consistently reported to be worth billions; in 1989 the American business magazine *Fortune* placed it at £7 billion, making her the world's richest woman and the world's fourth richest individual. It was wildly inaccurate, but in PR terms it didn't matter. While the rest of the country paid tax on their comparatively meagre incomes, she was exempt; and the Prime Minister's announcement in 1990 that her income from the Civil List was to be increased by more than 50 per cent as part of the ten-year deal simply added insult to injury.

Peat's first challenge was to convince the household that the Queen could in fact afford to pay tax and still maintain a lifestyle commensurate with her position as sovereign, and then to convince the Treasury and the Inland Revenue that this could be done without a change in the law. Once he had Airlie's support, neither challenge proved insurmountable; and in February 1992 he set up a small working group with representatives from both the Treasury and the Inland Revenue to work out the detail. The plan was to announce the scheme in April 1993.

On 20 November 1992, however, five months before the proposed announcement, catastrophe struck. Fire broke out at Windsor Castle, the oldest of all the royal residences and the only one that has been in continuous use since William the Conqueror selected the site for a fortress after his conquest of England in 1066. The fire began in the Private Chapel when a curtain that had accidentally been touching a spotlight for a prolonged period burst into flames. By the time the alarm was raised fire had taken a firm hold of the north-east wing and smoke was billowing from the roof. It took fifteen hours and

41

a million and a half gallons of water to put out the blaze. Mercifully no one was injured, and thanks to the Duke of York, who hastily organized a rescue operation, most of the artwork was moved to safety, but the fire caused millions of pounds' worth of damage to a glorious and historic building that was uninsured. Nine principal rooms and more than a hundred others over an area of nine thousand square metres were damaged or destroyed by the fire – approximately one-fifth of the castle area.

The Duke of Edinburgh was in Argentina at the time and spent hours on the telephone trying to console the Queen. She had stood watching her childhood home burn, a small, sad figure in a mackintosh with the hood pulled over her head. She was clearly distraught and the nation felt huge sympathy. But that sympathy quickly evaporated when the Heritage Secretary, Peter Brooke, announced that since the castle had been uninsured the government would foot the bill for the repairs, estimated at between £20 and £40 million. 'When the castle stands, it is theirs,' wrote Janet Daley in *The Times*. 'But when it burns down, it is ours.'

And so, when John Major rose in the House of Commons six days after the fire and announced that from 1993 the Queen and the Prince of Wales would pay tax on their private income and that Civil List payments of £900,000 to five other members of the Royal Family would cease, it looked as though the Palace had been bounced into paying tax as a placatory measure. How the tabloids crowed.

It was very bad luck, because all they had actually been bounced into was making the announcement earlier than they had intended – and instead of gaining brownie points for having volunteered the idea, the Palace was once again caught on the back foot apparently reacting to bad publicity. In fact Airlie and Peat had not yet talked to the Queen about the detail of their proposals. She knew that they had undertaken a study into the feasibility of her paying tax but the whole business had been enormously complex and, although they had almost completed it, it was not yet entirely ready when the flames took hold.

In the end the restoration work at Windsor Castle was completed at no extra cost to the taxpayer – and in a roundabout way at considerable pleasure to visiting tourists. The irony was that, having worked so hard to become masters of their own destiny, the newly formed Property Services department was landed with the awesome task of repairing the damage. It took five years to complete and turned out to be the biggest and most ambitious historic-building project to have been undertaken in this country in the twentieth century. Privately it was a nightmare. First, all the debris had to be cleared and the salvaged pieces sorted, dried out and numbered. Next the building had to be stabilized, then re-roofed. Some of the rooms were restored and reinstated as they had been before the fire to accommodate the original furnishings and works of art that had been rescued. Other areas, such as the Private Chapel where the fire had started, were so badly damaged they had to be built from scratch. Miraculously, it was completed six months ahead of schedule and came in £3 million below budget. The final cost was £37 million. To help pay for it, Michael Peat suggested opening the state rooms at Buckingham Palace to the public. This could only be done for eight weeks of the year, during the summer when the Queen was in Scotland, but it proved so popular that it paid for 70 per cent of the total cost of the work. The shortfall was met by the annual Grant-in-Aid funding by Parliament for the maintenance and upkeep of the occupied palaces. But it was a very difficult period and one on which everyone looks back in horror.

FIVE

Communication

Another major fault highlighted in Peat's report was communication; and it was certainly my experience over the years that the right hand never knew what the left was doing. Press officers seldom appeared to know what the private secretaries were briefing and vice versa, and there was no sense that the various members of the family were all working either for the same outfit or towards the same goal. Peat didn't criticize the private secretaries in other respects, but he found the idea of forward planning or discussing arrangements for their principal with other households within The Firm anathema. It was perfectly possible, and certainly not unknown, for two members of the family to have been visiting the same town on the same morning and know nothing about each other's visit until they met in the high street.

There was another problem. They were constantly being caught on the wrong foot, always reacting to problems and situations, waiting for criticism rather than pre-empting it. The solution, devised by David Airlie, Michael Peat, Robin Janvrin, then the Queen's Deputy Private Secretary, and Charles Anson, her Press Secretary from 1990, was The Way Ahead Group, which first met in September 1994. Hard to believe that so simple an idea had to wait until 1994. It was an informal meeting which took place every six months between the Queen, the Duke of Edinburgh, the Prince of Wales, the Princess Royal, the Duke of York and the Earl of Wessex plus their private secretaries and other senior courtiers to map out the coming half-year and discuss anything of importance. According to a leaked agenda from a meeting in 1996 that could mean a discussion about the possibility of abandoning primogeniture – and allowing the firstborn, whether male or female, to inherit the throne – abolishing the ban on heirs to the throne marrying Roman Catholics, ending the monarch's position as Supreme Governor of the Church of England and reducing those working for the Family Firm to include only the consort, children and grandchildren directly in line. The constant surprise is that the Royal Family doesn't discuss any of these sorts of topics with one another on their own; it takes prompting from their courtiers and the structure of a formal group. Privately their talk tends to revolve around the domestic scene: dogs, horses, sporting pursuits and Estate matters, interspersed with dirty jokes and nudges in the ribs. This is not a family that enjoys debate or intellectual conversation. 'Some people regard "bugger" as a term of abuse,' says a former courtier. 'The Royal Family uses the word "intellectual" in much the same way.'

'They do communicate in the oddest way,' agrees another, echoing everyone I have known who has ever worked for the Royal Family. 'It's a very close family, but they don't communicate directly. They let other people take soundings; they never say "I'll talk about it with whomever" over the weekend. They do it through private secretaries or press secretaries. It's very cumbersome.'

'They used to write each other memos all the time, but that's changed a bit,' says one lady-in-waiting. 'They no longer commit anything to paper that they wouldn't want to see on the front page of the *Daily Mail*.' Unfortunately for the Prince of Wales, an inveterate memo writer, old habits die hard. An internal memo sent to Mark Bolland, his Deputy Private Secretary at the time, about a secretary he thought 'so PC it frightens me' turned up in an industrial tribunal and was on the front page of every newspaper as recently as November 2004 and sparked off a massive row about education. The then Secretary of State for Education, Charles Clarke, weighed in and openly criticized the Prince of Wales for meddling in something he knew nothing about, thus breaking the convention that members of the government never criticize members of the Royal Family in public. In fact the Prince of Wales knows a damn sight more about education than most politicians, but it would be a shame to let the facts get in the way of giving the Prince a good kicking.

It has to be said that safe methods of communication are diminishing. The Duke of Edinburgh has seen his private letters to the Princess of Wales published for public consumption courtesy of Paul Burrell and his book, and the Prince of Wales knows all too well about the dangers of mobile phones, after finding his amorous late-night ramblings intercepted and dished up for the world's entertainment. No wonder he doesn't use email.

The Prince, in fact, still writes everything in longhand, pages and pages with plenty of underlining for emphasis. He fires off memos to his staff and to his charities – Julia Cleverdon at Business in the Community calls them 'black spider memos' because of the colour of his ink and the frantic scribbling as his pen tries to keep up with his thoughts. And he writes letters, a habit he acquired long ago, with no apparent thought about them falling into the wrong hands.

Says a former courtier:

He's one of the great letter writers, except he needs an editor; his letters are far too long. But most people find letters of condolence the most difficult things to do. He would just sit down, pick up his pen and do four pages, or whatever, and it was always absolutely brilliant. He's a very emotional man and his emotions, unlike 'British' emotions, are right there, available and articulated. That's why he likes the descendants of Winston Churchill so much; they're very given to tears. He likes the idea of people breaking into tears.

Charles finds he can express himself with a fountain pen. He has never used a computer and has no plans to start now, but his Luddite tendencies are not reflected elsewhere in The Firm. His father, now in his eighties – nearly thirty years older than Charles – was probably one of the first people in the land to own a laptop and has been writing letters on it and using email for as long as email has existed. Even the Queen is ahead of her eldest son. During a trip to Brunei in 1998 she remarked to the Sultan's family, 'I can't write any more. I can only write on computers. You can rub things out. It's so simple.' The Duke of York is another devotee and has all the very latest hand-held wizardry, like his younger brother. Having worked in the film business, Edward is entirely familiar with computers and better than most at knowing how they work. Wandering into the Press Office at Buckingham Palace one day he found Ailsa Anderson, Assistant Press Secretary to the Queen, staring forlornly at a dead screen and immediately fixed it for her. The surprising thing about Edward is that for all that exposure to the real world, and all the nice touches that people report time and again, he is the most regal of all his siblings and in some respects the least relaxed about royal protocol.

The brainstorming that produced The Way Ahead Group

threw up another good idea: the creation of a department that has no ties with the past and is staffed by no one with a military career behind them. The Coordination and Research Unit (CRU), which was set up in 1995, is currently run by Paul Havill, a civil servant who came from the Office of Fair Trading and is on secondment for three years, which has since been extended. He is the third incumbent. His two assistants are always from the private sector – usually from companies like Price Waterhouse or Arthur Anderson – and stay for a year, perhaps two. 'The idea is to keep the fresh thinking and dynamism from the private sector coming into the heart of the private secretaries' office.' He works directly for Robin Janvrin, his assistants for Janvrin's deputies.

With the best will in the world they need that fresh thinking and dynamism. It is very easy to lose touch with reality if your life is spent at Buckingham Palace. It may be more efficiently run than it ever was, but how many other offices in London have Old Masters on the walls, Georgian tables doubling up as desks and priceless works of art decorating every corridor? It's only when you catch sight of computers, fax machines and filing cabinets that you realize this is neither a museum nor an art gallery. If you are travelling with the Queen you may visit schools and hospitals and meet a wide cross-section of society but you still travel with outriders, still walk on red carpet, and still, in the main, meet people who are pleased to see you. It is an unreal existence and it's seductive, particularly when you stay for ten, fifteen or twenty years, as most of the Queen's private secretaries do. Staff at lower levels are very often in royal service for life.

Michael Peat tried to put an end to that, suggesting short-term contracts of five years or so and retiring most jobs at sixty, although government policy on retirement will up that in future. It was a revolutionary idea and one that has upset some of the old guard. 'In the old days people went there for life,' says one. 'It wasn't for the money – there never was any – but they were proud to work for the Royal Family, it was a privilege. Today they just go there to get something on their CV; there's no loyalty any more.' However, having a constant flow of new blood coming into the Palace, bringing experience of the outside world with them, looking at the business with fresh eyes, not indoctrinated by the protocol or intimidated by the hierarchy, is undoubtedly good. And the fact that they are no longer coming exclusively from the Armed Forces is another giant plus. Loyalty is another issue. In the wake of the *Daily Mirror* reporter Ryan Parry taking a job inside the Palace – the final straw after a spate of revelatory books from former servants like Patrick Jephson, Ken Wharf and Paul Burrell – the confidentiality clauses in all royal employment contracts have been considerably tightened.

The man in charge of personnel and all matters financial is Alan Reid, the Keeper of the Privy Purse – old title, new man. He arrived in 2002 aged fifty-five, having been Chief Operating Officer at KPMG. A Scot, educated at Fettes and St Andrews, he was one of 234 applicants for the job. As with all senior appointments at the Palace these days a headhunter was used, but the job was also advertised on the open market. One of the applicants, from Australia, either a wag or understandably confused by the job title, said he 'would be happy to carry Her Majesty's handbag'.

'People used to think we couldn't take action, but we took an injunction out against the *Mirror* and Ryan Parry, and all staff in the Palace have signed new, tighter undertakings of confidentiality.' Most of the challenges Alan Reid has faced since he began the job, he admits, have been to do with personnel and security. 'They could publish in the United States and over the internet here, so it's not foolproof, but we can and will take action in terms of anyone making money in this country; all money will go to charity. It used to be that if your principal had died, the undertaking of confidentiality died with him or her.' This is how those people who worked for the Princess of Wales were able to publish with impunity after her death. 'Now contracts are in the sovereign's name and the sovereign never dies.'

The point of the Coordination and Research Unit is two-fold, and, unusually for job titles within the royal household, implicit in the title. It coordinates the family's activities 'because we want to have a joined-up, working-together sort of family', as Paul Havill puts it. 'There was a feeling that the different households didn't know what the others were doing; each member has their own office and their own patronages and interests and there was a need to bring them together, to be more coordinated.' Paul goes to all the six-monthly planning meetings when each member of the family sits down with their own staff to map out their diaries for the following six months. He advises everyone of the Queen's movements. There is a pecking order in The Firm and she is at the top, then the Prince of Wales and so on down the line of succession (excluding, for these purposes, Prince William and Prince Harry who don't yet carry out official engagements), and their planning meetings are held in order of precedence. Each member needs to work around those higher up the food chain, and if someone is needed to cover for the Queen, a date that she can't make but an engagement which needs some sort of royal presence, Paul puts in his bid for another member of the Royal Family to take it on. And because he has an overview of what everyone is doing, if there is a disaster somewhere, such as the Madrid bombings, he can find a member of the family to drop everything and go.

And, as the name suggests, the CRU researches. 'It provides

an executive resource for the Queen's private secretaries', in civil service-speak; effectively it is a Palace think tank, picking up on what's going wrong in the Family Firm and coming up with ideas for doing things better. And in the aftermath of Diana's famous *Panorama* interview in 1995 – which happened at much the same time as the CRU was being set up – there was a strong feeling among the Queen's staff that quite a lot was going wrong and the Princess of Wales was stealing a march on them all.

SIX

Lessons Learnt

The public loved Diana for all sorts of reasons but not least
because people felt she was in tune with them; she went down
to the Embankment in London and met the homeless, she went
to drug rehabilitation centres and she visited AIDS victims and
held their hands. She connected with the public in a way that
they liked. It wasn't the royal way. Princess Anne once tetchily
remarked, 'The very idea that all children want to be cuddled
by a complete stranger I find utterly amazing.' She has a point;
but Diana's informality and the raw, controversial causes she
adopted, symbolized a humanity that compared badly with
the unemotional hands-behind-the-back approach of everyone
else.

According to one of the private secretaries involved in the
process of finding a new way forward:

> That interview showed what a very different model Diana
> was and would continue to be, and it certainly gave impetus
> to the work that was going on in the Palace for change.
> What was their attitude to her style? Less hostility than I
> would have expected. There was an acceptance she was very
> popular and I never heard the Queen criticize Diana, but
> there was almost a sense of bafflement and a feeling that

this wasn't the style of the rest of the family. The Queen had a very strong, admirable sense herself of the need to be herself and not be something different. The Duke of Edinburgh will say, 'We are not here to electioneer, to tout for short-term popularity', and there was an understanding that they couldn't adopt Diana's style and pretend to be the kind of people they weren't. But working out how they could be themselves and yet do somewhat different things, and show interest in somewhat different things, was something they needed a lot of help with.

The CRU began trying to steer the Queen and other members of the family towards official engagements that were more closely aligned to what was going on in society. They used MORI and other opinion surveys to track key issues and establish people's views on a variety of issues. They looked at current polls which showed how many people in the population held republican sentiments, how many didn't care and how many were staunch monarchists, and discovered that the ratio varied very little. The number of republicans was always between 8 and 12 or 13 per cent; a large majority was neutral and a small number of people were raving monarchists.

The Queen and the Duke of Edinburgh have no interest in tracking opinion polls themselves. It's a form of self-protection they have developed over the years. They read newspapers and the Queen watches the early evening news on ITV so they are well aware of what is being said and written about them, and they pick up the sarky comments in comedy programmes, but they don't pore over the minutiae, as Diana did, looking to see if they had a good report today.

It's the Private Secretary's job to talk these kinds of issues through with the Queen, to discuss the way the monarchy is currently being perceived in the country and to work through the implications, and when and if necessary, recommend change. And it is probably one of the toughest and most crucial parts of the job.

> You trod carefully as you would with a minister or Prime Minister, and probably more carefully because it is an intensely personal role. Generally if you are in public life you can console yourself that if you're being criticized, it's your official persona that's being criticized. But it's very difficult for the Royal Family because that boundary line between being a private and public individual is blurred for them. One of the things I took away from my time at the Palace was a feeling that there needed to be a clearer distinction between the two. I think they've learnt to protect themselves from taking the criticism personally to some extent, but only to some extent.

Criticism was at its fiercest, of course, in the days after Diana's death, and that was the second major impetus for change. By the end of the week, when the family had finally come back to London and the Queen's broadcast had showed the country that its sovereign was back in the driving seat, no one at Buckingham Palace was in any doubt that the future had been on a knife edge. The Queen pulled it off; catastrophe was averted but it could easily have gone the other way. No one had any illusions about that, and they realized that change in the way the Queen's programme was organized was now a priority.

First they mapped out how the Queen currently spent her time on official visits; how many organizations in the private sector she went to compared to those in the public sector, what parts of the country she visited; when she went to schools, how many of them were private, how many state; within the private sector, how often did she go to manufacturing companies compared with service companies. And they mapped it against the current structure of society in the economy and discovered, for example, that she was doing a disproportionate amount in the public sector for the number of people employed in it. When she did pay visits to the private sector she tended to visit manufacturers rather than companies in the service industry because it was easier to devise a visit for her when there was something specific being made that she could look at. So even though the service industry accounts for 80 per cent of the private sector she didn't go there. But the reason she tended to go to more public schools than state schools, they found, was simply because she received more invitations from public schools.

'What we tried to do was get the maps a bit more aligned, which wasn't difficult once you tried, and I think she found she was visiting rather fresher places, that were fun.' She started going to popular, touristy kinds of places, like a Center-Parcs, and an aquarium in Liverpool, an example of new investment in that part of the country. In London, where she had only ever done ceremonial events in the past, the Queen spent a whole day visiting the City of London; she had lunch at the *Financial Times*, visited an investment bank, a venture capital company, sat in on a Monetary Policy Committee at the Bank of England, bought a copy of the *Evening Standard* from a vendor outside Holborn underground station and met messengers biking documents all round the City; everyday experiences for most people, all new for the Queen. She spent another day in theatre-land, a huge source of tourist income, and among other things watched a rehearsal of the musical *Oklahoma!*, and visited the Almeida Theatre in Islington. They became known as 'theme days' and were as relaxed and informal as possible. On other days, the Queen has toured television studios and seen something of the world of broadcasting; she dipped into publishing when she visited Bloomsbury and met the Harry Potter author, J. K. Rowling; and last year the entire Firm (this was a first) spent the day visiting tourist attractions all over the country, each member of the family in a different region, culminating in a big reception at Buckingham Palace in the evening for leading lights in the tourist industry.

I was with the Queen on that day and I never cease to be amazed by how very informal she is when she is out and about meeting people. Security is tight but it's low-key and unobtrusive and in no way puts up a barrier between the sovereign and her people. She doesn't put on any great show, doesn't keep a grin on her face in the way that showbiz personalities do when they meet their public. She smiles when something amuses her or if someone hands her something particularly pleasing but her face is often in repose – and therefore quite glum, even when the cameras are on her.

Tourism is Britain's sixth most important industry. Visit-Britain (formerly the British Tourist Board), which markets the country abroad, estimates that there are 2.1 million jobs in the industry – 7 per cent of all people in employment – and the monarchy, with its palaces, history and pageantry, is one of the principal draws. The top five royal attractions in the country – the Tower of London, Windsor Castle, Hampton Court Palace, Buckingham Palace and the Palace of Holyroodhouse – account for more than four million visits each year. But they also go in their hundreds of thousands to the decommissioned Royal Yacht *Britannia* berthed at Leith in Edinburgh, to Sandringham, KP, Balmoral, and, more recently, Clarence House; and to watch the annual Trooping the Colour ceremony. The biggest free visitor attraction in London is the Changing of the Guard which happens every morning on the forecourt of Buckingham Palace at 11.00 a.m. and lasts for half an hour. The Guard is mounted by the two regiments of the Household Cavalry – the Life Guards and the Blues and Royals – each of which provides one squadron for a special ceremonial unit in London, which is housed in Hyde Park Barracks with more than one hundred horses, and men who do a two- or three-year stint before returning to their operational units. The man in charge is Major General Sebastian Roberts who sits at the Duke of Wellington's old desk in the aptly named Wellington Barracks with history all around and the awesome task of ensuring that the military aspect of state ceremonials goes according to plan.

Buckingham Palace is not just a magnet for tourists. It is a rallying point where people instinctively go when there's a problem or a cause for celebration – either personal or national. When in 1982 a schizophrenic named Michael Fagan had family problems, it was the Queen he wanted to talk to. 'I was under a lot of stress,' he said, 'and just wanted to talk to Her Majesty about what I was going through.' So he broke into the Palace, found his way to her bedroom and she awoke to discover him sitting on her bed with a broken ashtray in one hand and blood pouring from the other – and, incidentally, needed to make two calls to the police switchboard within the Palace before anyone came to her rescue. When in 2004 a divorced man wanted visiting rights with his children, he dressed up as Batman and scaled the front of Buckingham Palace to stage a protest on a ledge and refused to come down for five hours. He caused a major security alert and the Metropolitan Police commissioner warned that the next time anyone tried a similar stunt they might very well be shot. (The mother of the interloper's third set of children, meanwhile, walked out on him, saying that he spent twice as much time demonstrating as he ever spent with their children and she'd had it; but that's not the point. The point is that he made his protest at Buckingham Palace.)

Those of her subjects who don't drop in personally – and the Queen prefers it if they don't – tend to write to her. She gets about three hundred letters a day: some of them to do with political matters, some wanting help in solving a local problem such as housing or hospitals – or the difficulty for divorced fathers in seeing their children – and some are straightforward fan letters (and a few abusive), but others are also highly personal, just as Michael Fagan's conversation was personal.

And that is one of the functions of monarchy: providing a focus for people's emotions. Two women spend an entire morning each day opening and sorting letters. The Queen doesn't answer them personally but she sees them and gets a very good feel as a result for the issues that are worrying people. Her other great feeler for the mood of the nation is the conversations she has when she is on away days. People may only have a few seconds with her when she shakes their hand, and some are so overcome with nerves that they utter nothing intelligible, but some come straight out with whatever is on their mind, from Britain's engagement with Europe to the contentious issue of foxhunting.

The Queen's other opportunity to meet people outside her own social circle is at receptions and lunches at the Palace. A recent innovation has been themed receptions. There was one for pioneers, for example, to which people like James Dyson, of vacuum cleaner fame, were invited; another for people who had changed the life of the nation, for which the television cook Delia Smith was chosen; and another for women of achievement, which included all sorts from Lady Thatcher to Kate Moss.

The research for all of these activities is done by the CRU.

They plan the Queen's programme and research not only who the women of achievement, for example, are for the receptions, but also which parts of the country are due for a royal visit. They have the latest in IT – researched, you guessed it, by the CRU – and with this they can produce geographical analysis tables of royal visits, and can work out where each member of the family should go in the coming six months.

On one of the days I followed the Queen she was in Surrey, where amongst other things she opened a new orthopaedic wing at Epsom hospital and met a familiar face – Mr Roger Vickers, the surgeon who operated on her knees and the Queen Mother's hips so successfully. It was no random choice: she had not been to the county for five years. They also do research on patronages; if a charity approaches a member of the family asking them to become patron or president, they check it out. They research new thinking from the private sector, look at policy procedures, work with the Press Office on opinion polls, scrutinize travel plans; the list is endless, and, according to Havill, the unit is constantly changing, constantly modernizing, constantly evolving.

A longer-established tradition are small, informal lunches at Buckingham Palace for assorted members of the great and the good. It was an idea suggested by the Duke of Edinburgh, who has had many good ideas during the course of the Queen's reign. These lunches were held so that the Queen could meet interesting people and opinion formers who she didn't normally come across; and, just as importantly, so that they could meet her. The first lunch took place in 1956 and she has been holding them ever since. People who go are generally enchanted, my own father among them. There were ten guests the day he went, a typical number. At the time he was editor and columnist of the *Sunday Express*; his fellow diners were a Tory MP, Sue MacGregor, then the presenter of *Woman's*

Hour, a High Court judge, an interior designer, the coxswain of the Humber lifeboat and Anne Beckwith Smith, lady-in-waiting to the Princess of Wales. They gathered promptly at 12.50 in the 1844 Room where they were given a drink before lining up to meet the Queen and Prince Philip who came in and shook hands with each of them and engaged in small talk. There were corgis roaming around and my father jokingly asked the Prince whether they were dangerous. 'You mean are they in danger from you?' he retorted. He had clearly done his homework and had a journalist in his midst under sufferance.

At lunch my father found himself on the Queen's left-hand side, the judge was on her right, and throughout the first two courses – salmon, followed by braised ham – she addressed not one single word to him. He was beginning to feel more than a little miffed. At the other end of the table he noticed that the Tory MP was in exactly the same situation. He was on the Duke's left and for two courses had been completely ignored while Philip lavished attention on Sue MacGregor, seated on his right. The two of them looked at each other and shrugged their shoulders.

But as soon as the pudding arrived the entire table was transformed. The Queen and the Duke of Edinburgh both turned to the guest on their left and my father basked in the Queen's full attention for the rest of the lunch. They chatted, he said, like old friends and he was always certain that the key had been horses. On the way to the Palace his office driver, a very keen punter, had told him to ask the Queen whether her horse Height of Fashion was going to win the Oaks. This is precisely what he did and the Queen immediately lit up and explained that the horse's legs were possibly too long for the Epsom course but that its chances would be decided by whether the horse ran well at Goodwood. Bingo.

SEVEN

Diana

Someone should have taken them to one side and said, 'Make this work. Go out on to that balcony, hold hands, smile and when you come back down, one of you turn to the right, one to the left. Take a mistress, take a lover if you want, but for the sake of the boys, the family and the country, stay together.' No one seemed to have the long view; Diana was a huge asset. She'd have been in her forties by now; and one of the most interesting women in the world, the best ambassador for this country ever. She could have been UNESCO's child ambassador ... Wherever we went people's eyes widened – her mannerisms, her dress sense. What else did he want? In that position you've got to work together. Someone should have said to the Queen, 'This is the next generation coming through.' They should never have let her go.

These are not the words of an outsider who didn't understand the situation. This is someone who worked for the Prince of Wales before his marriage and for both the Prince and Princess for several years after the marriage. He was a member of the royal household for ten years in all and was loyal, devoted and dedicated. He is now in his early seventies and might still

61

have been there in some capacity or other had he not been caught in the crossfire of the warring Waleses. He was enormously fond of both the Prince and the Princess and would have wished the greatest personal happiness to them both, but this was not about personal happiness. It couldn't be. They were not just any couple; they were royal, they had obligations; and his principal concern is for the monarchy.

There is no doubt that he is right. The monarchy was very seriously damaged by the breakdown of that marriage; it destroyed the respect that a great many people instinctively felt for the Royal Family and it paved the way for much of the intolerable media intrusion that has now become a part of their lives. Charles and Diana would not have been the first couple to have lived separate lives under the same roof; they didn't even have to be under the same roof – they already had a roof each – Charles at Highgrove in the country, Diana at Kensington Palace in London. Aristocratic families have been doing precisely this for generations: staying married for the sake of their children and their estates, and discreetly taking lovers on the side. It should have been possible for the Prince and Princess, but this was such a mismatch, the relationship so volatile, Diana so unpredictable and the handling of it all so inept that in the final analysis bringing the marriage to an end was the lesser of two evils.

Michael Colborne first met the Prince of Wales in the Navy in the early seventies when, fresh out of Dartmouth, Charles had joined his first ship, HMS *Norfolk*, as a sub-lieutenant. Colborne was a non-commissioned officer, fourteen years his senior, unfazed by the HRH tag and quite unafraid to speak his mind. He was a grammar-school boy, with a wife and young son, who had joined the Navy at sixteen and been there all his working life. The two became friends and they would sit up at night, talking over a few drinks; Colborne would often pull his leg and when they were on shore leave he would show him the sights. This was the first time the Prince had mixed with people from a different social class and he was fascinated by every aspect of Michael's life; when the Prince left the Navy in 1977 and became a fully-fledged member of the Family Firm he invited Colborne to help set up his office. Officially he was in charge of his financial affairs, but in practice he became the Prince's right-hand man, and the only member of his staff prepared to tell Charles the truth, however unpalatable it sometimes was. The Prince welcomed his honesty and made him promise that he would never change. 'If you don't agree with something, you say so,' he had told him, but, of course, on those occasions when Colborne had disagreed and said so, there was all hell to pay.

Like his father and grandfather, George VI, the Prince has a terrifying temper that has reduced strong men to tears; it was that which finally drove Michael Colborne away. Lord Mountbatten, the Prince's great-uncle and mentor, had once said when he was on the point of leaving in the very early days, 'Bear with him, Michael, please. He doesn't mean to get at you personally. It's just that he wants to let off steam and you're the only person he can lose his temper with. It's a back-handed compliment really, you know. He needs you.'

The Prince did need him, not least in helping him cope with Diana. The story of Charles and Diana and their marriage has been analysed and written about *ad nauseam* – I have done a fair share of it myself – but I am now about to do it again. This is partly because no book about the monarchy can ignore the significance that that marriage and all the consequences of its failure has had on the institution; and partly because, in my view, despite all the books, articles and documentaries, there is still a profound misconception about the whole sorry tale.

Colborne was one of the first people the Prince told about his proposal to Diana. He was the one who organized flowers to greet her on her return from Australia where she had gone while making up her mind about marriage. The Prince had asked him to send her the biggest, most fragrant bunch of flowers he could find and had handwritten a welcome home note to go with them. They had been delivered by the Prince's police protection officer, yet years later, when the Princess was talking about her rotten marriage, she threw it out as a sign of his callousness: 'I came back from Australia,' she told Andrew Morton. 'Someone knocks at the door – someone from his office with a bunch of flowers and I knew that they hadn't come from Charles because there was no note. It was just somebody being very tactful in the office.' Nothing could have been further from the truth.

Colborne became like a father to Diana in her early years in the Palace, but he could see there was going to be trouble from the start. At nineteen, she was little more than a child when she first arrived, totally unprepared for the life that lay ahead and completely out of her depth. She was a romantic, an innocent, she knew nothing of life or work or relationships. The things she knew about were loss and rejection, the product of her parents' divorce; and she had been fatally damaged by the experience. She had no self-confidence, no stability, just a desperate need to be loved and wanted; and a determination to get what she wanted.

She wanted the Prince of Wales – she had fallen in love with him – but it was the idea as much as the man she was in love with. In reality she scarcely knew him; and he knew nothing about her because she hadn't let him. She had presented to him a Diana she knew he would be attracted by; a Diana who shared all of his interests, who loved the country, who was easy, loving, funny and uncomplicated. It was only once the ring was on her finger and she found herself transported from her all-girl, giggly flat in Fulham to an impersonal suite of rooms in Buckingham Palace, with no one of her own age for company and a fiancé who was always busy, that the real Diana began to emerge. The happy, easy-going girl became moody, wilful and suspicious. The moods swung wildly; one minute she would be laughing and joking, the next she would be kicking the furniture, displaying a terrible temper that Charles had never seen before. It came from nowhere, along with hysterical tears, and could be gone in an instant. She took sudden dislikes to people she had previously appeared to like, accused them of spying on her or being out to get her; she was jealous of friends and ex-girlfriends (not so surprising); she was even jealous of the Prince's relationship with his mother, and convinced that the Queen was writing about her in the letters and memos she sent her son.

To begin with Diana and Michael Colborne shared an office and she spent many an hour pouring out her heart to him. A more secure, mature nineteen-year-old might have coped, might have had a better understanding of what she was taking on, but Diana had none. She had a romanticized view of marriage and no experience of commitment. When she had encountered difficulty in her life – a school she disliked, a dancing job she didn't enjoy – she ducked out of it; no one had ever made her do anything she didn't want to do. With two sets of parents there had never been any real discipline. Discipline: the key to being a member of the Royal Family. She wasn't marrying the man, she was marrying the job; she was joining the Family Firm, and, as Michael Colborne tried to explain to her, it was a unique way of life.

One weekend she had been at Royal Lodge in Windsor and had decided to go for a walk without telling anyone. All hell broke loose because of the security implications, and on the

Monday morning she told Michael what had happened. She said she didn't know how she was going to cope.

'This is going to be your life,' he had said.

You're never going to be on your own again. And you're going to change. In four to five years you're going to be an absolute bitch, not through any fault of your own, but because of the circumstances in which you live. If you want four boiled eggs for breakfast, you'll have them. If you want the car brought round to the front door a minute ago, you'll have it. It's going to change you. Your life is going to be organized. You open your diary now and you can put down Trooping the Colour, the Cenotaph service, Cowes Week, the Ascots. You can write your diary for five years ahead, ten years, twenty years.

That was the reality. There would be no spontaneity, no last-minute plans, no ducking out of commitments. Her carefree life of being a nobody was over. For a nineteen-year-old that was a terrifying prospect.

Colborne is convinced that if Lord Mountbatten, murdered by the IRA in 1979, had still been alive a year later, Charles and Diana would never have married. He is probably right. Years later, Diana spoke about being the 'sacrificial lamb' on the day of her wedding, of how she had wanted to back out of it some weeks before but been told by her sister that it was too late: her face was on the tea towels. If she did have doubts, despite their frank and lengthy conversations she certainly never expressed them to Colborne.

Charles himself had serious doubts about whether he had made the right decision during their engagement, but he kept them to himself. He asked the advice of a number of people – official advisers, friends and family – before he proposed to

Diana, aware that this was no ordinary marriage and that he couldn't afford to make a mistake. Most people counselled for the marriage, including, significantly, the Queen Mother. She was very keen on the match; Diana was the granddaughter of her friend and lady-in-waiting, Ruth, Lady Fermoy, and in every sense, on paper, the perfect match. Ruth Fermoy knew it wasn't; but, socially ambitious for her granddaughter, she chose to keep quiet. Years later in 1993, only a month before she died, the old lady apologized to the Prince of Wales for failing to warn him. Diana, she knew, had been 'a dishonest and difficult girl'. Her father, who died in 1991, also admitted he had been wrong not to say something.

And so, having taken soundings, Charles went ahead and proposed, knowing that despite the consensus among those he'd spoken to, in his heart of hearts he was still uncertain. 'It all seems so ridiculous because I do very much want to do the right thing for this country and for my family,' he said, 'but I'm terrified sometimes of making a promise and then perhaps living to regret it.' He was in a 'confused and anxious state of mind', he confessed to one friend. To another, 'It is just a matter of taking an unusual plunge into some rather unknown circumstances that inevitably disturbs me but I expect it will be the right thing in the end.'

The fact that, when asked on television on the day of the engagement whether he was in love, he replied 'Yes, whatever love is', is irrelevant. It was a very tactless thing to say, hurtful to Diana and bad PR, and he should never have said it; but the truth is this was a marriage where being in love was not the most important ingredient. This was a marriage that had to last – look at the number of ordinary marriages that have fallen apart when the pair stopped being 'in love' and discovered that there was nothing else holding them together. Look at the number of innocent children who have suffered as a result. The Prince's own thoughts about this, articulated years earlier, have been quoted many times before but they cannot be bettered:

> I've fallen in love with all sorts of girls and I fully intend to go on doing so, but I've made sure I haven't married the first person I've fallen in love with. I think one's got to be aware of the fact that falling madly in love with someone is not necessarily the starting point to getting married. [Marriage] is basically a very strong friendship ... I think you are lucky if you find the person attractive in the physical and the mental sense ... To me marriage seems to be the biggest and most responsible step to be taken in one's life.
>
> Whatever your place in life, when you marry, you are forming a partnership which you hope will last for fifty years. So I'd want to marry someone whose interests I could share. A woman not only marries a man; she marries into a way of life – a job. She's got to have some knowledge of it, some sense of it, otherwise she wouldn't have a clue about whether she's going to like it. If I'm deciding on whom I want to live with for fifty years – well, that's the last decision on which I want my head to be ruled by my heart.

So what went wrong? Why did Charles allow himself to make what, by the time he walked up the aisle, he knew was the wrong decision? He took advice before he proposed, but once he had asked Diana to marry him the subject was no longer open for discussion. His old friend Nicholas Soames could see disaster ahead; what worried him was the intellectual gulf between them and the fact that they had so little in common. Penny Romsey, wife of his cousin Norton (Lord Romsey), Mountbatten's grandson, had an additional fear. She thought that Diana was in love with the idea of being a princess and had very little understanding of what that would involve. Norton agreed with all three observations and had very real fears for the future. He tackled the Prince on several occasions but was firmly told to mind his own business. None of them had the influence over him that Mountbatten had had. Mountbatten was like a father to the Prince – he called him his 'Honorary Grandfather' – and although Mountbatten was ambitious on his own behalf and would have dearly loved his own grand-daughter to marry Charles, he would have seen that Diana was the wrong person for him to be bound to for fifty years or more. But Mountbatten was dead, and Charles was still consumed by grief, lost without the older man to guide him; and alone.

He couldn't talk to his own father; he and the Duke of Edinburgh had never been able to talk. If they had this mar-riage might never have happened, because what prompted Charles to make a decision before he was ready was a letter from Prince Philip. He told Charles he must make up his mind about Diana: he must either marry her or let her go because it was not fair to keep her dangling on a string. Charles took it to mean he must marry her. Friends who saw the letter have said there was no such ultimatum; the Prince misinterpreted his father's words. Either way, over something so crucial, it is calamitous that they did not sit down and talk about it. And the Queen offered no opinion one way or another.

The Duke had written his letter because of the media frenzy; Diana had been hunted from the day her face first appeared on the front page of the *Daily Star* with a question mark about her identity. She had been spotted through a pair of binoculars by the paper's relentless 'Charles watcher', James Whitaker, on the banks of the River Dee. She was lounging around while Charles was fishing. He and his photographer, his companion in the bushes that day, quickly worked out who she was and from that moment until the engagement five months later, she was besieged – followed, photographed and occasionally tricked into talking – everywhere she went. And when a blonde was seen boarding the royal train in sidings in Wiltshire late one night, the press assumed, mistakenly, it was Diana. The Duke of Edinburgh realized that her honour was at stake and that any further delay in the Prince declaring his intentions would be damaging.

EIGHT

The Duty of an Heir

It is too easy to say that the media is responsible for the whole mismatch between Charles and Diana. It is true that, had James Whitaker not been spying on the Prince of Wales while he fished that afternoon, Charles might have been able to get to know Diana better before popping the question. The media has a lot to answer for, and its behaviour during the most troubled years of their marriage was disgraceful. The war over circulation robbed newspapers of all humanity as they scrabbled to get the juiciest, most damning story and the most intrusive photograph. But what really forced the Prince's hand was the system – a system that was thoroughly out of touch with modern thinking.

Charles's one obligation as Prince of Wales and heir to the throne was to perpetuate the House of Windsor. He could have chosen to do nothing with his life while his mother reigned, to make no contribution to the welfare of the country. He could have squandered his income from the Duchy of Cornwall, hunted three days a week, played polo all summer, gambled, partied and drunk himself into a stupor. None of that would have mattered, in theory at least, provided he produced a legitimate heir.

For that he needed a wife and that was more problematic.

By the time Charles was old enough to be looking for a suitable candidate in the 1970s, a sexual revolution had taken place in Western society. The contraceptive pill had removed the fear of unwanted pregnancy; we had had the swinging sixties, the age of rock and roll, the Beatles, flower power, free love and the beginning of women's emancipation. Educated, well-bred women no longer saw marriage as their only goal in life, they went to university rather than finishing school, were independent, capable, smart, and when they married they were no longer prepared to keep house, mind the children and be decorative adjuncts to their husbands. Mrs Thatcher, after all, was about to become Britain's first woman Prime Minister. Debutantes had had their day; virgins over the age of sixteen were becoming as rare as hens' teeth.

Yet when Charles and Diana became engaged in 1981, the system – society, the press – still insisted that the Prince of Wales should marry a virgin – nearly twenty years after virginity had ceased to be of importance for the rest of society. And in a piece of advice that owed more to his generation than his personal wisdom, Lord Mountbatten reinforced the need.

'I believe,' he wrote to Charles, 'in a case like yours, the man should sow his wild oats and have as many affairs as he can before settling down, but for a wife he should choose a suitable, attractive and sweet-charactered girl before she has met anyone else she might fall for . . . I think it is disturbing for women to have experiences if they have to remain on a pedestal after marriage.'

And to help with the sowing of the wild oats, Mountbatten made Broadlands, his house in Hampshire, available to the Prince as a safe hideaway to which he could bring girlfriends, away from the prying lenses of the press for which would-be-princess spotting had become an obsession. One or two of those girlfriends might have made perfect wives for the Prince. Several shared his sporting interests or his Goonish sense of humour and were good friends as well as lovers; they were intelligent, pretty, good company and from suitably aristocratic families. But any 'past' always ruled them out as possible brides. Camilla Parker Bowles, or Camilla Shand as she then was, fell into that category. But she pre-empted the problem by marrying Andrew Parker Bowles and in the process dealt a devastating blow to the Prince of Wales. Charles had been very young when that happened; he had met and fallen very much in love with Camilla in the autumn of 1972 when he was almost twenty-four and newly in the Navy. She was a year older and already seeing Andrew Parker Bowles (who was wonderful but hopelessly unfaithful). Her dalliance with Charles was a bit of fun – a brief fling while Andrew was posted in Germany – and it was destined never to go anywhere. She knew that she would not have passed the virginity test and had no desire to be a princess. The man she wanted to marry was her handsome Cavalry officer.

Four years later the Prince fell for another girl, Davina Sheffield, who could have been the soulmate he was searching for. She seemed ideal in so many ways, and they appeared to be very much in love, but she already had a boyfriend when Charles met her, an Old Harrovian and powerboat racer called James Beard. Davina initially rebuffed invitations to have dinner with the Prince, but he was so persistent that she eventually succumbed and the boyfriend soon fell by the wayside. He was subsequently conned into talking about his relationship with Davina by what turned out to be a Sunday tabloid reporter and the story of their affair, complete with photographs of their 'love nest', made headline news. It killed the relationship stone dead.

*   *   *

73

That was not the only time a girlfriend's past was raked over, but the strong message girls took from all of this was that, unless you wanted the third degree from the tabloids, Prince Charles was not the man to date. By the same token, if your public profile needed a bit of a hike, in the case of actresses and starlets, he was your man.

Unsurprisingly Charles became despondent about ever finding the perfect girl and sought refuge with a number of married women, one of whom was Camilla Parker Bowles. Meanwhile, the press continued to link him romantically with just about every eligible girl he had ever shaken hands with, and went so far as to announce his engagement to one, Princess Marie Astrid of Luxembourg, whom he had never even met. The pressure was almost intolerable and he began to think that no girl in her right mind would ever want to be involved with him, far less marry into the House of Windsor. So when he met Diana in 1979, and found her to be so fresh, funny and delightful, as well as suitably aristocratic, and at just seventeen, suitably innocent, he began thinking of her as a potential wife.

They had first met two years before when Diana was still a schoolgirl and, in his eyes, jolly and fun, but nothing more than the little sister of his current girlfriend, Lady Sarah Spencer. Two years later, when that relationship had ended, they met again and although still very young in some respects, she had surprising maturity in others and clearly seemed to adore him. They had a number of casual meetings, never dates, always with others; and then sitting on a hay bale in the summer of 1980 she had touched him deeply. They were at a barbecue near Petworth, in Sussex, and he mentioned the murder of Mountbatten. She either had compassion that was way beyond her years or knew precisely which button to press. She said how sad he had looked at the funeral in Westminster

Abbey; how she had sensed his loneliness and his need for someone to care for him.

Later that summer she went to stay with her eldest sister, Jane, married to Robert Fellowes, the Queen's Private Secretary, at their cottage on the Balmoral estate; his infatuation deepened and everyone in the household fell in love with her. That autumn he invited her to a house party at Balmoral, after the Queen had left, to see what his friends thought. They were bowled over. As Patty Palmer-Tomkinson said to Jonathan Dimbleby:

> We went stalking together, we got hot, we got tired, she fell into a bog, she got covered in mud, laughed her head off, got puce in the face, hair glued to her forehead because it was pouring with rain ... she was a sort of wonderful English schoolgirl who was game for anything, naturally young but sweet and clearly determined and enthusiastic about him, very much wanted him.

Imagine his surprise, therefore, when after their engagement she seemed suddenly to hate everything he had thought she loved. He was quite at a loss to understand the change in Diana and thought it must be his fault in some way; that the prospect of marrying him was all too ghastly. And yet he spoke to no one about his anxieties; and when concerned friends tried to talk to him, he refused to listen. Pulling out would have been unimaginable: the humiliation, the hurt, the headlines, the castigation; but in retrospect, it would have been infinitely less painful and less damaging to everyone involved, including the monarchy, than going through with a wedding that he knew was a mistake. At the very least he should have discussed it. As one relation says, 'In his position he bloody well should have spoken to people because he had to think of the constitutional side as well as the private side. He had chosen Diana with both sides in mind, but equally he needed to think of the consequences for both if it was going to go wrong.'

The trouble is that the Prince of Wales is fundamentally a weak man, and that is what has so incensed the Duke of Edinburgh over the years. He wanted a son in his own image – a tough, abrasive, plain-talking, unemotional man's man – but those qualities bypassed his first son and settled instead on his daughter. Charles has a generous heart, he cares hugely about the underdog, because, for all his palatial living, he is one, he identifies. He wants passionately to make the world a better place, to stop people feeling hopeless and helpless, to stop modernizers from destroying our heritage, chemicals from destroying our environment, ignorance and greed from destroying our planet, red tape from destroying our lives. He is admirable in so many ways, but he has never been a strong character and has never been able to cope with confrontation. Blisteringly angry at times, certainly, demanding, yes, and on the sporting field no one could question his courage, but he has never been brave when it comes to taking tough decisions. He gets others to do it for him. Perhaps it is because he has always been surrounded by strong women: his grandmother, his mother, his sister – even his nanny. Helen Lightbody was such a terrifying woman that the Queen kept out of the nursery while she was in charge. By the time the Queen had the two younger children Helen Lightbody had gone and Mabel Anderson, her deputy and a much easier character, was in charge, and she and the Queen were good friends and brought the children up together. As a result the Queen had much more contact with Andrew and Edward than she ever had with Charles and Anne, and is still infinitely closer to them today.

In marrying Diana, for all her emotional turmoil and frailty

Charles had found himself with another strong, determined woman. He didn't understand her rages – one day during their honeymoon, when they were staying at Craigowan Lodge, a small house on the Balmoral estate, she lost her temper and went for him with a knife which she then used to cut herself, leaving blood everywhere. That night as he knelt down to say his prayers – as he regularly does – Diana hit him over the head with the family bible. He has never been to the house since. He just couldn't fathom the emotional rollercoaster, the demands, the insecurities; he couldn't cope, needed others to help, which of course infuriated her more. Michael Colborne was the first of a long string of members of the Prince's staff who had to mediate with Diana while Charles backed away. Even during the honeymoon he was summoned to Balmoral to talk to Diana because she was so bitterly unhappy. She was already caught in the grips of an eating disorder, bored by the countryside, made miserable by the rain and baffled by the Prince's desire to spend his days shooting and fishing. And what was he doing while Colborne spent more than seven hours with Diana while she raged, cried, brooded in silence, ranted and kicked the furniture by turns? He was out stalking with his friends.

That night both men were taking the train back to London; the Prince had an engagement in the south, Diana was staying at Balmoral. As Colborne waited in the dark by the car, a brand-new Range Rover, he could hear a fearsome row going on inside. Suddenly the door flew open and Charles shouted 'Michael' and hurled something at him, which by the grace of God he caught before it was lost in the gravel. It was Diana's wedding ring; she had lost so much weight it needed to be made smaller. The Prince was in a black rage all the way to the train; the new car wasn't quite as he had specified and so he took it out on Colborne, calling him every name under the sun. Exhausted and defeated by his day with Diana, Colborne simply stared out of the window and let the abuse wash over him. Once on the train, the Prince summoned him. Colborne had just ordered himself a triple gin and was in no hurry to respond. The Prince offered him another. 'Tonight, Michael,' he said, 'you displayed the best traditions of the silent service. You didn't say a word.'

And for the next five hours or more they sat together and talked about the Prince's marriage; not yet two months old it was already a disaster. He was mystified by Diana's behaviour, simply couldn't fathom what was going on or what he could do to make her well and happy.

NINE

Not Waving: Drowning

It was never the case that Charles didn't care. Couldn't cope, yes; and as the months and then the years went by with no let-up from the unpredictability of Diana's behaviour, he became hardened and at times downright callous in his attitude towards her. He had found her a top psychiatrist; he had done what he could to appease her. He had cut out of his life the friends she disliked or of whom she was suspicious; good, loyal friends, some of them friends since childhood – and, in typical style, he took the easy way out and did it without telling them. They were left to wonder what had happened when phone calls, letters and invitations to Highgrove and Balmoral simply stopped. He even gave away his faithful old Labrador Harvey because Diana thought he was smelly. None of this seemed to make any difference; and when she burst into tears or launched into a tantrum, nothing he could say seemed to calm her. So he gave up. When she made dramatic gestures he walked away, when she self-harmed he walked away. Not because he didn't care but because he couldn't help; he felt desperate, hopeless and guilty and to this day he feels a terrible sense of failure for not having been able to make his marriage work.

That is not to say that there was no happiness. There were

moments of intense pleasure, the children brought huge joy and there was laughter and jokes and fun, but not enough to counter the difficulties, and as time went by the gulf between them became no longer bridgeable.

Diana had needs that Charles couldn't begin to address. Anyone who has lived with someone suffering from an eating disorder (which was very probably in Diana's case a symptom of a personality disorder and therefore even more complex) knows all too well what an impossible situation he was in. Anorexia and bulimia test and sometimes destroy even the most stable relationships and balanced homes. And all that we know of her behaviour – from her staff, her friends and even her family – fits every description that has ever been written about the disorders. The Prince didn't stand a chance. And yet to outsiders Diana looked like the happiest, most equable girl you could hope to find. She seduced everyone with her charm and coquettishness, men fell like ninepins, she was playful and funny and oh so beautiful, so young, so glamorous. Just what the Royal Family needed to invigorate it and make it seem relevant to swathes of young people who didn't see the point of it. She captured the hearts and minds of the nation. No wonder no one wanted to believe that behind closed doors Diana was deceitful, demanding and manipulative, and that the laughter was replaced by tears and tantrums. Much easier to believe that it was all a story put about by the Prince's friends to discredit Diana. And when Diana accused him of doing as much herself, because the woman he really loved was Camilla Parker Bowles, there was nothing more to be said. Nothing would convince the majority of the British people that Charles was anything other than a villain who used Diana as a brood mare to produce the heir and spare he needed; that their marriage was a sham from the start and the woman he really loved, and continued to bed throughout, was Camilla.

Not Waving: Drowning

Camilla Parker Bowles has seen a turnaround in her fortunes since Diana died. Having been arch-villain and probably the most hated woman in Britain for a good chunk of the 1990s, people now rather admire her. They have bought into a touching love story. Charles was a bastard for what he did to Diana, so the script goes, but this is a woman he has loved since he was twenty-three. They missed their opportunity to marry then, but the flame still burned bright and now, in middle age, they have finally found happiness together. It doesn't alter their view of what Charles did to Diana, but Diana has now been dead for nearly eight years, Camilla has behaved with dignity and discretion throughout, he has been true to her (if not to Diana), he's a pretty decent chap in every other respect: they deserve some happiness.

It's neat but it's not the truth, and it is important to state this if only for the sake of William and Harry, who must infer from this version of events that the father they love used, abused and destroyed the mother they also loved. He did not and the impression of their marriage that Diana left on the world, via Andrew Morton and *Panorama*, and repeatedly rehearsed in documentaries, is grievously unfair.

The Prince of Wales has plenty of shortcomings but he is not a liar; his great misfortune is that he has never been able to be even faintly economical with the truth. There are so many occasions when the smallest, whitest lie would have saved him a great deal of trouble – starting with that fateful answer on the day of his engagement to Diana about whether he was in love. It has come back to haunt him regularly, as for many years did his admission that he talked to plants. And when I interviewed him in 1986 and asked him whether having a wife to talk to who had done ordinary, everyday things before her marriage was an advantage in helping him know how the other half lives, he said he didn't really talk to Diana about that sort of thing, but conversations with Laurens van der Post were very stimulating from that point of view. His Private Secretary, Sir John Riddell, almost visibly clutched his head in his hands. But the most disastrous example was during his television interview with Jonathan Dimbleby when he was asked about his infidelity. The question didn't come out of the blue, and his reply was very well thought out.

'Were you,' asked Dimbleby, '. . . did you try to be faithful and honourable to your wife when you took the vow of marriage?'

'Yes,' said the Prince, and after a brief and rather anguished pause said, 'until it became irretrievably broken down, us both having tried.'

On that occasion his Private Secretary, Richard Aylard, had reinforced the Prince's determination to tell the truth, and it was the rest of the world that held their heads in their hands and gasped with incredulity. The Duke of Edinburgh was incensed, the rest of the family flabbergasted, the Queen's advisers and courtiers stunned, the Prince's friends appalled, and the blame fell squarely on Richard Aylard for having allowed Charles to make what many regarded as the worst mistake of his life. At the time many people thought it might cost him the throne.

'It wasn't being honest to Jonathan that was the problem,' protested Aylard in his defence. 'If you want to start placing blame, the fault was getting into the relationship in the first place.'

There is no doubt that Camilla has been an important figure in the Prince's life since he first fell in love with her at the age of twenty-three. They are the greatest of friends, they have all sorts of interests and enthusiasms in common and they love one another very dearly; it is clearly a warm, comfortable relationship and hugely beneficial to them both, but it hasn't been an exclusive, obsessive relationship since Charles was twenty-three. He has fallen in and out of love many times since then – probably never more deeply than with Camilla – but he has fallen in love none the less. She was certainly one of the women he was seeing when he started going out with Diana but it was never going anywhere. Camilla was married; even if she had been divorced he could never have married her, not in 1981; a divorcee with two children becoming Princess of Wales? It was unthinkable. Besides, what woman in her right mind would want to?

When Charles first started looking upon Diana as a possible candidate for marriage he talked to Camilla about her; he asked all his close friends what they thought of Diana, and Camilla was one of those who tried to befriend her and welcome her to the group. She invited Charles and Diana to spend weekends at her house. There was nothing sinister in any of this. The fact that Camilla knew Charles was going to propose and hence wrote a friendly note to Diana to await her arrival at Clarence House on the day it was announced wasn't sinister either. Look at almost any episode of the American TV sitcom *Friends*: soliciting friends' approval of the latest girl/boyfriend is par for the course. But the Princess took it as proof that something was still going on between them, and read into Camilla's friendly invitation to lunch the latter's desire to find out whether she was going to hunt when she moved to Highgrove, and therefore whether she would be in the way of their plans to meet.

There were no meetings, and virtually no contact until several years into the marriage, and certainly no sex, as the Prince so painfully and honestly explained, until the marriage had irretrievably broken down. And by that time he was close to irretrievably breaking down, too. Towards the end of 1986 he started making contact with friends once again, those he had shut out of his life at Diana's request some years before. As he wrote to one of them:

> Frequently I feel nowadays that I'm in a kind of cage, pacing up and down in it and longing to be free. How awful incompatibility is, and how dreadfully destructive it can be for the players in this extraordinary drama. It has all the ingredients of a Greek tragedy . . . I fear I'm going to need a bit of help every now and then for which I feel rather ashamed.

He was in such a chronic state of depression by then that they feared for his sanity, and it was Patty Palmer-Tomkinson who engineered a reunion with Camilla, knowing how much she had meant to him in the past. Camilla herself was not particularly happy; she and Andrew Parker Bowles were the best of friends but their marriage was an empty shell with Andrew in London escorting pretty girls all week and Camilla minding the home, dogs, horses and children in the country. At first she and Charles started to talk on the telephone, he pouring out his heart to her, she listening sympathetically, warm, understanding and supportive; then they met at Patty's house in Hampshire and started seeing each other again, and gradually the relationship developed and they took up where they had left off more than six years before. Camilla was a lifeline for Charles; she brought light and laughter into his life which for a long time had been so very dark.

This was not the outcome Charles had either wanted or anticipated. For years he had longed to be married, to have for himself the family atmosphere that he experienced in his friends' houses, to have children running around and a companion with whom to share his life. He was lonely; he was surrounded by valets, footmen, butlers, private secretaries and police protection officers. He was never on his own, but 'he was one of the loneliest men you'll ever meet. They all are,' says Michael Colborne. 'They go out to banquets and dinners and great dos, but when they get home at night they go up to their rooms and they are on their own. There's no one to have a drink with. They are very independent people; even their friends are mostly acquaintances.' Charles wanted a soulmate. In a thank-you letter to a friend written on Boxing Day in 1981, when Diana was first pregnant, he wrote, 'We've had such a lovely Christmas – the two of us. It has been extraordinarily happy and cosy being able to share it together . . . Next year will, I feel sure, be even nicer with a small one to join in as well.'

It had either been a rare moment of calm or wishful thinking. Not long afterwards she was throwing herself down the stairs in a desperate cry for help. The whole situation was a vicious circle. Diana's chronic need for love and reassurance meant she wanted Charles to be with her 100 per cent of the time – more than that; she wanted his full attention 100 per cent of the time. It was an impossible demand. If she didn't get it, she raged, and the more she raged the further she pushed him away. Even the most slavishly devoted partner would have found her demands unreasonable; he found them impossible. He was Prince of Wales, he had letters to write, papers to read, speeches to deliver and a diary full of engagements and ceremonial duties stretching ahead for ever. He could have given up all his sporting activities if he had wanted to, but he would never have been able to abandon his work; he simply couldn't be the husband Diana wanted.

The interesting question is whether he could have been a satisfactory husband for any woman. Charles wanted a wife, he wanted a companion to share his life with, and he needed a wife because he was heir to the throne and had a duty to procreate; but he had no need of a wife in the sense that most other men need wives. Everything was already done for him: his meals were cooked; his clothes bought, laundered and laid out for him; his bath run, his toothbrush pasted; his shopping done; his house furnished, cleaned and polished; and if he wanted four boiled eggs for breakfast and his car brought round to the front door a minute ago, it happened.

Michael Colborne had warned Diana that in four or five years with this sort of lifestyle she would change; she would become an absolute bitch. The Prince of Wales had known no other lifestyle and was perforce supremely selfish. It may be that he would have taken out of a marriage rather more than he put into it. Very few people have ever disagreed with him, still less said 'No' to him, or told him anything he didn't want to hear. He has never had to consider anyone else's plans or preferences – and still doesn't. His staff work all hours and are expected to jump when they are called whatever the time of day with little apparent thought for their families.

Materially he was spoilt but emotionally he was needy. And though he longed for a home, a family and security, as she did, like Diana he had never known a normal one and therefore had no model to work from. His parents loved him – there is no doubt about that – and friends remember the Queen sitting him on her knee at teatime when Charles was a small boy and playing games with him but she didn't spend the hours in the nursery that she did with the two younger boys because she was intimidated by Helen Lightbody, and any sort of overt affection stopped as he grew older. The Duke was and is a bully, and was equally sparing in his affection. He was rough with Charles, and, according to witnesses, frequently reduced the boy to tears. As a result Charles was frightened of his father and always desperate to please him, without ever apparently succeeding. Even now in his fifties, Charles is still eager to please his parents and earn their approval, and much of the time still feels he's failing. Hard to feel anything else when your father repeatedly makes sarcastic and cutting comments either to you or about you.

The Queen and the Duke were appalled by *The Prince of Wales*, the book Jonathan Dimbleby wrote about the Prince in 1995 following the disastrous film, and hurt by the picture he drew of his childhood. The Prince had given Dimbleby unprecedented access – which turned out to be decidedly foolish – allowed him free rein with private letters, diaries and even official papers and had given him many hours of his time. One former courtier was utterly bemused that his advisers had ever let it happen:

They released Jonathan Dimbleby and the Prince of Wales on to the Scottish moor together at 9.30 and they came back breathless and excited at 4.30; and when you go for a very exhausting walk with anybody – if you went with Goebbels – after a time the blood circulates, the joints ease up, the breath gets short – you'd pour out your heart to anyone, even Goebbels. Dimbleby has huge maieutic charm. Alan Bennett uses that word in his book *Telling Tales*; it means mid-wifely. Jonathan Dimbleby's charms are huge so the Prince of Wales gave him all that stuff about how unhappy when he was a boy – the Queen never spoke to him, the Duke of Edinburgh was beastly to him – and it very much upsets them.

Everyone was told this book would finally show what a marvellous person he was; and people were bored out of their wits by Business in the Community and the Prince's Trust; they wanted to know about their private life. We're interested in who they're going to bed with, except we got rather bored by that because we couldn't keep up with it.

Superficially the Prince of Wales is a carbon copy of his father; it is as though he has modelled himself on the older man. They walk and talk the same way, hold their hands behind their backs in the same way, they enjoy the same sports, share the same interests, and are both involved in charities with much the same agendas. But according to the Duke of Edinburgh there is a fundamental difference. 'He is a romantic – and I'm a pragmatist. That means we do see things differently. And because I don't see things as a romantic would, I'm unfeeling.'

If Charles and his parents had only been able to talk, the history of the last two decades might have been very different and thus also the future security of the monarchy. Prince Philip might have spoken to Charles about the need to make up his mind about Diana rather than sending him a letter which was open to misinterpretation. Charles may have discussed his fears that this marriage was going to be a mistake during the five months of his engagement, so that they could have devised a dignified way of calling the whole thing to a halt. And if all else had failed and they had gone down the aisle and given the public the fabulous fairy-tale wedding that so lit up the world, he might have asked his parents for help when things started to unravel at such terrifying speed. Instead, he said nothing and they said nothing. And, sure as hell, no one else was going to say anything, even though everyone in Kensington Palace and St James's Palace could see the disaster unfolding before their very eyes.

Sadly, the marriage was never going to have been bliss for either of them, that was clear from the start. There were too many differences, too many unrequited needs, too much loneliness; but they could have kept up a façade for the sake of their sons and the monarchy and the millions of people who had wished them well on their wedding day, identified, empathized and invested such hope in their union. By the time any talking happened it was too late. The Princess had gone public, she was out of control – and scaring even herself – and on course for destruction.

As a former courtier says, 'You might have thought the Prince could have found a way of dealing with Diana. Have said, "Let's have a high-level conference over tea to see how we're going to manage this." But it's part of his psychology that he can't do that, it's all part of not giving a PR answer, not telling the smallest of white lies, when he should.'

TEN

Camilla and the Future

The Queen has long held the wish that the earth would open up and swallow her newest daughter-in-law. It is nothing personal – they scarcely met during all the years of controversy – and when they did know one another, in the days when Camilla was a regular guest at Balmoral, Sandringham and Windsor, she was very fond of her. Everyone was very fond of Camilla, particularly the Queen Mother. She was there in those days as the wife of Andrew Parker Bowles, who boasted the unlikely title of the Queen's Silver-Stick-in-Waiting. It is a title from Tudor times – the incumbent kept close to the sovereign to protect him or her from danger and carried a staff of office, topped in silver. Camilla was easy, friendly, earthy and game for anything; she also loved horses and dogs – the perfect combination to endear anyone to the House of Windsor. But the Queen, like her former Private Secretary Robert Fellowes, believes that with few exceptions everything that has gone wrong for the monarchy in the last twenty years has been attributable to Mrs Parker Bowles. It is hard to disagree.

Whichever story you buy about the relationship – the Princess's version, that there were three of them in the marriage, so it never stood a chance; or the Prince's version, that he gave up Camilla before his engagement and there was no physical contact until more than six years later – Mrs Parker Bowles plays a central role. She was certainly the Prince's lover before Diana appeared on the scene, and she was definitely in place again after 1987. He told us so. Whether activity in the intervening years was all in Diana's imagination or not is largely immaterial. By 1992 the Princess of Wales was passionately jealous of her rival and wanted the world to know how unhappy she was about it. Her chosen method was through Andrew Morton, a charming, roguish former *Daily Star* journalist. He wrote a riveting book the like of which has never been seen before or since.

He once told me that he was able to write his book *Diana: Her True Story* in 1992 because of one I had written the previous year which had incensed Diana. That book was *Charles and Diana: Portrait of a Marriage* and in it I had said that the marriage was not a happy one for a multitude of reasons – something I had first mentioned in a biography of Charles four years earlier – and they were leading largely separate lives with separate friends, which was sad, but that it was a successful working partnership none the less. They both worked hard, both made a real difference in their charitable activities, were a terrific double act for the House of Windsor and were both excellent parents. Jonathan Dimbleby mentioned my book as a footnote in his own book three years later. He called it 'a sensitive account of a working partnership which judged that the marriage was, in those terms, "actually very healthy" – a conclusion which, pre-Morton, did not seem so far from the truth as it would do with the benefit of hindsight'. What incensed Diana was the suggestion that, ten years into her marriage, she was happy with this situation; and she set out to tell the world what her life was really like.

Morton used to play squash with a doctor friend of Diana's, James Colthurst, and he acted as a go-between. The full truth of Diana's participation only came out after her death. She had spoken into a tape recorder at Kensington Palace during the summer and autumn of 1991 and Colthurst had delivered the tapes to Morton. The result was explosive: eighteen thousand words on tape and a publishing phenomenon. *Diana: Her True Story*, which ultimately led to the break-up of the marriage, rocked the monarchy to its foundations. It talked about Diana's troubled childhood, her feelings of abandonment when her mother left, her bulimia, her husband's indifference towards her, his obsession with his mistress. The authority of the text was bolstered by on-the-record quotes from some of Diana's closest friends like James Gilbey (of Squidgygate fame) and old flatmate Carolyn Bartholomew. It talked about the Prince's shortcomings as a father and the loneliness and isolation Diana had felt for so many years, trapped in a loveless marriage within a hostile court, made worse by a cold and disapproving Royal Family. The book was serialized in the *Sunday Times*. 'Diana Driven To Five Suicide Bids By "Uncaring" Charles' screamed the banner headline, while the Palace went into meltdown. So many incidents revealed in the serialization, such as those occasions on which the Princess had self-harmed, happened at Sandringham; plans over who took the children where were discussed in the privacy of their office. Morton's sources were good; suspiciously good. And it wasn't the first time that stories had inexplicably been leaked.

Robert Fellowes, treading difficult ground, not for the first or last time, as both Diana's brother-in-law and the Queen's Private Secretary, asked Diana if she had had anything to do with the book. Diana swore she hadn't and Fellowes believed her. The Duke of Edinburgh also challenged her and again she denied it; lying, as it turned out in both cases. The chairman of the Press Complaints Commission therefore duly issued a statement condemning the serialization, and was left feeling very foolish and exceedingly angry when Diana went straight round to Carolyn Bartholomew's house (having telephoned the newspapers to ensure photographers would be waiting) and in a public show of approval embraced her on the doorstep.

During Ascot Week, very shortly afterwards, while Morton's book started vanishing from the shelves, the Queen, the Duke, Charles and Diana all sat down together at Windsor to discuss the situation and to see what could be salvaged from the marriage. This was the first time there had ever been a discussion of this kind. Parents of any couple having difficulties in their marriage would be naturally reticent about intervening, uncertain as to whether help would be welcome. But this wasn't any couple. The breakdown of this marriage had huge implications for the monarchy and yet both the Queen and the Duke of Edinburgh had held back and chosen not to get involved. Andrew Morton was the first person to discover that the Princess had been suffering from bulimia, and the detail in his book was obviously unparalleled, but plenty had already been written about the state of the marriage; it was no secret that Charles and Diana were leading separate lives, seeing separate friends and that the marriage was in trouble. Calling a conference now was too late. Diana had gone public, and, intoxicated with the power she had over the husband who had cheated on her, she announced that she wanted a trial separation.

The Queen and Duke were sympathetic but were firmly against the idea of separation, and urged them both for the sake of the boys as well as Crown and country to try and find a way of making the marriage work. They all agreed to meet again the next day to talk further, but Diana didn't show up.

Two months later the *Sun* published a transcript of an amorous late-night telephone conversation allegedly between Diana
and James Gilbey. Dubbed 'Squidgygate' because of the way
Gilbey repeatedly referred to her as Squidgy or Squidge, it
reinforced Morton's message. Between endearments, she railed
against the Prince and his 'fucking family' and said, 'I'm going
to do something dramatic because I can't stand the confines
of this marriage.'

By Christmas her wish had come true. It had taken one final
disastrous tour to Korea, and a botched weekend Charles had
planned to have with the children at Sandringham, for the
Prince finally to snap and agree there was no purpose in carrying on; the marriage was over and all hope that he and Diana
might still be friends was also over. On 9 December 1992 the
Prime Minister, John Major, announced their separation in
the House of Commons. Julia Cleverdon, chief executive of
Business in the Community, was with the Prince of Wales that
day. She had worked closely with him for nearly ten years and
in all that time, despite innumerable crises, she had never seen
him so utterly miserable.

Diana took the moral high ground. She seemed oblivious of
the fact that she too had been unfaithful during their marriage.
In fact, she had been the first to do so, and had had not just
one lover but a succession. Charles had been unfaithful with
one woman. The problem was that it was Camilla Parker
Bowles, the same woman he had admitted to having been in
love with before he and Diana ever met. In yet another example
of the Prince's unfortunate compulsion to tell the absolute
truth he had gone out of his way to explain this to Diana, to
reassure her that now that he was engaged to be married there
was, and would be, no other woman in his life. And when
Diana asked him point-blank if he still loved Camilla, he didn't
say, as anyone with an ounce of common sense would have

said, 'No. You're the one I love. She and every other woman I've ever known is history.' He said 'Yes' and went on to explain that Camilla was very special to him, but then so were a number of other women.

For a man who is so sensitive and really quite clever at times, it was utterly crass. Diana was insanely jealous of her and it had nothing whatever to do with having a wobbly background and insecure childhood. Find me a young girl who is not jealous of her boyfriend or husband's ex-lovers. Even if they have never met their predecessors they are jealous – jealous of the idea, jealous of the memories they have of each other; irrational, stupid, deeply destructive, I don't deny, but true.

An old family friend, who had also married a man much older than herself, tried to calm Diana. Yes, he'd had girlfriends and some quite serious, but he was thirty-two, that was to be expected. The thing to hang on to, she said, was the fact that it was none of *them* that he had married – the one he wanted to marry was *her*.

There was just one glaring difference here between Diana's situation and that of any other girl on the eve of her wedding; and Diana was no fool, she knew. Charles was Prince of Wales, he couldn't marry *them*; he certainly couldn't marry Mrs Parker Bowles – she was already married. As she said to Andrew Morton, 'He'd found the virgin, the sacrificial lamb.'

And so she became obsessed. A suspicious, insecure girl by nature she imagined an affair where none existed, she imagined him on the telephone to Camilla all the time, discussing his marriage, discussing her. The suspicion and the jealousy ate away at her. She had found a bracelet on Michael Colborne's desk, with GF engraved on it, that Charles had given to Camilla over lunch two days before the wedding. The GF stood for Girl Friday, his nickname for Camilla. It was with a collection of similar presents for other women who had been kind to him during his days as a bachelor. Diana simply saw it as a token of love and went berserk. Camilla gave Charles a pair of cufflinks and those were the ones he chose to wear on his honeymoon. Proof seemed to be everywhere. He might have stopped seeing her, she reasoned, but that didn't mean he had stopped loving her. She told Morton that Charles and Camilla had slept together at Buckingham Palace two nights before the wedding. It was fantasy. The Queen had hosted a dinner and ball that night and Charles was up until the early hours with guests; Camilla was long gone; and on the following night he spent most of it talking to his mother's lady-in waiting, Lady Susan Hussey, who he had known since the age of twelve. All sorts of wild ideas thrashed around inside Diana's head and no amount of reassurance from her husband helped. She couldn't exorcize the conviction that her husband loved someone else.

The Prince of Wales was utterly humiliated by *Diana: Her True Story*. It painted the blackest portrait; it not only called him a cold and faithless husband and a bad father, but it also questioned his fitness to be king. So much of it was demonstrably untrue and so many stories were a distortion of the truth. People who were witnesses to the events remembered them in essence, but they had a twist to them which always put the Prince in a bad light. He was adamant, nevertheless, that there should be no retaliation and instructed his friends to say nothing.

Charles has never publicly criticized Diana. Whenever I have pointed this out to people they say, 'Ah, but he got his friends to do it for him.' This is untrue. Some of his friends did feel that the injustice meted out to him by Morton's book was intolerable and I, for one, was encouraged by several of them to try to redress the balance, but they were not thanked for their trouble and neither was I. I had been planning to make the television documentary that Jonathan Dimbleby finally made, to mark the Prince's twenty-five years as Prince of Wales. I had had discussions with Christopher Martin, the producer of the Prince's previous films – one on his views about architecture, the other about conservation called *The Earth in Balance*. Christopher and I had been to a private lunch at Highgrove to discuss it with him. Suddenly I was dropped from the project and discovered very much later the reason why. I had defended him too vigorously in the media.

What Morton's book had done, as none other had done before it, was point the finger at Camilla Parker Bowles as the principal cause of Diana's unhappiness. Diana had seriously considered calling off the wedding two days before she walked down the aisle, he said, because of Prince Charles's 'continuing friendship with Camilla Parker Bowles, the wife of a member of the Queen's household'. Today the name Camilla Parker Bowles is almost as well known as that of the Prince of Wales, but until 1992 she was scarcely known outside her own circle of friends – and neither was her relationship with the Prince.

Morton's book changed all that. It didn't convince everyone that Charles and Camilla were having an affair. Some thought there was a chance that he had got it wrong, that it was just more tabloid tittle-tattle; but a substantial number of people did believe that what was written in *Diana: Her True Story* was true, and overnight Camilla's peaceful existence in the heart of the countryside was shattered. The press set up camp outside her house and followed her wherever she went. She wasn't safe even in her own garden; photographers were waiting with their long lenses. Hate mail began to arrive accusing her of breaking up the royal marriage. For someone with no experience of being the object of such hatred it was extremely unnerving. It also put her husband in a difficult situation, and wasn't easy for her two children, Tom and Laura (then both in their teens), or for her elderly parents. But Morton was as nothing compared with what followed in relatively quick succession: the Camillagate tapes, the Dimbleby documentary and *Panorama*. The first two put an end to Camilla's twenty-one-year marriage; the third brought the Prince's marriage to an end.

ELEVEN

From Bad to Worse

Having watched the Royal Family from the sidelines all these years, I never cease to be amazed by their resilience. Crises have come and gone, crises that would have crippled most individuals, families, even institutions, but they simply keep going, keep on doing what they have always done, nine times out of ten not even acknowledging whatever has happened, and miraculously the crisis fades. It is a brilliant strategy for survival and probably the only one that could work for a family so remorselessly in the limelight from cradle to coffin. They have no alternative but to take the long view, and recognize that, long term, very little really matters. But after an intimate late-night telephone conversation between Charles and Camilla was taped, published in the British press and devoured by millions over their breakfast cornflakes, I did wonder how the Prince of Wales would recover from this one. The man wanted to be a Tampax. How do you hold up your head in public after everyone you meet knows that? He wanted to be a Tampax to be as close as he could to Camilla. It was a playful conversation any two people very much in love and missing one another might have had and, read in its entirety, the eleven-minute conversation was rather touching; but you would rather slit your throat than contemplate one solitary soul overhearing you, let alone millions of people all over the world.

The tape was a compilation of several different conversations held over several months in 1989, but that was irrelevant. No one could deny that the voices were authentic; the Prince's humiliation and embarrassment were total. He knows that it will come back to haunt him – it will be dredged up at his coronation and at other serious moments in his life – and serve to humiliate his parents, his sons and Camilla's family, too. And yet the day the tapes were published he had an engagement in Liverpool and, instead of finding some excuse to cancel, as any ordinary person would, he stepped out of his car that morning to face the waiting crowds as though absolutely nothing had happened. The courage it took was immeasurable; he had no idea what kind of reception awaited him, but to the intense relief of everyone with him there were no sniggers, no shouts, no catcalls and no absence of people. Yet for all his cool, it was one of the worst days of his life, made worse by the damage he knew he had inflicted yet again on the monarchy.

There were lurid headlines and cartoons in the press, wide condemnation of Charles, questions about his fitness to be king, and, in the mounting fever of puritanical indignation, demands from Cabinet ministers that the Prince give up Mrs Parker Bowles.

The contents of her mailbag, meanwhile, took on an even more unpleasant tone and the press presence and pressure at her house became even worse. She became the butt of jokes up and down the country, her children at boarding school were teased and tormented and her husband stood publicly cuckolded.

It was at this point, with the documentary underway, that Jonathan Dimbleby and the Prince's adviser, Richard Aylard, discussed the question of the Prince's adultery. With the Morton book published, two sets of tapes in the public arena and screeds written in the press, it was an issue that no film about the last twenty-five years could duck. Dimbleby would have to ask the question; what Aylard and the Prince had to decide was how best to reply? There were three options. The truth, a lie, or evasion. Aylard advised the first, which accorded with the Prince's inclination. If he lied then sooner or later he would be caught out, argued the Private Secretary. The *News of the World*, he knew, already had both the Prince and Camilla watched and followed round the clock; it was only a matter of time before they were seen together or a disaffected servant sold his story. If he refused to answer the question on the grounds that it was a personal matter the surveillance would continue and the story would never go away until the media had evidence of an affair. After the 'Camillagate' tape, most people believed they were lovers, so why not be honest with the British public and admit the truth? The Prince wanted to tell the truth and Aylard encouraged him.

What they should both have foreseen was that the great British public was more interested in Diana's truth. She had got hers in first and it had a far juicier ring to it. They heard the 'Yes', and completely ignored the rest of his sentence which came after an anguished pause, 'the marriage having irretrievably broken down, us both having tried', and concluded that Charles had been an adulterer from day one. When Aylard confirmed at a press conference the next day that the adultery to which the Prince had confessed had indeed been with Mrs Parker Bowles, her goose was finally cooked. Andrew Parker Bowles filed for divorce and, less than a year later, married his long-term girlfriend, Rosie Pitman. The public blamed Camilla for breaking up the royal family home, and the reputation of the monarchy was once again dragged through the mire.

101

But there was more to come. Diana nursed her wrath until it was nicely warm, then she invited the television journalist Martin Bashir into Kensington Palace, who interviewed her for *Panorama*. Sitting demurely with head bowed, and looking up through kohl-darkened eyes, stopping only to wipe the occasional tear that welled, she eviscerated her errant husband and his frigid family with the skill of a samurai. She wanted to be 'Queen of people's hearts', she said. 'Someone's got to go out there and love people and show it.' And why had her marriage failed? Simply this: 'There were three of us in this marriage, so it was a bit crowded.'

The Queen had seen and heard enough. She and her advisers, like the Prince of Wales and his, were taken entirely by surprise. Not even the Princess's Private Secretary knew what she was about to spring on the world. The programme had been made in the greatest secrecy and the first the Press Office at Buckingham Palace heard of it was thirty minutes before news of her appearance was trailed on television, a week before it was broadcast. 'John Birt [Director General of the BBC] didn't judge it right,' says one of those in the Press Office at the time.

His idea that if the Palace knew any earlier we would try and stop the programme was ridiculous; the publicity would have been horrendous. But to prepare a public line on something as controversial as the marriage in that little time was impossible. And of course the press rang and said, 'Did she seek advice from the Queen and talk to her about this programme?' That week was very tricky, particularly as the Princess kept phoning and saying 'There's nothing to worry about in this programme, I haven't said anything against the Queen, I promise there's nothing that's going to cause you any problems.' But by then I knew enough about her condition to know that people with this level of anxiety can persuade themselves of anything to keep calm and the more in panic they are at the thought they've done the wrong thing, the more they go in the other direction, saying it's all going to be fine, it's just a little interview.

The Palace had no prior viewing and only saw a script of the programme half an hour before it went on air. But the minute they saw Diana, with all the melodrama and the heavy kohl on her eyes, instead of leaping to criticize most of the courtiers gathered round the Press Office television set felt a sudden wave of protective sympathy. As one says, 'I thought if this was my daughter I'd just want to help her, because what a terrible misjudgement to get on television and talk about all this, with her children at school.' The Queen and the Prince of Wales both agreed. Horrified and appalled as they all were, the overwhelming emotion was concern for Diana. Speaking on BBC's *Newsnight* immediately afterwards, Nicholas Soames made the immortal comment that Diana seemed to be exhibiting 'the advanced stages of paranoia' – something with which a number of people watching agreed, but very many more lapped up Diana's words, her accusations and her condemnation of her husband, his family and the institution without question.

The Queen decided that it was time to intervene and call a halt to the marriage that had brought such grief before any more damage was done. She was concerned, as much as anything, for William and Harry, who had been through enough in the last few years; and she was concerned for the monarchy and the damage that the War of the Waleses in all its guises was inflicting on the institution. After consulting with the Prime Minister and the Archbishop of Canterbury, the Queen wrote formally and privately to both her son and daughter-in-law asking them to divorce as early as could practicably be done.

The divorce was complicated and acrimonious. Negotiations lasted for months and although the Queen stripped Diana of her HRH status – an action widely perceived as petty – the settlement was unequivocally generous. The Princess received a package worth over £17 million: a lump sum of £15 million, reckoned to yield an income of £1 million per annum, plus £350,000 to pay for her private office (at Kensington Palace, not St James's which she had wanted) and an apartment at Kensington Palace to provide a 'central and secure home' for her and her children. They retained equal access to the boys and equal responsibility for their upbringing, and when she was with them she continued to be protected by armed bodyguards.

It was the end of fifteen years of marriage but it was not the end of the war. Diana was no happier outside the family she seemed to have hated so much than she was within it, and was still angry with Charles and determined to embarrass and upstage him at every opportunity. And, according to the opinion polls, she took the majority of the public with her. As the divorce became absolute a statement was released saying that the Prince of Wales had no plans to remarry. It was just as well; at a televised debate on the monarchy, run by Carlton Television with a randomly selected audience of three thousand, every time Camilla Parker Bowles's name was mentioned it was drowned by boos and hisses. The public was not about to forgive Camilla any more than Diana was and the Church was no comfort either. A poll on the day of the decree absolute showed that 56 per cent of all full-time Anglican clergy were opposed to a divorced Prince who remarried becoming king. A columnist in the *Catholic Herald* accused the Queen of having a flexible conscience and that, by not only agreeing to but urging divorce on her son, she had 'betrayed the ideal of marriage'; while the Dean of St Paul's said that divorce was all right but marrying again was the problem – that was what constituted adultery in God's eyes. For the next year Camilla remained firmly and quietly in the background; known to exist but knowing better than to show her face. And as a result the stakes were raised yet again on a photograph of the two of them together.

In the mid-1990s very few people knew what Camilla looked like. There had been very few photographs of her, even on her own, but during the latter part of 1996 that began to change. It was no accident. There was an attempt progressively to inch Camilla out of the closet and make her acceptable to the British public. The Prince did not want to spend the rest of his life hiding from photographers, behaving like some sort of criminal, unable to share the simple pleasures of life with the woman he loved. The person charged with making this possible was Alan Kilkenny, the PR consultant behind the Great Ormond Street Wishing Well Appeal in the 1980s, one of the most successful fundraising campaigns ever. He had been working quietly for the Prince on a variety of projects for most of the 1990s, which included minimizing the media fallout from the Parker Bowles divorce in 1994.

In April 1997 the newspapers published the first glamorous photograph that had ever been seen of Camilla, taken by Sir Geoffrey Shakerley. It accompanied the announcement that Mrs Parker Bowles had agreed to become a patron of the National Osteoporosis Society. This was none of Kilkenny's doing – the NOS involvement was entirely personal. Camilla's mother had died from the disease and when the society asked Camilla to become a patron her immediate instinct was that with her reputation she would probably do them more harm than good. It was only after much persuasion that she agreed.

But there were reports that this was the start of a PR campaign to sanitize Camilla, to raise her profile and make her acceptable to the British public. Diana was incensed; but it was as nothing compared to her rage when she heard of the Prince's plans to throw a fiftieth birthday party for Camilla at Highgrove in July 1997. And because Diana was cross, Robert Fellowes was cross and so too the Queen.

It was risky, as everyone knew, but the press seemed to be warming to Mrs Parker Bowles. There were no photographs of her and the Prince together, but there were plenty of her arriving bedecked with jewels that he had given her for her birthday and the reports in the following day's newspapers did nothing to calm the Princess. The *Daily Mail* began, 'She was the first to arrive, sweeping into Highgrove last night with all the confidence of a queen.'

Meanwhile, the Princess who would never be queen – and who would never be sweeping into Highgrove again either – was cavorting in a leopard-print bathing costume on a luxury yacht belonging to Mohamed al Fayed in the South of France. He was the foul-mouthed, high-profile Egyptian owner of Harrods, who had been repeatedly refused British citizenship. His great coup was that Diana was having a fling with his playboy son Dodi, which he hoped might lead to marriage. Nothing could have delivered a two-fingered salute more effectively to the British Establishment that had snubbed him. What's more, she took William and Harry to stay on the yacht with her, too. He had a plan that was coming together nicely. But the newspapers that had championed Diana over her rival for so many years were not impressed. 'The sight of a paunchy playboy groping a scantily-dressed Diana must appal and humiliate Prince William . . .' wrote Lynda Lee-Potter in the *Daily Mail*. 'As the mother of two young sons she ought to have more decorum and sense.'

Four days later Diana was dead and people like Lynda Lee-Potter were rapidly revising their opinions.

'They're all going to blame me, aren't they?' was the first question the Prince asked when he heard that she had been killed. Initial reports were that she had been badly injured but was still alive. 'The world's going to go completely mad, isn't it? We're going to see a reaction that we've never seen before. And it could destroy everything. It could destroy the monarchy.'

'Yes, sir, I think it could,' said Stephen Lamport, the Prince's Private Secretary. 'It's going to be very difficult for your mother, sir. She's going to have to do things she may not want to do, or feel comfortable doing, but if she doesn't do them, then that's the end of it.'

And for most of that week, while the nation's grief brought everyday life to a juddering halt, so much so that the death of Mother Teresa passed almost unnoticed, the Prince's prophecy came within a whisker of coming true. His mother finally did some things she didn't want to do, didn't feel comfortable doing and the crisis passed; the monarchy was not destroyed. But it was close; too close for comfort.

What he did get absolutely right was the prediction that he would be blamed. Had he loved Diana instead of his mistress, people argued in their anger, Diana would still be alive. She would never have been racing through the streets of Paris with Dodi Fayed. She would have been happily married and safely tucked up at Kensington Palace out of harm's way. And who's to say it wasn't true?

TWELVE

What If?

The history of the last twenty years could have been very different if Charles had been strong enough to bring an end to his relationship with Camilla Parker Bowles. And the prospects for the next twenty years would have been very much more certain than they are today. Diana talked about being a sacrificial lamb. But let's face it, Charles was too. Born into the Royal Family as eldest son and heir, he had to marry, had to breed and didn't have the luxury that most other men in life have of choice, either about a career or a partner. A stronger character might have been able to stand up to the pressures that were forcing him towards a hopeless marriage. But Charles had neither the strength nor the self-confidence to call a halt, and allowed himself to be swept along by others in the vain belief that he was doing the right thing; doing his duty. Charles has spent his life doing what was expected and required of him. That is the curse of his birthright. The upside is that he gets to live in beautiful palaces and castles surrounded by priceless treasures and genuflecting flunkies. The downside is that his life is not his own.

Charles grew up with the spectre of the abdication hovering over him. He had been weaned on stories about the disgrace brought upon the family by the Duke of Windsor who as

Edward VIII gave up the throne rather than the woman he loved. He abandoned his duty and that single selfish decision betrayed the Church, the Crown and the British people. No one felt so bitter and unforgiving about his behaviour, nor referred to it with more venom, than the Queen Mother, who was convinced that the strain of being thrust into the role in his brother's place eventually killed her husband, George VI. She never forgave Edward, and he and Wallis Simpson, whom he married after the abdication, were forced to live the remainder of their lives as exiles in Paris.

Nothing has spurred the Prince of Wales over the years quite like the terror that he might be compared with the Duke of Windsor. There have always been similarities, not least of all a selfish streak. Before his disgrace, Edward VIII was a charming and popular figure and much praised for his social conscience. His distress at the plight of the unemployed while visiting the mining valleys of South Wales prompted his famous remark, 'Something must be done to find them work.' Then added, 'You may be sure that all I can do for you I will.' Three weeks later he abdicated, thus abdicating all responsibility for the unemployed of South Wales and everywhere else. During the 1970s, when Charles was rattling his way through an alarming number of girls, with little apparent care or thought for anyone else, Mountbatten thought he was showing alarming signs. He warned him against 'beginning on the downward slope which wrecked your Uncle David's life and led to his disgraceful abdication and his futile life ever after'. The Prince was shocked that his 'Honorary Grandfather', Mountbatten, could have drawn such a devastating parallel and considered himself soundly rebuked.

Charles has never shown any signs of being a quitter. He has worked solidly fulfilling his predecessor's promise, doing all that he can not just for the disadvantaged of South Wales but for the disadvantaged everywhere, finding work for the unemployed, better housing, better schooling; he has fought for rural communities, for urban communities, he has built a model town; the list of what he has done in the last thirty years is remarkable and whatever you think of his stance on architecture or beliefs about complementary medicine, the commitment is hugely impressive, and he has already stuck at it for twenty years longer than his Uncle David.

But there is still one striking similarity: he refused to give up the woman he loved when it was abundantly clear that her existence was in danger of rocking the monarchy to its foundations. We will never know what would have happened if Charles had given up Camilla in the early nineties when Diana was on the rampage. It was probably too late for him and Diana to have salvaged any happiness from their marriage, but he might have prevented his jealous wife from pressing the self-destruct button.

This was never going to have been a marriage made in heaven. It was a mismatch of epic proportions and neither Charles nor Diana was emotionally strong enough to have given to each other what they needed. Charles did not cause Diana's instability by his love for Camilla. Diana came into that relationship with colossal problems that had nothing to do with Charles and everything to do with her unhappy childhood and her feelings of being unloved and unwanted by her parents. Charles was simply not equipped to handle her; he was the very last person who should have married Diana. He had never looked after himself let alone anyone else, and his position as Prince of Wales with so many demands on his time made it impossible for him to give her the attention she craved. She would have proved a challenge for any man she married, and I suspect might never have found true happiness with anyone. But I do strongly suspect that having a figure in the background like Camilla to fixate on made Diana worse.

Of the four incidents that stand out head and shoulders above the multitude of embarrassments and blunders that the Queen's other children have sprung upon the monarchy in recent years, Camilla Parker Bowles was at the root of them all: the Morton book, the Prince's admission of adultery, *Panorama* and the divorce. And if you push that to its logical conclusion, if Diana had still been married, she would never have been travelling through the streets of Paris at dangerous speeds with a drunken driver at the wheel and no police protection.

It is hard to understand how someone who is so dutiful and cares so passionately about the monarchy should have this blind spot. Not unlike the blind spot he has about his former valet, Michael Fawcett, whose bullying manner and the adverse publicity he has attracted has caused untold damage to the Prince's reputation yet who remains firmly favoured and in regular employment. My guess is that both anomalies are attributable to a mixture of insecurity and loyalty. The Prince has a tendency to become very dependent on people close to him; he seems to have an almost childlike need to have his thoughts, ideas and decisions, and hence his confidence, constantly bolstered and reinforced. Camilla has fulfilled that role; so have one or two of his private secretaries over the years and other members of staff like Fawcett. Richard Aylard was so close to the Prince at one stage that, according to another member of his staff, they were almost breathing the same air. Mark Bolland, who was with him for seven years, was another he needed to have either by his side or on the end of a phone night and day. Camilla, of course, fulfils other needs too and is in a different category; she understands him, knows where he's come from emotionally, has lived through the traumas with him, shares the history. But mostly she stems the chronic loneliness of the man so many outsiders enviously think has everything.

THIRTEEN

Mrs PB

Nearly twenty years ago, in a biography of the Prince of Wales, I made a stupid and very expensive mistake. I muddled up two Camillas – Camilla Shand, who became Camilla Parker Bowles and long-term lover of the Prince of Wales, and Camilla Fane, who didn't. Both had known him in his bachelor years and been photographed with him at polo matches, but the latter went on to marry a man called Hipwood – and not, as I had said, a man called Parker Bowles. 'The Prince fell deeply in love with Camilla,' I said, 'more, some friends say, than he has ever been again.' And unknown to me at the time, at almost the precise moment the book was published, Prince Charles was bailing out of his troubled marriage and he and Camilla were busy rekindling the relationship.

Both Mr Parker Bowles and Mrs Hipwood sued me for libel. The clear implication from my false and malicious words, they claimed, was that they had committed bigamy (or several alternatives too tedious to go into); and 'by virtue of the said publication', said Lady Camilla Hipwood, daughter of the sixteenth Earl of Westmoreland, in her statement of claim, 'the Plaintiff has been gravely injured in her character, credit and reputation and brought into public scandal, odium and contempt'. Blah blah blah. I sent a grovelling apology to each of them and offered to pay a sum of money to the charity of their choice. Neither was interested. And so the case proceeded and my publishers and I were left out of pocket.

Alan Kilkenny, who was charged by the Prince of Wales with the task of easing Camilla Parker Bowles into public life after his divorce and has been a friend for years, knew that I had long wanted to meet her, if only to tackle her about what I saw as a monumental injustice; in 1996 I had my opportunity. Two years earlier Camilla had become involved with the National Osteoporosis Society. Its director, Linda Edwards, who has sadly since died of cancer, had read in a magazine article that Camilla's mother suffered from the disease and had written to Camilla. By the time her letter arrived, Mrs Shand was dead – she had died a particularly painful death as a result of osteoporosis – and Camilla, who had known nothing about the disease before her mother's illness, and had never heard of the NOS, was keen to do anything she could to help other families who were facing what she had been through. Her one stipulation was that there should be no publicity. That was no problem for the charity – what it needed was money, which Camilla was happy to try and generate and as she spoke to friends – both her own and those she met through the Prince of Wales – donations started to roll in. She personally donated her half-share of £25,000 paid to her and Andrew Parker Bowles by the *Sun* for publishing private photographs stolen from their house at the time of their divorce. And courtesy of her friends the Earl and Countess of Sherburne, she was hosting a private soirée for two hundred guests at Bowood House in Wiltshire. Thanks to Alan Kilkenny, I was one of those guests and, eager for a bit of sport, he lost no time in introducing me to Camilla.

'This is Penny Junor,' he said. 'She tells me you sued her.'

'It wasn't me,' said Camilla with a wicked glint in her

eye. 'It was my ex-husband. Let me find him for you', and with our hands firmly clasped we fought our way through the crowded room until we found her rather florid-faced ex, whose face became considerably more florid as she explained why she was introducing us. I have had a very soft spot for Camilla ever since, and the sight of Andrew Parker Bowles's embarrassment when put on the spot by his ex-wife – and much to his ex-wife's merriment – was almost worth the settlement I'd paid to him all those years before.

Camilla has been very badly done by over the years. I happen to believe that for the sake of the monarchy the Prince of Wales should have given her up years ago, but it is not her fault that he didn't; and quite why she should have been the scapegoat for everything that befell the family is a mystery to me. Throughout this whole sorry saga, throughout all the years of provocation, criticism and abuse, she has never said a word out of place to anyone. She has never retaliated, never attempted to defend herself, not even when newspapers have published stories that are simply, grotesquely, untrue. Even when the Prince himself exposed her and her family by going public with their adultery, she said nothing. She has been the soul of discretion. True, she did sleep with the Prince of Wales but I don't think she exactly had to tie him down and threaten him first. His marriage was over, he was depressed, desperate, and she dragged him back to the land of the living. What she did was love him and value him as no one had ever done before and the effect she has on him is miraculous, even today. Charles felt he owed everything to Camilla. She had brought him back from the emotional abyss in the dark and desperate days of his marriage; she had restored his will to live, given him the confidence to carry on. She was his lifeline. She was and is a gentle, steadying force, down-to-earth, practical, sensible – mother, best friend and lover rolled into one, with an

115

ability to giggle at all the worst moments, to lighten his spirits and make him laugh. She helps him enjoy life, stops him feeling sorry for himself. She takes an interest in his work, listens to him, supports him; she even hosts receptions and dinners for him and chatters to all his boring guests. They go on holiday together, go painting, walking; they go to the theatre, they garden together, and until recently (but no longer) she used to hunt with him. She couldn't be happier that he finally went down on one knee to her, but she hadn't been desperate to marry and she had no ambition to be queen. She was happy being his companion, his lover, his soulmate. And yet, because Diana pointed a finger at her, she has been treated by everyone, including his family that are now officially in-laws, as a villainous marriage wrecker.

The Prince of Wales has a great capacity for feeling sorry for himself and after Diana's death that was particularly in evidence. Diana had been the ex from hell in many ways: she had spied on him, wanting to know where he was going, who he was seeing and why; she made it difficult for him to see William and Harry, she upstaged him, she embarrassed him, she leaked stories to the press, but deep down Charles loved Diana – she was the mother of his sons, after all – and he was overwhelmed by the tragedy of both her life and her death. In the weeks and months that followed he did a great deal of grieving for what might have been. There had been some moments of happiness in the morass of misery, but he was keenly aware that he had failed to make the happiness last, failed to make her his friend and failed to create the secure, loving home for their children that they both had dreamed of. However, headline writers who suggested he felt guilty were wide of the mark. Charles didn't feel guilty in any way, either about Diana's death or about his affair with Camilla. He knew he had done everything in his power to make his marriage work, but he had failed, and the failure was what hurt – and it still hurts him to this day.

It was several months before Charles summoned up the courage to face the public himself, and he knew it would be a long time before his name could be linked to Camilla's – and longer still before they could be seen in public together – but he was determined no matter what the obstacles, no matter what the cost, that she should remain a part of his life, and in many ways he needed her more towards the end of the 1990s than ever before. Before Diana's death they had been on the verge of coming out. Her birthday party at Highgrove had gone well; Diana, meanwhile, had been attracting increasingly hostile publicity for her flirtatious behaviour in the South of France with Dodi Fayed. Alan Kilkenny was easing Camilla gradually out of the shadows. They were two weeks away from a spectacular party to raise money for the National Osteoporosis Society at Camilla's sister Annabel's antiques business in Dorset. Seven hundred invitations had been sent out, at £100 apiece, and although nothing was official there were plans for the Prince to pay a surprise visit to the party. It would have been a second giant step along the path to making Camilla a legitimate part of the Prince's life – the phrase he used time and again – which was his ultimate goal. But those and every other plan screeched to a halt that Sunday in August when Britons awoke to the shocking news that Diana, Princess of Wales, had been killed in a car crash.

The Queen's desire for Camilla to disappear into the ether did not end with Diana's death. In some respects her troubles were just beginning, and the events of the next few years made the horrors of Morton and *Panorama* pale by comparison. Once again, it was nothing personal. Wearing her mother's hat the Queen was pleased that Charles, whose life had been so tortured and sad, should at last be free to enjoy the companionship of his long-term lover without fear of upsetting his ex-wife. Wearing her monarch's hat – or possibly even crown – she had very real reservations, as did all her advisers. Charles was determined that Camilla was non-negotiable. He was not prepared to give her up, no matter what anyone thought, from the Archbishop of Canterbury to the man on the Clapham omnibus – and certainly not Robert Fellowes. He was not prepared to keep her under wraps any more either. He was tired of coming and going from different entrances, hiding in the trunk of cars and playing games to foil the press. He wanted to be able to walk openly with Camilla by his side, and he wanted the British public to accept her as his partner. And in customary fashion he told members of his private office to make it happen. They did, but in their zeal to make Camilla acceptable to the British people they drove a wedge between St James's and Buckingham Palace and employed methods that the Queen and her courtiers felt did not belong in either royal household.

FOURTEEN

Lord Blackadder

The name Mark Bolland still sends shivers down a number of spines in both palaces. He was hired by the Prince of Wales in 1996, post-Dimbleby, post-divorce, when the Prince's reputation was at an all-time low and many of his friends were demanding Richard Aylard's head. Over dinner at St James's Palace, Hilary Browne-Wilkinson, who had been Camilla's divorce lawyer, and also happened to be a member of the Press Complaints Commission, asked the Prince if he had come across a man called Mark Bolland. Her husband, law lord Nico Browne-Wilkinson, was also at the dinner table that evening, and another couple, plus Camilla. As coffee was served Lord Browne-Wilkinson launched into a fearsome attack on the way the Prince's staff had handled the media in recent times, concluding that it was the legal profession's collective view that the situation could not be worse, nor more damaging for the monarchy. Sitting uncomfortably, playing with his coffee cup, was Richard Aylard, the man apparently responsible, a detail not lost, I am sure, on the assembled guests.

'He works for the Press Complaints Commission,' said Hilary, referring to Mark Bolland, in the ensuing silence. 'You should hire him and see if he can do anything to help.'

Two days later Bolland, who was director of the PCC at the time, had accepted a very minor role in the Press Office at St James's Palace. He'd been warned the job he would be offered would be 'crap' but had been told to take it; better things would follow. As indeed they did. Bolland, clever, charismatic and confident, very swiftly became the Prince's new best friend, the wonder man who would fix his life; and Aylard, whose loyalty and devotion to the Prince had cost the courtier his marriage, was spat out of the system like so many before him, as cherished as yesterday's bus ticket.

It was not the Prince's finest hour. He knew that Aylard deserved better but once again he took the weak man's course and allowed himself to be convinced by friends that Aylard was responsible for everything that had gone wrong – and after Dimbleby little seemed to go right. In truth, Aylard had probably been there too long and had certainly given too much of himself; he discovered at the end of the day the brutal reality, that working for a member of the Royal Family, however close the relationship, is only a job. There is often a gong at the end of it or a present of some sort and a card at Christmas – and in Aylard's case he continued to do some consultancy work on green issues – but in other respects it's no different from leaving a burger business or a merchant bank. Out of sight is out of mind, and some new face soon becomes equally indispensable.

Aylard had been Private Secretary for five years but he had been in the household for eleven, and had been with the Prince throughout his worst years. He was at Klosters in March 1988 when an avalanche killed the Prince's friend Major Hugh Lindsay, and with him through Morton, Camillagate, separation and divorce. They shared the same interests and enthusiasms – as a zoologist Aylard was an expert on environmental matters and conservation and wrote some of the Prince's best speeches on the subject. It was a very intense relationship; they spent hours together, round the clock, most days of the year, and if Aylard was not actually in attendance he was at the other end of a telephone, even on his days off. Aylard would never presume to have called himself a friend – no courtier ever would – but they were close and there is no doubt he enjoyed his position. 'Richard had all the armament required,' says a former courtier at St James's Palace. 'The Prince of Wales loved him, the chemistry between them was very good, but he became completely intoxicated. Late at night they used to sit in front of the fire at Sandringham and he would have all the problems of the Royal Family poured out to him. The Prince of Wales didn't understand how tremendously over-excited he was.'

And yet for all the talk down the years, and the unburdening of the Prince's problems, the Prince was blissfully unaware of Aylard's own problems on the home front. The Princess of Wales was always concerned about the people around her, attuned to the slightest vibration and aware of their personal circumstances. The Prince has no such antennae, and no awareness that the demands he puts on his staff might have an effect on their family life. Because he never stops working, it doesn't occur to him that they might need a break. Because he never has lunch, it doesn't occur to him that his staff might feel a little peckish in the middle of the day. In Aylard's case he had a wife who had suffered severe post-natal depression and two young children living in the country he never got home to see. He lived in a grace and favour apartment in Kensington Palace and when he did have enough time off to make it to the country, the Prince would ring and want to speak to him on the telephone all day long and half the night.

However, the minute he was alerted to what was going on by someone in the office – 'I had no idea,' he said. 'Why didn't anyone tell me?' – Charles was immediately on the phone to him full of sympathy. 'Thank you very much,' said Aylard in mock indignation as he came storming into the office the next morning. 'Thanks to you the Prince was on the phone from a quarter past ten until midnight last night sympathizing with me.'

Mark Bolland was never going to sacrifice his life for the sake of a job. Aylard had been a commander in the Royal Navy; he was traditional courtier material – courteous, understated, with a healthy understanding of the importance of tradition and hierarchy. By contrast, Bolland was a maverick. Educated at a comprehensive school in Middlesbrough and at York University, he had been nowhere near the Armed Forces and was in awe of no one. He was thirty, good-looking, gay, sophisticated and already on a highly successful career path. After three years at the Advertising Standards Authority and five at the Press Complaints Commission he knew his way around Fleet Street, knew all the personalities and loved wheeling and dealing.

At their first meeting the Prince of Wales asked him if he could bear to do the job. He could certainly bear to do it, he said, and he intended to have some fun the while. 'If you don't have fun in a job, there's no point in doing it,' he said. 'It doesn't all need to be so terrible. Things can get better.'

'If you say so,' said the Prince.

'Well, I do, actually.'

And he was true to his word on both counts. Things did get better, quite dramatically, and as Bolland settled into the job it was clear he was having fun. His predecessors seldom lunched and perpetually looked harassed and overworked. Bolland did lunch, very comfortably. He had a table at Le Caprice, conveniently round the corner from St James's Palace, and liked nothing more than a Kir Royale. In the evenings he dined at the Ivy or 1 Aldwych or wherever was fashionable, the food good and the clientele classy. He and his partner Guy Black, at that time director of the Press Complaints Commission, equally charming and accomplished, were very much a part of the London social scene – also the Gay Mafia – and by association took the Prince's name into a whole new constituency.

When Richard Aylard departed, Stephen Lamport stepped into his shoes as Private Secretary. A career diplomat, he had been in the Prince's office for three years handling foreign tours and the architectural brief. He was orthodox, cautious and clever but uninspiring. Mark Bolland was his deputy, but he was the one with the influence over both the Prince and the press. His brief was to rehabilitate Camilla Parker Bowles; to restore the Prince's reputation after Diana's various assaults on it; and to demonstrate to the world that he was not a bad father and, contrary to what his ex-wife had said, perfectly fit to be king.

Bolland was camp, flamboyant and dangerous – and those who didn't hate him loved him. He took chances, he spun stories, he had favourites, traded secrets, called in favours, and very quickly the Prince's name was in the headlines – and, for the first time in years, not because he was a bad husband or a lousy father but because he was hard-working, committed and entrepreneurial. But there was a sting in the tail. The *quid pro quo* was that selected newspapers were given occasional stories about his love life. A dangerous barter but, in the hands of a pro like Bolland, it worked.

To suggest Mark Bolland's life was one long lunch would be entirely misleading. He was at the Prince's constant beck, his mobile phone never further away than his breast pocket, and in all the years I knew him in that job I don't remember a meeting that wasn't either cancelled because he had been called away or wasn't uninterrupted by a call from the boss. As one former courtier, who, like many before him, had given up an extremely successful career to take up the job of working for the Prince, said:

> It is very odd to find oneself being treated like an office boy at my stage in life. I've never had to work so hard.
>
> When I told him once that he really ought to employ more boring people as courtiers, he said how awful courtiers were and how boring. But it's quite right, you need boring people to be courtiers, you don't want people who are going to be overexcited. Mark Bolland, he hit that comment off into mid-wicket. As a professional PR man you couldn't get better, putting engine oil all over Mrs PB so she could be readily reintegrated into the royal structure . . .

A large part of Bolland's job was looking after Mrs PB, as Camilla was universally called, and the engine oil he put all over her was very effective. When he arrived in the job, Camilla was a prisoner in her own home with two Jack Russells and sackloads of abusive letters for company. When he left seven years later, she and the Prince of Wales had been seen together in public so frequently that the newspapers didn't always bother to carry photographs – and more than 50 per cent of the British public thought he should marry her.

Mark included her in the office, invited her to diary-planning meetings; they were allies in handling the Prince of Wales, who is not always easy. She could often say things to him over the breakfast marmalade that anyone else would have had their heads bitten off for even mentioning. He would speak to her for hours on the phone each day, exchanging news and gossip or listening to one of her many minor crises. They would meet for lunch – he would always be given the best table in all the best restaurants – he gave her advice, took care of any problems, eased her anxiety, boosted her confidence and was kind to her – something she was not always accustomed to in the Prince's office. While Diana was alive there were many who had no sympathy for Mrs Parker Bowles at all. And surprisingly, after all this time and all she has been through, she doesn't have the hide of a rhinoceros. Mark looked after her, made her feel brave enough to take on the world.

Bolland gave the Prince of Wales courage, too. Charles was by now fast approaching fifty, still failing to please his parents, and, worse, still agonizing about it. It was a daily task to prop up the Prince's psyche. Bolland encouraged him to stop worrying; if his parents didn't approve of his lifestyle and his choice of companion that was their problem. This wasn't courtier-speak and did nothing to improve inter-family relationships, but Bolland was not traditional courtier material and the Prince loved that. For years he had felt himself surrounded by people who spent their time telling him why he couldn't do things. Here was someone telling him not only that they *could* be done but *how* they could be done; and the Prince loved him, listened to him and relied upon him – just as he had Richard Aylard and others before him. The Prince of Wales has always been looking for someone to solve his problems; sometimes he thinks he has found that person, but ultimately he is always disappointed. Perhaps this is because ultimately there are only so many problems that a Private Secretary can solve.

Bolland loved the power of his position. He never suffered from red-carpet fever, one great advantage he had over his predecessor. He was never in awe of anyone, never felt socially inferior to anyone, never lost sight of the Prince's shortcomings, never lost his sense of perspective, and never forgot that what he was doing was a job and that real life, his personal life, came first; but he did enjoy watching doors open and the effect that the Prince's name had on people. And he enjoyed the fame – and the notoriety – that he acquired over the years as a Machiavellian *éminence grise*. Other members of the Royal Family may have had good reason to curse him but he was never disloyal to the Prince of Wales and in the seven years he worked for him he achieved everything that the Prince asked of him. He was there for him night and day; there for his children and there for his lover, and, until shortly before the end, by which time he felt overused and underappreciated, he revelled in it.

FIFTEEN

Battle of the Palaces

By that time, however, a schism the size of the Mall had developed between Buckingham Palace and St James's and that had become the story. The Firm was split down the middle with one side sniping at the other and the senior courtiers from both camps hardly on speaking terms. The mistrust of Bolland became so chronic that he would now be excluded from meetings for fear that he would leak anything that was said during a meeting to the press. He professed a sincere belief in the monarchy, which I am sure was genuine, but felt that the entire institution needed a wake-up call, that they were 'totally out of touch with the real world'. Writing in 2003 after he had left the Palace – seen as an act of treachery – he said, 'Sadly, the Prince of Wales apart, they are blissfully unaware of real people's problems and ignore the hard choices that confront everyone else in public life. The declining audience they attract is almost as narrow as the ageing rump of support that sustains the ailing Conservative Party.'

The problem was a conflict of style and a conflict of interests. Mark Bolland was from a world that Robert Fellowes didn't begin to understand. There were no points of reference: he didn't hunt, shoot or fish, didn't inhabit gentlemen's clubs, hadn't been to Eton, hadn't been in the Army, hadn't even been in the City, didn't have a wife and children, and was twenty-five years younger. He was not steeped in the tradition of royal protocol; he was a meritocrat – he gave respect where it was earned and not where it was expected because of rank or status. And he was there to do a job which the Queen and Robert Fellowes frankly didn't want done. In their ideal world Camilla would have emigrated to another planet; they recognized, however, that Charles was not going to let that happen and their next best option was to keep her out of sight. Bolland was specifically instructed by the Prince to make Camilla visible, to bring her out into the open so that the day would dawn when the public would view her as a legitimate part of his life, which is precisely what he achieved. A clash was inevitable.

The first major problem arose over Camilla's birthday party. Robert Fellowes was furious when he heard that the Prince planned to give a party for her at Highgrove and said that if the party went ahead he would have to advise the Queen to tell the Prince that he must give up Camilla for good. There was a view that Fellowes didn't much like the Prince – a view shared by the Queen's great friend and racing manager, the late Lord Carnarvon – which, given Fellowes' relationship to the Princess of Wales, would not have been surprising. However, his colleagues Robin Janvrin and Mary Francis were both dismayed by his attitude over the party and told him that if he advised the Queen as he intended then they would have no alternative but to offer her very different advice. He backed down and the party went ahead.

The following year, in the spring of 1998, the Prince was giving a weekend party for a group of friends at Sandringham and wanted to invite Camilla. He asked Mark Bolland for his advice. 'Invite her,' he said. 'It will be a two-day wonder in the press and then it will go away. It won't be a problem.' That was the phrase he used frequently in his dealings with the Prince and that was what so endeared him to his boss. Diana had been dead for nearly nine months and the weekend was important in terms of defining Camilla's future role in the Prince's life. Besides, it was important for the relationship. She was beginning to tire of being left behind, kept in the shadows; they needed to spend some time together.

Bolland rang Robin Janvrin to tell him that it was happening and said there would be a story about it in the newspapers (leaked, inevitably, by an unnamed senior source within the royal household) which would, equally inevitably, beg the question of whether the Queen had known that Camilla had been invited to Sandringham and whether she had given her permission. He had deliberately chosen to ring Janvrin rather than Fellowes, knowing that he would meet less hostility. Janvrin was a younger and more conciliatory character than Fellowes: he said he would deal with it, and on his advice the Queen's reaction was that this was a private party, it was up to Charles to invite whoever he wanted and she would not have been expected to be consulted. Had Robert Fellowes made the call to the Queen her reaction would have been entirely different, and rows would have ensued.

Janvrin was sympathetic to the Prince in relation to Camilla and he endeavoured to keep the lines of communication open between the two palaces, but he wasn't prepared to go out on a limb for him. A few months after the Sandringham weekend, Prince William had a secret meeting with Camilla at York House, the Prince's home in London adjoining St James's Palace. A few months before Diana died, Charles had tried to introduce the subject of Camilla to his sons but neither of them had wanted to know. Now, a year after his mother's death, William had changed his mind and on a visit to London from school said he would like to meet her. They spent half an hour together on their own in William's flat at the top of the house, and, although terrifying for Camilla, it was the beginning of a very cordial relationship. But later that afternoon the Prince of Wales suggested that Robin Janvrin, who was by then the Queen's Private Secretary designate, might also like to meet Camilla. In all his years at the Palace he had never met Camilla. Charles was 'tired of all this nonsense'.

Janvrin had been at St James's Palace for a meeting and was in the waiting room when Stephen Lamport went to find him. 'Robin,' he said, 'the Prince of Wales would like you to come back upstairs because he'd like to introduce you to Mrs Parker Bowles.' Janvrin declined. 'I can't possibly do that,' he said. 'I couldn't do it without asking the Queen's permission and making sure it was the right thing to do.' He was not to be budged and when Lamport relayed this message to the Prince of Wales his language was unrepeatable. 'In my house . . .' he said. 'How dare he be so rude in my house?'

Janvrin was being neither rude nor judgemental. He had been placed in an impossible position and knew full well that if he had agreed to meet Mrs Parker Bowles without having first cleared it with the Queen, it would have been all over the newspapers and would have been a grave embarrassment to the Queen, and to him. His instincts were right. Camilla's meeting with Prince William found its way on to the front page of the following day's *Sun*, and there is every chance that his meeting with Camilla would have done so too. For once this was none of Bolland's doing; Amanda MacManus, Camilla's PA, who was married to a *Times* newspaper executive, had told her husband about the meeting over supper that night and he had subsequently mentioned it inadvertently to a journalist. But such was Bolland's reputation that the other newspapers immediately thought that he had given the story to the *Sun* and were enraged by such apparent favouritism.

A former Lord Chamberlain had a strict rule, which he maintains to this day, of never doing or saying anything in this area without first telling the Queen. Others who have worked for her say the same. Provided she is forewarned, the Queen is 100 per cent supportive if things go wrong. What she doesn't like are surprises. Some months later, Robin Janvrin did finally meet Camilla Parker Bowles at St James's Palace, but he told the Queen of his plan beforehand, and they have had a perfectly amicable relationship ever since.

Whenever stories appeared the finger of suspicion immediately pointed to Bolland. And as often as not he was responsible, but it was always calculated. He didn't issue formal statements as his predecessors had done. He gave non-attributable briefings to editors and journalists. He used the newspapers to get good, positive stories about Charles and Camilla into the public domain and stories that demonstrated that Charles was a good and loving father. But he also used these briefings as bargaining tools, and a great many explosive stories, particularly about the boys when they were first going to parties, never saw the light of day because of the relationship Bolland had developed with certain editors. There were some papers he disliked and gave nothing to, such as the *Daily Telegraph*, because he felt that its editor, Charles Moore, was hostile to the Prince. The *Daily Mail* had always had a special relationship with the Princess of Wales, via its good-looking royal correspondent Richard Kay, to whom Diana regularly fed stories. Being pro-Diana, it was inevitably, therefore, anti-Charles; but it was an important and influential market and after Diana's death there was a considerable amount of cross-wooing between Bolland and David English, editor-in-chief of the *Mail* and *Mail on Sunday*, and after his death with his successor, Paul Dacre. The two titles became his main outlet – also the *Sun* and the *News of the World*, whose editor,

Rebekah Wade, was a personal friend with whom he and Guy Black spent holidays.

The first ever photograph of Charles and Camilla together since their affair had been made public was a prime example of the way in which Bolland cleverly orchestrated the news for his own purposes. A photograph of the pair had become as sought after as the Holy Grail, worth a fortune to the paparazzo lucky enough to catch them in an unguarded moment. The Prince was determined this should not happen but equally resolved that he and Camilla should be able to do things together. And so Mark devised a plan. Camilla's sister Annabel Elliot was celebrating her fiftieth birthday with a party at the Ritz on the evening of 28 January 1999, to which both Charles and Camilla had been invited. It was the perfect occasion, informal and non-royal. Mark made a few discreet phone calls suggesting that they might be seen leaving the party together and by mid-afternoon the pavement outside the Arlington Street entrance to the Ritz Hotel in Piccadilly was thick with photographers. According to one, there were no fewer than ninety-seven sets of photographer's ladders on the street. It was a long, cold wait but they were richly rewarded. Shortly before midnight the couple emerged. They didn't pose for the camera and there was no touching, apart from the Prince's guiding arm around Camilla's waist as he steered her towards the waiting car, but it served a very useful purpose and proved a major landmark in the history of their relationship. No one had an exclusive shot, all the papers and television broadcasts carried the story, and it was the perfect way of gauging public opinion – which they found to their relief was surprisingly favourable. From that day on their relationship was effectively out in the open and life for the two of them became very much easier.

But what was good for St James's Palace was not necessarily

viewed in such a favourable light from across the Mall. Stories in the press that the Queen was still hostile to Camilla did nothing to amuse. For the Prince's own fiftieth birthday the Queen gave a party at Buckingham Palace to which Camilla was not invited. Since the guests were people from his public life that was not surprising. What did seem surprising was that the Queen refused an invitation to a private birthday party that Camilla gave for Charles at Highgrove. In retrospect the Prince realized he should have spoken to his mother about the party first and not just allowed her to find out when an invitation arrived out of the blue. More likely was that she found herself between the devil and the deep blue sea. There would be a media story whatever she did: if she went she would be seen to be condoning the relationship, which she was not prepared to do at that stage; if she didn't, she was snubbing Camilla. Damned if she did; damned if she didn't.

SIXTEEN

Master of Spin

One of the most damning charges levelled against Mark Bolland during his time with the Prince was the accusation that he briefed against other members of the family in his quest to portray his boss in a good light. The Wessexes felt particularly aggrieved, as did the Duke of Edinburgh. It started with Prince Edward's television company, Ardent. When Prince William went to university at St Andrews in October 2001, St James's Palace drew up a kind of Faustian pact with the press, generally known as the St Andrews Agreement. William's side of the bargain was that once a term he would give the press access in the form of a photocall and an informal chat. In return, the press would leave him alone thereafter and allow him to enjoy his university career unmolested. In the first week of his first term, no sooner had the press dutifully left the Scottish seaside town than Prince William spotted a television crew filming. It turned out to be a crew from Ardent.

In no time at all the newspapers were full of the story, with reports in the *Daily Mail* that the Prince was 'incandescent' with rage that the one company that should have flagrantly ignored the agreement should have been his brother's. He was so angry that he had refused to take telephone calls from Edward. The story blew up into a major attack on Prince

Edward and his competence as a film maker, and ran for some days. Then a further report claimed that Prince Philip, in support of his youngest son, thought William was being 'overprotected' by his father and that he had 'overreacted' to the Ardent film crew.

The stories had Bolland's fingerprints all over them, and once again Buckingham Palace was not amused. In a rare reaction, Prince Philip issued a strongly worded public statement saying that the views attributed to him by the *Daily Mail* were 'totally without foundation'.

His peers, however, had nothing but admiration for his endeavours. Shortly afterwards Mark Bolland won a public relations industry award for his campaign to improve the image of the Prince of Wales. In honouring him as PR Professional of the Year, he was commended for overseeing 'a massive sea change in the relationship between Charles and the press . . . and moving the subject of any potential marriage to Camilla Parker Bowles on to less negative ground'.

In January 2002 another extraordinary story came out of St James's Palace. The Prince of Wales had taken his younger son to visit a drugs rehabilitation centre after he confessed to smoking cannabis. The story was a *News of the World* exclusive and had come directly from the Prince's office. Prince Harry had been drinking under age and after hours in a pub called the Rattlebone Inn in Sherston, near Highgrove, as well as smoking cannabis. Prince Charles had discovered the previous November what had been going on while he had left Harry home alone during the school holidays, and had handled the incident well, so the story went. He had taken him for a short sharp shock to Featherstone Lodge in south London to talk to recovering drug addicts. What could have been a wholly negative story had a positive spin. Charles had handled the nightmare scenario – one that every parent with a teenager dreads – and reacted well. The story was so well sourced that there were suggestions in some sections of the media that maybe Bolland's friendship with Rebekah Wade was just a bit too cosy.

Not many people knew at the time that this was a masterful piece of damage limitation. The *News of the World* had published a photograph of a very spaced-out Harry in a nightclub in Spain during the summer. They had kept a watch on him ever since, spoken to associates, and had compiled damning evidence of far more serious behaviour than that which appeared in January 2002. Rebekah Wade rang Bolland to alert him to what they had and he brokered a deal which saved the young Prince's bacon and left his father smelling of roses. The Prime Minister headed the list of people queuing up to praise Prince Charles. 'The way Prince Charles and the Royal Family have handled it is absolutely right and they have done it in a very responsible and, as you would expect, a very sensitive way for their child,' said Tony Blair on *Breakfast With Frost*. Peter Martin, chief executive of Addaction, Britain's largest drug and alcohol treatment agency, said, 'The Prince of Wales has acted with deep sensitivity and very quickly, which is exactly what is needed.' To which the Department of Education added, 'Parents play a very important role, as demonstrated by Prince Charles, who has set an extremely good example.'

None of them pointed out that leaving a seventeen-year-old – particularly one as mixed-up and vulnerable as Harry – home alone for long periods of time with no parental guidance is bordering on the negligent, and is certainly a recipe for disaster. Of course Prince Harry is not home alone in the sense that he's a latch-key kid. The house is fully staffed and he always has a police protection officer with him, but these figures are not *in loco parentis* – and suggestions that a certain sort of behaviour might be inadvisable (such as wearing a Nazi outfit to a fancy dress party) are usually unwelcome.

By now Bolland was finding that the fun was wearing off. He had too many powerful enemies, not just those who worked for the Queen across the Mall but some of the Prince's friends with whom Bolland had clashed over the years and who had the Prince's ear and thought him a bad influence. He had been at St James's Palace for almost six years; he had had enough of the infighting and backstabbing and being on call for the Prince of Wales morning, noon and night. Stephen Lamport had already announced he was leaving in the summer and his replacement was to be Sir Michael Peat, architect of the modernization programme at Buckingham Palace, Keeper of the Privy Purse and a direct import from the enemy camp. Bolland knew it was time to go.

And so in February 2002 he announced his resignation and left to set up his own company, MBA, a public relations consultancy; but such was the Prince's dependency on this charismatic character (to whom Prince William referred as Lord Blackadder, after Rowan Atkinson's creation) that, following his departure, he paid Bolland £130,000 a year to act as an adviser to both him and Camilla in a private capacity.

'Mark has been a senior and much valued member of my staff for nearly six years,' said the Prince in tribute, 'and is now ready to move on to develop his career in new areas, but I'm delighted that he will continue to provide help and advice to my office.'

It suggested a calmness he didn't feel. For the next year Mark Bolland continued to spend hours on the phone to both Charles and Camilla, to hold their hands, handle their crises, all the while discovering that his other clients offered much less trouble for far more money. He began to tire of this, too. He wanted out; he didn't get on with Michael Peat but he wanted Charles and Camilla to drop him rather than vice versa. In February 2003 the perfect opportunity presented itself. Rebekah Wade claimed to have some stolen strands of Prince Harry's hair, taken so as to have them DNA tested to ascertain whose son he was – the Prince of Wales's or James Hewitt's. (This, by the way, is a physical impossibility since Diana did not know Hewitt until after Harry was conceived.) Peat handled it in what Bolland considered to be a ham-fisted way, and said so. A row ensued, it became obvious to everyone that the relationship wasn't working and Bolland had his out. He had been colourful and controversial, he had put up backs and sent shock waves through the immaculately carpeted corridors of Buckingham Palace, but he had done what had been asked of him. He had made Camilla Parker Bowles a legitimate part of the Prince's life. And the fact that in 2005 Charles was able to marry Camilla without the sky falling down is a major credit to Mark Bolland. He prepared the ground.

And yet he is the only member of the Prince's staff of that seniority who remained in his employ for that length of time who was not offered a gong.

SEVENTEEN

Planes, Trains and Automobiles

I was standing on the platform of a station in the small town of Mistley in Essex. It was ten o'clock in the morning and the royal train was expected. A shaven-headed policeman in fluorescent jacket arrived with a bouncy black Labrador. Half his tail was missing. What happened to his tail, I asked. He wagged it so much he kept hitting things with it and splitting it open, explained the handler. The dog raced the length of the platform, sniffing along the railings that bordered the station; his rear end wagging furiously, he leapt on to the small stone wall, investigated under the single railway bench where nobody sat and bounded briefly into the undergrowth at the far end. His handler called him back. The two of them then jumped down on to the rails, crossed the track and climbed up on to the southbound platform to do the same there. The dog was a delightful hooligan; the handler might have gone that way too, but the police force caught him in time. They made a good team.

There was a small reception committee waiting on the platform – several men in suits and the Lord-Lieutenant of the county in full fig with sword and spurs, gold braid and red stripes up his trouser legs. The men stiffened briefly as a train approached but passed straight through. Everyone relaxed and the forced laughter and chatter continued. People checked their watches. In the station forecourt a group of excited school-children had gathered, clutching a motley collection of flags and banners. They had been waiting a long time. And across the road, a beautifully restored nineteenth-century maltings, the object of the day's visit, was filled with nervous people in best bib and tucker, all of whom had some connection with the project. They too had been waiting a long time.

Suddenly we had action. At 10.07, two minutes late, the royal train came into sight and slowly and deliberately pulled up alongside the platform. Did the driver see the reception committee and calculate how far forward he had to go to make sure his passenger stepped from his carriage at precisely the right point, or had it all been recced and worked out in advance? I don't know. But I do know that there is no chance that the Prince of Wales walked along the inside of the train until he found the door that best suited his hosts. He is not in the habit of making adjustments; he expects everything to be perfect and invariably it is.

The train is not what you might expect a royal train to be; although, given how clean and shiny the paintwork and windows are, you know it can't be a regular passenger train. The engine that pulls it looks very ordinary – it is one of two, and does in fact pull other coaches when it's not wanted by the Royal Family, without anyone being the wiser – and the rest looks quaintly old-fashioned, rather like a train Miss Marple might meet. It is maroon with red and black livery and a grey roof and resides in Wolverton, just outside Milton Keynes, where aged retainers lovingly polish every nut and bolt. The Prince had spent the night on board, having had an engagement in Scotland the previous evening. Sometimes it travels through the night, sometimes it pulls into a siding, depending upon timing. Either way, the Prince and his entourage would have had a good night's sleep and been able to work as well. It is not quite the *Orient Express*, given that most of the coaches are thirty to thirty-five years old and could do with refurbishment, but the train is extremely comfortable by any standards, with armchairs and sofas, a dining room, office and communications equipment, decent-sized bathrooms, showers, soft down duvets and full-sized beds, and, in the Prince's coach, pictures of Highgrove on the walls. It is a home from home, and one of the most secure ways of accommodating the Royal Family overnight – as well as being one of their favourite – and of maximizing their time. Both the Prince of Wales's and the Queen's coaches are heavily reinforced; they are ten times heavier than the other coaches.

The man who organized that trip to Mistley was Group Captain Tim Hewlett, a pilot with the RAF for thirty years. He is now in his mid-fifties, has been at the Palace since 2001 and as director of Royal Travel runs the equivalent of a small travel agency from a narrow little office on the ground floor. He's informal, relaxed and friendly, and clearly enjoys his job, as everyone I have met inside Buckingham Palace seems to.

Hewlett is also the Queen's Senior Air Equerry (actually, post-Peat and his 188 recommendations, he is her only Air Equerry) and as such flies everywhere with the Queen. One of the requirements for the job was that he should have military fixed-wing experience, and although he doesn't fly the aircraft, if anything went wrong he could, and he is certainly in a good position to advise a course of action if an engine fails, for example, a not unknown occurrence. He travels in uniform, acts as a go-between with crew and passengers and stands at the foot of the steps when the Queen disembarks. Wearing his other hat he handles the travel arrangements for the entire Royal Family and is an expert on trains, planes and helicopters and how to get the best and cheapest deals. The private secretaries say where their principals need to travel to, when and why, and he and his team calculate the best and most economical way of getting there. It is often a combination of transport, and very often the answer can be for the entire journey or part of it to be on normal scheduled services.

On a recent visit to Cambodia and Vietnam, for example, the Princess Royal flew commercially to Bangkok, but once there used a BAe 146 which Hewlett's team had flown out separately because there was no other means of getting about, and she returned with British Airways.

Since 9/11, the Queen and the Prince of Wales no longer travel on scheduled airlines because of the security risk. Nor do they ever fly together in the same aircraft – they never have – and the Prince of Wales does not as a rule fly with his sons. He needs the Queen's permission to do so and there have been occasions in the past when she has refused it. The only exception was when the Queen Mother died, and Charles, William and Harry all flew home from Klosters together. But the Queen and Prince of Wales, like every other member of the family, can and do use normal scheduled passenger trains from time to time. For most of them no special arrangements are made. They travel first class and simply reserve a seat and travel with a royal protection officer. Princess Anne frequently travels on the train between Kemble and Paddington. She is met by a car on the platform in London and whisked away, but at Kemble, a small country stop near her home in Gloucestershire, she walks to the car park like any ordinary commuter. The Queen, of course, doesn't. She usually has a carriage to herself and always travels with a lady-in-waiting, a Private Secretary, an equerry and police protection officers and considerably more fuss is made – but not as much as you might imagine. The Lord-Lieutenant of Wiltshire was due to meet the Queen off a regular passenger train at Swindon one day. 'I was told what time she would arrive and there was no sign of her. I thought "Damn it, she's missed the train", then spotted a little lady walking down the platform swinging her handbag.' As Hewlett says, 'In PR terms it looks like a nice cheap option, and we can stand proudly in front of the accountants and say it cost £35 for a first class rail ticket for the Queen, but the security costs are quite considerable and those are not part of our budget. [The police pay for security.] It's not really so cheap. But the royal train is expensive . . .'

The train is owned by Network Rail and operated by EWS and is the most expensive means of transport they use. The cost of the Prince of Wales's journey from Edinburgh to Essex that day would have been getting on for £20,000; the audited figure for 2003–04 is £48 per mile by rail, compared with £14 per mile for air travel. (Curiously, there is no similar breakdown for travel by road.) He had to get to four separate locations around the county and home in time for a reception, followed by a dinner at Buckingham Palace. It was a very tight schedule; and after that first engagement in Mistley he transferred to a car – an insignificant-looking black Ford Sierra – and he and his staff were driven in convoy with a police escort at high speed from one place to the next. His schedules are invariably tight and it is always difficult to keep to the timetable; when a couple at the converted maltings, whose apartment the Prince was looking over, wanted to show him their collection of model boats, his timing went for six. The minute he hit the back seat of his car the convoy was off, five vehicles in all, with a marked Metropolitan Police car at the front and an unmarked one bringing up the rear that belonged to the local force. I was trying to follow in my own car and was warned if I couldn't keep up they wouldn't wait, and if I followed them through a red light, which they can do them- selves if necessary, I would be on my own. As we approached

143

a junction the lights duly turned red and I was forced to stop. I lost them but we were just about to turn on to a dual carriageway with scarcely any traffic on it; I had a fast car, I could easily catch up. Some hope. I was nudging 100 mph for the next twenty miles or more and didn't even catch sight of them. They had been doing 120 mph.

The Prince of Wales has two Aston Martins for his own personal use – one of which the Queen gave him as a twenty-first birthday present – and sometimes drives a Bentley, which is not his. It is heavily armoured and belongs to the police and when he drives it, it is at their insistence when they think security demands it. The cars he uses for engagements are leased, as are most of the Queen's fleet. Even the helicopter that the Royal Family use is now leased. They used to fly in two big, bright-red, noisy Wessex helicopters, which belonged to the Queen's Flight, something Peat disbanded in the interests of cost cutting. The Queen hated the Wessex, and helicopters are still not her favourite means of travel, but they now have just one, a little maroon six-seater Sikorsky (based at Blackbushe Airport) which is quieter and faster but smaller, with very little luggage space, and if it is fully laden is too heavy to take off from small fields. Hewlett is keen to encourage the Queen to make more use of the helicopter, but she is much happier in a car.

The Queen's official car is a specially adapted Bentley, a gift from the company for her Golden Jubilee in 2002; the oldest car in the fleet (of eight state limousines) is a Rolls-Royce Phantom IV built in 1948 – 5.76-litre with a straight-eight engine and a Mulliner body (for vintage Rolls-Royce lovers). There's also a Phantom VI which she was given in 1978 for her Silver Jubilee and a 1987 Phantom VI. Privately the Queen drives a Daimler Jaguar, and in the country a Vauxhall estate. The Duke of Edinburgh has a Land Rover Discovery and when he's in London gets about in his own black Metrocab, which looks like any other taxi on the road.

Cars, curiously, are not in the director of Royal Travel's brief; they belong in the Royal Mews along with thirty-two or so carriage horses and a collection of state coaches under the control of the Crown Equerry. His duties were once performed by the Secretary to the Master of the Horse, and the post has traditionally been held by experienced horsemen. Lieutenant Colonel Sir John Miller, who is president of every horse society you can think of, was Crown Equerry for twenty-six years – from 1961 to 1987 – and played a big part in the Royal Family's horse activities and was much loved by the Queen. He was a keen huntsman and polo player and very much in the picture when Charles and Anne were in their teens and beginning to hunt, play polo and, in Anne's case, to show an interest in three-day eventing. He was still in place when Prince Philip switched from polo to carriage driving. Miller retired at the age of sixty-eight and, now in his nineties, is still an Extra Equerry to the Queen; it was he who flew to California in 1989 on the Queen's instructions to investigate a horse trainer called Monty Roberts (about whom, more later). Colonel Miller's successor, Lieutenant Colonel Seymour Gilbart-Denham, is equally at home in the Mews. Now in his mid-sixties, he a carriage driver like the Duke, and, after a career in the Life Guards and the Cavalry, is suitably horsy for the post. Not surprising, then, that Michael Peat, when making his recommendations about bringing travel back within the household, decided that trains, planes and helicopters should go into a separate department and be run by someone with fixed-wing flying experience.

So Hewlett comes up with the options for getting from A to B, printed on a form with the costs and justification for the journey, which he passes on to Paul Havill at the Coordination and Research Unit. Havill looks at them from the public servant's point of view – wearing his taxpayer's hat, he says – and if he is happy with it all, the form goes to the Queen; she personally authorizes every journey made by a member of the family. If the cost is above a certain threshold, however, before the Queen sees it it has to be approved by the director of finance and if it is a serious expense, such as a foreign tour, it has be passed first by the Keeper of the Privy Purse.

'A member of the Royal Family can't say "I fancy doing that trip by helicopter",' says Havill. 'There are tough criteria to be met. I often turn things down or say I need more information, fill in the form properly. We are more open than government or anyone else. Every single journey is in the public domain so it has to stand up. You can only have a helicopter or plane if you've got enough engagements or you've got to come back for an evening engagement; not just because it's easier to fly. There are rules.'

Every journey costing £500 or more is indeed in the public domain – which member of the family made it, where they went, why and how much it cost. Overall, the bill for helicopters in 2003–04 was £2,270,000; for fixed-wing air travel, £534,000; and for use of the royal train and other rail journeys, £782,000. The Palace publishes Annual Reports – also available on the internet – on every area of its activity and expenditure, and they make fascinating reading. Everything is there, from Sir Robin Janvrin's salary (£151,131 in 2003–04) to the cost of food (£432,000), garden parties (£514,000), housekeeping (£279,000), stationery (£152,000) and legal advice (£117,000). 'We even publish how many glasses were broken during a reception,' says Havill. 'I don't know any other organization that is so transparent.'

Royal Travel was one of several Palace departments that had been farmed out to government over the years and until

Peat's report, which recommended radical cost cutting and bringing it back under Palace control, Travel had been shared between the Department of Transport, the Ministry of Defence and the Foreign and Commonwealth Office. This was partly to mask the amount of money the Palace was spending by hiding it in governmental departments. It is still paid for by the Department of Transport as Grant-in-Aid but since April 1997 it has been back within the household and a series of leasing deals negotiated. The Sikorsky is halfway through a ten-year lease and if they need extra capacity they charter helicopters. The fixed-wing aircraft that the family uses belong to 32 Squadron of the RAF, for which the household pays just over £2000 an hour, about half what it would have to pay commercially. And if any members of the family use an aircraft for private business they pay for it at the commercial rate.

32 Squadron has two BAe 146s, which can carry twenty-one people but have a flying range of only 1500 miles; they are very useful for getting in and out of small landing strips, but alas there are only two of them and although the royal household has first call, the Prime Minister and Foreign Secretary also use them. Actually, so too do the RAF. The aircraft's primary role is moving operational commanders around theatres of war and if they are needed in a war zone – as they were in Iraq in 2003 – the Armed Forces have very first call on them.

The other planes belonging to 32 Squadron to which the household has claim include six HS 125s, which have a range of 2000 miles but only carry seven passengers, and have no hold, and the same rules of precedence apply. Every other plane the family flies in these days – ranging from a huge 777 to a small Lear Jet – is chartered. The big ones, like the 777 chartered for the Queen's trip to Jamaica, Australia and New Zealand a few years ago, come from British Airways who put in a couple of divan beds for the Queen and Duke of Edinburgh, knowing that two legs of the journey were over twelve hours long. The real cost of that was £661,300, but the governments of New Zealand and Australia contributed, which reduced it to £304,667. Since then the Palace has repeatedly taken its business back to British Airways. (Virgin was invited to tender but didn't respond.) Tim Hewlett says British Airways give them such good service that if it wasn't for the accountants he wouldn't bother to tender. He charters the smaller planes – such as the Lear Jet that he organized to take Prince Harry and his friends from Cape Town to Botswana during his gap year – through a broker. There were suggestions he might travel on Air Botswana but, knowing its chequered history, Hewlett advised chartering a Lear. 'The Prince of Wales had to put his hand in his pocket to pay for it,' he said, 'but it was the only sensible way to go.'

EIGHTEEN

Beyond the Dreams of Avarice

The Queen is not hard up by any stretch of the imagination but she's not the richest woman in the world either – despite what you might read in the magazines that monitor and publish such things. The mistake they make is to assume that she owns the vast and priceless collection of art that furnishes Buckingham Palace, Windsor Castle and all the other royal residences. The Royal Collection was put together by generations of monarchs over the centuries and belongs to the Queen in title, but is no more part of her personal wealth than Buckingham Palace or Windsor Castle. The Royal Collection, as it is officially known, is held in trust for the nation. And the Royal Collection was another department that was radically restructured after Peat's 1383-page report.

The Royal Collection had previously been part of the Lord Chamberlain's huge and unwieldy empire but in 1987 it became a department in its own right, and was the first and only department within the royal household to be entirely and independently self-financing. At Michael Peat's recommendation, a subsidiary, called Royal Collection Enterprises, was set up which was effectively the trading arm of the business; it became responsible for managing public access to the palaces and galleries, and the money it earned from ticket sales and other retail activity – legally the Queen's money – was ploughed into the Royal Collection to pay for restoration, conservation and the costs involved in maintaining and displaying the treasures. But this was at a time when the Queen was paying no tax on her income. When that changed and she started paying tax in 1993, Peat set up the Royal Collection Trust, a charitable trust, under the chairmanship of the Prince of Wales, to administer the entire business and prevent 40 per cent of the money earned by Royal Collection Enterprises going to the taxman. This brought it into line with most galleries and historic houses that for tax purposes are run by charitable trusts.

The current director of Royal Collections, and also Surveyor of the Queen's Works of Art, is Sir Hugh Roberts, a friendly man who is as passionate as he is knowledgeable about his empire. From a modest office in St James's Palace he looks after one of the largest and most valuable art collections in the world. It runs to many hundreds of thousands of *objets*, from very well-known paintings by artists such as Van Dyck, Canaletto, Rembrandt, and Tintoretto to more pedestrian items like the chairs in his office. The vast majority in all the palaces – a total of thirteen residences, including those that are unoccupied, such as Hampton Court and Osborne House – belongs to the Collection and much of it goes out on loan to exhibitions and museums all over the world.

The Queen is not the first monarch to lend treasures from the Royal Collection; Queen Victoria was also a great lender. It is part of the tradition of the Collection that it be made accessible through loans – it is not unusual even for pieces to be lent from the Queen's private rooms – but what is new to this monarch's reign is the extent to which it has become accessible to the public.

The whole thing began with Prince Philip's suggestion more

than forty years ago that the old private chapel at Buckingham Palace – bombed and destroyed during the Second World War – should be turned into a public gallery. This opened in 1962 and by the time it closed for refurbishment in 1999 nearly five million people had passed through its doors. Three years later, in time for the Queen's Golden Jubilee, a brand-new state-of-the-art gallery designed by John Simpson opened, with an extension that provided three and a half times the original space.

The earliest pieces in the Collection date from the reign of Henry VIII. Charles I was an avid collector. He bought Dürers and Titians, Rubenses and Van Dycks, miniatures, sculpture, silver, jewellery, furniture and tapestries, but his treasures were sold off after his execution and the abolition of the monarchy in 1649. Although some of it was returned or bought back after the Restoration eleven years later, much was permanently lost, and some of its greatest masterpieces now belong in French, Spanish and Austrian collections. Like his father, Charles II was also a keen collector; he started the collection of Old Masters drawings by acquiring Holbein's portraits of Henry VIII and his court, and six hundred drawings by Leonardo da Vinci, and brought French and Huguenot craftsmen to England. William and Mary brought in more Huguenot artists, including cabinetmakers; Queen Mary collected oriental porcelain and Delft vases, while William III bought clocks and barometers. George III, whose sixty-year reign saw great advances in the arts, science and manufacturing, bought Buckingham House, as the Palace was then called, in 1762 for his young bride, Princess Charlotte of Mecklenburg, and commissioned a huge quantity of decorative arts to furnish it. He also bought a celebrated collection of paintings and drawings, books, manuscripts, medals and gems that had been put together by the British consul in Venice, Joseph Smith, among which was the finest group of Canalettos then in existence.

But the greatest collector in modern history was George IV. He had a voracious appetite for art, buying porcelain, jewellery, books, manuscripts, furniture, *objets d'art*, as well as Dutch, French and religious art, Rembrandts and Rubenses. He also acquired sculpture: French bronze statuettes, life-sized busts and giant Roman marble statues. He commissioned contemporary English artists such as George Stubbs, Joshua Reynolds and Thomas Gainsborough; and, inadvertently, he converted Buckingham House from a private royal residence into a magnificent royal palace. He had intended to turn it into a pied-à-terre for himself and commissioned John Nash for the purpose. Nash had built the Royal Pavilion in Brighton for him while he was Prince of Wales, as well as Carlton House and Royal Lodge. His plans for Buckingham House were so lavish, however, that George decided when they were finished that it should become the ceremonial centre of his court. And although he didn't live to see it completed, between them they had created the most magnificent palace, and the state rooms that visitors see today, as well as the Grand Staircase, the marble, the chandeliers and the inlaid floors, are virtually unchanged since 1830.

William IV was good for porcelain and gilt banqueting plate; it was also he who established the Royal Library in its present form at Windsor Castle. Queen Victoria was knowledgeable and brought some Landseers into the Collection, but after her marriage Prince Albert became the prime mover in terms of what was acquired and how art was subsequently promoted during her sixty-three years on the throne. After his death in 1861, she lost interest, but as ruler of a vast empire as well as sovereign of the most powerful country in the world, she was on the receiving end of a never-ending stream of gifts from foreign rulers. This is how the Collection came by the famous Koh-i-noor diamond as well as countless other precious stones, furniture, tapestries, metalwork, porcelain, curiosities and mementoes.

Edward VII wasn't particularly interested in art, but through his wife, the Danish Princess, Alexandra, he did add to what was to become the finest collection of Fabergé in the world. Edward's tours abroad as Prince of Wales on behalf of his mother, the Queen-Empress, resulted in more wonderful gifts including the Cullinan diamond, the largest ever found, which was presented to him by the Government of the Transvaal on his sixty-second birthday.

George V wasn't interested, but Queen Mary was the complete enthusiast. She was like a magpie, collecting everything that caught her eye; she had dozens of books on English furniture and loved going round sale rooms, fascinated by anything that had a royal provenance. She even commissioned books about the Collection. One of Prince Charles's earliest memories was being taken by his nannies to have tea with Queen Mary, his great-grandmother, at Marlborough House and playing with priceless pieces of jade, crystal and silver that she had lovingly gathered from all over the world. Her collection was normally housed in the safety of splendid display cabinets. They had been strictly out of bounds to her children and grandchildren, but her first great-grandson was indulged. The Queen Mother took an interest in the Collection too; she enjoyed the company of artists and invited people like Augustus John and John Piper to Windsor and Buckingham Palace respectively, and commissioned paintings from them, but, overall, the volume of additions in the twentieth century pales in comparison with the art that was bought in the past. And the present Queen is no great collector.

'The way the collection has been formed has been a matter of personal taste,' explains Sir Hugh Roberts, 'which is what makes it such a peculiar collection.'

153

It doesn't set out to be the national collection; it has extraordinary gaps: there are six hundred Leonardos, for example, and not a single drawing by Rembrandt. It's hardly representative of Western art; it's very much a personal collection with the personalities shining through. Some monarchs have been terrifically keen, others not. This Queen has added some interesting things. Part of my job is to inform her of what is available or coming up on the art market, and she's always interested and occasionally goes for things. Last year she bought a porcelain service made to celebrate the recovery of George III in 1789. It had gone to someone else in the eighteenth century. She's not like George VI, who thought the day wasted if he hadn't bought several works of art, but she has a fantastic memory about things in the Collection and she is interested.

She is not, however, a great enthusiast and modern art by and large leaves her cold. The most striking modern addition is a portrait by Lucian Freud but that was not a purchase; it was a gift from the artist. She is said to have given Freud no fewer than seventy-six sittings – seventy-two more than most artists get – but she is typically noncommittal about whether or not she likes the portrait. However, Freud presented it as a gift for her Golden Jubilee and it is already worth a fortune, and she was delighted to have it for the Collection and for the opening exhibition of the new gallery.

Sir Hugh is responsible for everything pertaining to the Collection, and a large part of the job is overseeing the cleaning, conserving and repairing of the pieces – a task not unlike the painting of the Forth Railway Bridge. As well as the London gallery he runs the new Queen's Gallery at the Palace of Holyroodhouse in Edinburgh, which also opened in Jubilee Year. The Palace has been open to the public for the last hundred years – and is among the most visited tourist attractions in Scotland – but there had never been a specific gallery space showing the art in modern conditions. And there had never been anywhere to sit down and have a cup of tea afterwards, either inside or outside the Palace . . . until now. The Queen has gone into the catering business. 'Not specifically what the Royal Collections is about,' says Sir Hugh, 'but that part of Edinburgh is a gastronomic black hole and we are always looking at ways of improving visitor services – and of course increasing the amount people spend.' There's a café in the Farm Shop at Windsor, but this is the first in an occupied residence. 'It was the Queen's decision. Every other gallery now provides somewhere, and she said "Well, there isn't anywhere for them to go here, is there? We'd better do it ourselves."'

The Royal Library at Windsor Castle is also part of the Royal Collection, and for almost twenty years it was the province of Oliver Everett, an early casualty of the Princess of Wales's curious behaviour. A former diplomat, he was her first Private Secretary and Comptroller to their household but was sent packing after just two years. He was given sanctuary in the Library, where it was always felt his talents were wasted, although this is no ordinary library. Housed in three rooms dating from the reign of Henry VII to that of Charles II, it is more like a museum of the British monarchy. Among its thousands of books is an important collection of illuminated manuscripts dating from about 1420; the original manuscripts of various poets and authors including Byron, Dickens and Hardy; more than 250 incunabula (the earliest and rarest Western printed books dating from before 1500); and the writings of several sovereigns, among them a signed copy of the book Henry VIII wrote against Luther in 1521, which earned him the title Defender of the Faith, and the description of her father's coronation that the present Queen wrote in an exercise book at the age of eleven. It houses Old Masters drawings, watercolours and prints, plus collections of fans, maps, coins and medals, orders and decorations and portrait miniatures. But it also has a collection of random objects ranging from the overshirt worn by Charles I at his execution in 1649 to the Duke of York's flying gloves from the Falklands War in 1982.

None of this is financed by the taxpayer, as Sir Hugh is proud to boast. He has no Grant-in-Aid for his empire, and no money from the Civil List. The income that keeps them all afloat comes from the lucrative business of opening the palaces to the public (Buckingham Palace, the Royal Mews, Windsor Castle, Frogmore House and Holyroodhouse) – another of Peat's recommendations – and from the galleries in London and Edinburgh, and a handful of shops at each of the above as well as online.

Nor do they get a brass farthing from the unoccupied palaces; Hampton Court, Kensington Palace State Apartments, the Tower of London, the Banqueting House, Kew Palace and Queen Charlotte's Cottage all come under the Secretary of State for the Environment and are run by the Historic Royal Palaces Agency. And yet all furnishings and works of art on display – not to mention the Crown Jewels – are part of the Royal Collection. The unoccupied palaces have always been maintained by the government but the department was restructured after the fire at Hampton Court in 1986, which killed an elderly widow who lived in a grace and favour apartment. (The next day the minister responsible went to inspect the damage; he decided something had to be done when, on asking who was responsible for Hampton Court, individuals from about ten different departments put up their hands.)

Maintaining the Royal Collection is incredibly expensive –
last year it cost about £4 million.

You can't give the finest works of art in the world to just
anyone to clean and restore, so everyone we employ is at
the very top of the tree. We have the painting conservation
team based at Windsor, the paper conservation team, also
at Windsor, which looks after books, drawings, watercolours and prints; the furniture conservation workshops in
London, which looks after furniture, ceramics, metalwork,
arms and armour and gilt-wood. We do all of that in-house.
The Forth Bridge has nothing on a collection like this.
We're dealing with a collection that's getting older by the
day, canvas gets weaker, paint gets thinner, gilt-wood gets
chipped, joints get weak, veneer falls off, porcelain chips;
it all requires constant maintenance. What sets this collection apart from a museum collection is it is very much a
collection in use. The Queen likes to use eighteenth-century
services for decorating tables for state visits. In a museum
these would be behind glass all the time and never touched.
This adds a completely different dimension to it; it's continuously in use. Paintings cannot be under microclimatic
conditions at all times, as in a museum, and part of our job
is to make sure things are kept in as good conditions as
possible.

That these treasures are not kept in museums is good news
for the people who visit Buckingham Palace, either as guests
or paying visitors. They see breathtaking art and a building
steeped in history yet one still inhabited by the most famous
family in the world. However, the boast that the Royal Collection is entirely independent and self-financing comes at a
price. They have stepped irrevocably into the grubby world of

retailing, and any shortcomings by Royal Collection Enterprises staff in dealing with suppliers – not unknown although inevitable, perhaps, in such a competitive and price-sensitive business – become a talking point and, because of the brand, it is the monarchy's name that suffers.

NINETEEN

All the King's Horses –
The Private Queen

Early in the 1990s a middle-aged Californian cowboy with an extraordinary talent for handling horses found himself on the verge of bankruptcy. He had worked with horses all his life. At the age of eight he was a Hollywood stunt rider and doubled for Elizabeth Taylor in *National Velvet*. He had bred, trained and ridden horses. He had produced champions but now he was *persona non grata* in the horse world because he had had the temerity to suggest that it was unnecessary to hurt and frighten horses in order to get them to do what you wanted.

His father was a trainer who had hurt and frightened horses; he had also hurt and frightened his son. He had endeavoured to break the child with the same brutality as he broke his young horses. By the age of twelve the boy had seventy-one broken bones in his body. As a result, he grew up with a passionate belief that there was another, kinder, way to treat both horses and human beings.

His name was Monty Roberts; he was the real life 'Horse Whisperer'. Now nearly seventy, his methods for starting horses have been adopted by forward-thinking, enlightened people all over the world, his books on the subject have sold in their millions and he no longer has to worry that he might be forced to sell the farm.

159

'The person who did all of this was Her Majesty,' he says.

She was the one who found me and believed in me and she said, 'There must be a book.' And she didn't let it go.

Sheik Mohammed could have endorsed it, but he wanted it for his horses, not for anyone else's, Walter Jacobs wanted it to be exclusive to Germany, Ronald Reagan said, 'You just keep that under your hat, we'll have some real nice racehorses', and Her Majesty's first words were 'We've got to get this out to the rest of the world'. She's the only one who came at it with a generous attitude. Her primary motivation I think is it's a better way, a kinder way, and we've been making a lot of mistakes. I also believe in the time she has watched and worked with me that she believes there will be better racehorses and horses and carriage and Household Cavalry horses as a result.

The Queen read about Monty's methods in a magazine when she was staying with horseracing friends in Kentucky. She was intrigued. A few days later she saw a second magazine with another piece about Monty. As soon as she arrived home she asked one of her trainers his opinion. 'It's a load of rubbish,' he said. She asked Sir John Miller, as Crown Equerry responsible for all the Queen's non-racing horses, what he thought. 'Rubbish,' he echoed. That was the standard view at the time. For centuries man had been dominating horses by inflicting pain on them if they didn't obey him. Monty's methods were revolutionary: he used no violence; he doesn't even raise his voice. He uses the language that horses use in the herd.

The Queen persisted. Knowing he had a friend in California, she bought Sir John Miller an airline ticket and asked him to go and visit the friend and check out this Monty Roberts. 'If you still think it's rubbish when you've watched him, fine; but if you think there's anything to it, I want to see him.' The friend lived six miles from Monty and knew him well; and when he said he was bringing the Queen of England's Crown Equerry to see him, Monty was convinced it was a prank.

'Sir John got out of the car and he looked like something out of Central Casting,' says Monty, a big man, gentle, generous and amused. 'Tweeds, waistcoat, white moustache, cane, perfect English accent. He watched me do several horses, got back to the house and said, "What are you doing on 1 April? I think the Queen will want you to come to Windsor Castle." Ten days later I had an invitation.'

The first of April fell during a very busy week for the Queen. The Russian President Gorbachev and his wife Raisa were in Britain on a state visit and they were due to have lunch at Windsor Castle the day Monty arrived. He was told he might not get to meet her at all, that she might only be able to watch his demonstration on video. Then he was told he would meet her; she would watch him for an hour in the morning before her lunch. He was nervous. At home he trained his horses behind a wooden fence; no good if people were to see, so he found a metal cage, which they erected inside the schooling ring at Windsor. The Queen, the Duke of Edinburgh and the Queen Mother all came to watch that first morning, as did the Queen's stud groom, Terry Pembury, and a number of female grooms. The Queen had selected twenty-three young horses with which to test him, including a filly belonging to the Queen Mother. Apart from the Queen, who had an open mind, the audience was deeply sceptical.

The morning went well but at lunch he couldn't help noticing Sir John Miller and the grooms speaking into walkie-talkies out of earshot. Exactly why became clear as they got up to leave. The girls thought he had in some way hypnotized the horses he had handled that morning. 'Her Majesty's very upset with what these girls are saying,' said Sir John, 'and she has sent a truck off to Hampton Court to get two three-year-old piebald stallions that are due to be drum horses some day.'

'These little babies were Suffolks, huge and raw as can be,' says Monty.

They weighed a ton. The two of them were in this little horsebox, there is steam pouring out of it and the truck is rocking from side to side, and they bring one of them out and bring him into the cage. There's a bigger audience in the afternoon, so Sir John goes into the cage to introduce me, and the horse runs him out of it. So he introduces me from the outside. I go in, and the other horse outside is screaming at the one inside and I think, I've just got to block everything out. You can't do my job when your adrenalin level is going through the roof; it was nothing to do with the horses, but with all those people there. So I blocked it all out like never before, and knew immediately he was going to be okay. In thirty minutes I had a rider on him and had him trotting around. The Queen was jubilant; the girls were sliding out and going back to the stables not saying a word. I said, 'No, no, there's another one outside.' They said, no they had things to do, and the Queen knew they did but she wanted them to watch, so they did, and the second horse was just as good.

The Queen was profoundly affected by what she had seen and had plenty of questions about why the horses had behaved as they had. The Duke of Edinburgh was predictably curt – 'I've got a whole lot of ponies out there that I don't think you could do that with' (during the next few days he was proved wrong) – but the Queen Mother, who had great difficulty walking at that time and was leaning heavily on two of her staff, had tears streaming down her face. 'That's the most beautiful thing I've ever seen in my life,' she said, stiffening only slightly when, without thinking, Monty put a pair of comforting arms around her.

The Queen watched him work with her horses all day, every day of that week – Monty is convinced she told her Private Secretary to clear her diary. On one day the editor of *Horse and Hound*, Michael Clayton, came to watch and asked the Queen whether he could write an article about Monty's method and use a photograph of her to accompany it; she agreed. 'There was the door-opening of all time,' says Monty. And at the end of the week she lent him a car – a Ford Scorpio, armour-plated underneath – and sent him off to give demonstrations in twenty-one cities around the country, telling Sir John Miller to set the cage up, get some horses for Monty to work on and organize everything. 'I want the people of Great Britain to know about this,' she said. 'Her Majesty was my first tour guide,' says Monty, grinning.

Since that week Monty Roberts has been a guest at Windsor Castle on more than twenty occasions. He stays in South Lodge or with Sir Richard Johns, governor of Windsor Castle, and his wife in the Norman Tower, but always sees the Queen for a private lunch or tea, and she is always fascinated to hear what he has been doing. All her horses are now started and trained using his methods; so too are the Duke of Edinburgh's ponies and driving horses, and he has been called in by the Household Cavalry on innumerable occasions. They normally take ten years to train a horse to take the lead; he had one ready within six months.

The Queen's patronage has been fantastic but it is Monty's books that have spread the word worldwide. 'And that was all Her Majesty's idea too. "You know there must be a book," she said. I told her I wasn't a book-writing type so I said couldn't we just do some more videos. "No," she said. "Videos go away, they are not for ever; the written word is for ever. There must be a book."'

Monty looks, sounds and dresses like the Californian cowboy he is and has, I suspect, spent more time on the back of a horse than he ever did in a classroom. The idea of a book was daunting and so he quietly forgot about it and hoped the Queen would, too. That autumn she asked him back to do some teach-ins with *Horse and Hound*.

Her first words when I saw her were, 'How are we coming on with the book?' I knew then that there was going to be a book, I didn't know how, but I knew she wasn't going to let it go. And so next time I brought her some pages and she was shocked at how badly I wrote. I thought it was going to be a How To book. She was very kind, she read them and did not throw them at me and say they're rubbish, but her body language did and she said, 'I've come to the conclusion that you can't tell a How To story of a discipline that no one's ever heard of before until you know the person and how they came to these conclusions, so you must give us a more autobiographical look at this and then maybe do the How To bit.' So I was sent away with my homework under my arm again, totally lacking in any talent.

After the Queen had read the next attempt she said, 'I don't think you should write a book. Get one of these little tape recorders and tell your story, because when you tell me your story I understand it; when you start to write it becomes very stiff and it isn't you, it isn't in your voice.' So Monty went back to the drawing board.

The Man Who Listens to Horses was published in 1996 in

14 countries and sold over three million copies. Monty Roberts has now written five books – one of them describing how his method of handling horses can be translated into the human world – and it is currently being practised with remarkable success at a failing junior school in Birmingham that was on the verge of being shut down.

Monty had just been visiting the school the day I met him. 'It's amazing what's going on there,' he says. 'My methods have been moving into the human field for thirty-five years now but it was all behind closed doors until Her Majesty made the doors open. They now want me to go to Australia and free the aboriginal people and help them to get violence and drugs out of their lives.'

It is not surprising that the Queen should have been so taken with Monty Roberts and his methods. He is the most charismatic man and she has always adored horses; they have been her escape from the unreal world in which she lives and they respond well to her. As Sir John Miller says, 'She has an ability to get horses psychologically attuned to what she wants, and then to persuade them to enjoy it.'

TWENTY

The Sport of Kings

Horses are the Queen's one indulgence, the one interest in her life on which she spends serious money. She has ridden since she was a small child, having been introduced to racing by her grandfather, King George V, who liked nothing more than to take his young granddaughter to visit the royal stud at Sandringham. It was he who gave her her first pony when she was six. He also loved dogs, the Queen's other great love in life. She breeds and trains gun dogs – all registered at the Kennel Club with the prefix Sandringham, which is where she has kennels. Her grandfather bred Labradors and reintroduced the Clumber breed of spaniels (particularly good for rough shooting) which were originally started by Edward VII. Edward VII was an avid breeder, he built kennels at Sandringham designed to house up to 100 dogs – which Edward VIII during his short reign closed down. George VI re-established them with Labradors and the Queen has continued the breeding programme, although in 1968 she demolished the old kennels and built a smaller complex. The breeding and training of gun dogs is one of her great passions, and as with horses, something about which she is a genuine expert. She has produced many Field Trial Champions over the years and Sandringham dogs are recognized in shooting circles as one of the top of the breed in the country.

But it is her corgis for which she is better known. It was her father who introduced the family to corgis, and who gave the Queen her first on her eighteenth birthday, from which most of her subsequent corgis are descended. She currently has a fleet of five corgis (one inherited from her mother) and two dorgies (a cross between a corgi and a dachshund) and was devastated in 2003 when one of Princess Anne's bull terriers attacked and killed one of them. The only thing that makes her cross is when a visitor treads on one of her dogs.

Her father had a passing interest in racing but his real love was foxhunting. Her mother loved National Hunt racing – a winter sport, because the horses need softer going for jumping hurdles and running steeplechases. The National Hunt season culminates in the Cheltenham Festival in the middle of March, which was the Queen Mother's favourite race meeting; the champion two-mile chase is named after her. The Queen's passion – as it is for a considerable number of her subjects – is flat racing. She is never happier than during the four days of Royal Ascot in the third week of June where she watches some of the finest flat racing in the world. It is without doubt her favourite week of the year. She fills Windsor Castle with friends, all of whom are fellow racing enthusiasts, and every day they lunch in the castle, where the talk is racing. But, like everything else in her life, there is a rigid routine that is followed year after year after year. After lunch, at 1.35 p.m., cars take her and her family and guests to the Ascot Gate of Windsor Great Park. There they transfer into waiting landaus, attended by liveried footmen in red tailcoats, white gloves and top hats, which take them the last two miles to the golden gates at the eastern end of the racecourse. At 2.00 p.m. they begin the royal procession up the straight mile which delivers them to the royal box in time for the first race. Royal Ascot, still a highlight of the social season, has become a hugely popular sporting event in recent years and much more commercial – crowds have doubled in the last six or seven years – but the royal enclosure, for which anyone who wishes to attend has to be sponsored by a royal enclosure badge-holder of at least four years standing (the rule banning divorcees was abandoned in 1955), is still a very grand affair. Men wear uniform or morning dress, women may wear smart trouser suits (since 1970) but are not allowed jeans or shorts, and hats are still obligatory.

But the Queen is there for the racing. Breeding is her principal fascination. She is one of the most knowledgeable bloodstock owners in the country and racing people say that if she wasn't Queen she could be a very successful bloodstock breeder. Some of her best friends are also extremely knowledgeable. Henry Porchester, the seventh Earl of Carnarvon, sadly no longer alive, was one. Known as 'Porchey' to the Queen, he had been racing with her since the 1940s and her racing manager for thirty-one years. He was one of her very closest friends and they saw one another or spoke most days. He was the only person, Princess Anne once said, who could be sure of being put through to her mother on the telephone at any time without question, and he was with her at every race meeting. His death, sudden and unexpected on 11 September 2001, the same day the Twin Towers were destroyed, was a terrible blow to her. It was with Porchey that she made her first visit to Normandy to look at French studs in 1967. She had been sending mares to French stallions for the past fifteen years but had never been herself and mentioned this to President de Gaulle at Winston Churchill's funeral. Two years later she went on a private visit with a small party to see how the horses were bred and to meet French owners and breeders. It was the first of regular trips first to France and then America. Porchey introduced her to Will Farish, until recently the US

Ambassador in London and a successful Texan racehorse owner and breeder with the farm in Kentucky where she stays often (and where, in fact, she was when she first heard about Monty Roberts). Any official trip thereafter to either country – like her state visit to France in 2004 – would invariably be finished off with a private diversion to one of these studs.

The Queen has owned several over the years but now has just one stud; breeding horses has been a royal pastime for centuries. She inherited the royal stud at Windsor, which had originally been founded at Hampton Court in the sixteenth century, and two studs established by the future Edward VII at Sandringham – the Sandringham and Wolverton studs, which now operate as one. In 1962 she leased and later bought Polhampton Lodge Stud near Overton in Hampshire for breeding racehorses; now she uses it to hold mature horses before and whilst they undergo full training. She also has jumpers now, having taken over the Queen Mother's horses after her death in 2002. She visits all her establishments regularly and often in the early morning goes to the stables where her horses are in training to watch them run along the gallops. At one time she was a very big owner breeder in this country, but no longer. Alongside people like the Maktoum brothers and Robert Sangster, who have come into British racing with vast sums of money, the traditional home-grown owner breeders, including the Queen, have found it hard to compete.

When Porchey died, his son-in-law John Warren, married to his daughter Lady Carolyn, took over as the Queen's racing manager. 'Under John Warren's aegis they run a tight ship,' says my racing expert.

Her racing interests are kept on a very cost-effective basis. It's all carefully budgeted, they don't waste money, and they take commercial opportunities – last year they sold a filly to the United Arab Emirates. It is always a bit of a surprise when one is told that anything to do with the royal finances is properly managed but this is an example of where it is. John Warren is one of the best bloodstock agents in the world. He has an incredible eye for horses; and he is an outstanding bloke and although he must be thirty-five years younger is close to the Queen. Not just because he runs her racing interests but because he can keep up with her knowledge. Not very many people can.

At Royal Ascot the Queen is closer to the general public and more relaxed and informal than on any other occasion anywhere else. Security is tight but it is subtle, which is what she likes. Before some races she goes down to the paddock – the grassy area that is open to everyone – and makes her way to the pre-parade ring where the horses are walked round before being saddled up. It's where the experts, the people who really understand about the conformation of a racehorse, like to go. She has a very good eye for a horse, a great memory about lineage, and will stand there for fifteen or twenty minutes discussing muscle and stride and the pros and cons of the day's going, before following the horses to watch them parade round the ring prior to the race.

John Warren will usually be with her, also her Representative at Ascot, Stoker, the new Duke of Devonshire, whose family she has known for years; he is a fellow owner, ex-senior steward of the Jockey Club, ex-chairman of the British Horseracing Board and a very knowledgeable man. He has been her Representative there since 1997 – it is the one appointment she makes entirely on her own – and as such is chairman of the Ascot Board which runs the racecourse. In October 2004 it closed for redevelopment – and for only the second time in the fifty-three years of the Queen's reign her

June routine will be different. The first time was in 1955 when Royal Ascot was cancelled because of a railway strike, and she went privately to the July meeting instead. This year it will still be in June but rather more than a landau journey from Windsor. After much competition, York was the racecourse chosen to stage Royal Ascot in 2005.

The redevelopment of Ascot is a huge project, the third largest sports scheme of the new millennium after Wembley and Arsenal Football Club – it will cost £185 million – and is being financed, unlike those two, without a penny of tax-payers' money. Commercializing Ascot and making it more accessible has paid off. Over the last ten years it has built up reserves of £75 million and on the strength of its forecasts for the future has been able to borrow the remainder. Without the royal connection Ascot would be a very different place. Over the five days Royal Ascot gets 5 per cent of the total turnout at British racecourses at 1300-odd fixtures throughout the year and attracts huge television audiences nationally and internationally as well as other media coverage. It is also about fashion and having a good day out, but the absolute core of Ascot is the royal connection and attendance by the Queen and the royal procession and everything to do with it. Without that Royal Ascot would not be the same.

The Queen does not get involved in the day-to-day business of Ascot – that is the Duke of Devonshire's job – but she takes a very keen interest and has been closely involved in the redevelopment at every stage, as have the Duke of Edinburgh and the Prince of Wales. The Duke always accompanies the Queen to Ascot, and most members of the Royal Family attend some stage of the meeting – supporting Royal Ascot is expected – but none of them is as enthusiastic about racing as the Queen, and none begins to share her knowledge. However, her husband and eldest son have had plenty to say about the new building. The Duke has been particularly interested in the technical details, while Charles has concerned himself with the architecture and the functionality of the building.

The main reason for the redevelopment is because the racecourse has become so popular in recent years – a victim of its own marketing success – that crowd circulation has become a real problem; but it was a problem, ironically, that the architect Rod Sheard also had in one particular part of the new design. Sports stadiums are his speciality; he designed the Millennium Stadium in Cardiff and the Olympic stadiums in Sydney and Brisbane, so he is not new to the pitfalls, but there was one particular area that looked perfect on the drawings but which he knew wasn't going to work. He and the rest of the team had looked at it again and again – computer experts using all the latest technology – and on the day when they presented the plans to the Queen, the Duke and the Prince they had still not found the solution. But it was a small detail, one which they would eventually iron out, and not something worth mentioning. The royal group was there to look at the overall scheme.

At the end of the presentation the Duke of Edinburgh, then eighty-two, stood up, walked across to the diagram and pointing his finger to the precise spot that was under scrutiny said, 'You've got a crowd-circulation problem there.' Rod Sheard was gobsmacked.

TWENTY-ONE

Representing the Nation to Itself

When King George VI and his ministers heard that Hitler had set August 1940 for his planned invasion of Britain, the Queen immediately commissioned John Piper to paint a series of pictures of Windsor Castle, 'so that it would be remembered as it was if the worst happened'. The paintings that Piper produced hang in Clarence House to this day. Hitler's plan was to destroy London and kill or capture the King, and he and Queen Elizabeth were advised to take their two young daughters, Princess Elizabeth and Princess Margaret, and evacuate to the safety of Canada or the United States. 'The children won't go without me,' was the Queen's famous reply. 'I won't leave without the King. And the King will never leave.'

She sent the children to the comparative safety of Windsor Castle but she and the King stayed on in Buckingham Palace for the remainder of the war. There were other, safer houses in London, less obvious from the air, which they could have used but George VI refused to move. Ordinary Londoners didn't have the option of moving out of their homes; remaining in Buckingham Palace was a visible and potent gesture of solidarity with the people.

But it wasn't safe. The Blitz began on 7 September 1940

and during the first night two hundred German planes bombed London, killing four hundred people and seriously wounding 4357. During the following years Buckingham Palace suffered nine direct hits from German bombs and the damage sustained was extensive. The swimming pool was hit, leaving a crater fifteen feet wide, ceilings came down, glass was broken and windows shattered; there was damage to the roof and the ground floor, to a conservatory, the West Front and lawn, the quadrangle, the forecourt and gardens, and the North Lodge was entirely demolished, killing a policeman. An equerry who had fought in the trenches during the First World War described the night when 'this great house continuously shook like a jelly . . . for two or three hours it was like a front-line trench under bombardment'.

In one attack on 13 September the King and Queen had a lucky escape. They had just returned to Buckingham Palace at about 10.45 and had gone to their rooms on the first floor to collect a few odds and ends before going down to the air-raid shelter in the basement. They delayed a moment while the Queen removed an eyelash from the King's eye, and, as she did so, a German bomber flew under low clouds straight up the Mall in broad daylight and launched a direct attack on the Palace. 'At this moment we heard the unmistakable whirr-whirr of a German plane,' said the Queen in a letter to her mother-in-law, Queen Mary, the next day. 'We said "ah, a German", and before anything else could be said, there was the noise of an aircraft diving at great speed, and then the scream of a bomb. It all happened so quickly that we had only time to look foolishly at each other, when the scream hurtled past us, and exploded with a tremendous crash in the quad-rangle . . . Then there was another tremendous explosion . . . Then came a cry for "bandages". My knees trembled a little

174

bit for a minute or two after the explosions!' The King and Queen then calmly retreated to the basement for lunch, where the chef, when asked by the Queen if he was all right, said with a broad smile, there had been '*une petite quelque chose dans le coin, un petit bruit*'. The '*petite quelque chose*' was the bomb demolishing the chapel next door – which today houses the Queen's Gallery.

When the all-clear sounded at 1.30 the King and Queen set off to visit the East End of London, where the bombing and the casualties had been heaviest. 'I'm glad we've been bombed,' said the Queen. 'It makes me feel I can look the East End in the face.' Her lady-in-waiting remarked, 'When we saw the devastation there, we were ashamed even of the glass of sherry we had had after the bang.' Describing the visit to Queen Mary, the Queen wrote:

> The damage there is ghastly. I really felt as if I was walking in a dead city, when we walked down a little empty street. All the houses evacuated and yet through the broken windows one saw all the poor little possessions, photographs, beds just as they were left. At the end of the street is a school which was hit, and collapsed on the top of five hundred people waiting to be evacuated – about two hundred are still under the ruins. It does affect me seeing this terrible and senseless destruction. I think that really I mind it much more than being bombed myself. The people are marvellous, and full of fight. One could not imagine that life *could* become so terrible. We *must* win in the end.

Day after day she and the King toured blitzed areas of Britain, travelling by train to those cities and communities that had been bombed, arriving as soon as possible after the air raids to comfort those who had lost relatives, friends and possessions. 'The war', in Winston Churchill's words, was to draw 'the Throne and the people more closely together than was ever recorded'. From its outbreak the Queen had been quick to visit Civil Defence points, Red Cross centres, hospitals, factories and troops. She made a point of dressing in her most cheerful clothes and went from group to group boosting morale and giving her support to local and national efforts to raise money or set up welfare schemes to help people who were homeless and hungry. The King visited troops; he travelled to France in 1939, to North Africa in 1943 after the victory at El Alamein and he was kept informed about the plans for D-Day. 'Once more a supreme test has to be faced,' he said in a broadcast to the nation on 6 June 1944. 'This time the challenge is not to fight to survive but to fight to win the final victory for the good cause.' Cornelius Ryan described the extraordinary flotilla that carried the troops on to the Normandy beaches in *The Longest Day*:

> They came, rank after relentless rank, ten lanes wide, twenty miles across, five thousand ships of every description. There were fast new attack transports, slow rust-scarred freighters, small ocean liners, Channel steamers, hospital ships, weather-beaten tankers, coasters and swarms of fussing tugs. There were endless columns of shallow-draft landing ships – great wallowing vessels, some of them almost 350 feet long ... Ahead of the convoys were processions of mine sweepers, Coast Guard cutters, buoy-layers and motor launches. Barrage balloons flew above the ships. Squadrons of fighter planes weaved below the clouds. And surrounding this fantastic cavalcade of ships packed with men, guns, tanks, motor vehicles and supplies ... was a formidable array of 702 warships.

Ten days later King George VI was there, visiting his Army on the Normandy beaches as they fought to liberate Western Europe from Nazi rule.

Being there, being visible, showing his support, sharing the danger – and being bombed in his home as others were being bombed – was an important part of sustaining morale during the terrible years of war. As Lord Mountbatten said to the King, 'If Goering could have realized the depths of feeling which his bombing of Buckingham Palace has aroused throughout the Empire and America, he would have been well advised to instruct his assassins to keep off.' The King and Queen symbolically held the country together; they supported, encouraged, thanked, praised and commiserated with their subjects. They united the nation under threat from the enemy. The troops felt proud to be fighting for King and country, and the citizens at home were comforted to know that the King and Queen were there for them. As one of the survivors of the devastating air raid on Coventry in November 1940 said, 'We suddenly felt that if the King was there everything was all right and the rest of England was behind us.'

Sixty years later, on 6 June 2004, it was the King's daughter who stood on a dais in the town square at the coastal town of Arromanches-les-Bains, in Normandy, and, with the Duke of Edinburgh beside her, took the salute while eight hundred soldiers, sailors and airmen, a sea of white hair, berets, blazers and regimental badges – the last survivors from that remarkable D-Day operation, proud liberators of Europe – marched past their Queen in a stirring and emotional climax to the 60th anniversary commemorations.

'What for you is a haunting memory of danger and sacrifice one summer long ago,' she told them, 'is for your country, and for generations of your countrymen to come, one of the proudest moments in our long national history.

'I take it upon myself to express the immense debt of gratitude we owe to you all. I salute you and thank you on behalf of our whole nation.'

She praised the work of the Commonwealth War Graves Commission, which looks after the graves of more than 22,000 Commonwealth servicemen who died fighting in Normandy. The sacrifice of those who died or who were wounded 'must never be forgotten', she said. Neither should 'the courage and fortitude and the dogged determination of the hundreds of thousands of servicemen who landed on the beaches on that day and then fought their way inland in the face of determined opposition'. And she quoted her father from his broadcast sixty years before.

It was stirring, emotional stuff, fuelled by a fly-past of the Battle of Britain memorial flight – the Lancaster, Spitfire, Hurricane and DC 3 Dakota – the Red Arrows with their vapour trails of red, white and blue; while on the ground cheers for 'Her Majesty' and the mournful lament of bagpipes, the bugles and drums of the Royal Irish Regiment band and the King's Division Band sent tingles down more than a few heroic spines.

At moments such as this, there is no question about what the monarchy is for; the pride on the faces of those old soldiers, their pleasure that the sacrifices they had made in their youth and their bravery all those years ago were being recognized and appreciated by their Queen on behalf of their country said it all. They hadn't fought for the Prime Minister or for a political party or ideology. They had fought for their King and country and to preserve the freedom and way of life for which their fathers before them had fought. And those fathers and mothers, grandparents, wives and children who lived through five years of fear, of rationing, bereavement and hardship while Britain was at war understood what monarchy was all about, too. When the King and Queen visited their bombed-out houses and offered comfort and concern for their loss they felt they were not alone.

Before her appearance at Arromanches, the Queen had laid a wreath at Courseulles-sur-Mer to commemorate Canada's role in the Normandy landings, she had reviewed a Guard of Honour, attended a service of commemoration in the Commonwealth War Graves Cemetery in Bayeux alongside President Chirac of France and had lunch with heads of state; she met and talked to veterans at every stop. Most members of the Royal Family were involved in some sort of activity over that weekend. The Prince of Wales was in various towns along the Normandy coast, laying wreaths, unveiling statues, meeting veterans from the Parachute Regiment, the Royal Navy, Royal Marines and Army Air Corps and, finally, opening a British Garden of Remembrance in Caen, created as a tribute to the fifteen British and Allied divisions which fought in the eighty-day battle for Normandy between June and August 1944 to try to bring the war to an end. The Earl of Wessex, the Duke of Kent and the Duke of Gloucester were all in Normandy, while the Princess Royal was in Canada visiting the regiments there of which she is Colonel-in-Chief. And for all those old soldiers, sailors and airmen recognition from a member of the Royal Family – whichever member of the Royal Family – has a very special significance which no politician could ever match.

Mercifully there has been no comparable threat to national security since the Second World War. There has been terrorist activity of a terrifying nature, civil war in Northern Ireland and wars in the Balkans and Iraq in which British forces have been engaged. Those wars have come into our living rooms via vivid, graphic images on our television screens and because of that we know more about the horrors of war and terror than we ever did before, but civilians in London, Sheffield and

Coventry and all the other cities that suffered the devastation of Hitler's bombs have not feared for their safety here in Britain. There has been no common enemy that has brought us together and generations of Britons have no memory of there ever having been one. No memory of needing a figure-head to hold the nation together in the way that the King and Queen did during the Second World War. When those veterans and their contemporaries die, there will be fewer people who unquestioningly accept the value of the monarchy.

Prolonged peace brought all sorts of changes, not just to the automatic acceptance of monarchy. Society has changed out of all recognition in the last sixty years. The values that once underpinned our lives have shifted. Hierarchy and deference have largely gone, and so has respect. We stick two fingers up to authority; we think traditional British institutions like Parliament, the police, the BBC and the Church of England are sleazy and corrupt; we swear, blaspheme and trample all over people, their property and their sensibilities. Our democracy is so secure, and politicians so discredited, that we have lost interest in politics. We believe in nothing, care about nothing and prepare for nothing, expecting the state to nanny us when things go wrong and technology to answer our prayers. We live vicariously through the media – newspapers, television and the internet – and through the lives of two-bit celebrities. And our young binge-drink and do drugs – mug old ladies if they have to, to get them – have iPods and mobile phones glued to their ears and £200 trainers on their feet; and see no point in anything.

Where in all of this (which, of course, I exaggerate) does the monarchy fit? The answer, I believe, is in being a fixture in this morass. The Queen is approaching eighty and has been there, her face on our money, our stamps and in the media, for most if not all of most people's lives. She has got older and greyer in that time and her face is lined – and occasionally she nods off on the final day of an exhausting foreign state visit – but her values, her routine, even her hats, have scarcely changed in all that time. And when our world crumbles, as it does in times of national horror like Lockerbie, Dunblane or 9/11, we seem to need a figurehead to put their arms around us, metaphorically, and direct and articulate our emotion.

In April 1966, the small coal-mining community of Aberfan in South Wales was struck by disaster when a slag heap collapsed and engulfed the village school, killing 146, most of them children and all from the vicinity. The Prime Minister, Harold Wilson, hurried there immediately, as did Lord Snowdon, then married to Princess Margaret, who surprised the Prime Minister by his emotion. As he wrote in his diary, 'Instead of inspecting the site, [he] had made it his job to visit bereaved relatives . . . sitting holding the hands of a distraught father, sitting with the head of a mother on his shoulder for half an hour in silence.' The Queen issued an immediate statement of sorrow, but, despite continuous prompting from her advisers, didn't visit Aberfan for six days on the grounds that her presence would cause a distraction from the rescue work. It was a plausible excuse, but a mistake. The people of Aberfan wanted their Queen, and when she did arrive the healing effect, by all accounts, was palpable. She stayed for two and a half hours, and had told the police not to keep people back. Everywhere she went she was surrounded by silent groups of villagers, dressed in black. A little girl presented her with a bunch of flowers with a card that read, 'From the remaining children of Aberfan'. 'As a mother,' she said to bereaved parents, 'I am trying to understand what your feelings must be. I am sorry I can give you nothing at present except sympathy.'

'There were tears in her eyes as she talked to us,' said one woman. 'She really feels this very deeply. After all, she is the mother of four children. We had four too and now we have only two.' After placing a wreath at the cemetery where eighty-one children had been buried, she and the Duke of Edinburgh had tea in the home of a couple who had lost seven relatives in the disaster. 'She was very upset,' said her hostess. 'She was the most charming person I have ever met in my entire life. Really down to earth.'

The indiscriminate shooting of six-year-old schoolchildren in the small Scottish town of Dunblane on 13 March 1996 was another local tragedy that transfixed the nation in horror, and where a royal visit – the Queen and the Princess Royal visited the families, poignantly, on Mothering Sunday – not only helped the healing process but in some way helped express the nation's sympathy; the Queen and her daughter's obvious distress mirrored the distress of the nation.

The dreadful event had started to unfold just as the first lesson of the morning was about to begin. A lone forty-three-year-old gunman, armed with four guns and 743 rounds of ammunition, walked into the gymnasium of Dunblane Primary School and, without uttering a word, fired rapidly and continuously at children and staff alike. He killed sixteen pupils and their form mistress and wounded many more, before killing himself. It had all the ingredients of every parent's worst nightmare, and, like Aberfan, ripped apart a small community. A great media debate about guns ensued, which resulted in a Firearms Bill being rushed through Parliament that led to a total ban on handguns. Given that there were 160,000 handguns in the country, most of them owned by perfectly sane and law-abiding members of shooting clubs, the ban caused huge controversy.

Speaking on Radio 5 Live ten months after the tragedy, as the Firearms Bill was going through the House of Lords, the

Duke of Edinburgh, in his inimitable way, caused outrage by stating rather bluntly what seemed to many to be glaringly obvious: that banning otherwise legal handguns would do nothing to stop guns falling into the hands of criminals. 'I can't believe that members of shooting clubs are any more dangerous than members of a squash club or a golf club or anything else,' he said.

I mean, they are perfectly reasonable people, like the great majority of the population in this country. If a cricketer, for instance, suddenly decided to go into a school and batter a lot of people to death with a cricket bat, which he could do very easily – I mean, are you going to ban cricket bats? I sympathize desperately with the people who are bereaved at Dunblane, but I'm not altogether convinced that it's the best system to somehow shift the blame on to a very large and peaceable part of the community in trying to make yourself feel better. This transfer of blame on to the sport shooters, I think, is a little unreasonable. I can understand the fury and unhappiness. But these are sensible people who belong to these clubs.

The gun lobby applauded him for his courage in speaking out but he won no friends in Dunblane, or among the gun-law reformers, and played straight into the hands of republican MPs. Alex Salmond, leader of the Scottish National Party, said he should keep out of it; his comments were 'crass, insensitive and typically Prince Philip'. Tony Banks, Labour MP, said that 'as ever, the Duke of Edinburgh has got it wrong ... This man is insensitive, selfish and ham-fisted. A prolonged period of silence on his part would be much appreciated.' And Alan Williams, a Labour colleague, concurred: 'I think it is very ill-advised of the Prince at this delicate stage in the fortunes of the monarchy to come blundering in on an issue on which most members of the public, as well as most MPs, would disagree with him. He has done his cause no good, nor the reputation of the monarchy.'

This was a highly political issue, and, technically, Messrs Salmond, Banks and Williams were absolutely right; the Royal Family should not get involved in politics, but I have to confess to a sneaking admiration for Prince Philip. He is not the monarch with a constitutional obligation to remain above politics – the Queen is and she does so, religiously. He is an intelligent man, better informed than most, who finds it incredibly frustrating to have to bite his tongue when every other man in every pub in the land is able to sound off about controversial issues that have divided the country.

At the same time, it is a perfect demonstration of why the monarch has to be above politics. The Queen represents the entire nation, whatever their colour, creed or politics, whatever their status or situation, whatever their age. She is a unifying force within the country, the glue that keeps us all together, and that is her great strength. She belongs to everyone, no one voted for her – and no one gave their vote to someone else. If she expressed an opinion that could be claimed by a political party, she would immediately alienate a section of the population and that would be divisive; and so she doesn't. She is utterly inscrutable. And in my view, provided she remains neutral, her husband lobbing the odd grenade merely opens up the debate and adds to the gaiety of nations. And as it happens he was quite right. There are now more illegal handguns in the hands of criminals in Britain than ever before and gun crime has gone up. According to Home Office figures, in 1996, the year of the Dunblane tragedy, there were 3347 firearms offences in England and Wales involving handguns. In 2002–03 there were 5549.

There are many more examples of tragedies over the years where the Queen has played an important role in representing the nation to itself. None more so in recent times, perhaps, than the shocking, horrifying events of 9/11 which we saw unfold on our television screens. Played over and over again on that unforgettable day in September 2001, we saw the two hijacked airliners plough into the Twin Towers and smoke billowing into the sky as the buildings collapsed like cards taking thousands of office workers with them. The Queen had watched it herself, she said, in 'total shock' and 'growing disbelief'.

'These are dark and harrowing times for families and friends of those who are missing or who suffered in the attack, many of you here today,' she said in a message to the memorial service for British victims held in New York. 'My thoughts and prayers are with you all now and in the difficult days ahead. But nothing that can be said can begin to take away the anguish and pain of these moments; grief is the price we pay for love.'

A separate service was held in London at St Paul's Cathedral, for which she and members of the family were out in force. She had been at Balmoral when the tragedy occurred and remembered all too well the last time tragedy had struck during her summer holiday. She immediately sent a personal message of sympathy to President George Bush, while Malcolm Ross, the master of all matters ceremonial at the Palace, pondered the problem of how to affect a two-minute silence – the obvious way to mark Britain's solidarity with America – during the Changing of the Guard. His solution, to play both the American and the British national anthems, with a two-minute silence in between, and American music as the guards marched down the Mall, worked a treat. Spectators outside the Palace that day, many of them Americans, wept as they heard the familiar tunes.

185

TWENTY-TWO

Coming to Grief

On 31 August 1997, the night Diana's car smashed in a tunnel in Paris, the Queen's reactions had been less popular. Her life has always been a juggling act between the private and the public roles – that is the nature of monarchy; the one merges into the other in a way that it does for no other human being in any other position in the land. And on that Sunday morning, as she woke up to the fact that her two vulnerable young grandsons had just lost their mother in the most violent and unnatural of circumstances, she allowed the private to override the responsibilities of the public. She closed her ears to what her advisers were saying; she chose to deal with her personal, family grief rather than the grief of the nation. The fact that this was her son's ex-wife and not a gymnasium full of six-year-olds in a primary school of which she had never heard, obscured the picture. And the nation was angry and confused. People may have said and thought they wanted some display of grief from the Queen because she was Diana's former mother-in-law – the one that Diana had always said was so cold and indifferent. But that wasn't it; what they were really missing was the figurehead who could direct and focus their heightened, uncontrolled and rather frightening emotions. They needed the Queen in the same way that those families in the East End had needed her mother and father, fifty-seven years before, when the Luftwaffe was destroying their homes and killing their loved ones.

And so they congregated around Buckingham Palace, where people have always congregated in times of national mourning or celebration; none more so than on 8 May 1945 when the war in Europe was over and the King, Queen and Princesses, accompanied by Winston Churchill, came out on to the balcony again and again to the roar of cheering crowds in the Mall below. Fifty years later the Queen, the Queen Mother and Princess Margaret were there again to celebrate the anniversary and, despite the lapse of time, tens of thousands of people came to watch and to cheer. The building, as familiar to most Britons as the Queen herself, has been the focus for national identity for generations. There was, of course, a link between Diana and Buckingham Palace; but as she was divorced from the Prince, the logical place to have gone and to have laid flowers and tokens was Kensington Palace, the house where she had lived. Millions of flowers were left there, certainly, but they were feet deep outside the gates of Buckingham Palace too and that was where hundreds of people were standing around waiting for some sort of lead from their monarch.

When the Queen finally returned to London, and on the evening before the funeral spoke about Diana, live on television, only the second time she had broadcast to the nation other than at Christmas time (the first being during the Gulf War in 1991), the crisis very quickly passed.

Since last Sunday's dreadful news we have seen throughout Britain and around the world, an overwhelming expression of sadness at Diana's death.

We have all being trying in our different ways to cope. It

is not easy to express a sense of loss, since the initial shock is often succeeded by a mixture of other feelings: disbelief, incomprehension, anger – and concern for all who remain.

We have all felt those emotions in these last few days. So what I say to you now, as your Queen and as a grandmother, I say from my heart.

First, I want to pay tribute to Diana myself. She was an exceptional and gifted human being. In good times and bad, she never lost her capacity to smile and laugh, nor to inspire others with her warmth and kindness.

I admired and respected her – for her energy and commitment to others, and especially for her devotion to her two boys.

This week at Balmoral, we have all been trying to help William and Harry come to terms with the devastating loss that they and the rest of us have suffered.

No one who knew Diana will ever forget her. Millions of others who never met her, but felt they knew her, will remember her.

I for one believe that there are lessons to be drawn from her life and from the extraordinary and moving reactions to her death.

The Queen's words were what people wanted to hear, and they were delivered in the nick of time, but she does not have her mother's gift. The Queen Mother exuded charm and empathy; her smile, her wave, her eyes – no one who stood within a sizeable radius of Queen Elizabeth, whether she spoke to them or not, ever felt they had been excluded. They knew she had noticed them and her look spoke volumes. Diana had the same gift, in a much more informal, modern way and her laugh charmed the birds from the trees. She had no fear of people's emotions. She invited them to open up, and was not afraid to hold a hand for longer than normal or to put a comforting arm around someone in need. The Queen finds it very hard; it is partly her character and partly a generational thing. She was brought up, as people were in the 1920s, with a stiff upper lip; she was taught not to wear her heart on her sleeve and to keep her emotions to herself. 'Nowadays people think differently,' says a former courtier of the same age, 'but if that's what you've been taught, as we all were, it lives with you. It might appear that we are not as simpatico as we might be, but it's just that we don't show our feelings and that's the way it is. It doesn't mean we don't care. It was demonstrated at the time of the Princess of Wales's death. It's the generation gap. A stiff upper lip is not all bad; it gets you through difficult times. You can't cry all the time.' The Prince of Wales has more of his grandmother than his mother in him in that respect; he is a deeply spiritual man and not alarmed by what lies beneath the surface – but, like his mother, he has sometimes taken some convincing to believe that his presence will help. He was once persuaded to stop at a school in Middlesbrough on his way to Teesside, where a child had been brutally murdered the day before. He was afraid he would be intruding on private grief but his Private Secretary said firmly not; this was what was expected of monarchy. The press were out in force and he talked to the headmaster and the parents of the murdered girl. Then, quite unexpectedly, the headmaster asked whether he would talk to the girl's classmates. Unprepared, but unable to say no, he spoke to them, told them about his own experience, how he had learned to cope with the murder of Lord Mountbatten. It was monarchy at its best.

Prince Charles drew on personal experience again when he went to Omagh in Northern Ireland in 1998, just after twenty-nine people, many of them women and children, had been killed by a Real IRA bomb. More than two hundred were injured, many of them seriously; one of the doctors performing amputations said afterwards that he had done so many he had lost count. Charles spent five and a half hours in Omagh, talking to the injured and relatives of the dead, meeting doctors, nurses and the people from the emergency services who had had the grim task of collecting the body pieces. And he visited the site where the twenty-nine had died. It was an emotionally draining day, he found everything he saw and heard deeply upsetting, but, like his grandmother, he appears to absorb other people's pain without cracking up himself. When asked how he does it, he says, 'It's fifteen hundred years of breeding. It comes from being descended from Vlad the Impaler!' Again, he was worried that he might be intruding on other people's grief but nothing could have been further from the truth. About a thousand people came to see him, all of them saying again and again how grateful they were that he had come. And it was clear in Omagh, as it is in the aftermath of every tragedy, that a royal visit helps. When a politician turns up, cynics can always say he or she is doing it to win votes. The same can never be said about a member of the Royal Family.

But if ever proof were needed that these aspects of monarchy were valued, the public reaction to the deaths of the Princess of Wales and, four years later, the Queen Mother, must surely have been it. Two very different reactions but, in their own ways, both equally as strong. I don't pretend for a second that I understand what was going on in the public psyche when Diana died – even psychiatrists have tried and failed to explain the extraordinary display of grief for someone who most of those grieving, some so badly they needed counselling, had never even met. It wasn't just the shocking way in which it happened, or just the fact that she was so young and beautiful and leaving behind two young children. I don't even think it was the tragic end to what had been a very tortured and tragic life. I think she provided on a small scale what monarchy provides in the wider picture. People seemed to identify with her, they felt that she spoke for them and cared about them, and was a part of their lives, utterly familiar, her face seen time and again, part of their identity, part of the national identity.

The Lord Chamberlain, the Earl of Airlie, who was responsible for organizing Diana's funeral, which had to be done from scratch with no precedent to follow, went out into the crowds outside Buckingham Palace on two separate occasions during the days after her death to try and understand what was going on. He concluded that there were two distinct groups of people among the mourners. There were the modernists, who were desperately unhappy, crying in the streets and wanting to demonstrate their feelings in the various ways they did; and there were the traditionalists, quiet, low-profile, who didn't openly express their views – very upset, no doubt, but not likely to have been milling around outside Buckingham Palace. It proved an important factor in deciding what sort of funeral procession to devise, one that took into account both the modernists and the traditionalists. The result was a cortège with Welsh Guardsmen on either side of the coffin to provide the formal, ceremonial and a bit of military; but to have all Diana's charities following behind higgledy-piggledy, which was perfect, and perfectly judged. The procession alienated no one.

Any fears that the public reaction to the Queen Mother's death when it finally came on 31 March 2002 – she was a hundred and one, had two new hips and up until the end looked as sparky and indestructible as ever – would be insignificant by comparison with their reaction to Diana's were simply not borne out. The BBC misjudged it badly. They did interrupt a programme in the early evening to make the announcement but the newscaster who delivered the news, Peter Sissons, was wearing an everyday burgundy-coloured tie (following BBC guidelines), and for the main evening *News At Ten* was still wearing burgundy rather than black – and was much criticized for it. There was no hysteria as there had been over Diana's death, but Diana's death had been unnatural and untimely; the Queen Mother's was a peaceful conclusion to a long, full and largely very happy life. But there was no shortage of mourners. Thousands of bouquets were left on the lawns at St George's Chapel in Windsor, and the queue for the lying-in-state in Westminster Hall, where each of the Queen Mother's four grandsons – Charles, Andrew, Edward and Princess Margaret's son, Viscount Linley – stood vigil, stretched for more than three miles. So many people wanted to pay their respects that the doors of the Hall were left open all night.

Prince Charles, who had been in skiing in Klosters with William and Harry, was distraught and on his return gave a very personal and moving tribute on television to his 'magical grandmother'. How much they had learned from the experience of four years ago. Then there had not been so much as a statement from Balmoral, and the family had all gone to church within hours of hearing the news, which looked, in this godless day and age, for all the world as though nothing momentous had happened.

Plans for the Queen Mother's funeral – Operation Tay Bridge – had been drawn up years before and were very straightforward compared with the complexity of Diana's. Queen Elizabeth's was a full-blown state funeral with full ceremonial regalia; and ceremony is something that The Firm does exceedingly well. One million people lined the route on the day of the funeral and one billion around the world supposedly watched it on television.

Why? Because of what she represented. She was an old woman with a penchant for pastel coats and matching feathery hats; a complete tyrant, rumour has it, but a much-loved mother, grandmother and great-grandmother. Bill Tallon, or 'Backstairs Billy' as he was known, her butler for many years, also loved her unreservedly. People of all ages, all religions and all colours queued in the cold for hours to walk past her coffin because she had touched their hearts, just as Diana had. She was part of their identity, the nation's identity, as familiar to them as the language, November fog or cancelled trains.

TWENTY-THREE

Pomp and Ceremony

Ceremonial is part and parcel of the monarch's ability to represent the nation to itself, and anyone who advocates a bicycling monarchy, like the Scandinavians, where the King of Sweden was once asked for proof of identity when he presented his credit card in a shop, has been a lousy student of history. The British love ceremonial – so do tourists. The sight of the Irish State Coach or the Golden Coach drawn by four pairs of immaculate Windsor Greys, uniforms dating back to Tudor times and serried ranks of soldiers, moving with the precision of a Patek Philippe watch, is not just stirring, it touches the very heart of what it is to be British.

It is something that critics of the monarchy seize on regularly; why, they ask, does the Queen have to travel by coach and horses with all the paraphernalia to open Parliament? Why can't she just go by car?

These are the sort of questions that come up for discussion from time to time inside Buckingham Palace, a custom encouraged by Lord Airlie when he was Lord Chamberlain. He would get papers written on the subject – not just platitudes but genuine, thought-provoking papers which got out into the open issues, many of them difficult, that it would have been much more comfortable to have left forgotten. They would then discuss the paper, look at the pros and cons and try to form a view. And find, as in the case of the ceremonial, that there might be changes that they could make at the margins, but that there was not a strong argument for doing away with it. Once you have done away with it, it is gone for ever.

Lord Airlie's view is that they do it very professionally and it is something the British love. Ceremonial is an important part of the image of the monarchy and the respect that people have for it. They want to see the Queen up there in her magnificent coach – even if not every car driver and bus passenger caught in the resultant traffic jam in London agrees.

The State Opening of Parliament is a tradition that goes back centuries and is the very essence of what our constitutional monarchy is all about. It establishes the Queen's role and Parliament's role and the relationship between them. And the ceremonial aspect, rooted so deeply in history, and so incongruous with modern life, serves as a vivid reminder, even if only subliminally, of the continuity and stability of our system. Society may be changing rapidly, technology turning our world upside down, but in the sea of so much change and uncertainty there is a rock – a landmark that is reassuringly constant. No matter which individual is wearing the crown, the sovereign performs the same ritual year in year out.

In October or November, or at other times if there is a change of government, the Queen makes the journey from Buckingham Palace in the Irish State Coach (on view in the Royal Mews) drawn by four horses with a Household Cavalry escort. They take the traditional processional route down the Mall, across Horse Guards Parade, through the Horse Guards Arch into Whitehall and along to the Palace of Westminster where a guard of honour awaits – three officers and 101 men with a colour and a band. The Queen wears a long evening dress with long white gloves and the George IV diamond State

Diadem on her head, which normally resides with the Crown Jewels in the Tower of London. The rest of the regalia travels in its own coach ahead of the Queen's; the Comptroller of the Lord Chamberlain's Office carries the Imperial State Crown (set with three thousand precious stones and weighing two pounds thirteen ounces) for which she exchanges the diadem during the ceremony. His assistant carries the Cap of Maintenance, and other bits of regalia are carried by Gentlemen Ushers and Serjeants-at-Arms. Before he became Diana's rock, Paul Burrell was at one time one of the Queen's personal footmen at Buckingham Palace; on the eve of the State Opening one year he found his boss, late at night, working on her boxes with pink mule slippers on her feet and the Imperial State Crown on her head. She was practising carrying the equivalent of nearly two standard bags of sugar on her head – as she does every year – but the absurdity of the picture she presented was not lost on her. Before the Trooping the Colour ceremony, the Prince of Wales practises wearing a bearskin, which is also several bags of sugar, and he has the added hazard of having to sit on the back of a horse at the same time.

Before the royal party sets out a detachment of ten Yeomen of the Guard – the oldest of the royal bodyguards (formed by Henry VII in 1485) and the oldest military corps in existence – search the cellars under the Houses of Parliament with lanterns to make sure the building is safe. This dates back to 4 November 1605 when they found Guy Fawkes busily preparing to blow up the place; nowadays they are helped in their task by policemen with sniffer dogs and other devices but the ten Yeomen of the Guard in their scarlet doublets still go too.

The ceremony itself takes place in the House of Lords – the Commons are summoned from their chamber to hear The Queen's Speech – and when the Queen arrives at the Sovereign's Entrance she is met by the Earl Marshal and the Lord

Great Chamberlain, both in scarlet court dress, the latter carrying the golden key to the Palace of Westminster. The entire ritual is performed by a collection of officers with ancient titles in ancient costumes and when the Queen finally arrives in the chamber of the House of Lords (having been up the Royal Staircase past two lines of troopers of the Household Cavalry in full dress uniform with swords drawn) to the Robing Room to put on the crown in the ceremony for which she has been practising, plus the Garter collar with diamond George (the figure of St George and the dragon) and the same parliamentary robe she wore for her coronation – eighteen feet of crimson velvet and ermine – she is ready for a throne to sit on.

The Lord Chancellor then advances – and, despite the present incumbent Lord Falconer's attempt to abolish the ancient office in 2003, much to the Queen's surprise and dismay – removes The Queen's Speech (written by the Cabinet) from its special silk bag and on bended knee hands it to the sovereign. Before she reads it, the 'faithful Commons' have to be summoned. What follows is a reminder, dating back to 1642, when Charles I burst into the Commons with troops in the vain hope of arresting five MPs, that the Commons have the right to exclude everyone from the chamber except the sovereign's messenger. The Gentleman Usher of the Black Rod is that messenger; dressed in black cutaway tunic, knee breeches, silk stockings and buckled shoes with white lace jabot and cuffs and a sword at his side, he makes his way to the House of Commons and as he approaches the Serjeant-at-Arms slams the door in his face. Black Rod knocks three times with his rod – three and a half feet long and made of ebony – the Serjeant-at-Arms looks through the grille to make sure there are no troops and opens the door. Black Rod then says, 'Mr Speaker, the Queen commands this Honourable House to attend Her Majesty immediately in the House of Peers.' With traditional lack of haste, the Speaker and the Serjeant-at-Arms baring his mace then lead MPs to the Upper Chamber, chatting deliberately as they go to demonstrate they stand in no awe of 'the other place'. The other place can't hold the full complement so a token 250 MPs stand at the opposite end of the Chamber to the sovereign to listen to 'the most Gracious Speech from the Throne' at the end of which Parliament is officially open.

'On the face of it, it is the Queen giving these common folk their instructions about what they are to do,' says Lord Garel-Jones, the former MP (as Tristan Garel-Jones) and pairing whip and, as such, for seven years held sinecure positions within the royal household.

> But everyone knows the government has written it. Well, what is the first thing the House of Commons does when it gets back? It approves, on the nod, no debate, supply for the Armed Forces. It votes money so that the monarch can pay her soldiers, and the symbolism of that is, 'You may be head of the Armed Forces, all those soldiers may have sworn an oath of allegiance to you but, we, Parliament, the people, we actually pay for all of this.' It is a symbol but it doesn't do any harm to remind people about these things.

As vice-chamberlain, comptroller and treasurer, Garel-Jones played a part in the State Opening, walking backwards with his rod of office at the ready. 'It's all part of the pantomime but there's no harm in it and a lot of the pantomime represents part of Britain's evolution from absolutism to being widely regarded as one of the most solid democracies in the world. Each one of these things that goes on reminds us. It hasn't happened by chance. It has happened through history.'

TWENTY-FOUR

Charity Begins at Home

It was steaming hot in the hospital. There was no air condition-
ing and, despite the pioneering work going on here, not many
creature comforts. This was Tashkent in Uzbekistan, once part
of the Soviet Union and still communist to its fingertips in
everything but name. Life was still bureaucratic, cheerless and
very hand-to-mouth.

The hospital specialized in treating children with cerebral
palsy and the Princess Royal had come to visit. It was July
1993, she had recently remarried and this was her first foreign
trip with her new husband, Tim Lawrence. They had already
been to neighbouring Mongolia, where they had narrowly
avoided eating sheep's eyeballs in a nomadic camel breeder's
yurt – a great honour in those parts – and been soaked to the
skin in a sudden storm in the Gobi Desert; from there they
had travelled to Kazakhstan. The trip was a mixture of Foreign
Office fixtures, the British Royal Family extending the hand
of friendship abroad, and charity, which more often than not
in foreign parts is Save the Children. Uzbekistan was the last
leg of the ten-day trip.

As is the way of these things, the people she was due to
meet had been ready and in place for well over an hour, and
so as to look good for their important visitor the children were

199

out of their beds and standing to attention in their pyjamas. One little boy's body was so buckled that he had been strapped to a board to keep him upright; whether it was the wait, the discomfort or general anxiety about what was going on around him, he whimpered as a trickle of pee ran down his leg to form a puddle on the linoleum floor.

These children had no idea who the Princess Royal was; neither had their carers. But someone somewhere had singled the hospital out as a place of excellence which she should visit on a tour of the country. And so it was sandwiched, if memory serves me right, between a visit to a poet's grave, a look at some very splendid Islamic architecture and a wander round the spice market in Samarkand.

If the Princess's expression changed for any of these sights, I didn't notice it. It certainly didn't change for the cameras; if anything, she simply scowled more fiercely. As she walked round, hearing about the work of the hospital – which clearly fascinated her – she turned to the doctor in a white coat escorting her, removed one hand from behind her back – where, Duke of Edinburgh-style, they spent most of the day – and pointed at two or three of the children as if they were exhibits on a trestle table at a WI fête. She seemed quite unmoved by the sight of their twisted limbs, bright, brave little faces and liquid brown eyes. She didn't reach out to one of them; she didn't smile; she didn't even make eye contact. The visit was an academic exercise for her: the children were incidental. What mattered was the question of how you diagnose and treat cerebral palsy and fund research in a country which has so many inherent problems.

That same week the Princess of Wales was visiting sick and starving children in Africa, spoon-feeding gruel into their open mouths, comforting lepers and AIDS victims and hugging emaciated babies, watched and admired by the world's media. Those children wouldn't have known who Diana was any more than the Uzbeki children knew who Princess Anne was, but almost instantaneously the world knew about their plight; heart-wrenching images were on television screens and in newspapers and magazines all over the globe and the funds for humanitarian aid began rolling in. Publicity is what charities feed on and the bigger the star they can enlist to the cause the better the public awareness and the greater, therefore, their generosity. Diana was so glamorous and photogenic that any picture was certain to be front-page news, and when she announced she was retiring from public life in December 1993 and giving up all but a handful of her charities, the remainder were horrified.

'Your Royal Highness,' wrote the director of the Welsh National Opera, Brian McMaster, in one of several hundred similar letters from others equally aghast. 'It is just so helpful to be able to use your name. We only ask you to do one engagement a year which is a reception followed by an opera, but 20 per cent or so of all our fundraising is achieved that night. What are we going to do now?'

Four years earlier the WNO had accepted a highly prestigious invitation to play at the Brooklyn Academy of Music in America – the apogee of its forty-three-year history, but expensive. The tour was going to cost almost a million pounds. Diana agreed to fly to New York for the first night, to attend a reception in the interval and a fundraising dinner after the performance for a thousand people each paying $1000 for their meal and the privilege of eating it in the same room as the Princess of Wales. She looked a million dollars, charmed everyone and in that one evening the charity recouped the entire cost of the tour.

And yet, Save the Children, the charity of which Anne has been President since 1970, wouldn't have swapped her for two

Dianas, nor, I suspect, for anyone else. Because although she has probably never cuddled a stranger's child in her life – and one wonders even about her own – and has never knowingly smiled for a press camera, the Princess Royal is the most effective President they could hope to have. She is professional to her fingertips; she chairs meetings with utter precision, has a memory like an elephant's, speaks superbly and usually without notes and is always completely on top of her brief. She is also a brilliant fundraiser.

Her attitude in that hospital in Uzbekistan shocked me at the time. I longed for her to reach out to one of those children, as any mother – as anyone with an ounce of humanity – would. But she is very clear about her role in life and doesn't believe being touchy-feely forms a part of it. There are other people who can do the hands-on stuff. Her value, she knows, is to get things done, to persuade governments to give money to hospitals such as the one in Tashkent, to bring in funds to run them or to buy beds and equipment. And she is not going to stand and pose with a sickly child in order to do it.

Charity work has become one of the monarchy's main and most important functions. The tradition of a charitable monarchy goes back to the reign of George III, but in the Queen's reign it has become an integral part of her family's daily work. In the immediate post-war years, the assumption that the welfare state would take care of the poorer and weaker in society and make charitable giving unnecessary, did not materialize. What the welfare state did was make people think they didn't need to look after their neighbours any more, and wealthy employers felt that ageing employees, their widowed spouses or orphaned children were no longer their responsibility. And although the rich have continued to grow richer, and those at the bottom of the heap poorer, the rich have become increasingly tight-fisted.

ABOVE The Family Firm in about 1945. Waving to the crowds, being famous, being feted and photographed was something Princess Elizabeth had grown up with. And something she never questioned.

LEFT Diana had had no such preparation. She was working in a kindergarden when she began seeing Charles – and knew nothing about dealing with the media. But it didn't take her long to learn. She became an expert.

LEFT Happy families on the balcony to watch the Royal Air Force fly past, ending the annual Trooping the Colour ceremony – a fixture in Royal calendars since 1748. But appearances were deceptive – the Prince's marriage was already in trouble.

ABOVE Back on the balcony during the Queen's Golden Jubilee. Diana gone, the dynamics changed but life goes on. And, despite the horrors of the Nineties and media predictions that it would be a flop, huge crowds greeted the Queen as she toured the country and hundreds of thousands flocked to the Mall.

RIGHT The Party at the Palace – the night the Queen hosted a pop concert for 12,000 people in the gardens of Buckingham Palace. Nothing like it had ever happened before. Modern music but old-fashioned protocol: Camilla Parker Bowles was seated in the row behind the Prince of Wales.

LEFT Prince Charles shooting at Sandringham accompanied by Michael Fawcett, at that time his valet. He resigned after the Peat Report but still has great influence.

LEFT A young Paul Burrell in happier days, carrying one of the Queen's corgis off the Queen's Flight as the household returns to London after the summer break in Balmoral.

ABOVE The Queen and Prince Philip arriving at Riyadh in Saudi Arabia on Concorde in 1979. Important – not just for strengthening links between the two countries, but also to be flag-waving for British industry.

RIGHT Not all travel is supersonic when you're Queen. The Gold State Coach, used only three times during the course of her rein, was built by George III in 1762 and has been used for every coronation since 1831. The Queen and the Duke of Edinburgh also used it to take them to St Paul's Cathedral for the service of thanksgiving for the Queen's Silver and Golden Jubilees.

ABOVE LEFT Prince Philip on parade during the Trooping the Colour. He no longer rides a horse at the ceremony – to his indignation – but he is there beside the Queen as he has been for more than 50 years. Most men of his age have been retired for twenty years.

ABOVE RIGHT The Queen Mother, a diminutive figure beside the regimental mascot of the 1st Battalion Irish Guards. She had a magic touch with everyone and a very soft spot for all her regiments – and their dogs.

RIGHT The Queen in her element – rain or shine – at the Windsor Horse Show. She was insistent that the people of Britain should know about Monty Roberts, 'the Horse Whisperer', and his revolutionary training methods.

'Here is the stuff of which fairytales are made' declared the Archbishop of Canterbury as he made Charles and Diana man and wife. And the nation roared in approval as the Prince kissed his bride.

But the fairytale had an unhappy ending. By the time they were touring Korea they had given up pretending. Official separation was only weeks away.

LEFT Diana reached out to people in a way that royalty never had before.

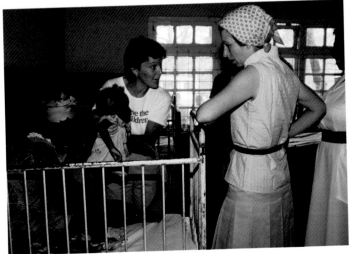

RIGHT Anne's approach, by comparison, looked cold and unfeeling.

LEFT Diana understood instinctively what put people at their ease – and the importance of being on the same level.

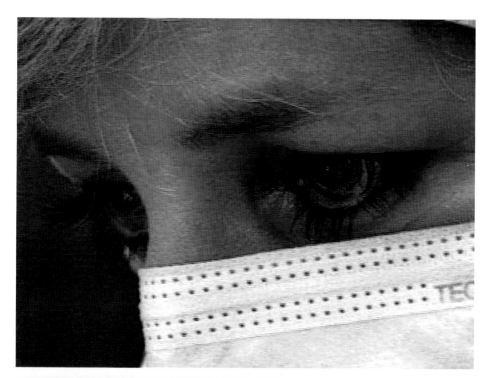

ABOVE She wanted to be the Queen of People's Hearts.

LEFT William at 18 – already showing signs of being his mother's son.

RIGHT The King is
dead. Long live the
Queen. Elizabeth II's
coronation in 1953.
Individuals come and
go but the institution
is what matters and
the institution
carries on.

BELOW The Queen
Mother's funeral at
Westminster Abbey.
She lived to the
age of 101 and
enchanted the
nation. Queues for
the lying-in-state
stretched for
three miles.

ABOVE Prince William learning to cook at Eton. The photo was one of a series shot for his 18th birthday, which caused 'a storm in a Fleet Street teacup' and lost the Prince's Press Secretary her job.

LEFT It was a good experience for William, however, and helped him to relax with the media that he had grown up hating.

It's a Royal Knockout was a turning point. It was done with the best of intentions but it placed royalty on a par with showbusiness personalities.

That doesn't mean all good works have to be serious. William and Harry replace ponies with bicycles to raise money for a charity polo match in Wiltshire.

A country woman at heart with a love of dogs and horses and not a trace of vanity.

The Queen, Princess Anne and Zara Philips. Three generations of equestrians.

The mask seldom drops, but the enormity of 9/11 – and the memorial service for its victims at St Paul's – was almost too much.

LEFT Charles and Camilla on the night their engagement was announced in 2005. After years of hostility the Queen finally gave them her blessing – and a family heirloom for an engagement ring.

RIGHT The tragedy was that his marriage to Diana had failed so spectacularly. Posing after their engagement in 1981, the future had seemed secure. But she was young and ill-prepared and the spectre of Camilla haunted her from the start.

The first and second in line to the throne on the 50th anniversary of Victory in Japan day, August 1995. An early glimpse for Prince William about what the future holds.

A photo call on the Home Farm near Highgrove in 2004. The night before William met journalists in a local pub for a pint of cider – a new approach by ex Manchester United man Paddy Harverson.

RIGHT Prince Harry being restrained after taking a swing at a photographer waiting outside a West End nightclub. He's vulnerable and volatile – an accident waiting to happen.

BELOW Diana in her misery was another loose cannon. Her interview with Martin Bashir – a masterly performance – was the final straw. The Queen decided it was time to call a halt to the marriage.

ABOVE The Queen's great curse is that in repose her face looks glum, and if she's watching the Derby and her horse is beginning to flag what can you expect? But if the horse comes in . . . jubilation.

ABOVE People who work for the Queen say they are in 'the feel-good business'. Meeting people is an important part of the job and if she overlooks someone, the Duke of Edinburgh is always there to notice and make amends.

LEFT Arriving on the Royal Train at Bristol for the Maundy Service. It's an expensive option but – comfortably furnished and kitted out with full office and communications equipment – it's a very secure and reliable means of transport, and one of her favourite.

William and Harry – the future. Service, dedication, duty is in the genes. But what if self-destruction is too?

As Will Hutton, journalist and chief executive of the Work Foundation, wrote in 2003, 'As inequality of wealth balloons back to nineteenth-century levels there is no sign of nineteenth-century levels of civil engagement and philanthropy by the rich.' Six per cent of the British population provides 60 per cent of the money given to charity, but it is the poor who give away proportionately more of their money than the rich. In America, giving is part of the culture – to be rich and not give to charity is to be a social outcast – and there is a tradition of the super-rich setting up charitable foundations. Bill Gates, the Microsoft billionaire, is the world's biggest philanthropist. His foundation is worth $30 billion and he plans to give away 90 per cent of his $50 billion fortune. When Ted Turner, the founder of CNN, gave a billion dollars to the United Nations in 1997 he mocked his fellow billionaires: 'What good is wealth sitting in the bank?' he asked. The rich lists were really lists of shame – encapsulated in the words of Andrew Carnegie a century earlier, who gave away his fortune to finance free libraries and a peace foundation: 'He who dies rich, dies disgraced.' There seems to be no such stigma in Britain, where old money finds ingenious ways of passing it on to its children and new money simply flaunts it. But if anyone can squeeze money out of the rich it is the Royal Family.

According to one historian the charitable work done by the monarchy today has 'made a genuine contribution to national wellbeing, but one which is largely ignored or misunderstood ... It may sound curious to those obsessed by constitutional niceties or royal spectacles, but the humdrum, day-in day-out charitable activity of the monarchy may be far more important than the "dignified" duties.' The charitable sector is now a huge industry and covers all manner of areas of society which government seems to have chosen to leave underfunded. The Charity Commission has 166,129 'main' charities on its register which last year raised a total income of £34,567 billion. The Queen is currently patron or president of 635 organizations and charities, the Duke 863, the Prince of Wales 619, Princess Anne 270, Prince Andrew 161, Prince Edward 30 and his wife, Sophie, Countess of Wessex, 61. And as was painfully clear when Diana ducked out of hers, those charities that manage to secure a royal patron to put on their letterhead do appreciably better in the fundraising stakes than those that don't. The WNO claimed that Diana's presence brought in 20 per cent of the charity's annual income – others have put the value of a single royal appearance at 10 per cent. Either way, it is a major contribution – and however you do the sums, the monarchy raises far more for charity than it receives in payment from the Civil List and Grant-in-Aid funding put together. In the last year Prince Charles has helped raise around £100 million for his own seventeen core charities and millions more for the others with which he is associated – and on the polo field alone he raises about £800,000 a year for charity.

The Queen has less time to devote to charity than the other members of the Royal Family because of her constitutional obligations, so for the most part the value she brings to her charities is the respectability of the sovereign's name on the letterhead, which sets them in a class of its own. She has added a few to the list during the course of her reign but most of them were taken over from King George VI at the time of her accession – and in those days patronages were given far more readily than they are today. Prince Philip also inherited a large number of patronages, but he took the view (which his children have followed) that it was better to limit the number of new patronages to those organizations in which he could take an intelligent and active interest.

The first he took on was the National Playing Fields Association in 1949, the only national organization, then and now, devoted to stopping Britain's open spaces and playing fields being sold and concreted over by developers. It 'has specific responsibility for acquiring, protecting and improving playing fields, playgrounds and playspace where they are most needed, and for those who need them most – in particular, children of all ages and people with disabilities'. George VI had been involved with the charity before his own accession and thought it would be a useful vehicle for his son-in-law to forge links with the community. 'I want to assure you,' said Prince Philip at his first meeting, 'that I have no intention of being a sitting tenant in the post.' He immediately redrafted a £500,000 appeal that was to go out in his name and masterminded an elaborate publicity campaign to back it up. He worked regularly at the NPFA office, then in Buckingham Gate, walking there from Clarence House, and went all over the country raising money and opening new playing fields. He played charity cricket matches, held fundraising lunches at Buckingham Palace and made an appeal film; he even persuaded Frank Sinatra to donate the royalties from two of his best-selling records – although associating with a divorcee, as Sinatra was (and dancing a samba with Ava Gardner, the voluptuous film star), thoroughly shocked his critics at court. He raised hundreds of thousands of pounds through his efforts – by 1953 playing fields were being opened at the rate of two hundred a year – and he is still at it, still President and still active. And the need is still as great as ever. The government makes noises about refusing planning permission but they have allowed nearly two hundred playing fields to be sold since 1998.

TWENTY-FIVE

The Rough with the Smooth

The charity for which Prince Philip is probably best known is the Duke of Edinburgh's Award Scheme, which he founded with Kurt Hahn in 1956. Nearly ten years ago I was asked to present Gold Awards on his behalf to young people who had achieved the top accolade and duly put aside a morning to spend in St James's Palace. The Duke's rudeness is legendary but his behaviour that morning took my breath away. With so many Gold Award recipients these days – about five thousand each year, which is a real testament to its success – he can't do them all in person so celebrities of one sort or another are asked to help. In this instance each of us was given a group of award recipients and put into interconnecting state rooms; we were to present the awards and the Duke, we were told, would come into each room to meet us all and talk to the recipients. I did my stuff and the Duke came into the room as planned; he spoke genially to all the young recipients, quizzed them, joked with them, congratulated them heartily on achieving their Gold Award, but when he was introduced to me the smile vanished from his face, he looked me up and down – I swear he snorted but I could be making it up – and walked on past without a word. But I am in good company – he did the same, I am told, to Jennie Bond, for many years the BBC's royal correspondent.

However, having now watched him on many occasions and spoken to dozens of the organizations with which he is involved, including the NPFA, I have had to swallow my pride and prejudice. They all agree that he can be unspeakably rude, he has a fearsome temper – which he has handed on to most of his children – and is not unknown to have reduced people to tears, but he is the ultimate professional, is as sharp as a razor, and still, despite being well into his eighties, phenomenally hard-working. There is no excuse for being rude to people who are not in a position to answer back (or failing to be civil to someone who has given up time on your behalf) but he is very much a product of his age and circumstance, and those who work with him appear to forgive him.

The Duke of Edinburgh's Award Scheme was not the Duke's invention although he has been the driving force behind it for nearly fifty years. The educationalist Kurt Hahn formed the basis for it back in 1934 but it was not launched in its present form as a national youth programme until over twenty years later, when he approached Prince Philip. Hahn was the man who founded Gordonstoun, the outward bound-type boarding school in Morayshire in the north of Scotland where Charles was so miserable during his teens, and where his brothers followed. Hahn also founded Outward Bound, another of the Duke's charities. Prince Philip had been one of the first pupils at Gordonstoun, after Hahn was forced to flee Nazi Germany and move his revolutionary school from Salem to the Moray Firth. Gordonstoun was his solution for civilizing adolescents; the other feather in his cap was United World Colleges, which he founded in 1962 as an international sixth-form college, preparing adolescents for life. He believed that education could tear down national barriers and promote international cooperation and therefore peace.

The idea behind the Award Scheme was to give young people between the ages of fourteen and twenty-five from every background and situation a chance to experience challenge and adventure, and thereby a sense of achievement and personal fulfilment. It was inspired by the same philosophy that drove his schools. He wanted to make the tough compassionate and the timid enterprising, to create citizens who would not shrink from leadership and, if called upon, could make independent decisions and put the right moral action before expediency and the common cause before personal ambition. The young people who sign up for the Award know none of that; they do it because it's fun and their mates are doing it, but they come out at the other end with a lot of the qualities Kurt Hahn was rather pompously striving to foster.

Vice Admiral Mike Gretton, who was director of the Award from 1998 until 2005, had known the Duke of Edinburgh in a naval context 'where his reputation for telling you that you were talking nonsense went before him', so there were no particular terrors for him in working for the Duke on dry land.

And I've been told I'm talking nonsense quite a few times since – usually with a huge guffaw of laughter and as long as you argue back and make your case it's fine. One of the most fascinating things I've found about him is when you're having one of these ding-dongs – good discussions I would call them – at the end the outcome was not always clear – had HRH accepted my point? Then I'd go to Miles Hunt-Davis, his brilliant Private Secretary, and say, 'We had this discussion and he didn't actually say "Yes, Mike, I totally agree with you", or "No, that's nonsense".' And Miles would say, 'Mike, if he's said nothing, you're okay. It means he's accepted it, he just doesn't say so quite so clearly.' The first time this happened was over a very technical detail about the Duke of Edinburgh's Award age limits. I went to brief him about this and he was pretty grumpy about it; he wasn't liking it and I was arguing it backwards and forwards, and I came out not really knowing whether I had got his mind or not. Two weeks later we were at the Waterside Hall in Belfast having our General Council, with a thousand people there from the Award, and someone asked a fairly hostile question from the floor about this change to the age limits. It was fourteen but it's more sensible to apply it as Year Nine in the English system when some children are thirteen and some fourteen – that would allow the younger ones to join with their peer group. He answered that question from the floor with all of the points I had deployed to him, much better than I could have quoted them, and that shut the audience up and there was never another word about it again. It was a minor but contentious issue, which he had hoisted in totally and transmitted logically. Very, very impressive. I just wish he had told me earlier; but that's not his style. I think he just likes to think about things and keep people on their toes, so they cannot presume which way he's going to jump.

There are three different awards – Bronze, Silver and Gold – and four components to each award, but there is no element of competition. It has nothing to do with ability; each individual sets his or her own goals, has help from an adult mentor, and success is measured on a personal level by how far he or she advances. So it is as valuable for people with handicaps, special needs and social disadvantages as it is for the ablebodied sons and daughters of the middle classes. Indeed, in 1956 the scheme was initially aimed at young men who left school as early as possible and who did not get jobs before starting National Service at eighteen. So making the Award available to young people with different backgrounds has always been a priority for the Duke of Edinburgh.

It also thrives abroad. It is now operating in 115 countries – not always under the same name but always the same programme – and since 1956 over five million people have taken part in it.

Paul Arengo-Jones was, until he retired recently, general secretary of the International Award Association.

> In very simple terms, it encourages young people to do what they like doing better, to learn more about it and to find an adult who will encourage them. The outcome is their own feeling of self-worth goes up in leaps and bounds because, for the first time in their lives, they are doing what they want to do, not what teachers or parents want them to do, and they are finding they can do it better and are having a relationship with an adult who is only there to help that person do what that young person wants to do.

A high percentage of the Award Groups are operated at schools and youth organizations but they are also run in prisons where, according to Arengo-Jones, there have been extraordinary results:

> In South Africa they conducted a survey to see how many of the seven thousand young people who had been through the President's Award programme – as it is called there – had re-offended and found that seven had. That figure would normally have been 86 per cent. It's incredible and a bit risky because they sometimes change their name. But even if that figure is wrong by 100 per cent or 200 per cent, it is still so substantially below the normal as to be unbelievable.

But every time I go there I get another set of figures which is the same. It stops them re-offending, and the prison service makes it available to all young people who go through the system.

In Britain the figures are also good. In one area in the south-east the re-offending rate of young people engaged in the Award Scheme was 2.5 per cent compared with 32 per cent of young people on final warnings and 85 per cent on probation orders who were not in the Award.

The Duke has handed over much of the practical day-to-day running of the International Award Association to Prince Edward; but Prince Philip is still Patron, and although the 50th anniversary in 2006, when he will be eighty-five, might seem the ideal moment to step down from the entire operation, he shows no inclination to do so. He is still involved, still influential and still participating in the triennial International Forums, last held in 2003 in Barbados. Father and son were there together, both staying in the same unglamorous holiday block as everyone else, in simple rooms with a double bed and bathroom, no valets, just protection officers. Prince Philip doesn't enjoy the fuss that so often goes with the territory. At a conference in Auckland one year he was irritated by the convoy of cars with flashing blue lights that the local police had laid on to escort him. When he arrived at the event he walked down the line of policemen and said, 'When we leave I want three or four cars; no more.' Five cars were waiting for him when he came out of the conference; he counted them. 'Come on,' he said to his companions, 'we're walking', and they walked the mile or so back to the hotel. It caused total confusion but it was the last time there were too many cars in the convoy. He hates the use of sirens, hates driving through red traffic lights. 'Why can't we stop?' he will ask.

Paul Arengo-Jones, twenty years his junior, is in awe of the Duke's stamina.

He works incredibly hard for us. We did a tour of the West Indies; seven countries in five days. He was seventy-nine or eighty at the time and I had managed to borrow a private jet and met him in the Bahamas and had crammed the programme. There's a rule with his programme: never leave empty spaces. What's the point in being there if you're not going to work? is his attitude. So when we were planning it I drew up this horrendous programme. I sent it up to him saying, 'This is the maximum we can fit in. I hope Your Royal Highness will draw some lines.' It came back, tick. At the end of it I was absolutely on my chin strap, exhausted; private aircraft, chauffeurs, it didn't make any difference. He was utterly unfazed by the whole thing, striding forward, 'What do I have to say now? Where am I going? What do I have to do?'

He is also impressed by how hard the Duke works. He can write to him 365 days of the year and no matter where the Duke is, whether at Balmoral, on a foreign tour or on holiday, he will get a response within three or four days, and often will have typed it himself. If he has asked for a message, for example, the Duke will draft something and send it, saying, 'Is this okay, do please just scribble on the paper so I can make the changes on my computer.' Says Arengo-Jones, 'I've given up writing notes for speeches, I just provide bullet points that I'd like included or names he might mention, and he will do it all himself. I believe every evening before he goes to bed he clears his desk. I've certainly been phoned at 11.00 at night by a Private Secretary saying, "We need that brief, could you get it delivered to Government

House at 6.30 a.m. so he can read and absorb it before breakfast?'"

He always comes to everything very well briefed, he's always on time, knows when to be there and when to leave; both him and the Earl. You say you'd like them to come to a cocktail party from 6.00 to 7.00. They say, 'Okay, how many people?' You say, 'About a hundred and twenty', and they say, 'Okay, forty minutes'. They know exactly how long it takes to work a room and come out the other side without having to go round twice or feeling spare at the end. They will talk to everybody. Once in South Africa they were going round meeting everyone and one group moved because they thought they were going to be missed and the Duke got to the end and I said, 'Right, I think that's the lot' and he said, 'No, there's one missing', and looked round and spotted them and was off, had a chat with them, then said, 'Now we go'. He had noticed when he went in who the groups were; he's an utter professional. You go back into the room and everyone says 'Wow' because he's talked to them all and he's interested and he's very knowledgeable.

Another well-known charity with which the Duke's name has long been associated is the WWF (World Wide Fund for Nature as it's now called). He agreed to be President for five years and is just clocking up his 33rd year and still going strong. Making conversation over lunch with girls and staff from the Cheltenham Ladies' College in March 2004, during a visit with the Queen to mark the school's 150th anniversary, he asked the chairman of the Council how long he had been in post. Having originally taken the job on for five years, the answer was very many more. 'I did exactly the same thing

213

with WWF,' said the Duke. 'Goodness,' said one of the girls, 'I didn't know you had an interest in wrestling.'

Dr Claude Martin who has worked with him at WWF for many of those years says he has been a very good Chair. He's been on hundreds of trips to see wildlife and endangered species, and opened doors all over the world to the most influential people. 'We were once on a trip into the Congo basin and on into forest. Prince Philip complained he never saw any wild animals because there were so many bloody policemen hiding in bushes they scared everything away. So we took him into forest with no one and saw masses of wild-life. He loved it.'

Like everyone who works with the Duke of Edinburgh, Arengo-Jones believes sixty-six-year-old Brigadier Miles Hunt-Davis is the key. They joined within a year of each other, had military backgrounds – Paul was a colonel – and had mutual friends.

The relationship with the Duke was also helped by a shared military background. Arengo-Jones viewed Prince Philip as his divisional commander.

> To me he would have been a four-star general or admiral, regardless of whether he married Her Majesty. He has the intellect and the bearing and the strength of character to have reached that rank, no doubt. I get so annoyed when the press picks up on his comments. Remember the Indian fuse box? He went up to Scotland, looked at a fuse box, it was a mass of wires, said 'That looks like an Indian fuse box', the press reported it and the Asian community went through the roof. My Indian counterpart wrote to me a few days later and sent the leading article from their equivalent of the *Sunday Times*, and it said, 'At last someone speaks

the truth.' It was a long article extolling the virtues of what the Duke said. 'He's absolutely right, our electrical systems in India are appalling, every Indian has to have about six transformers and seven circuit breakers between the grid and their computer because of the surges and the blackouts and so on. We really have got to get a grip.' Two days later he sent me the letters that the newspaper had had in response; about two disagreeing and ninety saying quite right; so I said don't send them to me, send them to the Duke, which he did and he got a nice letter back.

But not everyone can cope with the Duke of Edinburgh's challenging manner. One former director of the Award couldn't. He was so intimidated he broke out into a sweat whenever he saw the Duke; his shirt would be wringing wet. He couldn't and didn't stay. Yet the young people who have done the Award seem to thrive on his provocation. Put him with a group of rough, tough teenagers and he is in his element. 'What did you do for your Award?' he'll ask. 'That's not very challenging, couldn't you do better than that?' 'They respond wonderfully,' says Mike Gretton.

They come straight back at him, they're not overawed at all. They think, 'Who is this gaffer?' His technique at Gold Award presentations is to head for the prettiest girl in the front row because he knows she will be fun to talk to and she'll be confident and vocal, so it starts the conversation which quickly spreads out to the shyer boys and girls. It's brilliant. He was a superb chairman to me, he remains a superb patron, and just to see him wandering around St James's Palace or Buckingham Palace or Holyroodhouse when he's awarding the Golds . . . he hasn't missed a Gold Award presentation in forty-eight years. He's passionate about it, utterly dedicated, it's his baby, his thing, and I'm quite convinced that when we cut him in half after he moves to a better place we'll find a rock running through his insides saying The Duke of Edinburgh's Award.

Nevertheless, those who work for him have to be prepared for the whole package, to take the rough with the smooth. The Duke is punctilious about time and anyone greeting him is wise to be in position five or ten minutes early. On one occasion he was late, by five or ten minutes, for a UK Award General Council at the Barbican. Finally the car arrived – his personal black cab – he leapt out, growled at Mike Gretton about terrible traffic and it all being his fault, and, as they walked to the Green Room backstage at the Barbican, said, 'And your bloody brief was absolute nonsense.' He then went on to the stage and conducted the meeting perfectly and in total accordance with the brief. 'He loves having a little poke to see how you stand up and as long as you don't burst into floods of tears it's all fine.'

Apart from such rare exceptions, meetings he chairs always start and end on time and it is a brave committee member who turns up late. He will walk into the room with no ceremony and start chatting, and then he'll look at his watch and the meeting begins. Prince Edward, however, is a favourite and, some say, indulged son. He once arrived five minutes late for a trustees' meeting after the chairman had begun. Edward said, 'I'm frightfully sorry, sir', and Prince Philip stood up, kissed him warmly on both cheeks and welcomed him with open arms. His skill at conducting meetings, like that of his daughter, is legendary. He allows everyone their democratic say but is very skilled and enough of a diplomat to end up with a consensus view which leaves everyone thinking they have the answer they were looking for.

Nothing has been confirmed but Edward, who will inherit his father's title in due course, is almost certain to take over the Award, too. He is just as passionate about it as his father and, having done it himself – which his father never could because he was over age for the Award when it was launched – he is the best possible ambassador for the organization. Since giving up Ardent, his production company, in 2002, the Award has become his main interest; he is a trustee of both the UK and International Awards and also chairman of the International Council of the International Awards Association and when he is not swapping stories with current participants – who I suspect he gets on with better than adults – he goes all over the world making presentations and raising funds. 'People say, "What shall we do with him?"' says Paul Arengo-Jones. 'I say, "Put him in a room full of young people and close the door."' Next year he is lead trustee for the Award's 50th anniversary celebrations – and some of his riskier ideas are already resurrecting nightmares from the past.

TWENTY-SIX

A Moment of Madness

Many people date the beginning of the monarchy's recent troubles to that fateful television spectacular, *It's A Royal Knockout*. Everyone at Buckingham Palace, including the Queen's Private Secretary, Bill Heseltine, was against the idea. He had tried to get it stopped but Prince Edward was too far down the road with the negotiations, adamant that he should be allowed to do it, and the Queen, never good at confrontations, was unable to say no to her youngest son, even though she too had misgivings. Nearly twenty years on, Edward is older and wiser having not been allowed to forget the disaster. *It's A Knockout* is the benchmark for every idea that is floated at the Award. 'As long as it's not like *It's A Knockout*' the cry goes up and he will be on a short leash this time around.

Bad publicity and royal scandals appear to have surprisingly little impact on the charities with which members of the Royal Family have links. The Duke of Edinburgh's remark about Indian fuse boxes had one Award field worker saying he was not prepared to continue, but there has been no evidence of donors pulling out. Mike Gretton admits he worries about it but says that scandals reverberate very little.

Big corporate donors are usually ensnared over lunch at

either Buckingham Palace or Bagshot Park, invitations to which – with the promise of Edward, usually Sophie, and occasionally the Duke for company – have chairmen and chief executives responding by return of post. Edward gives a presentation, there is a discussion, lunch and the suggestion that they might like to give £20,000 per annum for five years. In the last six months they have had a 50 per cent strike rate and are purring.

'It's partly altruism – the corporate world would like to support young people in their development across the board – but, secondly, they can mix with other captains of industry and, by the way, it's in St James's Palace or Buckingham Palace and you can bring your clients along and you introduce them; the royals have a strong cachet, that counts for one hell of a lot,' says Gretton.

We've done a lot of research on corporate giving, and people say they've done it entirely for altruistic reasons, but you scratch a little bit harder and actually there is bound to be some self-interest. If I'm a shareholder or a private company owner, I want to know that my donation is doing something for me. It might be called corporate social responsibility – fine, but they're doing it because there might be something in it for them and I don't blame them, they're hard-nosed businessmen. We do think about that quite a lot – the debasing of the monarchy or a bicycling monarchy would have a huge effect on us on the fundraising side – and we have our thoughts and are building other planks to our fundraising which will be less dependent on the royal scene because that makes sense in itself and as a back-up – but it would be very damaging if the royals disengaged.

There's no question about the value of having a royal around – other charities would bite my arm off to have what we have. Whatever criticism there is of the Royal Family there are enough people around who want to meet a royal and be associated with something royal, for good reasons and bad, but that makes it a very, very positive advantage.

Privately he worries about what will happen when the Duke of Edinburgh goes because he is a stronger brand than Edward, but he has absolutely no doubts that in fundraising terms, and also operationally, having the royal connection is very important to the organization.

As Arengo-Jones says, royal patronage is a priceless commodity. It allows charities to offer their donors access to the most exclusive address in the country and the chance to shake the hand of a member of the British Royal Family. That is something that money simply cannot buy.

'It doesn't matter how much money you've got; unless you know the person with the key to the door, you won't get through.'

TWENTY-SEVEN

The Key to the Door

The member of The Firm who has perfected the art of using his position – in the interests not just of charity but of issues – is the Prince of Wales. He discovered many years ago that an invitation to Highgrove or Kensington Palace would be accepted before it hit the doormat. This enabled him to bring together disparate collections of people with a common thread, who without his intervention would never normally have met. He put them round his dining-room table, posed searching questions and coerced them into finding answers. What could have been read as impertinence had chairmen and chief executives twice his age returning to their desks and working for their lunch. The result, to cite but one example from twenty years ago, was that after listening to the needs of the disabled, at least one of the major builders of modern housing estates was persuaded to add an extra fifty millimetres to standard door frames, to lower the sills and build ramps instead of steps into the landscaping so that their houses could accommodate wheelchairs; and the disabled, who were so badly served by society, could feel less alienated.

Since 2003 the government has made it statutory for all public buildings to be wheelchair-friendly but that was long after the Prince of Wales first put heads together and effected a change, albeit small, via less draconian methods.

He discovered he could do the same internationally, too. In the early nineties he convened a two-day meeting in Charleston, South Carolina, for 120 senior executives from the United States, Britain, Europe, Japan and Australia. Declaring himself merely a 'catalyst', he posed one question after another to which he wanted written answers. With the Prince as their guide they wandered through the old streets of Charleston to try to capture the romantic essence of a traditional community and to admire the local architecture. 'How are we going to tackle the huge challenges facing us,' he asked them; 'vast population-growth rates, poverty, hunger, mass migrations, environmental degradation, potential conflict over diminishing natural resources – unless business, with its presence in these crucial areas and with so many people, their children and families, revolving around such business, takes a long-term view?'

As the businessmen there commented, no one else in the world, not even the President of the United States, could have got so many top people together at such short notice.

Architecture is the area in which the Prince's amateur involvement has earned him probably more enemies than anywhere else; and where (apart from his private life) he has most divided opinion. From the night when he stood up at Hampton Court in 1984, as guest of honour at the 150th anniversary dinner of the Royal Institute of British Architects, and, as his audience of seven hundred settled back with brandy and cigars expecting to hear a few congratulatory words, tore the profession limb from limb, he has been accused of abusing his power. Architects, he said, were consistently designing buildings without a thought for the people who were to live in them, and called the proposed extension to the National Gallery in

Trafalgar Square 'a kind of vast municipal fire station . . . like a monstrous carbuncle on the face of a much-loved and elegant friend'. Inevitably, some people agreed with him, others disagreed and the architectural practice which had designed the monstrous carbuncle lost the job and their business took a nosedive.

A few years later, he was at it again, criticizing the planned development for Paternoster Square next to St Paul's Cathedral. Following a competition, Charles had been invited to see the plans submitted by the seven finalists. He was appalled. Facing what he knew would be a hostile audience at the Mansion House he said, 'You have, ladies and gentlemen, to give this much to the Luftwaffe: when it knocked down our buildings, it didn't replace them with anything more offensive than rubble. *We* did that.' Richard Rogers, one of the finalists, described the Prince's remarks as 'very vicious – and very questionable democratically', a charge that has repeatedly been made against Charles in the last twenty years by those who disagree with his views.

'I believe I have been accused of setting myself up as a new undemocratic hurdle in the planning process,' said the Prince of Wales, 'a process we are supposed to leave to the professionals.'

But the professionals have been doing it their way, thanks to the planning legislation, for the last forty years. We poor mortals are forced to live in the shadow of their achievements. Everywhere I go, it is one of the things people complain about most, and if there is one message I would like to deliver this evening, it is that large numbers of us in this country are fed up with being talked down to and dictated to by the existing planning, architectural and development establishment . . .

Richard Rogers's words rankled. 'Sadly, in recent years,' he told commentators, 'our Royal Family have had a poor record as patrons of arts and sciences. As yet there is little to suggest that the Prince is an exception in this respect. As a man with strong views about architecture, a high public profile and enormous private wealth, he has an extraordinary opportunity to commission buildings for his large estates. But he has yet to produce a noteworthy construction . . .'

As it happened the opportunity had already presented itself. In 1987 West Dorchester District Council had selected a four-hundred-acre plot of open farmland belonging to the Duchy of Cornwall to the west of the town for development to meet local housing needs. This was the second time the Council had commandeered Duchy land for expansion. The first development had been entirely conventional and the Duchy was again preparing plans for a conventional housing scheme for between two and three thousand dwellings on the second site when the Prince intervened and brought in the distinguished classical architect and urban planner Leon Krier as master planner. 'Rather than see development of another zoned conventional housing estate with its accompanying separate industrial estate,' he said, 'I was determined to break the mould and to ensure that such growth should recapture the organic form and sense of place of our historic towns and villages.

Poundbury represented a challenge to achieve this without compromising its unspoilt rural setting. It also presented the opportunity to build a community which included a wide range of housing intermingled with economic activity.'

Poundbury has been a reality now for over ten years, yet it doesn't feature on *www.Streetfinder.co.uk,* and although it is on my 2004 road map there is no road signage to it, not even off the Dorchester ring road just a few hundred yards away, so you can – as I did – sail straight past. I am sure this is not the intention but it all adds to the feeling of unreality when you arrive – as though you might be in a dream. It sounds clichéd to suggest it feels like a toy town – his enemies have been writing it off as a joke town from the start – but it does at first blush and even the locals in the old town refer to the buildings as Noddy houses.

Poundbury seems altogether too perfect and the scale too small to be real. The streets are all perfectly named, and black iron signposts, the sort you find in the pedestrianized parts of historic towns, guide you to places such as the Middlemarsh Clinic, the Enterprise Centre and Pummery Square, the heart of the community with the Poet Laureate pub, the Octagon Café, a parade of little shops and the Brownsword Hall, that stands on chunky, honey-coloured pillars (a dead-ringer for the town hall in the Prince's home town of Tetbury) – where all the clubs and societies meet. The houses might have been models made for a child's play set. They are a hotchpotch of different designs and sizes but all have chimneys and tasteful front doors; they have lintels and bow windows, brick and sandstone, tiles, slates and gables, with not a telephone wire, aerial or satellite dish in sight, and not one with a car parked out front. Some are detached, others are terraced and at odd intervals there are fountains, water features and trees. I was looking for the Duchy development office – 'just beyond Sunny Days nursery' – and was being talked in on my mobile phone. I followed the roads I was told to follow and although I was horribly late and instinctively, therefore, inclined to hurry, I suddenly found myself driving at a snail's pace. The road surface was uneven and mostly gravelled, it had no markings, no white lines or triangles, no indication of whose right of way it was at a junction, none of the signs that drivers are so familiar with and which allow us to drive on autopilot. As a result I felt uncertain and dropped my speed dramatically.

This, I discovered, is all part of the plan, not, as I assumed, because the development was as yet unfinished; it is one of the major differences between Poundbury and other new housing estates built since the war. In rubbishing the development, the Prince's critics tend to focus on the architecture, which is unashamedly traditional, and accuse him of being stuck in an earlier age. Simon Conibear, development manager for the project, urges me not to follow that line. That is the least important part of the experiment.

What is interesting about Poundbury is that the design has created an instant community, and that is what the Prince was after: a development on a human scale that puts people before cars. It has a mixture of private and social housing in the same street, to prevent the formation of either rich enclaves or poor ghettos and a mixture of homes, offices and factories (including a chocolate factory that sells seconds at the back door) within the same area. And because garages and car parking areas are all in courtyards behind the houses, and walkways run between the buildings, the whole village is permeable, which makes it very user-friendly – but not so friendly, evidently, for burglars: crime levels are significantly lower than in any other part of Dorchester, and so far nothing more than petty. The streets are designed for pedestrians first and cars second, as I discovered. The result is that people can – and do – walk down the middle of roads in such safety that parents let their children walk to school and even five-year-olds go to the shops for their mothers. What Poundbury has done is to break the mould in which town planners and house builders have been stuck for the last fifty years, in which the car dominates everything; in doing so it has created – to hear the residents talk – a safe, friendly community that people are proud of and want to look after, where neighbours know one another and look out for one another.

'The whole concept has worked remarkably well,' says Kim Slowe, one of the developers, who now lives in one of his own houses in Poundbury,

> . . . and I admire the Prince for doing it. He put his neck on the line without question and it has genuinely worked. If people move in Poundbury they move to another place in Poundbury, from house to flat maybe. That's very telling. There's no question it could have gone the other way, if the factories had created problems, if the highways – every single highway rule is broken because the planning officer was broadminded enough to listen to what was being explained to him and accept it. If he had changed and a by-the-book man had come to Poundbury, it would have been destroyed overnight. If someone had said 'You've got to have bollards, yellow lines, and county-standard street lights' it could have gone off the rails. If the social housing experiment had not worked it *would* have gone off the rails and would have turned very sour, very quickly.

The developers have had to agree to work very closely to a highly prescriptive building code imposed by the Duchy of Cornwall that governs everything, from the materials and detail of the brickwork to the colour of doors and window frames and the positioning of house names.

Although traditional on the outside and built from local materials in the local style, the houses in Poundbury are wholly contemporary in terms of energy efficiency and eco-friendliness. They all have double glazing – all wooden window frames, no plastic allowed – and some, like Kim Slowe's, are 'interjer' houses with sheep's wool for roof-space insulation and thermomax vacuum tube solar heating, heat recovery systems and grey water – too technical for me, but ground-breaking to those in the know, and all without using concrete and glass.

Poundbury had a rough start. They began building Phase One in 1993. It was the middle of a recession, the media was taking potshots at the Prince of Wales over all sorts of issues and his private life was all over the newspapers; he was accused of wrecking the countryside, of getting special treatment to build on a greenfield site because of who he was. They got the mix between social and private housing wrong – too much social – and there were tensions. Social, owned by the Guinness Trust, a housing charity, and rented to council tenants at a fraction of the market value, now accounts for between 20 and 35 per cent – and it's impossible to tell which it is. As one resident who takes round hundreds of visitors a year says, 'I offer a pound for every one identified and I've never lost my pound.'

Developers have always avoided mixing social and private housing for fear of depressing house prices; for the same reason, they have never put factories and commercial buildings alongside private housing. But the experience at Poundbury has turned that theory on its head; property prices are higher in Poundbury than on the executive estates or anywhere else in Dorchester. And with its mixed use, Poundbury fulfils all the government's ideals of reducing journey times to work and being able to walk to schools and shops.

But that didn't happen overnight. It was five or six years before Phase One suddenly gelled and began to work and what emerged was a highly bonded community, where everyone spoke to everyone else no matter which front door they emerged from. 'People identified with it and liked the architecture,' says Simon Conibear.

Then you got the Market Square and the Octagon Café which became a social venue; we procured a Farmers'

Market here in the square, bought covered umbrellas – that cost us £3000. I used to have to get up at 6.00 a.m. on a Saturday to put them up, then gradually residents took over and they now do it. Local organic producers came round and created a little fair in the square, then a musician, a fiddler, and suddenly these vital little human ingredients were showing that this experiment of creating a place based on the human scale, providing what people really wanted and not what was imposed by planners and plc house builders was actually beginning to work. There are later milestones, like the opening of the pub. All major brewers said it won't work, too small a catchment, not standard format, the *Daily Mirror* was running a long story saying no one wants the Prince's pub. Then someone took it and it worked and met its annual financial targets within six months. Will Hadlow is the youngest publican in England. It's a thriving business.

One reason the pub has worked is because it's a mixed-use environment – one of the principles of Poundbury – what towns and villages that grew organically used to be. It's not a housing estate or residential suburb. With all these employers there are now six hundred people working in Poundbury and 750 people living here. Business people use the pub at lunchtime, residents in the evening – double whammy. It's the same with village stores which opened six months after the pub. Tesco Metro turned it down, everyone said it wouldn't work, wouldn't trade. But it's busy. Private individuals took it, Budgens are their franchisers, so 80 per cent is Budgens and the rest they select themselves, some of it is Duchy stuff. They now want to open another. It has disproved the major retailers.

Poundbury is about disproving shibboleths that have confounded good design for the last fifty years, it has confounded the national house builders' precept that people want detached little boxes all looking the same round a cul-de-sac. Prince Charles deserves a lot of credit for sticking with these ideas through a lot of criticism.

Critics are still sneering at Poundbury – mostly people who haven't been to see it – but it has had a major impact on planning in this country. Poundbury is listed in PPG3 (Planning Policy Guidance Note 3, to you and me) and council engineers, traffic experts, highways officials, architects, developers and planners – great coach loads of people in the urban development business – come from all over to see this model of urban planning which, without the Prince of Wales, would never have happened.

Despite an absence of street furniture, white lines or stop signs, there has not been a single casualty on the roads in ten years. 'The Prince didn't dream all of this up in the bath,' says Simon Conibear.

He was extremely well advised by people in the know. That's the great advantage of his position, he can take advice, have a lunch at Highgrove and call in the top people and ask questions. He spoke to a highways engineer called Alan Baxter who has done things round the Tower of London and Trafalgar Square; he says don't look at roads as things for cars to get round, think of them as spaces between buildings, public space. This myopic view that says 'get the highway book out – 7.2-metre highway, 2.8-metre footways on either side, then do your houses' – has been so wrong and so damaging for Britain in the last fifty years and you needed someone like the Prince to challenge those standards and stand up and say some things and stick by those people who were saying those things. I doubt whether we would have had the success in challenging the highways and planning authorities without the Prince. The fact that he was fronting the challenge made them sit up and listen and work to make it work, particularly on highways.

Some might call that an abuse of power; but if the Prince of Wales hadn't stood up and challenged the planners, it's possible that no one would ever have done so, and the remorseless march of identical, soulless housing estates across Britain's green fields would have continued with no thought about the community needs and the welfare of the people who were buying them. Financially he would have been much better off if he had kept his nose out of it. As Duke of Cornwall, he gets the revenue from the Duchy – that's what keeps him in his very comfortable lifestyle and the Duchy would almost certainly have got more money for the land if they had sold it to a mass developer who would have built eight thousand boxes.

He put his head on the block for something he believed might make a difference to the quality of people's lives – and it certainly seems to have done so. It could have gone badly wrong and it is still early days. Not much more than 15 per cent of the whole project has been completed and it is not scheduled to be finished before 2020. But John Prescott, First Secretary of State, is a big fan, has visited several times, and Poundbury is being seen and promoted by government as a blueprint for the future.

TWENTY-EIGHT

Community Spirit

His experiment at Poundbury is by no means the first time the Prince of Wales has had an influence on government. The Department of Work and Pensions New Deal for getting the unemployed back into work is straight out of the Prince's Trust and the work they have been doing for nearly thirty years; the only difference is that the government's scheme is doomed to failure. It provides money to encourage employers to recruit the long-term unemployed; it doesn't provide the back-up, the practical help, the mentoring, the team building that the Prince's Trust provides – essential in giving real help to young people who lack motivation – with the result that most of those who have been given employment under the New Deal don't turn up on time, don't have the right attitude and have been swiftly sacked. The government's Public Sector Food Procurement Initiative is another example; this is pure Business in the Community – and in this instance pure Prince of Wales.

The Prince didn't found Business in the Community (BITC). It was started by Stephen O'Brien in the early eighties with a simple idea for inner-city regeneration: to involve companies in the communities in which they operate. If you can persuade business to invest, train and recruit from within those com-

232

munities then you solve unemployment and improve the whole depressed inner-city environment. O'Brien, aware of the Prince's Trust's work in that area, initially asked the Prince for support with a project called Fullemploy, to help unemployed young black people in the inner cities. What followed was a daring event known as the Windsor Conference. For two days the chairmen of sixty major companies in the UK were shut up with a crowd of articulate black people. Racism, the Prince told the assembled gathering, was a failure by the white community to recognize the potential of the black community. It was a brave thing to do, it could have backfired; instead it was widely regarded as one of the most significant advances ever made in race relations, and which people involved in the field still talk about today. Charles felt he had found a man who shared the same ideals and an organization where he could make a difference. He became President a year later and has been passionately and inextricably bound up with the organization ever since – personally initiating several major programmes. Like the Prince's Trust, BITC is a huge success story. It turns over £22 million, employs four hundred people and has seven hundred member companies – one in five of the private sector workforce and three-quarters of FTSE one hundred companies.

O'Brien's successor, Julia Cleverdon, an equally dynamic character, is frequently driven to distraction by the Prince.

He's like an extraordinary campaigning terrier with a memory like an elephant's – he remembers the detail of every character he's met on every visit, which is why, when junior ministers start arriving with shiny suits and shoes like conkers and being enthusiastic about inner-city problems, the Prince rolls his eyes to heaven. 'What do they think I've been doing for the last thirty years?' There's a lot of

frustration, a lot of here-we-go-again, new policy, new politician, new minister, having to explain all over again, 'Yes,
we know about this; yes, that would be a good idea; no,
you'll never make that happen in Bradford – unless you get
the private sector going in Bradford you haven't got much
of a hope . . .'

She imitates him well but she's a big fan. 'He's always had an
extraordinary ability to push the agenda further than most of
us thought it could go and spot things that other people haven't
seen,' she says.

A year before Britain's rural communities were devastated
by the foot and mouth epidemic in 2001, Julia Cleverdon was
hit by 'the first onslaught of black spider memos' saying that
he wanted BITC to look at the issues facing the rural communities. 'We now know the answers in the inner cities,' he wrote;
'we know what to do, the examples and the evidence are there;
all we need to do in the inner cities is to make it happen. What
no one has a bloody clue about is what you do in the rural
communities where the tide has gone out. There is no way in
which those Cumbrian hill farmers are going to be able to
continue; what is going to happen to large swathes of rural
Britain and does the business world not think this matters?'
'And the business world on my board,' says Julia, 'rolled their
eyes slightly and said, "Oh God, we can't cope with any more
and we don't really know what the answers are and perhaps
someone in government can do something about it." My chairman at the time, Sir Peter Davis from Sainsbury, did his best
to keep the Prince in play but the Prince wasn't having any of
it. Absolutely furious he was. He said, "If BITC won't do
this and won't take an initiative on this, I shall start a new
organization called Rural Business in the Community."'

At that point the board caved in – he had, after all, been

President for nineteen years and his instincts by and large had always been right – and so they set up a feasibility study to discover whether there was a business case for business being involved. The Prince personally took 150 business leaders to Cumbria with him – ten visits with fifteen business people on each – to show them what the issues were and they came back convinced. The situation was chaotic – there was no affordable housing, no jobs, pubs and village shops and post offices were closing, communities dying, and there appeared to be no one in Cumbria who thought it was any part of their job to advise hill farmers on diversification. In one instance they found five generations working on a single farm – and average incomes in the countryside were £5200 per farm, per year. The only hope in this family was the daughter who had started a recycling business, collecting black plastic sacks off everybody's fields and sending them to a recycling plant in Scotland. One of the chief executives ran a company that owned half the hill farms in Cumbria (but he had never been to talk to the farmers on the ground before). He jumped on the girl's idea – black plastic was a menace in the waterways, they had been frantically looking for ways of solving the problem, they could fund her business, provide the cash flow . . .

The case for business to get involved was proven; and then foot and mouth hit. The countryside was closed down, tourism stopped overnight, hotels, pubs and restaurants had no custom, hundreds of thousands of perfectly healthy animals were slaughtered, farmers faced ruin and the rural community was brought to its knees. But thanks to the Prince of Wales BITC was ahead of the game; the business world already had an understanding of what the problems were, Julia had put together a leadership team and some of the major food retailers were beginning to look seriously at the Prince's ideas about local sourcing – his belief that the only way that Britain's small farmers can survive is if the food retailers, in particular the supermarkets, buy from and thus support their local producers.

And now government has seen the logic – but, as Julia Cleverdon says, 'Would the government at this moment be making so much fuss about local sourcing by the public sector on public procurement if the Prince of Wales had not written to Margaret Beckett every day for most of the past two years moaning on about it?'

It all arose from a dinner the Prince gave at Highgrove. With all the retailers gathered round the table he asked where they were on local sourcing – he just wanted to go through a few points. Julia takes up the story:

> They held their temper very well and were able to produce some quite good examples of where they had been able to improve their performance and change their behaviour in this area and then Sir Peter Davis said as the final coup de grâce, 'Well, thank you, sir, it's been a very nice dinner and very good of you to harangue us for three hours on the whole subject and I do hope we have managed to make some points back on what we're trying to do. But I would just point out that although 50 per cent of all food is, of course, sold through the retailers in the UK, a stonking amount of food is bought by the government of the day for use in the prisons, the hospitals and schools and the local authorities – and I don't see them sitting round the table.'

'You're absolutely right!' said the Prince; seized a pen, wrote it down, letter off to Margaret Beckett the next morning: 'What are you doing about public procurement?' Discovers a bloody example in Wales of the Powys Public Procurement Initiative, rings me up at midnight, says he's found an amazing initiative being run in Powys, did I know the man? Of course I didn't know the man; would I get on to the man at once? Yes, I'd get on to the man at once. They had produced the most amazing thing in the Powys Education Authority which says that the food that is to be served in the schools of Powys is to be dew-fresh, sunrise-plucked, right through the Treaty of Rome with a coach and horses, and all of that food is now being driven as a Welsh food initiative. 'Why can't this be done everywhere else? What are the reasons why not? Send me the name of the man, get him into my study; would it be helpful if I went to Powys, would it be useful if I led a Seeing Is Believing trip to Powys to produce other examples for other procurement initiatives . . . ?'

The Prince is tireless. When I saw Julia she was just back from holiday and by Tuesday had had five 'black spider memos', each one four or five pages long, about things that had caught the Prince's imagination, or concern, or to find out what she was doing about something he had mentioned previously; had she followed up a suggestion he had made, where was she with chasing up a company or an individual? He spends a phenomenal amount of time and interest on causes he thinks are not popular and not listened to and she senses that he is more desperate now than ever before. 'It's not that time's running out exactly, but because he feels he's been at it so long, he's got to make more difference than he has already been able to.'

When Michael Peat published a booklet early in 2004 called 'Working for Charity', setting out for the first time some facts and figures about the Prince's charitable activity, Julia, like the chief executives of his other core charities, was astonished by just how huge his charitable empire had grown. An idea, scribbled on the back of an envelope in 1972 that became the

Prince's Trust, had spawned dozens of similar and sometimes rival charities; and for many years Allen Sheppard, who was chairman of Grand Metropolitan as well as the International Business Leaders' Forum, the Prince's Youth Business Trust and BITC, had been telling the Prince that he needed to coordinate all these subsidiary charities. He needed to get them together on a regular basis to make sure that they were singing the same tune and sharing the same brand values. His advice fell on deaf ears; coordination was not a priority for Stephen Lamport and nothing ever happened. 'Stephen Lamport let go of the tow rope on that,' says Julia. 'He wasn't particularly keen to get too much coordination going because it was going to produce a lot of work for everybody and we were much more concerned about the quick wins in the tabloids than understanding and communicating more clearly what had been achieved and how it had been achieved, and so now you wake up six years on and discover there are seventeen organizations.' But since Peat's arrival, the Prince's charitable house – as well as his domestic house – has been put in order and set out clearly and transparently for all to see.

Having no prescribed role in life was one of the Prince of Wales's great problems. He and his first Private Secretary, David Checketts, who was with him during most of the seventies, had to feel their way with nothing to go on but the knowledge that the example of the previous Prince of Wales was not the one to follow. The young, sensitive and dutiful Prince wanted to give something back to society, to justify his position in some way, and Checketts, a serviceman at heart rather than a hidebound courtier, encouraged him in this direction. He was a squadron leader in the Air Force who had been equerry to the Duke of Edinburgh and was then persuaded to look after the Prince of Wales in Australia during his schooldays and to stay on as his equerry. He became his Private

Secretary when Charles was twenty-one – he was thirty-nine – and his role as Private Secretary was as ill-defined as the Prince's, but they had a good relationship. And when Charles felt moved to set up some means of helping alienated and disadvantaged young people, he had no qualms about supporting him. The result, from that idea in 1972, was the Prince's Trust, which today, thanks to its high-profile Parties in the Park, is a brand that is as well known as the Duke of Edinburgh's Award Scheme.

It was sparked off by pure chance. Charles happened to hear a radio programme in which a probation officer called George Pratt was talking about a new scheme of community service for young offenders in London. Charles was deeply moved by what he heard, and unaware there were so many people growing up in such deprived conditions and turning to crime because they had no one in their lives to encourage them to do something positive. Spurred on by Checketts, he got in touch with George Pratt and asked what he could do to help. After much discussion with representatives from all the professional groups working with the young, his scribblings evolved into a charitable trust, formed in the spring of 1976 with the Prince's severance pay of £7500 from the Navy. Its purpose was to help individuals aged between fourteen and twenty-five (now thirty) turn their lives around. Applicants had to write down what they felt would most help them improve their lives and, in the early days, the Prince saw every application and chose which ones the money – usually a maximum of £75 – should be given to. At that time he was paying the grants anonymously out of his naval allowance; and then, as now, there were no strings attached. The Prince hoped it would challenge young people's sense of responsibility and show troubled teenagers that someone trusted and believed in them.

It worked. Today, the Prince's Trust is the largest youth charity in the United Kingdom. It employs twelve thousand staff and volunteers, has an annual turnover of nearly £60 million and has helped more than half a million young people. Its activities have mushroomed but the core principles are the same. The facts and figures that drive it are simple. There are nearly 120,000 young people unemployed long term in Britain and many of them have no skills to take up jobs, even if they could find them. Increasing numbers of children are being excluded from school, particularly among the ethnic minorities. Young black men are twice as likely to be unemployed as their white counterparts. And according to studies commissioned by the Prince's Trust, crime committed by unemployed youth costs the nation more than £7 billion a year.

Some sections of society have a lot to be grateful to the Prince of Wales for. Others would wish him airbrushed from history. He has certainly made some powerful enemies along the way, and, inevitably, the people he has helped, the most vulnerable, are those least likely to be heard. He has upset all sorts of revered bodies, from architects to the medical establishment, from the agro-chemical industry to wind farmers; and a lot of his activities have brought him dangerously close to politics, which in his position as part of a constitutional monarchy is out of bounds. Privately, though, he has been meeting and corresponding with politicians for years, telling them of his findings as he has visited communities around the country, expressing his concerns about all sorts of issues, from racial tension to the rural economy, asking for their reactions and impatiently waiting for their answers. He is remarkably knowledgeable; he sees and talks to many more people in the course of a year than any politician ever does, and through his charities has seen at first hand so many of the problems and needs which the politicians are trying to address. Occasionally his letters have been leaked to the press, almost certainly by politicians irritated by being made uncomfortable by his questions, and, predictably, press indignation and outrage have followed with the familiar cry that the Prince of Wales is abusing his power. Once again, it all depends on whether or not you agree with what the Prince is saying.

The difficulty is that social ills are always essentially political, so a prince who would like to improve the lot of the underprivileged, help minority groups, tackle unemployment, racial discrimination, school truancy or any other of the hundred and one other things he tries to help, is almost certain to run into trouble. And it is a problem that has produced tensions within The Firm too, from the very first time he acted on impulse many years ago. On that occasion he was on a visit to Lewisham during the Queen's Silver Jubilee year. There was an ugly demonstration going on behind the police barriers and, against all advice, the Prince stepped out of the safety of his crested limousine to find out what the problem was. According to one of the demonstrators, a black man sporting a badge which said 'Stuff the Jubilee', the black community felt they were being harassed by the police. Twenty-four black youths had just been arrested and the community felt that blacks were being targeted and picked up off the streets for no better reason than the colour of their skin. The Prince called over the police commander in charge and suggested that the two groups should get together and talk. Eight days later the two groups were invited to Buckingham Palace, under the auspices of the Prince's Trust, and the situation was defused – but not before the Prince had been roundly rebuked by the press for having interfered in a matter that was none of his business and by his father, who broadly agreed.

He retired hurt but undefeated and continued to work towards improving relations between police forces and minority communities in Britain 'to dampen down a potentially disastrous situation'. His instincts were right about the mounting tensions. A year later violent race riots broke out in inner cities all over the country.

The Queen doesn't notice colour. She is scarcely happier than with Commonwealth leaders from former African or Caribbean colonies. The Prince of Wales is the same – although their joint record of employing black people within their households has been a wasted opportunity to take a lead on race. Buckingham Palace employs 1100 people, of whom 6 per cent are from ethnic minorities and only thirty of those in senior positions (and only 25 per cent of those are women). They are acutely aware of the position and are working to improve it, but turnover of staff in senior positions is very slow. The Prince of Wales has a faster turnover of staff. However, Colleen Harris, the Prince's Press Secretary until last year, was the only black woman to be employed in a senior position at St James's Palace but she left (to take up a job in race relations, as it happens) because after three years of firefighting she was exhausted. The Prince also has a black police protection officer, but, as the statistics show, coloured faces are not a noticeable feature of life in either palace.

One of the Prince's former courtiers thinks that the influence the Royal Family has in leading public opinion is very important and could be a potent force for good.

They have squandered the opportunity to lead by example in the last ten years, but there was a time when a known royal preference or interest expressed publicly was powerful. The Princess of Wales shaking hands with an AIDS patient was a potent piece of publicity. I always think in this country, where we all find the business of race and colour so difficult, that the best thing that happened in the eighties was when the Prince of Wales went to a tram shed on his 40th birthday and was seen in the following day's papers to be dancing with a black girl. It's a very interesting thing about the Prince of Wales. He doesn't feel bothered by colour differences, plus the fact that he's rather given to religion, I don't mean orthodox religion; he's very interested in the whole spiritual thing, and my own speculative view of Africans, having visited Africa with him, is that the principal interest of Africans is not organizing themselves politically or making money or being intellectual, but being religious. The place has absolutely thousands of churches – Muslims, Christians – they are very religious. And there was one marvellous moment when we went to Finsbury Park, I suppose to look at that regrettable mosque that was put up as a result of his visit to Saudi Arabia. [The same mosque that was taken over by Al Hamza, the one-eyed, hook-handed Muslim fanatic who was eventually deported in 2004.] The Keeper of the Holy Places, King Fahd, agreed to give an awful lot of money for it after the Prince went to Saudi Arabia. He went to look at it and the programme said he should have ten minutes walking through. What actually happened was there were a whole lot of black men in a Portakabin and he disappeared into the Portakabin, and it was two minutes, five minutes, ten minutes, fifteen minutes and roars of laughter coming out of the Portakabin. He has no feelings about black and white, and I think one of his greatest gifts to this country could be to put everyone's anxieties at rest about that sort of thing.

TWENTY-NINE

A Thankless Task

Charles has had conflicting advice over the years on how he should be behaving and what is and is not his business. David Checketts was behind the Prince's social conscience, and would have been relaxed about detours into a Portakabin full of black labourers; but it is interesting to conjecture whether the Prince would have become quite so involved with the social issues that have taken him so perilously close to political intervention if he had been guided by a different man when he was scribbling ideas on the back of an envelope at the age of twenty-three.

The Hon. Edward Adeane, who replaced David Checketts in 1978, was a very different man with much less understanding of the philosophical, tortured soul for whom he had come to work. He was a traditional courtier – Eton, Cambridge, a barrister, a fiercely clever man – cerebral rather than spiritual or emotional. His father and grandfather had been private secretaries, so he was third-generation courtier; closer in age to Charles than Checketts had been, and kindly but stiff. He had traditional ideas about what royal behaviour constituted and the path a Prince of Wales should be following. And as the Prince grew more and more mystical, the more Adeane despaired. The Prince fell under the spell of the writer Laurens van der Post and there was an Indian Buddhist woman who pursued him relentlessly and introduced him to a spiritual world beyond Christianity. She was responsible for his brief flirtation with vegetarianism.

Adeane tried to rein in the Prince but the Prince is difficult to rein in, as Adeane has not been alone in discovering. If Adeane had had his way Charles would never have delivered his blistering attack on the architectural fraternity. Horrified by the speech that was destined for the RIBA's 150th anniversary dinner, all the way in the car to Hampton Court he tried to persuade the Prince to tone down his words but to no avail.

During the early years of his marriage, when the Prince was struggling with the demands of domesticity and fatherhood, Adeane was at a loss. Unmarried himself, he couldn't understand the pull that these new responsibilities had on the Prince – yet another instance of the difficulty the Royal Family faces in having no clear distinction between the public and the private roles. No government minister, no company chairman, would have his PPS or managing director taking instructions from his wife, but in late 1984 the Princess of Wales sent Adeane a note saying that the Prince would no longer be available for meetings early in the morning or evening because he would be upstairs in the nursery with William. He was flabbergasted. Mornings and evenings were their best time of day, the only time within a busy schedule when there was a moment's calm to talk and to go through letters, paperwork and briefings.

Their relationship was heading for the rocks and when the Prince lashed out at Adeane once too often – just as he had with Michael Colborne a few months earlier – Adeane handed in his notice and left at the beginning of 1985. It was six months before a permanent successor could be found. The Prince wanted his own man, not in the traditional mould, not someone imposed upon him by Buckingham Palace, which was where Edward Adeane had come from; someone of a high calibre with business and administrative skills who would run his office efficiently. But, given the Prince's interest in mysticism and alternative lifestyles, there was much relief in the Big House when Sir John Riddell arrived to take up the post wearing neither a long beard nor open-toed sandals. Riddell had been found by a headhunter; aged fifty-one, he was a successful merchant banker, a director of the Independent Broadcasting Authority and the Northern Rock Building Society, a man who met all the necessary criteria. And as thirteenth baronet from an old Northumberland family, with estates to match, educated at Eton and Oxford, he had the pedigree to fit in with the hierarchy of court. Equally important, so stunned and flattered was he to be offered the job that he was prepared to take a drop in salary. And, with a wife and three young sons, he was entirely sympathetic to the Prince's domestic situation; with no previous experience of working within royal circles, he came to the job with a fresh approach and no preconceptions.

John Riddell is a delightful, funny and charming man. I first met him when I interviewed the Prince of Wales in 1986. I was writing the Prince's biography and to my great joy my request to meet him was granted and, although it took months to set up, I was finally invited to Kensington Palace. After the faintly jaded grandeur of Buckingham Palace, arriving at Kensington Palace was like being a guest in a very comfortable smart town house. A friendly young butler greeted me at the door, knew my name (it is a nice touch, and the same happens when you arrive at the Privy Purse door at Buckingham Palace) and offered me coffee. The decor at KP was bright and pretty (Diana's doing), the carpet lime-green and pink, interwoven with Prince of Wales feathers. Good oil paintings, mostly portraits, covered the walls and the furniture was a mixture of antique and modern with vases of scented fresh flowers everywhere.

Sir John greeted me and we sat and took coffee together. He was relaxed and chatty; I had once filmed with his wife and middle son – a video about bringing up babies – so there was instant rapport, and, anyway, he is very easy company. Then he took me to meet his boss in a modest little study on the first floor, with a portrait of the Queen hanging on the wall above his desk. It was the first time I had met the Prince of Wales and I was immediately struck by his size – smaller and slighter than I had imagined. After shaking my hand he offered me a chair, and then took his own behind his desk where he sat and throughout our conversation fiddled nervously with his signet ring, his pen or his tie knot, every now and again bringing out a crisply laundered handkerchief to blow his nose. Sir John (fifty-one) sat opposite the Prince (thirty-eight) and to my left, a notebook on his lap, knees together, pen at the ready, his demeanour suddenly quite changed, like a fifth former in the company of a rather unpredictable headmaster.

The study was a picture of disorder: the desk covered with papers and books, envelopes with jottings on the back of them and a large diary filled for every hour of every day for every month, with scarcely a white space – people to see, places to go, receptions, ceremonies, presentations, openings. More books and clutter were piled around the room, as you might find in any home, and paintings – including a still life he had painted himself – stood on the floor, propped up against the wall. Next to them a brown canvas fishing bag which contained his painting equipment – sketchbooks, pencils, pens and a small tin box of watercolours. I know this, because, when at the end of our meeting I said I'd like to see more of his painting, he opened it up; while Sir John Riddell cleared his throat to indicate that the Prince had already overrun by forty-five minutes and there was no time for art, he slowly turned the pages of two sketchbooks, explaining each sketch as he did, while I looked over his shoulder.

We had talked about the inner cities, about his concerns and anxieties for people, for society and for the environment, about his attitude to politics and his disillusionment with politicians, about his admiration for the black community and the need to harness the talent of its people and not alienate them. He talked about his love of the countryside and his spiritual awakening. He had become more philosophical in his thirties, entering what Jung would probably have described as the 'middle period'. Intuition now played an important part in his life, even in his speech writing. He explained how his speech to the British Medical Association on its 150th anniversary in 1982 had come about. (This was where he suggested that modern medicine was 'like the celebrated Tower of Pisa, slightly off-balance' and horrified his hosts in much the same way as he did with the architects two years later.) 'I agonized over what on earth I was going to say,' he told me, 'and then the most extraordinary thing happened. I was sitting here and I happened to look at the bookshelf, and my eyes suddenly settled on a book about Paracelsus. So I took the book down and there was my speech; and the response to it was extraordinary. I've never ever had so many letters. I've been a great believer in intuition ever since.'

I came away from Kensington Palace that day with two impressions. One, what a very genuine but sad and tortured character the Prince of Wales was but with a very big heart; and two, what artificial relationships he seemed to have. Perhaps he and Sir John did have frank and fruitful discussions and relaxed together occasionally over a glass of wine at the end of the day but I doubted it. I suspected instead that the Prince, for all his insecurity – and perhaps because of his insecurity – was that unpredictable headmaster, and if Riddell had put up too much resistance he would have been slapped in detention. And John Riddell didn't strike me as the sort of man who enjoyed being in detention. As one member of staff said of him, 'I cannot count the number of times I have been into John's office with a disastrous problem to solve, to come out again with the problem still unsolved but feeling that the world was a much nicer place.'

Riddell admired what the Prince was trying to do and gave him his wholehearted support and enthusiasm, but he was not used to dancing attendance on anyone. Nor was he used to working round the clock; when the day was finished he wanted to go home to his wife and children. But the work began to escalate as the Prince embraced more and more causes and ideas, and became more and more excited by the challenges that presented themselves that he could take on now that he had a Private Secretary who was in tune with him. But Riddell was not an administrator so the office was as disorganized as it had ever been with too few people trying to do too much for a man who had no real understanding of the effect his demands had on his staff. When his five-year contract was up, Riddell went back to the City and a decent salary. He had, as he would put it, a marvellous opportunity to reconnect himself into his pension fund and took it, knowing that while he and the Prince had worked perfectly well together, their chemistries were ultimately different. And by that time Richard Aylard was working for the Waleses and the Prince had identified someone whose chemistry did match his own.

Before Aylard stepped into Riddell's shoes, however, the post was occupied by Sir Christopher Airey, whose feet hardly touched the floor beneath his desk before he was on his way back to retirement in the West Country. A former major general commanding the Household Division, he was in his late fifties and entirely out of his depth trying to control a chaotic, understaffed, overworked office and an impatient and demanding boss who quoted Paracelsus and Jung and flitted between the ills of the inner cities, effluent in the North Sea and homeopathy in the space of a morning. He was utterly charming but never fully understood the difference between the Prince's various organizations, never fully grasped where the Prince's Trust ended and Business in the Community began, what the Prince's Youth Business Trust had to do with either of them, or where the Prince's interest in organic farming or wildlife fitted into the picture. And when, after a year, he was little the wiser, he began to irritate the Prince and was persuaded that the time had come for them to part company.

THIRTY

Changing the World

I have every sympathy with the poor man's situation. The Prince's life is extremely hard to fathom even today, when his interests and organizations have been rationalized; at that time everything was much less professional. He has seventeen core charities which focus on seven main areas – youth opportunity, health, education, responsible business, the natural environment, the built environment, and the arts – so there is a bit of overlapping. It is a massive enterprise, collectively the largest multi-cause charitable enterprise in the country, and he appears to take an active interest in all of them. Then he is patron or president of another 350 charities, for which he raises money and attends functions, and nominal patron – on the letterhead but otherwise scarcely involved apart from writing messages of support and so on – of a further 252 groups. One wonders when he ever gets any sleep – and to listen to those who run his charities, they sometimes think he doesn't. The black spider memos go out 365 days of the year – even on Christmas Day; the phone calls arrive at all hours of the day or night – the later ones are usually when he's in another time zone or when he has met some fascinating character over dinner who he thinks would be good to harness.

His involvement with BITC took him to Boston in 1986 –

a lot of the models on which the charities' inner-city work was based were American – but fundamentally the focus of his core charities has always been British-based, with the exception of one. The Prince of Wales International Business Leaders' Forum (since shortened simply to IBLF, International Business Leaders' Forum) which he founded in 1990 as an offshoot of BITC, along with a group of international CEOs worried about the impact of unbridled capitalism in the emerging markets of the world. The aim was to promote good business practice in sustainability and corporate social responsibility (CSR) and most importantly, the engagement of business as a positive contributor to economic and social development around the world. For all his faults and foibles, the Prince has managed to attract and keep a number of remarkably dynamic, genuine and unsycophantic people over the years, and the man who runs IBLF, Robert Davies, is one of them. Davies was Stephen O'Brien's deputy at BITC and had already worked with the Prince for seven years; now it's more than twenty. 'The only reason twenty years on I am still engaged in it in this way is that he is a very unusual person,' says Davies. 'He is someone who has a set of values, an unusual way of thinking, a most bizarre willingness to take risks, to back you on risks and shelter you from all sorts of organizations that would otherwise conspire to prevent you taking those risks.' The Foreign Office, for one, was very hostile for the first two years – thought they were amateurs meddling and could undermine British interests; then it accepted IBLF, now it is so enthusiastic that ambassadors around the world call often on the charity for help in their new development and CSR agendas. The World Bank didn't want to know at first, neither did the United Nations – both of which the Forum now works with and both of which now recognize it as one of the leading organizations in this area. Not long ago IBLF's policy director, Jane Nelson, was seconded to work in Kofi Annan's office and IBLF wrote the UN's first ever policy on Partnerships with Business.

At the end of its first year, the Forum had five staff, five member companies, a small office in an attic in the City of London and a turnover of less than £200,000. Today it has smart offices in Regent's Park, staff of forty plus, seventy member companies, over 70 per cent from overseas, works in fifty countries and has a turnover of about £4 million. It rarely uses its own name or sets up branches, preferring to develop locally owned initiatives, never gives money, only more valuable know-how, it uses its unique convening power, and only ever works in partnership with others, often building the capacity of local partners. 'Many of these stem from the founding values of local sustainability of the Prince,' says Davies, 'even though it results in a lower profile for the organization.' Right now it is working with the World Health Organization to try and get the food and drinks multinationals together to combat the global epidemic of obesity. In 2002 more people died from overeating than undereating in all parts of the world except sub-Saharan Africa; by 2020 the prediction is that obesity will be the largest cause of death from non-communicable disease. It was IBLF that instigated the debate on environmentally sustainable tourism – and brought the hotel industries together to find solutions there. Robert Davies explains how

Our ability to win trust to get competitors to work together is a precious part of our franchise. The Prince is very involved. We speak once every three weeks and there's an endless stream of notes. On most of his foreign trips, three or four times a year, he does something for us – some privately, some publicly. He is very influential. We've loaned someone to the prime minister's office in Bulgaria to help him sort things out and the Prince single-handedly helped arrange that. Working with people who can be very influential is valuable but you can't sustain things on that basis. Our reputation is not just for talking about things but for doing things. Across Eastern Europe we've got about a thousand companies working together on enterprise and education programmes, we've set up a careers service in the Czech Republic, we've taught the Hungarians how to restructure their coal and steel closure towns, we've helped bring management skills into the arts in Russia and we're now working with the Russians on corporate governance.

After Boxing Day 2004 the phone calls and black spiders went into overdrive when, following the tsunami disaster around the Indian Ocean, the Prince and Robert Davies were in contact across the Atlantic almost every day for the next ten days in helping mobilize and engage the hotel industry and other corporate industry leaders in the relief and recovery effort where the IBLF had local presence. In the first week IBLF members had committed over $40 million and were actively involved in relief logistics, water purification, medical aid and coastal village recovery, as well as rescue in the hotel properties belonging to IBLF members, some of whom lost hundreds of guests and staff in the disaster.

His charitable life has not only become the central part of what he does in his role as Prince of Wales, it has also become a major industry. The Prince scarcely hiccups these days without raising money for the Prince of Wales's Charitable Foundation. Visitors to his garden – of which there are 20,000 a year – even the Prince's dinner guests in Gloucestershire find themselves in the Highgrove shop, classy wicker basket in hand, shelling out for delights such as jams and marmalade, chocolates and biscuits, fudge and fancy oils – all adorned with Prince of Wales feathers – before they feel able to return to their cars.

Last year the shop raised nearly £90,000 from such unsuspecting visitors to Highgrove.

The Foundation, which he set up in 1979, gives money to a wide range of other charitable causes and projects – in 2001, for example, during the foot and mouth crisis, the Foundation gave £400,000 to support farmers. It is funded by profits from the shop, royalties from the sale of the Prince's lithographs (made from his watercolours) and royalties from books he has written or contributed to, but the bulk of the money comes from Duchy Originals, the food business the Prince launched in 1992. The original idea was to sell organic produce from Duchy farms, thus promoting the organic message as well as making money for charity. It had a very inauspicious start, was derailed early on by a sequence of unprincipled or hopeless characters, exposed on the BBC's *The Food Programme* for passing bog-standard food off as organic and came very close to hitting the buffers. However, in 1998 it underwent a resurrection. The Prince recruited a new managing director and since then the company has taken off, becoming a major brand and making profits last year of £1 million.

Belinda Gooding saw the Duchy job advertised in the *Sunday Times* – it simply said MD required for organic company – she applied and soon found herself in front of the Prince of Wales, feeling totally overwhelmed but not lost for words. She had spent ten years with Mars and was then group marketing director of Dairy Crest where she had introduced an organic range; she knew her subject. She and one helper then shut themselves away in 'a horrid little room in the Palace' and analysed the business, put a plan to the board and watched it grow. In five years turnover has gone from £6 million to almost £40 million, staffing levels from two to fourteen and, as well as supplying the Highgrove shop, products are in just about every shop and supermarket that stocks premium brands. She inherited a limited product range – mostly bread, biscuits, sausages, bacon, preserves, a couple of drinks and chocolates. Today it is extensive, no longer exclusively organic (sausages and bacon – the difference is that now it says so on the label) and no longer all edible – there are Duchy shampoos and even furniture from Duchy woodlands. The Prince takes a very personal interest in his shop and in the business and tries to find ways of marrying up his various interests. The fish pâtés are made with sustainably fished fish, for example; the vegetable crisps are made from ancient varieties of vegetables, which preserves the gene pool. He tests every new product idea and if it is something of which he is not particularly fond, he gives it to friends. Pork pies and Cornish pasties recently went to Joanna Lumley. Camilla gets chocolates and anything with ginger. He's fascinated by the business world and retail margins, likes meeting retailers and is constantly on the phone. 'Why doesn't anyone know about my ice cream, Belinda?'

More to the point, why didn't his mother know about his biscuits? A visitor taking afternoon tea at Sandringham some years ago complimented the Queen on the Prince's delicious biscuits. She was apparently quite unaware that he made biscuits.

THIRTY-ONE

Maundy Thursday and Fixtures in the Calendar

It was Thursday, the day before Good Friday, with the Easter weekend looming. The Queen was on her way to Liverpool Cathedral for the Royal Maundy service. It was a bitterly cold day, an icy north wind drove straight through every layer of clothing and there was a forecast of rain – April showers. But the city had a carnival atmosphere about it. Good-natured crowds held flags and flowers and chatted to the policemen manning the barriers. A band played and a procession of Life Guards mounted on immaculate black horses rode, as though choreographed, in perfect formation down the wide empty road. Outside the cathedral people wrapped up in anoraks and woollen scarves were taking up their pitches behind the barriers, and greeting one another as they unpacked their thermoses and sandwiches. It was before eight o'clock when the first ones arrived. The Queen was not due for nearly three hours.

She and the Duke of Edinburgh were on the royal train. They left London late the previous night and slept en route. I was in a jam on the M6. A lorry had overturned and shed its load, two lanes were closed in both directions, and by seven o'clock in the morning the motorway had ground to a stand-still. Royal schedules take just such eventualities into account.

For short distances, the Queen will often use a helicopter although the weather sometimes means she is forced to rely on the traffic. But on a long journey the most secure and comfortable way for her to travel is by royal train. It is the safest place for the Queen to sleep away from home; she's in familiar surroundings, it's well equipped and, barring some kind of rail disaster, delivers her to her destination bang on time – important when the Lord Mayor, the Lady Mayoress, the Lord-Lieutenant, the High Sheriff and Uncle Tom Cobbley and all – collectively known in royal circles as 'the chain gang' – are waiting to greet her.

By the time I arrived in Liverpool at 9.30 the police had closed the streets around the cathedral and were out in force. They were dressed in bright yellowy-green fluorescent jackets and carried walkie-talkies. Uncertain of the way, I stopped at some lights and asked directions from one of them. She started to explain, the lights changed and a kid on a superbike revved his engine so aggressively that we both jumped. 'Watch it, sonny,' she said, and carried on directing me while he was forced to wait. Maybe she was always friendly to strangers in town, or maybe, as all her colleagues seemed to be, she was excited. Never have I met such universally good-humoured policemen – and never have I seen so many. It was a month after the Madrid bombings, large quantities of explosives had been discovered in the suburbs of London and several al-Qaeda suspects had been arrested. While the Queen was on their patch, West Mercia police were taking no chances.

As I passed the Roman Catholic cathedral – not the one I was looking for – which stands out like a giant tubular cooling tower, I spotted a man who looked as though he belonged in a Gilbert and Sullivan operetta chatting idly to a policeman. It was surreal. There we were in 2004 at 9.30 in the morning and this man was dressed in a scarlet Tudor doublet and hose, with a ruff round his neck. It was only when I saw a whole lot more like him that I realized they were the genuine article – they *were* the Yeomen of the Guard – and part of the proceedings. They are the sovereign's official bodyguard. They had been bussed up from London and had spent the night at the Marriott Hotel, causing more than a little consternation at breakfast when they arrived downstairs for their bacon and eggs in all the kit.

The cathedral stands on a hill, a huge pink stone building, designed by Giles Gilbert Scott (among his other great designs was the red telephone box – and there is one inside the cathedral), and last year this great edifice celebrated its centenary, the reason, no doubt, why it was chosen to host the annual Maundy service. Every year during her reign the service has been held in a different cathedral – another of Prince Philip's ideas. (Before that they were always held in London.) But this is a date, like Trooping the Colour and the service at the Cenotaph, which has been in the Queen's diary every year for the last fifty-two years and will be there every year for as long as she is physically able to be there.

It is a wonderful piece of pageantry dating back centuries. What happens today is a shortened version of a ceremony that has been known in England since about AD 600, when it was referred to by St Augustine. It has its origins in the Last Supper, and it was only in the Tudor period that it became associated with the sovereign. As St John recorded in his Gospel, Jesus rose from the table, laid aside his garments, girded himself with a towel, poured water into a basin and proceeded to wash the feet of his disciples. Afterwards he gave them a command, or *mandatum* (the Latin word from which Maundy is derived), to love one another as he had loved them. The Queen neither girds herself with a towel nor washes any feet, but every Maundy service opens with the words of this 'new commandment', and it is this new commandment that is commemorated by the service.

There is a broad stone seat in the East Cloister of Westminster Abbey, known as the Maundy Bench, where the ceremonial foot washing used to take place. King John is recorded as having taken part in the ceremony at Knaresborough in Yorkshire in 1210 and at Rochester in 1213. And by the early fourteenth century it had become customary for the sovereign to provide recipients – the number of which, since 1363, has corresponded with the sovereign's age – with a meal as well as gifts of food and clothing, and female sovereigns gave up their gown, too. Elizabeth I put a stop to that. She carried out the ceremony at Greenwich in 1572 and washed the feet of the poor once they had already been washed by the Sub-Almoner and the High Almoner; she then gave them cloth, salmon, herrings, bread and claret, the towels and aprons used in the ceremony, and rather than her gown she substituted a red purse containing additional money.

It would seem than none of the Queen's predecessors was that keen on washing poor people's feet. Charles I skipped it in 1639 at York Minster because of the plague. Charles II at Whitehall in 1667 left the feet washing to the Bishop of London, the High Almoner of the day. In 1685 James II wiped and kissed the feet of fifty-two poor men; at that time the recipients had to be the same sex as the sovereign, but that changed in the eighteenth century. William III delegated the task of the feet to his Almoner and gave women money instead of clothing. A hundred years later the men were given cash instead of clothing, too; but by the time William IV was seventy-two, the whole thing was becoming too expensive and the House of Commons suggested a change. Thus in the first year of Queen Victoria's reign in 1838, when she was only nineteen, so that there were comparatively few recipients, a new pattern was set for the future. Thereafter the distribution of Maundy money became symbolic and a means of recognizing service faithfully given by ordinary men and women. From the mid-eighteenth to the mid-twentieth century the sovereign was no longer personally conducting the service at all but delegated it to the Lord High Almoner or the Sub-Almoner. In 1932 King George V was persuaded to give out the Maundy money himself; Edward VIII did it once and George VI did it seven times during his reign. Queen Elizabeth II, however, has made it an important fixture in the royal calendar and in fifty-two years there have only been four occasions when the Queen has not handed out the Maundy in person. On two of those she was away on a Commonwealth tour and on the other two she had just given birth – to Andrew in 1960 and Edward four years later.

And in the Queen's seventy-eighth year it was quite a large gathering of ordinary men and women – seventy-eight of each – that waited nervously in their side-facing seats for their sovereign to arrive in Liverpool that bitter April morning. The Royal Maundy is often seen as nothing more significant than one of the fixed state ceremonials of the year, but it's more than mere ceremony: it is very much a Christian event, a commemoration on the eve of Good Friday – and only a matter of time perhaps before it is deemed as unacceptable in our multicultural, multi-faith society as hot cross buns. The recipients are pensioners of all denominations who have been selected by their clergy and ministers for their good works in either the church or the community – they no longer have to be the poorest – and it was a joy to see the delight on their faces as 1400 years of history settled around their shoulders. The oldest amongst them that day was Alice Fagan of Widnes who was ninety-eight and in a wheelchair; she had devoted her life to good works in the church and had fostered children when her own had grown up. The oldest man was ninety-three-year-old Leslie Roberts of Thornton, who had been involved in the local youth club and a drop-in centre to support families in difficulty. There were eleven nonagenarians last year, four fewer than in Gloucester Cathedral the year before, but the average age was the same – eighty.

They had been arriving at the cathedral since 9.45 along with their families and carers, and for the next hour and a quarter sat listening to soothing organ music while various grand processions made their way from doors to the east and west: the Ecumenical Procession – leaders from other faith communities in Merseyside; the Choir Procession, including the Children and Gentlemen of Her Majesty's Chapels Royal and the Organist Choirmaster and Composer of HM's Chapels Royal; the Procession of the College of Canons – Fellows, Canons, Archdeacons and Bishops; the Royal Almonry Procession including the Yeomen of the Guard who had so surprised the Marriott guests at their muesli earlier that morning; the Wandsmen, the Almoners and the Keeper of the Closet; and the County and Civic Procession – Mayors, Mayoresses and the High Sheriff.

Suddenly the calm was shattered by the sound of great fanfares from the Royal Liverpool Philharmonic Orchestra. It was eleven o'clock. The sovereign had arrived at the West Door in her specially converted Bentley with the royal standard flying on the roof. While the Queen and the Duke of Edinburgh had let the train take the strain overnight, the car had been driven down from London without her and was ready and waiting at the station along with a great reception committee to welcome her to the city when the royal train pulled in. She and the Duke had then driven through streets lined with flag-waving, cheering Liverpudlians, past the Roman Catholic cooling tower and up the hill to what John Betjeman called 'one of the great buildings of the world'. It is the largest Anglican cathedral in Britain and Europe and the fifth largest in the world, and it is an inspiring and awesome sight – 104,275 square feet in all, 619 feet long and its bells have the highest and heaviest peal in the world. A great cheer went up as she stepped from the car, waving at the crowds of friendly, smiling, flag-waving spectators, many of whom had now been there in the freezing wind for three hours and would be there for nearly another two before they felt any kind of warmth in their bones.

At the West Door the Queen and the Duke of Edinburgh were presented with the traditional nosegays of sweet herbs, originally a guard against infection, which all the principal players in the ceremony carry. Then the Queen's Procession – all of Liverpool's finest who were not yet seated – including the Beadle, the Bishop and the Lord-Lieutenant – made its way down the aisle past all the pensioners and their guests, past the dignitaries, all the way to the eastern transept, their progress projected on large screens (a nice mix of ancient and modern) so that those seated behind pillars could see what was going on. And while they walked, with the Royal Almonry Procession that had been waiting in the wings bringing up the rear, the organ began the first hymn, and all those able to rose to their feet and sang 'Praise to the Holiest'. The music and the singing were glorious. The sovereign's own choir, choirmaster, composer and organist all travel with her. Originally called the Gentlemen of the Chapels Royal, they are very much a part of the royal establishment and have been for centuries – they sang at Agincourt and were present at the Field of Cloth of Gold in 1520. Nowadays they are six Gentlemen and ten Children (educated at the City of London School as the Queen's Scholars, and when singing they wear scarlet and gold state coats that date back to 1661). They sing at every Royal Maundy and Remembrance Sunday service, and every Sunday for the morning service at St James's Palace in either the Chapel Royal or the Queen's Chapel, except when the Queen is at Balmoral in the summer.

By the time the last chords of the organ had died away, everyone was in their places and the Lord High Almoner, standing at the High Altar, began the service with the words from St John, chapter 13, verse 34, which have been used every year for the last 1400 years:

Jesus said: 'I give you a new commandment: Love one another: As I have loved you, so you are to love one another.'

After a psalm, some prayers, another hymn and the First Lesson, read by the Duke of Edinburgh – also from St John, chapter 13 – the distribution of the Maundy money began, during which the choir sang a succession of anthems. The Queen, who was the only one of those officiating not in fancy dress, walked slowly down the line of pensioners on the south side of the aisle handing each one two purses, one red, one white, which she took from one of the five alms dishes that the Yeomen of the Guard carried, which date from the reign of Charles II. The red purse traditionally contains £5.50 – on this occasion it was a special £5 coin to commemorate the Centenary of the Entente Cordiale (which the Queen had been celebrating in France the previous three days) and a 50p coin marking the 50th anniversary of Dr Roger Bannister breaking the four-minute mile. This money is traditionally an allowance for clothing and provisions – not that £5.50 would buy many of either these days. The white purse had 78p in the special silver Maundy coins, freshly minted – the only silver coins still minted and the only coins minted which always bear the young head of the sovereign – as opposed to normal coins which reflect the sovereign growing older. The coins are silver pennies, twopences, threepences and fourpences. They are legal tender, so after decimalization in 1971 they became new pennies. Originally twelve coins were given, symbolic of the Apostles, or thirteen, of the Apostles plus Jesus, but in 1363 Edward III changed it and thereafter the number of coins reflected the age of the sovereign.

The end of the Second Lesson, from St Matthew, was the cue for the Queen to distribute the second half of the Maundy to those on the north side of the cathedral, then, after prayers, another hymn and the National Anthem – an hour in all – the frozen souls outside caught another glimpse of the Queen before she disappeared into a reception in the Lady Chapel for a further half-hour before finally coming to walk along the length of the police barrier collecting flowers and tributes and talking to her loyal and doting subjects.

THIRTY-TWO

Pressing the Flesh

There must have been several hundred people in the crowd immediately outside the cathedral that Thursday in Liverpool. Most of them were local and there were big groups of school-children, but about thirty of them were royal groupies, who travel hundreds of miles from their homes to watch the Queen carry out her public engagements. After the Queen had left I was chatting to Peter Wilkinson, an ITN cameraman who is on permanent secondment to the Palace to film the Queen's activities. She knows him and likes him and is comfortable with him hovering over her shoulder or rapidly walking back-wards just a few feet in front of her. He shares an office at Buckingham Palace with Peter Archer, the court reporter for the Press Association; one Peter provides film footage for all the TV networks, the other puts news stories out on the wires. As I turned to go, I heard my name called and turned to see four or five people left behind the barriers. The whole area was emptying fast; the show was over and all that remained was the odd crisp packet and flag lying in the street. I went across to talk to them; they were curious about what I was doing. They had seen me in Cheltenham two weeks before and in Surrey the week before that. Was I writing a new book?

They were a fascinating bunch and more joined us as we

266

talked. The youngest was a small boy of seven who had been coming to royal engagements with his mother since he was seventeen days old. They were the only ones related to each other. The rest, guessing wildly, were probably in their thirties, forties and fifties, most of them women; they were bright, articulate and at great pains to convince me they were neither mad nor sad. This is their hobby, a strange one, they admit, but one that gets them out of the house, takes them all over the country to parts they otherwise might never visit, and provides them with friends from all over that they enjoy meeting up with. They know where the Queen will be from a list published on the internet and when their families and friends go off to football matches or on shopping trips, they pack up their picnic gear, their warmest jackets, hats, scarves and gloves and set off to watch the Queen and, less frequently, other members of the family, too. Some of them lived so far away they had had to spend the night in a bed and breakfast in Liverpool; others had set off well before dawn. They were all hugely knowledgeable about the Royal Family and great admirers of the Queen but not unconditionally so. One of her long-standing ladies-in-waiting had died a couple of weeks before and they were disappointed that the Queen had not gone in person to her funeral. 'She should have done. She should have been there.'

The Queen recognizes her fans and has spoken to them all several times, and also to the little boy – and remarks to his mother about how much he has grown. There are other regulars too who are more obsessive. One man who dresses in funny hats with Union Jacks on them is always giving the Queen poems, and engages her in conversations from which she clearly finds it difficult to extricate herself.

Meeting the public in these circumstances is one of the least enviable parts of the job. There are always many, many more hands outstretched, posies offered and children thrust to the front than the Queen or anyone else can possibly acknowledge: old faces, young faces, people in wheelchairs and pushchairs, people in woolly hats and anoraks, in uniforms and in their Sunday best, all of them looking expectant, excited and hopeful that they will catch the Queen's eye, that she will stop beside them and say something they can tell their family and friends about and remember for ever. There are hundreds of eyes on her and dozens of cameras. People seem to feel the need to capture their moment in the Queen's gaze for posterity and very often the Queen is left trying to communicate with faces hidden behind flashing instamatics. But she is used to it and seems unfazed by anything that anyone says or does, moving slowly along the line, smiling, taking flowers and passing them to her lady-in-waiting or her equerry, who are never far from her side. She doesn't take everything that is offered, doesn't respond to everyone's pleading, doesn't pick out every elderly or handicapped face at the front and doesn't sign autographs. It is inevitable that people will be disappointed – that is the nature of walkabouts – there are just too many people and she doesn't have youth on her side. But some people get lucky and their day is made, all the hours of standing in the cold rewarded in a thirty-second exchange.

The Queen does not have youth on her side. On that Thursday she was two weeks short of her seventy-eighth birthday; the Duke of Edinburgh, who is beside her and supporting her on every engagement, talking to dignitaries, talking to people in the crowd as she does, was two months short of his eighty-third birthday. Most people of their age have been retired for years, and many do nothing more strenuous with their days than potter in the garden, do the crossword or play with the grandchildren.

The Queen has supposedly slowed down a little. The Prince

of Wales has done a number of foreign tours on her behalf, particularly the long-haul ones, and he conducts an increasing number of investitures, but that week you would never have known it and there is absolutely no chance of the Queen retiring to potter anywhere. When she was nearing sixty, her then Press Secretary had his knuckles rapped; he rang the Queen from the squawk-box on his desk and told her that Queen Juliana of the Netherlands had just abdicated. 'Typical Dutch,' said the Queen and hung up on him. Even if she became incapacitated in some way it is still unthinkable that she would abdicate; far more likely that a regency would be adopted. She promised at her coronation to give her life, whether it be short or long, to the service of her country and that is the premise on which our hereditary monarchy is based. She, Prince Charles and Prince William all understand that, and although it asks a lot of the individual, to have a Head of State who has been in the post for over fifty years, been around the world several times, met most other heads of state, witnessed events and observed and absorbed more than fifty years of national and international politics is a priceless commodity. And one that often seems to be better appreciated outside Britain than it is at home.

France, for example, which shed its monarchy more than two hundred years ago, greets the Queen with rapture. At the beginning of the week that I saw her in Liverpool she had been on her fourth state visit to France and it had been a dazzling success. Her previous state visit, in 1992, happened to begin the day after the first instalment of Andrew Morton's book, *Diana: Her True Story*, in the *Sunday Times*. Robin Janvrin and Charles Anson had been across to recce the tour some months before. They were given the red-carpet treatment themselves. They went to a huge meeting with the chief of protocol and a collection of very senior officials in a magnificent glittering state building. The chief of protocol opened up a book and said, 'This is how we do state visits.' Then he closed the book firmly and in front of a hundred functionaries said, 'Now, what would the Queen like to do? Just tell us, we'll do anything she wants.' When the Queen arrived in Paris on the Monday the British press were in a frenzy, desperately trying to get a reaction to Morton's revelations. No one would speak to them. The French – officials and ordinary people in the street alike – couldn't have been less interested in the story that was sending shock waves the length and breadth of Britain. 'Listen,' they said, 'we've got the Queen here. We're not interested in this story – it's just gossip, just someone writing a book.' Their entire focus was on the Queen, who they regarded as a very special visitor.

Her visit in April 2004 was to celebrate the centenary of the Entente Cordiale – celebrations that concluded with a return visit by the French President Jacques Chirac to Britain the following November. It had been a hundred years since her great-grandfather Edward VII had sailed across the Channel to set in train the 'special agreement' that put an end to years of hostility between the two countries. When he arrived he had been booed, but by the time he left Parisians were crying, '*Vive notre Roi*'. The Queen arrived to a much warmer welcome than her great-grandfather and her journey was very much more comfortable. She and the Duke of Edinburgh travelled with Eurostar in a specially named train – *Entente Cordiale* – its nose freshly painted with the flags of both countries with two drivers, one French, the other British. The symbolism of having come through the Channel Tunnel, which now links the two nations, was not lost on either side.

Rail workers had sprayed the tracks with melon-scented air freshener by way of welcome and schoolchildren waiting on the platform at the Gare du Nord cheered. At the place de la

Concorde, the very spot where King Louis XVI and Marie-Antoinette lost their heads during the French Revolution, she was accorded full military ceremony – proof that while the French may have dispensed with their monarchy they still treasure some pomp and pageantry – and 150 mounted members of the Republican Guard trotted behind her as she progressed through the streets of Paris. In the Champs-Elysées she inspected the Guard of Honour, but security was so tight that only a few schoolchildren could see her. The French had deployed 2400 uniformed officers and an unspecified number of plain-clothes policemen to guard their special guest. Sharp-shooters on the rooftops tracked her movements and the shops she visited in the rue Montorgueil had been thoroughly searched beforehand. The last time France had had a state visitor, security had been so intense with roads blocked off and diversions everywhere that any goodwill that might have been generated by the sight of a foreign president in the city evaporated in the chronic traffic jams. The Queen hates the security she is forced to live with, as do all of the family. She recognizes that, sadly, it is a necessary part of modern life, but insists that it shouldn't come between her and the public who want to see her. She specifically asked for the security in Paris to be low key and, as if to prove the point, went on a short walkabout outside the Elysée Palace where hundreds of Parisians had gathered to cheer.

'I believe that we mark this week a most significant anniversary for our two nations,' she said at the state banquet held in her honour at the Elysée Palace.

If I may be allowed tonight one small British understatement, our historical relationship has not always been smooth. For centuries we fought each other fiercely, often and everywhere – from Hastings to Waterloo, from the

Heights of Abraham to the mouth of the Nile. But since 1815 our two nations have not been to war. On the contrary, we have stood together, resolute in defence of liberty and democracy, notably through the terrible global conflicts of the twentieth century.

This was far from inevitable when we reflect on how close we came to war over our colonies at the end of the nineteenth century. That we turned away from conflict to the path of partnership was due to the single-minded efforts of a small number of enlightened individuals dedicated to Franco-British rapprochement. Their immense achievement was the Entente Cordiale signed one hundred years ago this week. I am proud of the part my great-grandfather, King Edward VII, played in this historic agreement. It was his initiative, and that of your President Loubert, to insist on reciprocal state visits in 1903 which did so much to create the popular atmosphere for the successful political negotiations to settle our colonial disagreements the following year.

I hope that this state visit, and the season of Entente Cordiale celebrations closing with your visit to London, Mr President, in the autumn, will likewise contribute to a new era of Franco-British partnership. Our circumstances a century on are perhaps not entirely dissimilar.

For just as our statesmen and my great-grandfather realized a hundred years ago, we too need to recognize that we cannot let immediate political pressures, however strongly felt on both sides, stand between us in the longer term. We are both reminded that neither of our two great nations, nor Europe, nor the wider Western Alliance, can afford the luxury of short-term division or discord, in the face of threats to our security and prosperity that now challenge us all.

Of course we will never agree on everything. Life would be dull indeed, not least for the rest of the world, if we did not allow ourselves a little space to live up to our national caricatures – British pragmatism and French élan; French conceptualism and British humour; British rain and French sun; I think we should enjoy the complementarity of it all.

Exchanges of visits by heads of state have been happening for centuries as a way of demonstrating friendship between two countries – and one of the earliest was with France, when in 1520 Henry VIII invited Francis I of France to join him in the Field of Cloth of Gold to put a seal on a new treaty of friendship between them; Edward VII's treaty, so far, has been altogether more successful. The convention until recent times was that sovereigns only made one state visit each way during the course of their reign, unless the head of state changed, but since there are now more republics than monarchies and presidents change more frequently than monarchs, the rule has become more relaxed. The Queen usually makes two state visits a year and has two incoming visits from heads of state, selected after discussions between the private secretaries of the Queen, the Prime Minister and the Foreign Secretary. There used to be three a year but Margaret Thatcher reduced the number when she was Prime Minister, partly because having been on the throne for forty years the Queen had already entertained most long-term heads of state, and partly on the grounds of cost – which is borne by the government. The cost is considerable: £0.7 million in the year to 31 March 2004, and that's not counting the cost of police and Army security and of the Armed Services ceremonial. The Queen made just one visit abroad during that year, to a Commonwealth Heads of Government Meeting in Nigeria, and received two visiting heads of state – the President of the Russian Federation,

Vladimir Putin, and the United States President, George W. Bush, the security for which was the tightest ever mounted, and therefore one of the most expensive visits ever made.

Ceremonial is something the British do to perfection and it is at state visits that the splendours of our national heritage and the pomp and pageantry really come into their own. Visiting heads of state are treated as genuine guests of the Queen and want for nothing. She oversees all the plans, chooses all the menus, checks the suites that her visitors will stay in at Buckingham Palace or Windsor – or occasionally Holyroodhouse – to make sure that the flowers, the books and everything that has been laid out for them are right for the occasion; she decides on the presents that will be given to her guests and even checks the dining arrangements once the table has been laid for the state banquet on the first evening. From the moment a decision is made about who is to be invited, the organization falls to the Comptroller of the Lord Chamberlain's Office, Lieutenant Colonel Sir Malcolm Ross, who has been in charge of all things ceremonial since 1991. In his early sixties, with an Eton and Sandhurst pedigree, followed by twenty-three years in the Scots Guards and now nearly twenty years at Buckingham Palace, he can do state visits, weddings, jubilees, investitures and state funerals standing on his head. And in between times he is in charge of a whole host of things including the Crown Jewels, the Queen's chapels, chaplains and choirs, styles, titles, protocol, royal warrants, swans and the fifteenth-century ceremony of swan upping.

It is a popular misconception, a hangover from the Middle Ages, that all swans in Britain belong to the Crown. They don't. It was only ever swans on the Thames that belonged to the sovereign, and in 1473 a royal charter was granted to the Worshipful Company of Vintners allowing them to own swans on the river too, and a few years later the Dyers were also given permission. From then on it became necessary to mark the swans so they could tell who owned which. Unmarked birds belong to the sovereign, those with a mark to the right of their beaks to the Dyers and those to the left to the Vintners. And every year since then, on the Monday of the third week in July, the royal swan keeper, accompanied by a representative from the Lord Chamberlain's Office, the Queen's swan uppers and the swan marker of the Vintners' Company and the swan master of the Dyers' Company and their men – all dressed in special uniforms – set off upstream from Blackfriars in London to Pangbourne in Berkshire, in six rowing boats known as Thames skiffs. The journey takes five days and the task is to find the broods of cygnets and their parents, identify the adult birds and mark the young in the same way. The first man to sight a brood shouts 'All up!', warning everyone to get into position to catch the swans.

State visits follow a formula. The visiting heads of state arrive before lunch on a Tuesday at Gatwick Airport, where they are met by a junior member of the Royal Family and taken on the royal train to Victoria Station. Until ten or twelve years ago, the Queen and the Duke of Edinburgh, possibly other members of the family and various dignitaries, including the Prime Minister, would meet their guests – head of state, spouse and cast of fourteen – at the station in carriages. A long procession, escorted by the Household Cavalry, would then make the journey to Buckingham Palace along Victoria Street to Parliament Square, up Whitehall, through Horse Guards Arch and into the Mall, thus knocking out seventeen bus routes for the day that run from the north of London to the south. In response to public criticism the procession was scrapped and the Queen now meets her guests at Horse Guards Parade. An informal lunch for sixty follows – six round tables for ten with a member of the Royal Family heading each, which the Queen describes as an 'ice-breaker' – then an exchange of gifts and occasionally decorations.

That evening the state banquet takes place, at which 165 people sit down to dinner in the Ballroom round a horseshoe-shaped table that will have taken up to seven hours to prepare. There are no tablecloths: the tables are highly polished, lavishly decorated with floral arrangements and gold candelabra, laid out – using a ruler to measure the space between each setting – with gleaming George III or George IV silver and gilt cutlery and porcelain from one of the many priceless services in the Royal Collection. Some of it is kept in the vaults; the rest of it, when not in use, lives in one of the display cases in the Queen's Gallery and it is only handled by people who have been specially trained to work in the china and silver pantries. If the banquet is at Windsor Castle, in St George's Hall – as it was for President Putin in 2003 – the tableware is transported from London, as are the staff to prepare for the evening, to cook and wait at table. The glassware is cut-crystal made for the coronation in 1953 and hand-engraved with EIIR, the Queen's royal cipher; the wine that is served in it, the finest from the royal cellars, is looked after by the Yeoman of the Cellars. The family are not wine enthusiasts but others in the Palace are; there is a tasting committee which includes Masters of Wine from among the Royal Warrant Holders, and wines are bought *en primeur* through the Clerk of the Cellars and laid down until such time as he advises they are ready for drinking. According to the accounts for 2003–04, there is currently £365,000 worth of wine in store.

The Royal Family turns out en masse for state banquets – the women in long dresses and tiaras, the men in uniform with full decorations – and is on hand throughout the three days to entertain the visitors and show them parts of the country that may be of particular interest. Other guests are members of the government and other political leaders, high commissioners and ambassadors, members of the royal household and prominent people who have trade or other associations with the visiting country.

One of the most important tasks before a state banquet, or any dinner that the Queen hosts, is to establish what the guests can and cannot eat. And when the Queen travels it is equally important that her host knows what she likes and dislikes. She has a travelling yeoman who goes ahead to make sure that everything about her visit is acceptable. The only diet the Palace kitchens can't cope with is kosher because they don't have the facilities; in such cases they use an outside caterer. Everything else can be accommodated, and once the Master of the Household knows a particular guest's preference it will be logged, thus, if ever they come to the Palace again, the drink they particularly liked before lunch will miraculously appear or the herbal tea they drank in preference to coffee.

Day two of the visit is largely political: there is a reception at St James's Palace with the high commissioners and ambassadors in London, followed by talks with the Prime Minister and lunch at 10 Downing Street, after which there is often a press conference; and meetings with the leaders of the main opposition parties. That evening there is another banquet in the guest's honour in the Great Hall at Guildhall as guest of the Lord Mayor of London, and a guard of honour to inspect beforehand. And on day three, having spent the day seeing something of Britain – either by royal plane, train or automobile, the visiting head of state hosts a return banquet for the Queen and the Duke of Edinburgh, to which members of the Royal Family are once again invited.

Vladimir Putin's visit in 2003 was a return of hospitality. The Queen had been to Russia in 1994, three years after the end of the Cold War and the disintegration of the Soviet Union. It was her first visit and the fact that Boris Yeltsin was the first Russian leader ever to have been chosen by democratic election was no coincidence. While the successors of the Bolshevik regime that had murdered the Romanovs were in power she had refused to go as a matter of principle, but Russia had entered a new era. The visit was a great success and the Queen chose to include film clips from it in her Christmas broadcast that year. She had never met Yeltsin before but, thanks to some bright spark at the Foreign Office, the relationship got off to a good start. They had discovered that the President's wife Naina loved gardening and so the Queen's gift to her hosts had been a delicate set of crystal drawers containing seeds specially harvested from the gardens at Buckingham Palace. They were thrilled. By the time President Putin landed on British soil nine years later, relations between the two countries were secure, British companies had been investing heavily in the new democracy – and her eldest son's International Business Leaders' Forum was about to celebrate ten years of work in St Petersburg.

Prince Charles was already acquainted with Vladimir Putin. He had met him first in 1994 when he too visited Russia. The year before he had been approached by Anatoly Sobchak, then Mayor of St Petersburg. He wanted money to save the city's crumbling art and cultural heritage, its health institutions and civil society organizations. 'We don't do money,' said the Prince, 'this is not Venice in Peril. But we do advice.' And so a small task force organized by the IBLF went to St Petersburg in 1993 to see what could be done. The next year the Prince of Wales went to see for himself, taking with him a group of European experts and business leaders; the man escorting them round the city was the then First Deputy Mayor, Vladimir Putin. One of the typical sights on their tour was the

Marinskaya Hospital, where they saw rusty surgical instruments, skilled eye surgeons who were paid less than UK shop assistants and a desperate shortage of drugs. They also saw the city's newly opened Littlewoods department store. Long-term practical projects to help the city were developed as a result of that visit, working in partnership, as always, with Russian organizations and individuals. Ten years on they have made a significant impact.

'In the early days in Russia,' says Robert Davies, the IBLF's CEO, 'it was remarkable to work with someone who had such a very strong sense of history and destiny for Russia in a way that no one who is a politician ever could have.'

He was invited by the then Mayor of St Petersburg, the late Anatoly Sobchak, to the burial of the Tsar's bones in St Petersburg and I remember asking should he not go? For me it was a matter-of-fact thing; an issue to be judged here and now in relation to the politics and circumstances of the day. He took a four-hundred-year view of this, saw the historical context; and it is this sense of where we have all come from and where we are all going that helps pin my organization into thinking about the world in longer time scales and contexts.

Tsar Nicholas II, the last Russian Emperor, was buried in St Petersburg in July 1998, eighty years after his death. He and his family and several close servants had been murdered by the Bolsheviks in 1918 and their bodies thrown down an abandoned mine in Yekaterinburg; their remains were finally laid to rest alongside their ancestors in Peter and Paul Cathedral, where all Russian tsars from Peter the Great to Alexander III are buried.

The Prince of Wales didn't go to the burial; neither did the

Queen nor any senior member of the British Royal Family. They all work on a different historical time scale from the rest of us.

'Those of my generation in Britain have special cause to remember the unimaginable sacrifice the Russian people made to defeat fascism in the Second World War,' said the Queen in welcoming President Putin and his wife at the start of the state banquet.

Nothing – not even the fact that our countries became estranged in the war's aftermath – has ever dimmed our memory of the scale of your loss. That experience should continue to inspire us as we seek to build a more peaceful and secure world.

When I visited your country in 1994, I recall saying to President Yeltsin that he and I had spent most of our lives believing such a visit could never happen, and that I hoped he was as delighted as I was to be proved wrong. I am just as delighted now, nine years later, to be able to welcome you here and to learn about the great changes which have occurred in your country since I was there. Russia has established itself as our partner and our friend: we work together bilaterally and on the international stage, and we are developing new links all the time, in fields of commerce, culture, and counter-terrorism, of energy, education, the environment.

THIRTY-THREE

Crossing Continents

State visits in both directions do a great deal to strengthen links and friendships between nations. Sir Richard Needham, who was Minister for Trade between 1992 and 1995, says that he relied a lot on the support of the Royal Family in promoting Britain's commercial interests overseas and they were extremely good at it. The Prince of Wales and Princess Anne have been travelling the world for years, combining charity work with commercial flag waving, but more recently their brother, the Duke of York, has joined the fray and now plays a significant and much more specific role. When he left the Navy in 2001 after twenty-two years, he became a Special Representative for UK Trade and Investment. He has travelled all over the world since then opening up markets abroad for small to medium-sized companies and encouraging overseas traders to invest in the UK; and in that capacity he has been involved in inward state visits. He spent time with both President Putin and President Bush during their stay – 49 per cent of inward investment in the UK now comes from the United States.

Richard Needham has been heavily involved in business since he retired from the House of Commons in 1997 and is deputy chairman of Dyson, which, because of planning restrictions in the UK, has moved its manufacturing operation to Malaysia. He has encountered the Duke of York in a variety of settings.

On a good day, there's no one more charming, affable, amusing and capable of getting hold of the brief you've given him then getting it across in a non-partisan manner promoting Britain's interests, whether it's investment or gaining orders for power stations. He manages to get into places, to see people and get through doors which even with an ambassador you couldn't do. Part of it is that monarchy can attract a much higher level of participation – both in the countries he visits and the people he takes with him. On a bad day some people felt the Duke hadn't read the brief very carefully and seemed more interested in playing golf than doing what was wanted of him. He's much better now. He came along to a British Export Association reception at the House of Lords recently and gave an extremely good speech. I think he's got himself together. He does a very, very good job.

A former courtier at Buckingham Palace once got into a lot of trouble for suggesting that Prince Andrew would make a better king than the Prince of Wales. It was a long time ago, but his view then, which has not essentially changed, is that Andrew was more dutiful, would do what he was told, wouldn't agonize so much about things as the Prince of Wales does, and would be easily manipulated and therefore 'reliable' in governmental/civil service-type context. 'Here is your speech, you read it, don't start rewriting it; and this is where you are going next.' He would do it magnificently, he would be smartly turned out, very soldierly and look the part. 'He has a huge sense of duty,' says the ex-courtier. 'I'm not saying Charles doesn't but he wouldn't argue, he would just do the job. He's not stupid by any means; he's very astute, very loyal.'

One of Andrew's commanders at sea in the early 1990s agrees.

Prince Andrew is a lovely chap, less bright than Edward. He was flight commander, senior aviator in a frigate, seconded to my staff for about six months. I enjoyed his company, he's fun, he enjoys a laugh and a rumbustious laugh some-times, too. He is fanatical about his golf; he was just learning it then and whenever he could he was away with his golf clubs to the nearest course. What I admired about him particularly was this: when we parked alongside anywhere, he was on duty as a royal and his Private Secretary would arrive and say here's your itinerary, and he would go off and do official business and I was occasional dog's body tagging along at the back – complete role reversal. And he would do all that stuff and do it well; he would also play his golf every spare moment and get quite cross if there wasn't room for golf. Then we'd come back on board and do the military stuff and he was so keen to show that he wasn't just a royal playing at having a job so he could deflect criticism for being a playboy. He was very serious about his job on board. It was clear he was not in the forefront of tactical thinking about use of naval airpower, that wasn't his forte, he wasn't a questioning sort of person. But in producing schedules of flying, producing a safe plan, he was bloody good and he took it very seriously indeed and I admired that hugely. He was a typical aviator, they are great in their aeroplanes and they love it, but anything beyond that . . . You cannot put incompetents into aeroplanes, they kill themselves and people around them. He was a good aviator.

On shore he was Your Royal Highness and on board he was Andrew to the other officers, and sailors would call him sir, as they did every officer. He looked and behaved like a bog-standard officer. I think he enjoyed it enormously; he gave every impression he loved what he was doing and the environment in which he was doing it. It's a lad's environment and he was a lad, thoroughly uncouth.

Prince Andrew's great misfortune was in not being able to marry Koo Stark, the American he fell in love with in the early eighties. She was a model-turned-actress-turned-photographer, very pretty, very sweet and very much in love with Andrew but in her youth had appeared naked in the lesbian shower scene of a soft-porn movie. Throughout the relationship with Andrew she behaved admirably – also afterwards, and has remained a good friend – and the Queen was very fond of her, but the photographs ruled Koo Stark out as a potential royal bride and, much to Andrew's distress, they parted company. 'He was in love with Koo Stark,' says a former courtier, 'and she behaved immaculately and she was very honourable. He was deeply upset about Koo and the Queen liked Koo enormously.'

It was no secret that Fergie, Sarah Ferguson, the girl Andrew subsequently married, had a colourful past. Daughter of Prince Charles's polo manager, Major Ronald Ferguson, she had lived with playboy racing driver Paddy McNally and was clearly something of a good-time girl, but no damaging photographs were ever published and Fergie ran the course. The public warmed to her, she was the girl next door – not wafer-thin like Diana – she was fun, sexy, cheerful and informal and in 1986 she became part of the Family Firm. But the marriage fell apart and when the nation was not riveted by the Charles and Diana show, they could switch channels and see the embarrassing highlights of the Yorks' home life. By 1992 Fergie was having her toes sucked by her scantily-clad American financial adviser and enjoying herself with his Texan oil millionaire friend. They separated that year and by 1994 they were divorced. She was, in the words of Lord Charteris, the Queen's former Private Secretary, 'vulgar, vulgar, vulgar'.

Fergie was indeed vulgar, but she had a very kind heart and an indomitable spirit, and I can't help admiring her. She was wildly extravagant, she exploited her position and had amassed colossal debts by the time of her divorce, but she set to work to pay back the money she owed. She went to America, where they simply adored her; she became involved with WeightWatchers; she wrote children's books; she went on chat shows; she used her Duchess name-tag shamelessly to open doors and did everything she could think of to make money. But she never even came close to selling her story or betraying the Queen. She and Andrew remained good friends and for the sake of the children, and to save money, she moved back into the house they had once shared. They lived in opposite wings, and at Christmas and Easter he would take the little Princesses to their grandparents for a family get-together and Fergie would be left alone, excluded from family events.

On 11 September 2001 Prince Andrew was thirty thousand feet over the Atlantic on his way to an Outward Bound visit in America when the news came through that four American passenger airliners had been hijacked by terrorists. His plane immediately turned back but he felt in some way closer to the tragedy as a result. He was very keen to join the United States Ambassador in London at Buckingham Palace on the day that 'The Star-Spangled Banner' was played during the Changing of the Guard, by way of tribute to those who died at the World Trade Center. He was also at the memorial service at St Paul's with the rest of the family. And on a trip to New York not long afterwards he changed his schedule in order to visit Ground Zero. He was also prominent during President Bush's state visit in 2003.

'The first US President to stay in Buckingham Palace was Woodrow Wilson, in December 1918,' said the Queen in her banquet speech.

America had then been fighting alongside us in the First World War and was to do so again in our hour of need during the Second World War. And at the very core of the new international and multilateral order which emerged after the shared sacrifices of that last, terrible World War was a vital, dynamic transatlantic partnership, working with other allies to create effective international institutions. The Marshall Plan led to the beginnings of the European Union, and the establishment of NATO became the bedrock for European security.

Sixty years ago, Winston Churchill coined the term 'Special Relationship' to describe the close collaboration between the United Kingdom and United States forces that was instrumental in freeing Europe from tyranny. Despite occasional criticism of the term, I believe it admirably describes our friendship. Like all special friends, we can talk frankly and we can disagree from time to time – even sometimes fall out over a particular issue. But the depth and breadth of our partnership means that there is always so much we are doing together, at all levels, that disputes can be quickly overcome and forgiven.

I in my turn have had the pleasure of paying three state

visits to your country. The last was in 1991 – the end of the Cold War. Your father, Mr President, was instrumental in leading the way through those heady but uncertain months from the fall of the Berlin Wall in 1989 to the break-up of the Soviet Union two years later.

In this twenty-first century we face together many unforeseen and formidable challenges. The leadership you showed in the aftermath of the terrible events of 11 September 2001 won the admiration of everyone in the United Kingdom. You led the response to an unprovoked terrorist attack which was on a scale never seen before. Your friends in this country were amongst the very first to sense the grief and horror that struck your nation that day – and to share the slow and often painful process of recovery. And our troops have served side by side in Afghanistan and Iraq to lead the fight to restore freedom and democracy. Our two countries stand firm in their determination to defeat terrorism.

The Queen's speeches at state banquets are never entirely her own, either in this country or abroad. She acts and speaks, officially, only on ministerial advice. So although she might write them, in conjunction with her Private Secretary, and express her own sentiments, these speeches are always checked and approved by the Foreign Secretary. Any speech on any matter, however trivial, is always checked and approved by the minister responsible for that particular portfolio. There are just two speeches each year that have no governmental input: her message to the Commonwealth on Commonwealth Day each March, which is sound only; and her traditional Christmas broadcast on television. Conversely, the only speech she delivers that is pure government with not a nuance of her own, is the Speech from the Throne at the State Opening of Parliament.

The same is true when she is in any of her realms. Speeches in, say, Australia, New Zealand or Canada have to be acceptable to ministers in that country and sometimes to state or provincial ministers, too. And if ever a speech causes controversy, it is the minister and not the Queen who shoulders the blame.

According to Robert Lacey, the Queen's biographer:

> The Commonwealth has provided Elizabeth II with more sustained pleasure than any other aspect of her work – and an area in which her power and prestige have actually increased. In 1952, Britain's Commonwealth seemed a poor apology for a lost empire. In the course of her reign it has developed, in a quietly persistent and low-key style that rather echoes her own, into a pragmatic international organization from which its members have generally profited. It helps its less developed members get aid, and has played its part in such events as the ending of apartheid and the coming of majority rule in South Africa.

The Commonwealth is unlike any other international organization such as the United Nations, NATO or the European Union. It didn't come about through contract or treaty but through history; it grew organically as Britain lost her empire. During the first half of the twentieth century, almost all of the territories that had been subjugated during the reign of Queen Victoria – which made the British Empire the largest the world had ever seen – formed themselves into a voluntary association of free and independent states which today comprises 30 per cent of the world's population. 'In all history,' declared the Queen to the City of London during the Silver Jubilee celebrations in 1977, 'this has no precedent.' Following the re-entry of

South Africa to the Commonwealth in 1994, it now comprises nearly one-third of the world's independent states, fifty-three in all. Its total population is estimated at 1.8 billion people. Sixteen of the fifty-three members are monarchies ruled by the Queen, six are separate indigenous monarchies and twenty-nine are republics. 'To ask,' as Vernon Bogdanor says, ' "What does the Commonwealth do, what is its purpose?" is perhaps to ask the wrong question. The Commonwealth is an association which exists, not for any particular *purpose*, but for what it is, a group of countries connected by a common heritage and historical experience, and also by the English language. "The Commonwealth," Professor David Dilks has said, "is the only international organization which has no need of interpreters." ' It is 'a kind of international Rotary Club'.

The first Head of the Commonwealth was King George VI and it was a title made specific to the King, in 1949, not conferred as an hereditary title. When the King died less than three years later, Nehru, the Prime Minister of India, sent Elizabeth II a message welcoming her as the new Head of the Commonwealth and on 2 December 1952 her status – which is quite distinct from her role as Queen of the United Kingdom – was formally proclaimed. The role is entirely symbolic and the Queen holds it not by right of succession but by common consent – and so will her successor, whoever that might be.

A lavish state visit to Britain, with the full pomp and ceremony, is the highest form of diplomatic compliment the government can pay to a foreign head of state. His or her reception at Buckingham Palace or Windsor Castle and the images beamed home send a strong message to the people of his or her native country – and, in the case of George W. Bush, proved to be not a bad start to a re-election campaign. There are not many heads of state who are embarrassed by riding down the Mall in a horse-drawn carriage with the Queen of

England by their side, most of her family behind them, and half the British cavalry bringing up the rear. One exception was President Chirac on his first visit to London after his election as President of France in 1995. The Prime Minister, John Major, wanted to cement their friendship with an early invitation to pay a state visit and secured the Queen's agreement. To everyone's surprise, the Elysée Palace was slow to respond. It transpired that the invitation had put Chirac in a quandary. He had been elected as a people's president and had already done away with some of the grandiose habits of his predecessor, including sweeping through the streets of Paris in motorcades with motorcycle outriders. He was worried that the pomp and glamour would send the wrong message home, but he was reassured that his visit could include practical, down-to-earth events, too.

'Monarchy is glamorous,' says John Major, 'and in being glamorous it has an immense value for this country.'

> If you're not going to maintain that value you're doing some harm to the country. Cut it down but don't cut away its central attraction. The Royal Family see themselves as a focal point for the country and I think they are. They believe they are there to offer service to the nation in whatever form that service is needed, whether in terms of trying to bring people together – which is what the Queen tries to do with her Christmas broadcast – whether it's their charitable work and voluntary service, or whether it's their immense support and interest in the military. In much the same way as civil servants are servants of the policy of government, their job is to carry out the policy of the elected government; the Royal Family see themselves as servants of the nation with a responsibility to carry out those things that are self-evidently good for the nation.

Lord Hurd, who was Foreign Secretary between 1989 and 1995, agrees that the monarchy is a unique selling point.

> I travelled with Mrs Thatcher abroad a lot, also with the Queen; and of course Mrs Thatcher is the more dynamic, dramatic personality with more personal achievements to her name – of course she is – but when you travel hour by hour with the two of them there is no doubt which has the greater impact. It's the Queen. She has a wider range of interests and it is a different thing . . . It's like the difference between having dinner on board the Royal Yacht *Britannia* as opposed to dining in a hotel. It's hard to explain why, but when you see it, experience it, this is just true. The two last dramatic trips were to Russia and South Africa. In France it's very strong too, a little less so in Germany and America, but it comes and hits you rather unexpectedly. It's a magic really. And it continues to make a very strong case for Britain in the eyes of the rest of the world.

Douglas Hurd has also travelled with the Prince of Wales and says that he too is 'a unique asset to this country in its dealing with foreigners'. Particularly memorable was a visit to Hamburg fifty years after substantial parts of the city had been destroyed by Allied bombing in 1943 with a loss of fifty thousand civilian lives. His reception could have been cool, but the Prince, who doesn't speak German, had specially learned some of the language so that his audience would understand what he was saying. Thousands packed into the big square in Hamburg where he spoke in the open air for twenty minutes. 'He didn't have to do it,' says Hurd, 'and that he should have gone and taken such trouble, they thought remarkable.'

Last year the Queen made a fourth visit to Germany and was again warmly received, but the question that occupied the

German press during the trip was whether or not she would apologize on behalf of Britain for the Allied bombing of Dresden. Three months before the end of the Second World War a series of five air raids virtually flattened the city of Dresden, killing thirty-five thousand civilians and burying centuries of culture and history under 18 million cubic metres of rubble. Two months later the Soviet army occupied Dresden and, until the reunification of Germany in 1989, it was part of the GDR.

Reconstruction has been ongoing ever since, and the second night of the Queen's visit was spent at a fundraising gala concert at the Berlin Philharmonic in aid of the restoration of the eighteenth-century Frauenkirche in Dresden; hence the thought that she might apologize. She didn't. She referred to the past, to the human suffering on both sides during the Second World War, and urged both countries to 'learn from history, not be obsessed by it' and to 'look beyond simple stereotypes'.

'Britain's part in Berlin's re-emergence as one of the world's great cities is a source of pride for me,' she said during the state banquet in the Zeughaus.

Berlin symbolizes the remarkable achievement of German reunification; the British contribution to your skyline also symbolizes the reconciliation between our two countries. My admiration for your achievements is not limited to Berlin. The reconstruction of the Frauenkirche in Dresden is an inspiration to us all. I recall in particular the moment at Windsor Castle in 1998 when Prince Philip and I stood beside President and Frau Herzog to see the new orb and cross for the first time. At the Berlin Philharmonic tomorrow night we shall renew our support for this cause so full of powerful symbolism.

Measured and diplomatic to her toes; and wise. As *Die Welt* argued, to have apologized would have been a disservice to British–German relations. 'It would release animosities that have been kept in check by the very fact that each side has learnt to deal with the past in its own way.' Such sentiments might have been written by the Queen herself.

THIRTY-FOUR

Gongs and Garden Parties

The Queen is due to arrive at 11.00 a.m. The orchestra of the Coldstream Guards is playing a stirring march. Everyone is eagerly watching the dais at the front, waiting. Five members of the Queen's Body Guard of the Yeomen of the Guard are in place on the dais, the red stockings, ruffs and gold of their uniforms adding a touch of the surreal. The Ballroom is a sea of hats with feathers, crisply ironed shirts, shining shoes and matching handbags. Proud husbands, wives or partners, children – three guests per person – temporarily parted from their jeans and T-shirts, each clutching a programme, scanning it for the name of the friend or relative they have come to see receive an honour. Each one will go home remembering some detail about their two hours inside Buckingham Palace to treasure and to relay to friends and relatives.

In the Green Drawing Room and the Picture Gallery, meanwhile, a short walk away, with priceless Old Masters on the walls, Lieutenant Colonel Sir Malcolm Ross, Comptroller of the Household, is drilling the recipients about what to do when their turn comes; when to approach the Queen, how to acknowledge her, when to speak, how to receive their gong and when and where to go when Her Majesty has done with them. He is tall, good-looking, beautifully turned out in full dress uniform and punctilious as only a military man can be. He treats his audience like slightly simple schoolchildren but no one seems to mind; they are all slightly hyper anyway. He has been doing this for years; the jokes are hackneyed but effective in putting the class at ease, and he knows a proportion of them won't remember a word he's said when the time comes. Even the actress Maggie Smith forgot which way to leave the stage when she collected her Damehood. 'A lot of them do,' says Ross, 'and the stars of stage and screen are usually the worst.'

He explains the geography of the Palace, what room they are in, and the rooms they will have to go through – the Silk Tap Room, the East Gallery – to reach the Ballroom, which they will walk straight through at the bottom end to wait in line for their name to be called so they can come in through a door at the top. They are shepherded by Gentlemen Ushers (traditional at court since the fifteenth century – now retired servicemen) at every move except for their moment of glory when they are on their own. 'Your surname is your cue,' he tells them. 'When you hear it, walk forward to the centre of the room, turn to face the Queen and stop. The Queen is on the dais; you do not go on to the dais with her. Gentlemen give a little bow, if you will, ladies a little curtsey; there's no need to go right down', and he demonstrates – to slightly louder laughter than the extravagant gesture demands.

He repeats it all, complete with gestures, using the width of the room to demonstrate, and I wonder quietly whether he does amateur dramatics in his spare time. He is in the centre with people to left and right, his patter a very welcome antidote to their nerves. He sets the tone for the day, which is relaxed and friendly but deeply formal. He asks how many people have met the Queen before and a few hands go up. As at all investitures this is a mixed group receiving everything from Knighthoods of the Most Distinguished Order of St Michael and St George to the more common Most Excellent Order of the British Empire. Senior soldiers and distinguished diplomats stand alongside care workers, lollipop ladies and firemen – a mixture of citizens who are genuinely the great and the good. Tim Henman, having just fallen dramatically out of Wimbledon in the second round, is there to receive an OBE for services to lawn tennis; and Dr Frederick Dibnah, the country's favourite steeplejack (who sadly died a few months later), for services to heritage and broadcasting; they are the only famous faces today.

Knights kneel and are dubbed with a sword; other awards are on a neck-ribbon that the Queen places over the head, or clips on to a hook on the lapel – brooches for women, medals for men. 'Move forward so you are close enough for her to attach your award,' says Ross. 'She can't reach you if you're standing four and a half feet away.' He demonstrates how the Queen might look under these circumstances, to more nervous laughter. 'While she is putting it on she will be talking to you. Feel free to respond. She will then shake your hand. It is a firm and positive handshake – you will not miss it. It is an indication that your time is up. Gentlemen give a little bow, ladies a little curtsey' – another demonstration – 'turn to your right and walk to the door ahead of you.'

'I always tell them not to curtsey too deeply,' says Ross. 'I've seen them go down and not come back up again – their knees lock.' 'What on earth happens then?' I ask. 'A Gentleman Usher appears and holds them by the elbow.' 'Doesn't the Queen get the giggles?' I ask.

The Queen has great trouble but she can't laugh; this is ceremony. There was a terrible occasion I remember – if I'm being naughty – when the Lord Chamberlain read out the name of the Reverend Someone who was being awarded for services to Morris Dancing, and this fellow of over ninety came hobbling towards the Queen on two sticks. That was very difficult. On another occasion someone was so fazed that they walked straight past the Queen who said, 'Oi!', and they turned back. And we quite often have bolters who are fine until the last bit and then go back the way they came in or go straight into the audience.

The Ballroom is simply magnificent. It's huge – 14 metres high, 34 metres long and 18 metres wide (46 × 111 × 59 feet) and, built in the 1850s for Queen Victoria, it is the largest state room in the Palace and one of the largest rooms in London – and this is where state banquets and large receptions are held. Malcolm Ross describes all the state rooms as being like a theatre; they can be configured in any way. Today the Ballroom is an auditorium and the audience is sitting on rows of red and gilt chairs. Above hang six of the finest chandeliers in the Palace. They are vast: 5 feet 6 inches in diameter, 11 feet tall, each one has 5000 pieces of English lead crystal, 120 bulbs and weighs 450 kilograms – that's 1100 pounds, nearly half a ton. Like all the chandeliers in the Palace they are cleaned once a year. These are on a winch system so someone goes up into the roof space to lower them down, then a scaffold is built underneath them and they are sprayed with a gentle detergent to loosen the dirt; then the crystals are dried with a soft cloth.

At three minutes past eleven the Queen arrives, a small figure dressed in bright green, flanked by a couple of Gurkha orderly officers. The orchestra, in the Musicians Gallery at the back of the room, begins to play the National Anthem, and – whether it was the music or the pageantry or the sight of the Queen standing silently staring into the middle distance, while we called upon God to save her, to send her victorious, happy and glorious and implored her long to reign over us – I have to own up to a distinct shiver down the spine and some embarrassing wet stuff in my eyes, making it very difficult to read my programme.

Gurkhas have been escorting the monarch at official functions since 1876 when Queen Victoria became Empress of India, but the Yeomen of the Guard, on the dais behind the Queen throughout the ceremony, have been on royal duty even longer. Henry VII created their Order in 1485 after his victory at the Battle of Bosworth Field, and for centuries they were 'absolutely responsible for the safety of their sovereign' at home and abroad and also in battle. They used to live in the royal palaces, sleep outside the sovereign's bedroom and taste and serve the sovereign's food. Today that responsibility falls to policemen, and the Yeomen of the Guard are largely ceremonial, although I wouldn't fancy the chances of anyone who made a hostile move on the Queen on their watch. They are retired Army officers, warrant officers and non-commissioned officers and their uniform dates from Tudor times. The horse-drawn carriages they arrive in are not much newer, but they still carry swords and seven-foot halberds.

Also escorting the Queen is the Lord Chamberlain, The Right Honourable The Lord Luce, who stands on the Queen's right and calls out the name of each recipient (cue to walk forward), while Major James Duckworth-Chad, the Queen's Equerry-in-Waiting, a tall, eager, fresh-faced young officer who is never far from the Queen's side, whispers the salient details about each as they approach the front of the dais. The Master of the Household, Vice Admiral Sir Tom Blackburn, a friendly, down-to-earth character, holds the appropriate decoration out to the Queen on a velvet cushion, the decoration having been placed there by the Secretary of the Central Chancery of the Orders of Knighthood who is responsible for making sure that it is the right one. And the Queen presents it to her delighted subject in just the way Malcolm Ross has described it. I can't think why A. A. Milne starts creeping back into my head.

When asked in 1992 which of the many different aspects of her job she considered the most important, the Queen replied 'investitures'. She puts a tremendous amount of effort into them, not just on the day but also beforehand. She is given a list of recipients well in advance with several paragraphs about each, so she knows precisely what they have done to earn their award, and she picks out a few key words which provide the basis of a useful and personal remark to say when she presents it. She has an astonishing memory for a brief – something she has handed on to her two elder children – because once the investiture is underway, with nothing more than a quick, whispered reminder in her ear she recalls immediately the salient facts about each and every one of the 110 men and women who pass through the system at a rate of five every three minutes. They all come away feeling that they have had a personal conversation and tell Malcolm Ross that she spoke to them for a good three or four minutes when it was forty seconds at most. She also gives the impression of being sincere, which she clearly is, and makes people feel that the honour she is bestowing comes with heartfelt gratitude for outstanding service. The whole ceremony is over in one hour and ten minutes flat; although longer if Prince Charles is in the driving seat, as he often is. The Queen gives her handshake and turns to pick up the next medal; the Prince of Wales keeps eye contact until the person he has just invested is on their way. 'It's very special,' says Ross. But it adds an extra ten or fifteen minutes to the ceremony.

The impression is that these people, who come in all shapes, sizes, ages and colours, have been specially selected by the Queen for their award. The list of those selected is published twice a year, at New Year and on the Queen's official birthday in June, which reinforces the notion that they are her choice. This is not so. The only honours that are in the sovereign's gift today are the Most Noble Order of the Garter, founded in 1348 by Edward III and limited to twenty-five knights with the motto *Honi soit qui mal y pense* (Shame on him who thinks evil); the Most Ancient and Noble Order of the Thistle, founded in 1687, limited to sixteen knights, all of whom must be Scottish – motto *Nemo me impune lacessit* (No one provokes me with impunity); the Order of Merit, which Edward VII founded in 1902 to reward outstanding contributions to science, art, music, literature and public life – with a corresponding award for exceptional military leadership in times of war – limited to twenty-six; and the Royal Victorian Order for services to the Queen and other members of the Royal Family, which is usually conferred on long-serving members of the household on their departure. Apart from those, whose number is limited, the Queen's role in the honours system is almost exclusively constitutional; the bulk of the names are chosen in Whitehall and she has little power to affect the honours given in her name.

Each list has about 1350 names on it and a large proportion of them are civil servants, diplomats and the military – a hangover from the days when civil servants were poorly paid, for which a gong at the end of their career compensated. And for the high-flyers it denoted rank (despite vastly improved salaries, it still does); they rise from the CMG (Call Me God) to the KCMG (Kindly Call Me God) to the GCMG (God Calls Me God) to a Knighthood. In recent decades media figures have also been increasingly showered with honours, leading to the inescapable suggestion that the gongs have been given either as inducements or rewards for favours or support, and that the system is therefore rotten to its core.

Harold Wilson began the trend when he was Prime Minister in the sixties and ennobled no fewer than six journalists from the Labour-supporting *Daily Mirror*. Margaret Thatcher, in turn, knighted a number of prominent Tory supporters including the Jeremy Paxman of his day, the inquisitorial television journalist Robin Day; Peregrine Worsthorne; Kingsley Amis; and three loyal editors, Larry Lamb of the *Sun*, Nicholas Lloyd of the *Daily Express* and my father, John Junor, of the *Sunday Express* – he who had always insisted he would never accept a title if it were offered, any more than he would take a freebie, on the grounds that it would compromise his freedom to write what he believed. But he wasn't the first or the last to be so seduced. 'The English really *are* in the grip of the religious passion of monarchy,' wrote Richard Eyre, director of the National Theatre, in his diary when he received a CBE from the Queen in 1992. 'How can it change? It can't if people like me go on accepting honours.' Mrs Thatcher was well aware of the influence that all three of those newspapers had on the outcome of the general election that swept her to power in 1979 and knew the value of their continued support. John Major widened the scope of the honours system by introducing nominations by members of the public but he too used the system and Tony Blair has been no different – except that he cunningly honoured the then editors of the two major Tory broadsheets, Max Hastings of the *Daily Telegraph* and Peter Stothard of *The Times*.

In November 2003 Benjamin Zephaniah, the Rastafarian poet, broke with convention and announced publicly that he had rejected the offer of an OBE because he claimed it stood for colonial brutality and slavery. Would-be recipients are always sounded out by letter to see whether they will accept an honour before the list is passed to the Queen – 98 per cent accept. In rejecting the honour, Zephaniah did not pull his punches: 'It reminds me of thousands of years of brutality – it reminds me of how my foremothers were raped and my forefathers brutalized.' He added, 'Stick it, Mr Blair and Mrs Queen – stop going on about the empire.'

The next month documents leaked from Whitehall, hitherto secretive about the whole matter, revealed just how many prominent figures from the world of literature, stage, screen and sport had also turned down honours; and also how confidently a committee of civil servants, chaired by Sir Hayden Phillips GCB of the Lord Chancellor's department, decided who was to be honoured and who left out – revelations which once again brought the whole legitimacy of the honours system into question. The result was two reports, both published in July 2004. One, written by Sir Hayden Phillips, came up with thirty-one recommendations to ensure that the system would be seen to be fair and more accessible to the population at large. 'Some people believe the whole system should be swept away,' he wrote. 'Others would abolish traditional titles and historic orders. Some of those who hold these views hold them with a passionate intensity. But I do not believe that there is a broad public opinion that is seriously opposed to having a national system through which the Queen, as Head of State, confers recognition on the contribution of individuals to our society. Put more simply the honours system is our way, within our cultural history, of saying thank you publicly.' The other, a House of Commons Select Committee, attracted rather more attention, however. Under its recommendations, top civil servants and diplomats would also lose their entitlement to more 'exclusive' honours – the Order of the Bath and the Order of St Michael and St George; Knighthoods and Damehoods would be abolished and the Order of the British Empire re-named the Order of British Excellence. Knighthoods, so they said, were 'redolent of past preoccupations with rank and class, just as "Empire" is redolent of an imperial history'. It was roundly condemned by traditionalists and constitutional experts as 'damaging political correctness that could undermine the monarchy'.

Nearly forty years ago, however, the Queen tried to change the name of the OBE herself. In 1966, according to the author Anthony Sampson, she handed the Prime Minister Harold Wilson a four-page memo written by Prince Philip proposing the name be changed as the empire had been 'virtually eliminated'. He suggested alternatives like the Order of St James's or the Order of the Lion and the Unicorn. 'But senior civil servants were horrified,' Sampson wrote in *Who Runs This Place?*, 'and revealed all their conservatism in opposition to the Palace, the supposed "fount of honour".'

The head of protocol Sir Lees Mayall mockingly suggested that St James might recall a Tudor nunnery which was home to 'fourteen leprous maidens'. The head of the diplomatic service Sir Saville Garner complained that any change would arouse 'a good deal of unnecessary controversy'. The head of the Treasury Sir Laurence Helsby argued that it would be too expensive, and 'the less relation the name of an order has to reality, the better, and the further the empire disappears into the sands of time, the less difficulty there is in retaining the name'.

The mandarins won the day.

Garden parties are another great Palace institution. Three times every summer nine thousand people, most of them mystified as to why they have been invited, make their way from all over the country to Buckingham Palace – and once each summer to the Palace of Holyroodhouse. The men are mostly in morning dress or uniform (although increasingly it is lounge suits or national dress), women in their best summer suits, hats and handbags – all clutching their prized and exceedingly stiff and embossed invitations from the Lord Chamberlain who 'is commanded by Her Majesty to invite' them. As with every invitation issued by the super-efficient Malcolm Ross, who also organizes the garden parties, there are detailed instructions about where to find the Palace and which entrance to use, what clothes to wear, what time to arrive (4.00 – gates open at 3.15) and what time to leave (6.00), accompanied by car park stickers for their windscreens and instructions about where to park should they elect to come by car. The guest list is a hotchpotch of people from every walk of life, pulled together by a variety of list makers – the government, the civil service, the Armed Forces, professional bodies and the Lord-Lieutenants – and they are another means by which the Queen acknowledges and rewards good works and community service.

As with everything the Queen does, the pattern is the same party after party, year after year. She and the Duke of Edinburgh and members of the Royal Family walk out on to the terrace outside the Bow Room at four o'clock, at which point one of the two bands that play a selection of music throughout the afternoon stops and plays the National Anthem. Everyone stands to attention, including the royal party; a handful of people are then presented formally to the Queen – new Lord-Lieutenants, chaplains to the Queen or tenants of the Duchies of Cornwall and Lancaster. After that members of the Royal Family disperse themselves among the crowd mingling on the lawn, each one taking a different route, weaving their way between groups, talking at random to people who catch their eye. There is no formality and it is largely a matter of luck as to whether a guest will meet one, several or none of the family, but unless they are off exploring on the other side of the lake they are certain to come close. Besides, just to be inside the secret garden, behind the high brick wall with the black iron spikes on the top that seals off royalty from the rest of London, has a certain magic in itself. There are almost forty acres of garden at the back of the Palace, to the west, with a tennis court, wonderful rose beds, shrubberies, a huge herbaceous border, and more than two hundred mature trees, many of them specimens, gifts from different Commonwealth countries. The lake covers four acres and is a haven for wildlife. Tea and cakes are served in huge open-sided tents and for those guests who are rather more special than others – ambassadors, high commissioners, government ministers and the like – there's a royal tea tent. On the dot of 6.00, the band launches into a second rendition of 'God Save the Queen', she and the rest of the family disappear into the Palace and everyone else flocks out into the Mall, their day of excitement done, and heads home.

THIRTY-FIVE

Voluntary Service

Lord-Lieutenants are the Queen's representatives in the country; there is one in every county, appointed by the Queen on the advice of the Prime Minister. They are usually retired, can be men or, nowadays, women, aristocrats or commoners but are recognized as figures of distinction and good standing in the community. Glory comes with the job but not hard cash. The position is voluntary and although they get mileage, telephone and postage reimbursed, and have part-time use of a secretary, they have to provide their own car and meet all other expenses, which can during their tenure run into many thousands of pounds, out of their own pocket. As one of them said to me:

> Everywhere you go as Lord-Lieutenant, you go to church, you sit in the front pew and the collection plate comes to you first, you can't just put a couple of coins into it, you have to put at least £5; you go to a charity do and you can't buy a single 10p raffle ticket, you buy a £5 strip – and I am patron or president of fifty organizations. Heaven knows what I spend but I don't begrudge it. It's a huge privilege to be Lord-Lieutenant. You represent the sovereign which is a great honour, everywhere you go you're in the front row

of the stalls, you're greeted properly, your wife is hugely esteemed and you meet wonderful people we would never have met before – little people, big people, good people doing nice things, just beaming all over when someone says 'What a wonderful job you're doing'. One of best parts of the job is finding people to pat on the head and say well done to.

Lord-Lieutenants may be out of pocket but they are the top dog in the county, and except when the Queen or another member of the Royal Family comes to visit – which they organize with military precision right down to the last millisecond – they reign supreme.

They were originally appointed in Henry VIII's reign as part of the reorganization of local government, to control the military forces of the Crown in each county, and for a couple of hundred years had full control of the militia; but under the Forces Act of 1871 control reverted back to the Crown. The military flavour remains, however. The men wear military-style navy blue uniform with scarlet stripes down the trousers. On formal occasions they dress it up with overalls, swords, sashes, spurs, medals and peaked hat with a scarlet band – the full fig. Less formally, they leave off the sword and spurs and on other occasions can wear ordinary suits or blazers. The women – helpfully also called Lord-Lieutenants – are positively drab by comparison. All they have to show for themselves is a diamond brooch in the shape of the Queen's crown and emblem of the nation which hangs on a red and white striped ribbon that they wear with normal clothes.

Lord-Lieutenants are in demand, in much the same way as members of the Royal Family, to be presidents or patrons of charities, to open schools, factories and new buildings, to attend local functions and present awards and prizes including the public service Long Service and Good Conduct medal, the Queen's Awards for Export and Technology and the Queen's Scout and Queen's Guides Awards. It is a pretty full-time job and involves most evenings, too. They are automatically senior magistrates, they chair the Lord Chancellor's advisory committee, which appoints and sacks local Justices of the Peace, they are Keeper of the Rolls – the county archives – they are head of the county's Reserve Forces and Cadets Association, president of the St John Ambulance in the district and by tradition they are made Knights of St John. And at midnight on their 75th birthday they are sacked.

'Once appointed, we used to do it for life,' says Lieutenant General Sir Maurice Johnston, former Lord-Lieutenant of Wiltshire since reaching the magic age last October, 'but allegedly the Queen went up to the furthest reaches of Scotland and a nonagenarian drooled over her hand and she came back and said, "Up with this, I will no longer put. Sack them at seventy-five!"'

It is very often out in the country, at the grass roots away from the city cynics and chattering classes, that you get a more accurate sense of how the monarchy is viewed and valued. And the Lord-Lieutenants are useful in feeding the mood of the nation back into the system.

> Occasionally you get nobbled: 'Would you tell the Queen that . . .' People sometimes assume you see the Queen after breakfast every day, which of course you don't, but the relationship with the Private Secretaries of all members of the family is very close and we talk a lot. We are one of the avenues for advice and temperature gauging which goes to Sir Robin Janvrin. He used us a lot during the Golden Jubilee to sound out attitudes and opinions. Wiltshire is a conservative county with small and large C – except for Swindon

which has two Labour MPs. The attitudes of people are pretty conservative, they don't like change, they like order and authority, they don't like disorder and disharmony, and, as I discovered when I started, and during Jubilee Year, the Royal Family is held in huge esteem in the county. If, for instance, I have laid on a programme for a visit, there is massive disappointment if the visit has to be cancelled. And there is huge excitement when I bring a minor member of the family – the Duchess of Gloucester, for example – people go wild with excitement; or the Duke of Kent – he's a very valuable member of the family, does a good job and people are thrilled to see him. When Prince Philip came to open the new Great Western Hospital everyone knew where he was by the gales of laughter.

The Queen and Prince Philip spent a whole day in Wiltshire in December before the Jubilee Year. They went to Chippenham, Calne and Malmesbury; it was wonderfully successful, the programme encompassed big things, small things, walkabouts. I didn't announce that they would be travelling from Chippenham to Calne at such and such a time and the car would go past houses on the A4, but every single house had Union Jacks hanging from the window and every single house had someone standing on the pavement waving and taking off hats. People don't do that if they are longing to become a republic.

At the other end of the country, parts of which are considerably less Conservative, Sir John Riddell, the Prince of Wales's former Private Secretary and now Lord-Lieutenant of Northumberland, had the same experience.

I can tell you in the county of Northumberland when the Queen and Duke came on a pre-Jubilee visit I took them to

Ashington, which is a very melancholy and very large ex-pit village; it used to be the biggest pit village in the world. When I said the Queen was going to walk down Station Road there was a slightly bored response and I was expecting that no one would turn out and no one would make much effort. And they didn't make much effort, but it happened to be a sunny day and you'd have been in floods of tears if you'd been a monarchist because Station Road was absolutely full of people waving Union Jacks; you may say it doesn't take very many people to fill Station Road, Ashington, but by God they were all there, and that's a very important thing.

Sir Maurice regards Princess Anne as one of the hardest working members of the family and quite the most professional in terms of doing her homework and knowing what she's looking at. He once took her to a very high-tech cutting-edge firm:

It invented and manufactured a prism which basically split fibre optics and instead of ten thousand conversations going through a fibre optic, with the prism, there were eight times the number going through the same fibre optic. She knew all about that; could talk to the people in white coats about refraction and technical terms. From there she went to a hospice and she sat beside a dying lady's bed and knew exactly what to say, also to a nurse with a problem. It's because they've done it so many times before.

The Queen is less interested in the technical.

When she came to open a multimillion-pound extension of Motorola in Swindon, I briefed them that the purpose of the visit was for her to talk to the people, the work people, not to get involved in technicalities of what went on inside. Halfway down the line a white-coated expert said, 'Ma'am, this is our latest toy and if you look inside here . . .', and asked her to pop her head inside something the size of a deep freeze and was explaining that the wires connected to this and that; the Queen turned round and gave me a great wink. They're not interested in seeing computers – they've seen hundreds – nor looking at the layout of a factory. They're there so people can meet them and talk to them and have that wonderful satisfaction of saying 'I met the Queen today'.

One of the factories in Wiltshire that several members of the Royal Family have visited over the years is Dyson Appliances in Malmesbury, which found fame with the revolutionary bag-less vacuum cleaner. James Dyson is its equally revolutionary inventor and chairman, and is as unconventional as his vacuum cleaners. 'I spent a lot of my life thinking the Royal Family didn't have much to offer,' he says.

Recently, since I've got to know them because they've come to see me at the Design Museum [of which he has been chairman for the last five years, and trustee for eight], here at the factory and at the Chelsea Flower Show [where he had an award-winning garden design in 2003] it's rewarding and important to have someone who comes round and encourages, and congratulates people without having a political or any other motive. There's a place for that. It's like being at school and the headmaster or his wife comes round and says 'Well done'. It's very nice to know that someone has noticed and cares – as much for me as for my workforce. There is a role for someone saying what you are doing is good and good for the country. If the Prime Minister had done that, it would have been nice but it's different. We've had Gordon Brown here and I've been on a trip to Japan with Tony Blair. It's nice but there could be another motive, a political agenda. With the Royal Family there may be a social agenda but not a political one. When they came here and when Prince Philip went to the Design Museum, they said, 'What are you doing here? What are your problems?' They asked intelligent questions – I've never heard a member of the family ask a stupid question.

The Queen came eighteen months ago with the Duke. They weren't invited. They decided they wanted to come and see us. There was a lot of arranging to do – sniffer dogs and all that. There's a protocol; the Lord-Lieutenant of Wiltshire, Lieutenant General Sir Maurice Johnston, writes to you and comes to see you to discuss it. You don't hear from Buckingham Palace at all until afterwards, when you get a thank-you letter. It all goes through the local royal man. It was the same with Prince Charles two years before. The Lord-Lieutenant says they'd like to come and works out what they will do when they are here. He says they'd like to meet as many people as possible. There was no time to do the offices and the production line, so we got everyone into the factory, and at one end of the line was the whole of the finance department, and at the other end all our engineers from the office floor. When you go on to the production line you have to wear yellow safety jackets and safety boots and the Duke of Edinburgh kept going up to people and saying 'Which forklift do you drive?' and they would be one of our top scientists. The Queen happened to talk to a lot of people in the finance department and she turned to me and said, 'Why do you have so many people in your finance department?' I said, 'You just happen to have met them all bunched up.' When I brought her up on to the office floor to use the loo – you have to have a designated lavatory – she was supposed to be brought up by the lady-in-waiting but there wasn't one around so I brought her up. In a way that was the most interesting part of the whole trip because she talked much more freely when there weren't lots of people around and was much more interesting and relaxed and chatty. I have a feeling she's quite shy and finds it difficult.

The Queen is very easy-going. Other members of the family can be more difficult and Sir Maurice would not be the first person, when awaiting the arrival of the Duke of Edinburgh, to be quietly praying that his royal visitor was going to arrive in a good mood. A former director of the Royal Society for the Encouragement of Arts, Manufacture and Commerce (RSA) says that his views changed a lot over his seventeen years of working with Prince Philip, but he never lost his admiration for him.

He was pretty fantastic, he was pretty daunting and could be pretty awful. He would turn up here in a foul mood and make life very difficult. He could be quite rude to people and unkindly rude, but by the end of the time, two or three hours, he was invariably in a good mood again; the bad moods weren't very often. Generally he was fantastically supportive and pro and I thought as far as the environment was concerned he was brilliant, and he was a complete master of his brief. That was what amazed me. He did his own homework, wrote his own speeches. He asked for ideas, rough drafts, and he would never use anything verbatim but you could tell he was taking an interest in what you'd say and out came his own stuff. In environment committee meetings with lots of real experts, the Attenboroughs

313

of this world and others, he was the master of the total brief, no doubt. He had a very small staff, a very efficient office in complete contrast to the Prince of Wales's office. Going back twenty-five years, his was the little tight, well-run group of ex-servicemen mostly, pretty classy sorts. First woman equerry one before last was very nice, but they have become much more relaxed. A lot of the formality has fallen away; when I first encountered Prince Philip it was a very formal occasion. One gets very blasé about contact with the Palace. I have a letter from the Palace every week or a phone call. I joke that I see him more than my sister sometimes because he does do an awful lot for us. And he has a capacity to get into the detail of things. We sent him a governance review about six years ago and he asked to see the by-laws and he discovered four or five drafting errors that the lawyers had completely missed and he obviously enjoyed going through it.

Prue Leith, who happens to be my sister-in-law as well as a former chairman of the RSA, finds him perplexing. 'He's an enigma: really hard-working, well-briefed, intelligent, controversial and good company,' she says.

> He is the most challenging and terrific RSA president, reading everything and commenting forcefully on anything he doesn't like. When we were changing the RSA governance, I remember us sending out the new proposals to all forty-odd council members. He was the ONLY one to return it, annotated with suggestions and corrections handwritten in the margins.

But . . . and there is always a but, 'Sometimes he is extremely rude and a real bully.'

One day he came to an RSA event in honour of Dame Judi Dench, in a thoroughly bad mood, and was cross that there were two photographers present, loudly demanding an explanation from me in front of the half-dozen VIPs waiting to be presented. Since I had no idea why we had two photographers and anyway was unaware that we should not have, I joked, 'No idea, sir, maybe it's because one of them is useless and the other is back-up.' 'What utter rot,' he says and turns on his heel and stamps away, leaving me looking like a prat, unable to present anyone to him, and everyone embarrassed. I hissed at the barman to get him a drink pretty damn quick, and left him to his own devices. Of course, being the pro he is, he got on and talked to everyone else, and by dinner time he was completely delightful and great company. By then I'd found out that the unwanted extra photographer was in fact a Palace photographer, and we'd been asked by his staff to accommodate him. I told him this, but didn't get an apology – just a flat denial. 'Nonsense, I don't have a photographer.'

But he can be unexpectedly un-grand and relaxed. Once, in a discussion on world population, he was banging on a bit about how too many people had too many children and I found myself saying, 'That's a bit rich coming from someone with four children' – the sort of crack you are not meant to make at royals. He just laughed and said, 'Touché' or something similar.

And I remember remarking to one of his equerries that I'd just had a pleasant conversation with Prince Philip and that for once he wasn't determined to put me down, and he said, 'That's because you stand up to him. He likes that.'

Princess Anne, who is made entirely in her father's image, was due to open the Millennium Footpath in Bradford-on-Avon one day. At 10.30, driving her own car, she arrived, and Sir Maurice Johnston opened the door and said, 'Good morning, Your Royal Highness, welcome to Wiltshire', and she said, 'It is not a good morning', and strode swiftly on towards the chain gang he was presenting to her. When he caught up with her and asked what that was all about, she said, 'For the last twenty-five minutes I've been watching you from the multistorey car park there with a copy of *The Times* over my head hoping no one would see who I was, because my policeman got me out of bed half an hour early.' No one she met during the course of her visit would have known how cross she was, but her policeman is certain to have had better days.

The chain gangs are an inevitable part of royal visits, but something the Royal Family would prefer to see less of. When they are tying to cram so much into a day, and time is therefore limited, they want to meet the people they have come to see – the people who actually teach in the school, who take care of patients in the hospital and the people making widgets on the floor of the factory – not the local dignitaries. The Lord-Lieutenant is there every time a member of the Royal Family comes into his county on official business, his wife or husband is always there, the High Sheriff, the local Mayor or the Chairman of the District or County Council, the Chief Constable and the local MP and sometimes their spouses as well. 'One tries to limit them,' says Sir Maurice, 'but they are dying to be there because it's a great day in their lives.'

A new way of patting people on the head, as Sir Maurice puts it, is themed receptions at Buckingham Palace. The first one last year was for Women of Achievement. Perhaps there were some who had stayed away. Perhaps an invitation to lunch with the Queen at Buckingham Palace was not something for which they would have cleared their diaries; but I doubt it. And so on one cold March day, gathered 180 of Britain's highest achieving women – artists, athletes, academics, actresses, writers, models, politicians, scientists, doctors, businesswomen. Famous names, famous faces – J. K. Rowling, Janet Street-Porter, Kate Moss, Twiggy, Baroness Thatcher, Jennifer Saunders – and many you would never have heard of, but all of whom have done something remarkable – like an Indian woman who started off making curry in her kitchen and now has a business that supplies millions of pounds' worth of ready meals to one of the leading supermarket chains.

Before they went in to lunch there were drinks and much chattering. Whatever they may have thought of the monarchy, the women invited to the Palace that day were enjoying themselves. Some said their mothers were pleased they were there, others admitted it was for themselves, several had met the Queen before; two were wearing the same outfit but all seemed to be on a high. Many of them already knew one another, others were meeting for the first time, but seemed excited to be meeting heroes. It felt like a particularly good party and with 180 women talking at nine to the dozen the decibel levels were probably higher than I would guess the state rooms have heard in a century or two. And chatting with just as much enthusiasm were the Queen, the Princess Royal and the Countess of Wessex – the female members of The Firm – who had shaken everyone's hand formally as they arrived, and then mingled with the guests, walking informally up to groups and joining the conversation as any hostess would at any normal drinks party.

It is not often that members of The Firm work together. Indeed it used to be the first thing that new recruits to the private offices were told – to avoid putting members of the family together on the same platform, apart from the Queen and the Duke of Edinburgh, because they were all used to

317

being stars in their own firmaments and happier that way. Even at events like the Chelsea Flower Show they arrive in quick succession in a fleet of separate cars but immediately split up and make their own way around the exhibits.

The guests congregated in three interconnecting state rooms on the first floor overlooking the garden, one of them the Blue Drawing Room – so-called because of the blue flock wallpaper hung by Queen Mary in the early twentieth century. It is huge – George IV intended it to be a ballroom but died before the building work was finished. Queen Victoria built her own ballroom – where lunch was served that day – and the Blue Drawing Room became a reception room. It is one of the grandest rooms in the Palace, designed by John Nash, as all the state rooms on the first floor were, sumptuously decorated, particularly the ceiling, with moulded plaster reliefs, Corinthian columns and vast chandeliers. Big windows look out over the garden, and, were it not for the full-length net curtains, would offer a wonderful view across the lawn and down to the lake. Why the curtains are there I have yet to fathom. It isn't as if buses trundle past and passengers on the number 25 are going to see in. That side of the Palace is not overlooked; and the garden was deserted, except for a flock of greylag geese grazing greedily on the lawn.

From this height you could see that the lawn was still showing signs of strain from the two Golden Jubilee concerts. They may have lasted no more than two days but the effect on the lawn, where the colossal stage had been erected many months in advance, was every bit as great as that on the country. First there was a classical concert with great names from the world of opera at which the Queen, the Prince of Wales and Camilla Parker Bowles were all seen for the first time together; then there was the Party in the Palace, the biggest Golden Jubilee party of all – an evening of rock and pop with a spectacular pyrotechnic finale. Nothing like it had ever been seen at the Palace before. Twelve thousand people lazed on the lawn of the most famous building in Britain and listened to music spanning the fifty years of the Queen's reign. The *Telegraph*'s music critic was disappointed, however.

Queen Elizabeth II came to the throne in the same year Britain got its first singles charts. Her reign has coincided with the explosive birth and ongoing evolution of a vibrant pop culture. Although it may have had little impact on Her Majesty's dress sense, she has presided over rock and roll, the beat boom, psychedelia, heavy rock, prog rock, reggae, punk, ska, indie, new romance, electro pop, acid house, hip hop, trip hop, Britpop, jungle and garage. Yet precious little of this astonishing diversity was reflected in a Jubilee line-up almost exclusively divided between veterans of the sixties and the latest crop of all-singing-and-dancing, twenty-first-century stage-school graduates. It was a Royal Variety Show in everything but name, emphasizing the light-entertainment aspect of pop that has changed little over the decades.

The content was immaterial. The event was ground-breaking. Never before had the Palace gardens been opened up to the general public. These were not people who had done good works in the community or served the country in two world wars; they were not diplomats or civil servants. They were ordinary people of every age and background, in work, out of work, pro-monarchy, anti-monarchy – all they had in common was that they had been successful in the ballot for tickets. The tickets were free, and each person was given a hamper with a picnic and a small bottle of champagne in it. They were the lucky ones; outside in the Mall and Green Park a million people watched the action on a series of giant screens while the noise of the music boomed across the Palace walls into the night; and a further two hundred million watched it on television worldwide. And not only did they get to see such global superstars as Paul McCartney, Rod Stewart, Eric Clapton, Tom Jones, Phil Collins, Cliff Richard, Shirley Bassey and Annie Lennox – with Brian May of Queen standing on the roof blasting out the National Anthem to signal the start of the concert – they also got to see the real Queen – and Charles, Camilla, William and Harry all together for the first time in public. The Queen (wearing ear plugs) and the Duke of Edinburgh – neither known for their love of rock music – joined twenty-five younger members of the Royal Family in the royal box for what they thought was the last half-hour, but the concert so overran that they had to listen for an hour before taking to the stage to thank performers and to hear the Prince of Wales pay tribute to both the Queen and the Duke.

He also thanked the stars for their performance, which he said had made him 'feel extraordinarily proud of this country'. He then turned to his mother and, to deafening cheers, said:

Your Majesty ... Mummy. We are here tonight because, above all, we feel proud of you. Proud and grateful for everything you have done for your country and for the Commonwealth over fifty extraordinary years, supported unfailingly throughout by my father. You have embodied something vital in our lives – continuity. You have been a beacon of tradition and stability in the midst of profound, sometimes perilous, change. Fifty years ago, I would probably have been playing in the sandpit in the garden just behind this stage. But now you have generously invited everyone in here for a thoroughly memorable concert. So, Your Majesty, we are all deeply grateful to you and, in the words of the National Anthem, you have certainly given us cause to shout with heart and voice, 'God Save the Queen'.

And to a rousing three cheers from the audience, the Prince then kissed his mother. It was the climax to a day of street parties, fêtes and festivals, and at the end of it the Queen lit a fuse to ignite a rocket which sped along a wire suspended over the Mall that in turn lit the National Beacon on the Queen Victoria Memorial, the last in a chain of 1985 beacons across Britain and the world, and triggered the fireworks spectacular. It was all the work of Major Sir Michael Parker, who has been doing this sort of thing for a while. He has produced, to name but a few, twenty-seven Royal Tournaments, the Queen Mother's 80th, 90th and 100th birthday celebrations, the Silver Jubilee chain of beacons, and VE and VJ Day anniversary tributes. But that weekend's festivities in London – with 25,000 participants and no opportunity for rehearsal – was his most ambitious project yet.

From all his past glories there was one moment that he would not want to relive. It was when the Queen stood, torch in hand, ready to light the huge beacon he had organized to celebrate her 1977 Silver Jubilee. The only problem was it was already alight, prematurely ignited by an overeager squaddie.

The Queen turned to him and exclaimed: 'Look, look. It's lit already.'

'And it was lit,' Sir Michael said. 'But not only that, the main BBC generator had just blown up so we had to lend them one of ours, which meant half the site was in darkness.

'I had to say to the Queen, "Your Majesty, I am very sorry but I have to tell you that absolutely everything that can go wrong, is going wrong", and she turned to me and smiled and said, "Oh good. What fun."'

THIRTY-SIX

Media Menace

Walter Bagehot, who famously warned against letting daylight in on the monarchy for fear of losing the magic, would have spun in his grave the day that the phoney footman began his tale of life inside Buckingham Palace. Photographs of royal bedrooms, bathrooms, sitting rooms and the Queen's breakfast table, laid with marmalades and Tupperware boxes at the ready, finally expelled the last traces of magic. Bagehot was writing in the 1860s when Queen Victoria was on the throne. Parry's exposé was monarchy in the twenty-first century and a proof positive of just how intolerable life has become for her descendants.

Some people believe that the beginning of the end was in 1969 when the Queen, with encouragement from the Duke of Edinburgh, agreed to the making of a documentary called *The Royal Family*. It was an idea William Heseltine, who was then Press Secretary, hatched with Lord Brabourne, Earl Mountbatten's film director son-in-law, who then sold the idea to Prince Philip. There was a feeling that the Royal Family was almost too dull and that pulling back the curtain to give a glimpse of the domestic side of their lives, to reveal them as ordinary human beings, might add interest. According to the late Lord Charteris, 'There was a view that the Queen needed to sell herself a bit.' Sir Edward Ford, who worked alongside Charteris as Assistant Private Secretary to the Queen for the first fifteen years of her reign (and for six years to King George VI), had left by the time the film was made but thought letting the cameras in on their private lives was a mistake. Like Charteris, he had been at the Palace in the days when Richard Colville, the Press Secretary, had called in the two court correspondents (formally dressed) each morning to brief them about the day's public engagements and give them details of what clothes and hat the Queen would be wearing.

> Our remit – and that of Richard Colville, the much abused Press Secretary – was there should be maximum coverage of anything they did in the public sector, at any publicly announced engagements, tours, visits to provinces, audiences – provided that it was done in their roles as Queen and Consort – then we would give the fullest liberty to the press. But they very much resented their private lives being invaded in any way and particularly when it began to be by the paparazzi. But that meant they were remote figures. People didn't know about them unless they happened to work as an official or be involved in some sort of official contact. They didn't see them – the press were kept at bay.

The film certainly made the Royal Family less remote. It followed them for a year and showed the formal and the informal sides of the Queen's life; and caught the family off duty and at play in a way that had never been shown before. In one of the most memorable scenes it showed them on holiday at Balmoral, barbecuing their supper by the loch. A rather gauche teenage Princess Anne lit the fire, the Duke of Edinburgh was chief cook, Prince Charles mixed the salad dressing, while one of their younger brothers played around on the roof of the

Land Rover; and the Queen, wearing rubber gloves, washed the plates at the end of the meal. It was fascinating – partly to see how very ordinary they were. They looked and behaved like any other family, ill at ease with the camera, self-consciously making banal remarks and silly jokes, but riveting television in the same way that reality television is sometimes riveting. These characters normally associated with red carpets, golden coaches and grand palaces were disarmingly human – a fact that they had always jealously guarded. Marion Crawford, whose book, *The Little Princesses*, was a harmless and affectionate memoir about her years as governess to Elizabeth and Margaret, was cast into outer darkness for her revealing anecdotes and never forgiven to the day she died, almost forty years later.

This film was far more revealing than anything Crawfie wrote; the difference was that this time the Palace wanted those titbits put into the public arena – and they had full editorial control of them. *The Royal Family* was arguably the first example of royal 'spin' nearly twenty years before the term became common currency. 'I think it's quite wrong that there should be a sense of remoteness or majesty,' said Prince Philip, when asked his views about the film. 'If people see, whoever it happens to be, whatever head of state, as individuals, as people, I think it makes it much easier for them to accept the system or to feel part of the system.'

What it actually did was make people hungry for more – thus in a sense the Queen and her advisers were the architects of their own misfortune. They were the ones who first let the daylight in – although society was changing so rapidly and respect for institutions disappearing so quickly that it was only a matter of time before the media tore down the curtain that *The Royal Family* had so discreetly and fleetingly lifted; if they hadn't jumped they would surely have been pushed. And in choosing the BBC to make the film – and choosing the BBC again to interview Prince Charles before his investiture as Prince of Wales the same year – they bred resentment among its rivals who felt all the more inclined to do a bit of pushing. As Ben Pimlott wrote, 'Was it right for a Fourth Estate worth its salt, to accept such a calculated piece of media manipulation as a given? If royal "privacy" was no longer sacrosanct, why should its exposure be strictly on royalty's own terms?' Kenneth Rose observed, 'The sight of Prince Philip cooking sausages meant that after that people would want to see the dining room, the sitting room, then everything except the loo.' As it happens, they had to wait for Ryan Parry thirty-four years later to see all the rooms, but they saw an awful lot of other things in the meantime.

'Heseltine was acutely aware that the Queen did so much more than public engagements,' explains Sir Edward Ford, 'and people were just beginning to say "Do we need to pay quite so much money for so little return?"'

Heseltine thought people ought to know how hard the Queen works, that her day was so full, also that she was a human being and not just a remote figure out of the fairy-tale books; and so he had the idea of having a film showing her at work at her desk, seeing her private secretaries, and other heads of departments, approving programmes for visits and speeches. Her day was very fully taken up but I don't think people were worried about how hard she worked. There was a little bit of criticism starting up about her 'long holidays' at Balmoral; no one realized that every day the Aberdeen train brought up a red box or two for her to go through which she did regularly through the holiday. She didn't go to the Mediterranean or Caribbean, as most of us do. It was the relentlessness of her life, the relentlessness of the job. Even when she was having children, she never gave up doing her daily work; she used to ring within two days of the birth. She was tied to the job. She had very enjoyable holidays at Balmoral in the summer and Sandringham at Christmas time, but she never used them as excuses for not doing the job. She has never really taken a proper holiday. It was a great pity, I always thought, that the government did away with the royal yacht because that was the one place to which she could get away, because it was sometimes quite difficult to get the papers from Whitehall to the yacht, say, when it was off the west coast of Scotland. They could come by helicopter and be dropped. Urgent things could always be got to her. Even in Australia twice a week papers were flown out that required her signature on decisions.

The film certainly opened the door and once that door is open it's very difficult to shut it. You can open it wider but it's difficult to shut it. It was a mistake, but this is with a bit of hindsight. I'm not sure at the time I didn't think, 'Oh bully, they're going to discover the Queen that only we knew.'

The Royal Family reinforced the image of the Windsors as a model family, which with four children still to grow up was a dangerous card to play. 'If I had to point to one thing in that film, which was a hostage to fortune, it was the image of one big happy family,' says Guy Black, former director of the Press Complaints Commission, 'because we all know families don't work like that.' And as the family started to fall apart the media took the greatest delight in reporting it. 'But I guess *It's A Royal Knockout* was an absolute low point in their relationship with the media because they became a laughing stock and it takes years and years to rebuild your reputation after being a laughing stock.'

That programme in 1987 did immense damage to the Royal Family; not only because it turned them into a laughing stock but because it put them on a par with the sort of celebrities they had been competing with and against. As one of the Queen's former press secretaries says, 'It was a climacteric in terms of equating the young monarchy with showbiz because that's what they were doing, they were dressing up and making fools of themselves. Okay, it was for charity but so what? If you equate yourself in that direction you're going to be written about in that direction and it was a serious turning point.'

In today's celebrity culture it is a fine balancing act to keep the Royal Family in the news but to prevent them becoming embroiled in the razzmatazz that goes with modern celebrity. Celebrity today means nothing more than being famous. Fame can mean being a brilliant sportsman and winning a gold medal at the Olympics or being last out of the *Big Brother* house, being a talented, award-winning actress, a disgraced politician, or being an It Girl. It's vapid, rapid and comes with no sense of responsibility. Their private lives and their sex lives, past and present, are greedily devoured by the tabloid media in exchange for exposure and publicity and sometimes cash, and most of them thrive on it. They go to the places they know they will be seen, where they know the paparazzi will be waiting, and if they put their hand up to the lens or attempt to hide their faces it is nothing more than a con. There are plenty of places where rich and famous people, who truly don't want to be seen, can go; plenty of places where even princes can go. But if they mix with celebrities they get treated like celebrities – as Prince Harry discovered when he was provoked by a photographer outside a fashionable Mayfair nightclub in 2004. And that is dangerous. Even if we know that the Royal Family is made up of men and women with feet of clay, we still need to believe there is something special about them.

Reduce them to the status of two-bit celebrities and the illusion is gone for ever.

On the other hand, the monarchy cannot afford to become dull. Nor can it afford to be invisible; and in today's world the only way of being visible is through the media. They have no other form of direct communication. As Guy Black says, apart from the Queen's two broadcasts – to the Commonwealth and at Christmas – 'they don't make set-piece speeches, they don't have recourse to party political broadcasts, they don't go out campaigning and they don't put literature through people's doors. They have to rely on the media to get their message across, so when that relationship goes wrong it is very bad for them.'

A number of incidents in the sixties and seventies showed that the relationship was strained. Princess Anne's loathing of the press dates back to her competing days when she famously told photographers to 'Naff off' at horse trials, but the real problems started in the eighties with the arrival of Diana, who was such a gift for the media. Young, beautiful, glamorous, photogenic and, on top of everything else, a princess. And this princess didn't scowl and swear at photographers, she smiled at them, called them by name and charmed the socks off them. The public was charmed too and a photograph of Diana on the front page of a newspaper or magazine sold copies, whatever the story that went with it, which was often little more than a caption. And when the marriage started to fall apart, the stories became more and more salacious, people's natural appetite for gossip was well fed and circulations started to soar. Then the Princess began a direct dialogue with the media – and reaped the whirlwind from that in the end.

Her misfortune was that at much the same time the fundamental nature of newspapers started to change. For the first two decades of the Queen's reign proprietors of the main groups were members of the Establishment, monarchists to a man, who valued their relationship with the Royal Family. Lord Beaverbrook and Lord Rothermere owned the *Express* and the *Mail* respectively; two branches of the Astor family owned *The Times* and the *Observer*; the Berry brothers, Lord Camrose and Lord Kemsley, owned the *Daily Telegraph* and the *Sunday Times*. They were wealthy men who owned their newspapers more to fulfil their political ambitions or for reasons of vanity than to increase the family fortune. And had they wanted to make real money out of their newspapers, the print unions in Fleet Street were so greedy and so powerful they hadn't a hope.

Rupert Murdoch changed all that in the mid-eighties. He challenged the unions. He secretly moved his operation from Fleet Street to Wapping in east London and printed newspapers using new technology, without union manpower. A long and bloody battle ensued, known as the Siege of Wapping, but the unions were defeated and a new era dawned. No longer in the stranglehold of militants, all the newspapers invested in new technology and at last began to make real money. The advertising and marketing departments suddenly became as important, and in some cases more so, as the editors who in the past had been gods. The result was that the industry, already having to compete with television, became fiercely competitive and desperate to attract readers. Stories of royal discord were everything they could have hoped for.

And there were no more patricians to protect them, no one for whom sentiment was more compelling than the bottom line. Today's proprietors have different priorities. Rupert Murdoch whose News International owns *The Times*, the *Sun*, the *News of the World* and BSkyB, not to mention an entire book publishing empire, is an Australian living in America with no sentimental attachment to the monarchy or any other

British institution. He is a republican by inclination, but first and foremost he is a businessman and while royal stories continue to make money he won't kill the golden goose, but he doesn't lose sleep if he causes it distress. As Anthony Sampson says, 'Murdoch probably did more than any single individual to undermine the old British tribal Establishment. He promoted cheeky Australian journalists and crusading anti-Establishment editors who thrived on debunking toffs and stuffy institutions, and used class warfare to boost circulation ... He avoided paying British taxes, and remained uncontrollable and unaccountable, like an eagle swooping down on his prey and soaring back into the sky.' The Express Group, once owned by Lord Beaverbrook, is now owned by Richard Desmond, a man who made his millions publishing soft porn. The Hartwell family, which founded the *Telegraph* titles, are long gone, replaced by businessmen. Only the Harmsworth name survives. Jonathan, the fourth Viscount Rothermere, is chairman of Daily Mail and General Trust which owns Associated Newspapers, but he is answerable to shareholders and his are therefore as aggressively competitive as every other title. And as newspapers became more competitive, particularly the red tops, they became less scrupulous in their story gathering – paying criminals, entrapping public figures, fabricating stories and creating a lucrative market for kiss-and-tell tales: the perfect climate for disaffected royal servants to make a bob or two.

'I've always had a very simplistic view about newspapers,' says Guy Black.

They are there to make money with the probable exception of the *Guardian*, which is run in a complex fashion as a sort of charity because of the Scott Trust. Every other newspaper is there to show increasing profits and returns

330

for shareholders, and so, although they might stand up for great principles, those are, in reality, always secondary principles to whether or not they are going to increase their circulation. That too is very prone to fashion. During the late eighties and early nineties in the period of the Wars of the Waleses and others, I have absolutely no doubt the Princess sold huge numbers of newspapers; she was the most important thing that happened to newspapers in the course of the last twenty years. Now they are much more sceptical about the value of the royals to the task of shifting copies. Piers Morgan [then editor of the *Mirror*] would say and Rebekah Wade [editor of the *Sun*] has said, 'Put pictures of royal kids on the front cover, it won't shift any extra copies.' It is certainly long since the case that the Queen's picture sold copies. The story of Prince William's romance probably did but that's an exception because it was an intriguing royal story, and it's stories that sell newspapers not pictures.

THIRTY-SEVEN

Temporary Stand-off

The Press Complaints Commission wasn't set up until 1991, by which time the behaviour of some of the newspapers had become so excessive that the government was threatening to intervene. Faced with the prospect of legislation the newspapers proposed self-regulation and were given a last chance. The PCC was formed to enforce a Code of Practice that turned out to be completely toothless. The excesses continued almost unabated until Diana's death, which her brother immediately blamed on the tabloids. The reason her car was screaming through the Paris tunnel at such speed on the night it crashed was because it had a collection of paparazzi in hot pursuit. Earl Spencer said the tabloids had blood on their hands and they took it to heart. In November 1997 a new Code of Practice was drawn up covering every aspect of intrusion that the Prince and Princess of Wales had suffered and ensuring privacy for their sons. It was a code which, it claimed, 'both protects the rights of the individual and upholds the public's rights to know' – which left plenty of room for interpretation. However, the ruling was specific about children being 'allowed to complete their time at school without unnecessary intrusion' which was aimed specifically at William and Harry, and which for the most part the newspapers honoured.

The question was what would happen once they left school. Prince William was left unmolested during most of his four years at St Andrews. The deal the Palace made with the media worked. There was the Ardent episode, which got things off to a bad start, and there were photographs of him walking down the street with a Tesco carrier bag, also a couple of stories about girlfriends, but overall it was successful. And in the filmed interview he gave in November 2004 – which he would never have given had the media not behaved well – he made it clear that he was grateful to them for having allowed him to live life as a relatively normal student: doing his shopping, renting videos, going to the cinema and to pubs and generally enjoying himself. He said the agreement had been 'invaluable' and hoped it would continue once he left university.

The chances are it might. William has a kind of natural authority – and so far no labels attach. He is very much his own man – a much stronger character than his father – he knows what he wants and will do what he wants. He grew up with a profound dislike of the media and a hatred of cameras, having been subjected to so much of it with his mother and seen what havoc and unhappiness it caused to all their lives. But since his mother's death he has been well served by a series of good, kind and sympathetic individuals in his father's Press Office who have broken him in gently, carefully hand picking journalists to interview him and photographers to take pictures, gradually building up his trust, teaching him that not all media people are out to hurt or take advantage of him, that not all publicity is damaging. He knows that, like it or not, the media is going to be an essential part of his life – essential for the monarchy and the role he will have to play in The Firm. He will need the media as much as the media will need him – and, like his mother, he is playing the charm card, but where Diana spent most of her life out of control, William is in command and my guess is that he will command respect.

Sandy Henney was the first Press Secretary to take William under her wing. A former civil servant, she was warm, genuine and devoted to both boys. She had flown up to Balmoral after Diana's death at the Prince's request to talk to William and Harry and to try to prepare them in some way for what they would find when they came to London for their mother's funeral. Being there, helping them during that emotionally difficult time, made the relationship slightly special, and when Sandy fell on her sword after arrangements for William's eighteenth birthday photographs went wrong, they were sorry to see her go. Colleen Harris, her deputy, took over. She was another former civil servant and another caring, solicitous mother figure who also built up a good relationship with William and Harry and loved them dearly. Both women were ideal when the boys were vulnerable teenagers without a mother; but the new press supremo at Clarence House is perfect for them now that they are young men. Paddy Harverson, who came from Manchester United, arrived in October 2003. He's an imposing figure, a former journalist – he was sports correspondent on the *Financial Times* and still loves football – stands six foot four and is bright, straightforward, fair, forty and unflappable. And having spent his time at Manchester United, the world's biggest and most successful football club, dealing with giant egos, millionaires and megastars like David Beckham and perpetually managing intense tabloid interest, he was neither overawed by Clarence House nor the challenges of his new surroundings.

Sir Michael Peat had taken up his position a year earlier as an antidote to Mark Bolland, with the express intention of getting the Prince of Wales's private life out of the newspapers and his good works into them. Paddy Harverson's arrival cemented the plan. He doesn't spin, doesn't have favourites and is straight as a die. He also made it plain early on that Clarence House was under new management. When the *Daily Express* columnist Carol Sarler viciously attacked Prince Harry in February 2004 he immediately fired off a furious letter to the editor for publication. Harry had just arrived in Lesotho on his gap year, having previously been working on a cattle farm in Australia, and there had been stories of him visiting London nightclubs. Sarler had written:

> That Prince Harry is a national disgrace is scarcely news. His exploits have been making headlines for years: the drinking, the drugging, the yobbing, the waste of the costliest education in the land, the explicit disdain for the lower orders, the increasingly sexual public romps. But now there's a new note creeping into the royal revelations that turns my already queasy stomach: all of a sudden there's a nudge-nudge, wink-wink in the air, along the lines of good old Harry, eh? Just like any other lad his age, just a regular kinda guy . . . No, he's not. And I swear, if I really thought all nineteen-year-olds, in whose hands our future lies, were anything like him then I'd emigrate. He has never once done anything because it was the right thing to do and has rarely lifted a finger unless it's to feel up a cheap tart in a nightclub. Harry has opted for eight lavish weeks in interesting parts of Africa, where he has reluctantly agreed to spend a bit of the trip staring at poor people.

Her words, said Harverson, exercising commendable restraint, 'made it entirely clear that Ms Sarler has little or no understanding of Harry as a person and no knowledge of how he has so far spent his gap year. Like any other nineteen-year-old fortunate enough to be able to spend time travelling and working abroad, Harry should be allowed to enjoy and benefit from his experiences without being subject to the kind of ill-informed and insensitive criticism made in your paper by Ms Sarler.'

It was the first time either of the two Palaces had responded to an opinion piece in a newspaper; two months later, he made it clear that this was not a one-off. When the *Sun* published paparazzi photographs of Prince William on the slopes at Klosters with his girlfriend Kate Middleton – just days after he had performed for the cameras in a set photocall – Harverson punished the paper by banning Harry Arnold, the veteran *Sun* photographer, from future photocalls with William. It wasn't Harverson's doing but before he arrived Clarence House also went after the *Mail on Sunday*, an action which came to fruition in June. The paper had published a story that Prince William had speared and killed a dik-dik, a dwarf antelope, during his time in Kenya. Clarence House claimed the story was wrong; the *Mail on Sunday* had a good source and refused to back down and so Clarence House lodged a complaint with the PCC and the newspaper finally gave in. Speaking on the BBC Radio 4's *Today*, Harverson said, 'Now, hopefully, they will understand that we do take things seriously and will hold them to account where we feel that they are wrong and have evidence to prove that they are wrong.'

'The one thing the Royal Family can never ever succeed in is litigation against the papers,' says Guy Black.

It should never even attempt it. The example of the *Mail on Sunday* and the dik-diks in Kenya is an interesting example of where things are stacked in the media's favour. At one point the Royal Family started involving lawyers and threatening legal action. I talked to the newspaper a bit about it and we both reached the same conclusion, that the idea of taking legal action was laughable. How do you put Prince William, with his well-known views on hunting, in the witness box on a trial about killing animals? 'So what is your view about hunting? Do you approve of foxes being clubbed to death, in which case what's your problem with dik-diks? Tell us about your hunting exploits.' They would have a field day. The newspapers would love to get one of them in court; it would be worth having to pay hundreds of thousands of pounds in libel expenses just for all the information that would come out during a libel trial. So the media has got them where it wants them on this. They could never sue over libel or privacy. The courts have already fashioned some jurisprudence on privacy under the Human Rights Act, but a lot of it relates to the issue of 'If you court the media a bit, if you put aspects of your private life into the media, then you must expect the media to pay attention in return, and if you are a public figure you must expect the public to be interested in you'. That is a doctrine of the courts now laid down and Prince William is a public figure. Again, anyone who goes into the witness box to defend their privacy ends up with their reputation shredded. Naomi Campbell, Michael Douglas and Catherine Zeta Jones; okay, they may come out of it with a bit of money – but that's not important to the Royal Family – but their reputation is in tatters. So I've never seen the case for a privacy law to protect the rich and famous because they wouldn't benefit from it and the people who would least benefit from it are the royals because they couldn't use it.

THIRTY-EIGHT

Burrell

The Royal Family, however, did come close to appearing in court in the notorious Burrell trial in 2002 – not initiated by them but by the Crown Prosecution Service, driven by the Spencer family, Diana's executors. It was a trial that should never have come to court and, but for the behaviour of one of the arresting officers, probably never would have done. The damage and the subsequent fallout were inestimable. Paul Burrell, who began life as the Queen's footman and moved on to become Diana's 'rock' (and thence to fame as a celebrity), was accused of stealing more than three hundred items belonging to the Princess of Wales's estate. His house was a veritable Aladdin's Cave of items that he had either been given by the Princess or taken for safekeeping, and when police arrived on his doorstep early one morning in January 2001 looking for Diana's mahogany box – the box that supposedly contained letters from Prince Philip, James Hewitt's signet ring and tape recordings that came to be known as the 'rape tapes' – which they never found, they arrested him for theft. Their pretext for the dawn raid was the theft of an eighteen-inch-long jewel-encrusted model of an Arab dhow worth £500,000 which had been a wedding present to the royal couple from the Emir of Bahrain. It had been offered for sale in a London antiques shop, and the man accused of stealing it was Harold Brown, another of Diana's butlers. He claimed that Burrell had authorized its disposal. In October 2002 Burrell was brought to trial for the theft of the items found in his house and a month later the trial was abandoned after the Queen apparently 'remembered' a conversation with him in which he had told her that he had taken a number of items from Kensington Palace for safekeeping. Harold Brown's trial for the theft of the dhow collapsed a few weeks later, also before he took the witness stand and supposedly because of this evidence from the Queen.

The Queen had not suddenly 'remembered' anything. After Diana's death in 1997, the Queen had been encouraged by the domestic staff at Buckingham Palace to see Burrell, who was utterly distraught. Because she was fond of him and felt sorry for him she agreed. And so they met but because it was not a formal meeting – Burrell had come in from the staff side – Robin Janvrin knew nothing about it. During the course of the conversation Burrell mentioned that he had taken a few papers from Kensington Palace for safekeeping, about which the Queen took little notice. Four years later she read about Burrell's arrest in the newspapers, still thought nothing of their conversation but was saddened that such a nice man should have been up to no good. The Prince of Wales had similar sentiments, as had William and Harry, who had grown up with Burrell, knew his wife and as children had played with his two sons. The Prince of Wales would have liked to help but was warned by his lawyer, Fiona Shackleton, to stay out of it. He was told it was a legal process; he must not try to protect Burrell or get involved in any way. His private secretaries at the same time were telling him that Burrell in court would be a disaster and should be averted at all costs. And so Mark Bolland set up a meeting between the Prince of Wales and Burrell – who at that point had not been charged – for

3 August. The hope was that if Burrell apologized, confirmed that he had intended only to retain the property for safe-keeping, agreed to return it all and not reveal information personal to the Princess of Wales, then they would tell him that it might not be necessary for the police to press charges.

The meeting never took place because that same morning the police met the Prince of Wales and others at Highgrove and indicated to him that they were 'in a position to show that Mr Burrell's lifestyle and finances altered drastically after the death of the Princess of Wales'. Also that 'police are in a position to produce evidence that large quantities of items have been sold abroad to several dealers. In addition an independent source has shown police photographs of several staff members dressing up in clothing belonging to the Princess of Wales at a party before packaging them up and sending them abroad.' With what seemed like incontrovertible evidence that Burrell had been profiting from Diana's belongings, all thought of reasoning with Burrell vanished. The meeting was cancelled and Burrell was charged on 18 August and came to trial that October. When the Queen heard about the police evidence, all sympathy she may have had for Burrell also vanished.

The trial went ahead with some uncomfortable revelations filling the newspapers for several weeks. During the course of it Maxine de Brunner, one of the arresting officers, who had been at the 3 August meeting at Highgrove and had told the Prince of Wales that Burrell had been profiting from Diana's belongings, was interrogated by Burrell's leading counsel, Lord Carlisle QC. Had she, he wanted to know, been to Highgrove to tell the Prince of Wales that his client was believed to have been selling items abroad? She agreed she had, and agreed that there had been no evidence to back it up. Had she ever corrected the false impression she gave to the Prince, he wanted to know? No.

The Queen read all of this in the newspaper reports of the trial and began to wonder whether Burrell might not have been rather harshly treated. She had never thought that her conversation with him in 1997, which referred to a few papers, could have been in any way relevant to the trial, since the three hundred-plus items he had squirrelled away were furniture, pictures, ornaments and clothes. Nevertheless, having heard that what the police told Charles wasn't true, perhaps, she reasoned, Burrell wasn't guilty after all. She mentioned it to Prince Philip and the Prince of Wales while the three of them were together at Buckingham Palace before setting off for St Paul's Cathedral for a memorial service after the Bali bombing. The journey took them past the Old Bailey where the trial was underway. After the service the Prince of Wales rang Sir Michael Peat, newly installed as his Private Secretary, and asked him if the Queen had ever mentioned to him that she had seen Burrell after Diana's death. He hadn't and asked whether the Prince was sure she had. Yes, he said, she had told both him and the Duke of Edinburgh. Peat then said they should mention it to the police. Yes, said the Prince, but thought that Peat had better speak to the Queen first to make sure he had the story absolutely right. Having ascertained that the story was right, Peat then rang Fiona Shackleton who rang the police and, to everyone's surprise, the trial that had cost £1.5 million was suddenly brought to a shuddering halt. Why evidence that Burrell had told the Queen that he had a few papers should have undermined a trial for theft of more than three hundred items found in his house and under his floorboards remains a mystery to everyone in both Palaces.

Paul Burrell had had a devastating experience. He was a sad character, obsessed by the memory of Diana, but his life had been shattered, he had felt abandoned, he had contemplated suicide, he was out of a job, he had no money. And waiting

341

in the wings was the *Mirror*, the persuasive Piers Morgan and its reporter Steve Dennis who had become a friend. No fewer than four hundred media organizations approached Burrell, offering up to a million pounds for his story, but he decided to tell all to the *Mirror*, who gave him editorial control, for £300,000. 'He will protect the memory of Princess Diana,' said Morgan the day the deal was done, 'and will honour his pledge to always protect the Queen. But I think there will be many others in the Royal Family and close to the Royal Family who will be quaking in their boots tonight.'

It must have been one of the best deals that Piers Morgan ever made. Not only did he have riveting stories day after day pushing up his circulation, but a year later, despite promises that he would never betray the Princess or the Royal Family, Paul Burrell came out with a book, *A Royal Duty*, which was sensationally serialized in the *Mirror*. 'This particular phase of my life,' wrote Diana in a letter supposedly written ten months before her death, published in the first instalment, appearing to support conspiracy theories about her accident, 'is the most dangerous – ******* is planning "an accident" in my car, brake failure and serious head injuries, in order to make the path clear for Charles to remarry.' It wasn't long before they overcame the 'legal reasons' and named the Prince of Wales as the person she feared was trying to kill her – although serious doubt has since been cast on the date of the letter. It appeared to have been genuine in as much as it was written by Diana but written years, not months, before her accident. In another letter written shortly before her death she said, 'I have been battered, bruised and abused mentally by a system for fifteen years now ... Thank you, Charles, for putting me through such hell and for giving me the opportunity to learn from the cruel things you have done to me.'

By the end of the first week the Prince of Wales authorized

Colleen Harris to release a fierce condemnation on behalf of his sons. It was instigated by Prince William, whose blood began to boil with the first day's revelations and by Friday he had had enough. He was at St Andrews at the time, rang Harry in Australia and they agreed a statement that accused Burrell of 'cold and overt betrayal'. Prince Philip was also furious. Some of his letters to Diana had been published, one of which said, 'We do not approve of either of you having lovers. Charles was silly to risk everything with Camilla for a man in his position. We never dreamed he might feel like leaving you for her. I cannot imagine anyone in their right mind leaving you for Camilla.' He sought legal advice but was advised action would be unwise. In the midst of their discomfort, Mark Bolland, by now cut loose and fancy free, and more than a little disenchanted, wrote an article in the *Daily Mail* criticizing the Royal Family's 'disgraceful' treatment of Paul Burrell and suggesting that Britain could become a republic unless aides served their masters better. His invitation to Colleen Harris's leaving party at Clarence House the following night was summarily withdrawn and he sat in the car outside while his partner, Guy Black, enjoyed the Prince's hospitality.

One of the Queen's former press secretaries agrees about the quality of advice, but says that the Prince of Wales is a difficult man to advise. Looking back through the catalogue of disasters as far as the Dimbleby interview, he says:

It's bad enough dealing with your infidelities within your own home but to go parading them in public, and then not just to do it but to do it without telling anyone you were going to do it. The Prince told some people, yes, and his Private Secretary advised against it. It was madness, and everyone at Buckingham Palace thought it was a huge mistake. The Duke of Edinburgh was livid at the whole thing, thought it was disgusting and so infantile. Who was the Machiavelli in all that, do we think? Were people just going along with what he wanted to do? Everyone needs advice, particularly in moments of crisis.

The trouble with the Palace is always there are advisers and courtiers; advisers are in the best professional civil service type, they will give impartial advice, the courtiers will blow with every wind that's blowing and their main objective is to keep in their job and to tell their principal person what they want to hear. That's what I saw in my time, and why you have a whole lot of private secretaries to the Prince of Wales walking; like Edward Adeane and John Riddell and the man who was there for a year, Christopher Airey. The Prince of Wales didn't want to hear impartial advice; he wanted to hear people agreeing and he's always been a bit like that. The Prince of Wales has a fearsome temper. It's never been directed at me, but I've seen several members of the Royal Family break down and cry in my presence over the years. They are human beings like everyone else, with tempers; fury is inbuilt in several of them. I've never seen Prince Andrew furious; he's a very reliable, honourable man.

He might very well say that ... but the Press Secretary had never woken him up for breakfast in the morning. According to Ryan Parry, the *Mirror* plant, the Duke of York, depending upon his mood, would either say 'Good morning' or tell the footman to 'Fuck off'. I would like to believe Parry was making it up but I suspect he's not. Some years ago the Prince of Wales gave a concert in memory of Lady Fermoy, Diana's grandmother and old friend and lady-in-waiting to Queen Elizabeth. Belinda Harley in the Prince's office had organized it and she and her colleagues were all deputed to meet members of the Royal Family and show them up to the room in which it was being held. 'They all behaved entirely in character,' recalls one of them. 'The Queen Mother was charming, Princess Margaret said, "I hope it won't last too long, there's something good on TV at 9.30", and Princess Michael said, "What handsome young men".' After the concert, Prince Andrew, who was the only one not dressed in a dinner jacket, walked up to three of the Prince's staff who were standing at the side of the room. 'Who are you three?' he said in a particularly graceless manner. 'We work for the Prince of Wales,' they said. 'Oh. Well you three are in big trouble for not telling me it was black tie,' and without waiting for a reply stalked off. 'It was childish and stupid and his office *had* been told,' says one of the three. Two of the three were private secretaries. 'Robert Fraser had been chief barrister in the Navy, Stephen Lamport had been a diplomat at major embassies in the world, he'd been Private Secretary to Douglas Hurd, and compared to them I thought what has this chap ever done in his life apart from fly a helicopter? How dare he speak to us like that? Loyalty has to be earned and I'm not sure how good some of the family are at doing that.' Princess Anne could be equally rude, according to Parry, and swore at servants if they made a mistake, but Sophie, Duchess of Wessex, was everyone's favourite, always kind and grateful.

The Queen was furious about Ryan Parry's intrusion – although no one, no matter what they do, can ever hurt her as much as Crawfie did. 'Though few books were written so mawkishly,' wrote A. N. Wilson in his preface to the reprint in 1993, 'few can have been written with such obvious love.' For the Queen, however, the sentiment was secondary to the abuse of trust, but it inured her to further acts of betrayal. She was angry that she had given house space to a liar and a cheat but her anger is always immediate and rarely articulated.

Those around her simply know that she is thoroughly displeased. But then she moves on. It is not in her nature to dwell on what is past and the Queen doesn't go looking for scalps. She is enormously loyal to the people who work for her. As Charles Anson, her Press Secretary during the turbulent nineties says, he only ever had to look out for enemy fire. No matter how bad things were, and during the War of the Waleses when the publicity was disastrous at times, he never feared a bullet in the back. He knew that provided he had consulted and kept the Queen and Robert Fellowes, her Private Secretary, in the picture about what was happening, he could count on their support. 'And you would know that support was going to stay with you right through, whether things went right or wrong. The Queen expects loyalty and she gives all of it back. She's terrific. However wrong it goes, she'll either say, "Look, just keep going", or "This is simply untenable, let's look at it again". She would never say, "Who got me into this position?" or even imply it. She would take it on; you never had to worry for an instant.'

The Prince of Wales doesn't have such a good track record. Sandy Henney should never have lost her job over Prince William's eighteenth birthday photographs, and if the Prince didn't know the detail of what went on he should have made it his business to find out. She had wanted to find a way of getting some good, relaxed shots of William and knew that if she organized a general photocall dozens of photographers would turn up, William would be tense and none of them would get close enough to produce anything very special. And so, without announcing it to the rest of Fleet Street, she approached two easy-going, likeable photographers, Ian Jones from the *Daily Telegraph* and Eugene Campbell from ITN. She thought they would both get on well with the young, shy Prince and they would get some good shots that could be distributed to all the newspapers and television channels. It was a good idea; they got on famously and some wonderful photographs were produced as a result. The deal was that there would be no exclusives, no preferential treatment, and the photographs would be embargoed so that they all appeared on the same day. She discussed this entire deal at every stage with Stephen Lamport, the Prince's Private Secretary, with Mark Bolland, also with Les Hinton and Guy Black at the Press Complaints Commission. Everyone gave it their blessing.

However, when Charles Moore, Ian Jones's editor at the *Telegraph*, saw the photos, which he had electronically stored on the office system, he liked them so much he wanted to maximize the impact by running them in the glossy Saturday magazine which goes to print earlier than the main body of the paper. He therefore wanted them before the agreed date. Sandy Henney cleared this with Lamport and Bolland and the photographs were released. Shortly afterwards someone tipped off the *Daily Mail* and *The Times* about what was happening and Lamport agreed to let them have a set of photos early for their magazines too. Charles Moore was indignant and refused to let the photographs go. The *Telegraph* had provided the photographer, who had worked for five months on the project, it had provided the facilities and had undertaken to release the photos to every other newspaper free of charge; it was not unreasonable, he felt, for the *Telegraph* to have this slight advantage over its competitors. At this point Piers Morgan, then editor of the *Daily Mirror*, got wind of the story, turned on Sandy, wound up the rest of Fleet Street and it all turned very ugly. Sandy had nothing in writing; she had relied on a gentleman's agreement and, crucially, had not secured the copyright of the photographs. The final outcome was not catastrophic. The photographs were released to every newspaper at the same time, they all honoured the embargo and Ian Jones surrendered the copyright of his pictures to St James's Palace. As one commentator said at the time, it was a storm in a Fleet Street teacup.

Sandy offered Stephen Lamport her resignation as a matter of formality, never for a moment believing it would be accepted. How could it be? She had consulted at every stage, she had had everyone's agreement at every stage; her mistake had been to trust men she thought were honourable. If it was a cock-up it was a collective cock-up. But she was wrong. Her resignation was accepted and by three o'clock that afternoon she had cleared her desk and was out on the street and out of a job. And the Prince of Wales, to whom she had given years of loyal service, and whose sons she had helped, guided and looked after with such care, didn't even say goodbye.

Yet Michael Fawcett, his former valet, who has caused terrible damage to the Prince's reputation – and continues to do so – and who countless people have tried to unseat over the years, remains firmly in favour. Although he resigned from the staff in 2003, and is now running his own event-management business, he continues to work alongside the Prince. He handles all his party arrangements, makes decisions for the Prince in this area and earns thousands of pounds from those jobs and from other highly prestigious jobs that his association with the Prince has brought him.

THIRTY-NINE

Allegations and Denials

The Burrell trial opened a very large can of worms and revealed the undisciplined and chaotic nature of the Prince of Wales's household. Taking home unwanted gifts that had been given to the Prince and/or Princess of Wales had been seen as a perk of the job; some people kept them as mementoes, others flogged them. Gifts of any sizeable value were often sold and the proceeds given to charity, or the Prince might buy something he wanted with the money in place of the gift he couldn't use. And Michael Fawcett, nicknamed 'Fawcett the Fence' by the newspapers, had handled those sales. The media stirred up the nation's sense of indignation, planting in its mind the image of presents lovingly given by loyal pensioners being callously cast aside. Some things were even put on the bonfire at Highgrove, although, in truth, most of the presents were impersonal corporate gifts that the Prince of Wales had no use for and thought his staff might enjoy. However, it was not good housekeeping and it was disastrous public relations.

But it was what happened after the trial that really caused the damage. Male rape was the topic that gripped the nation – and the intriguing mystery of what the footman saw. The missing mahogany box, which came up in the course of the trial, had contained a tape recording made by the Princess of

Wales, in 1995 or 1996, which Lady Sarah McCorquodale, Diana's sister, had told the police contained 'sensitive' material. It was common knowledge in Fleet Street that the tape was a recording of George Smith, a former valet, telling Diana that another member of the Prince's household had raped him in 1989, some six or seven years earlier.

Ten days after the collapse of the Burrell trial, at the end of a week of sensational stories in the *Mirror*, the *Mail on Sunday* topped them all. 'I WAS RAPED BY CHARLES'S SERVANT' screamed the headline alongside a picture of a dapper-looking George Smith. The aide he accused wasn't named, but through his solicitor this man strenuously denied the allegation that Smith had been raped in his own home one night in 1989 when he was very drunk. Smith, now in his mid-forties, was a Falklands veteran, who had been severely traumatized. He had a history of depression and alcoholism and was in every sense an unreliable witness, which is why, when the story first came to their attention as a domestic matter in October 1996, the Prince and his advisers quickly dismissed the allegations. He had not reported the rape at the time, and when he did report it to the police in 1996 he almost immediately decided not to pursue it. He had a record of ill health, and, given the situation, could not continue working alongside the man he had accused of raping him. And so, in an attempt to see him right and stave off further accusations, he was given a £30,000 payoff by the Prince – which was inevitably interpreted as hush money.

In the same edition of the *Mail on Sunday* there was a character assassination of Michael Fawcett, who had not made many friends during his years with the Prince of Wales. Promoted to a position of influence never before enjoyed by a valet, he was arrogant and a bully who made many people's lives in the Prince's office a misery. He had extraordinary sticking power, and having the Prince's ear, he was able to damn anyone he didn't like or who was foolish enough to cross him. There had long been suggestions that he exploited his friendship with the Prince, particularly in relation to suppliers, but that the Prince chose to turn a blind eye.

Early in 1998 it looked as though Fawcett had finally come unstuck but the rejoicing throughout the office was short-lived. Although Fiona Shackleton was one of a group who persuaded the Prince that Fawcett must be removed – and the story that he was leaving appeared in the press – he never went. The Prince changed his mind, decided he couldn't live without him and Fawcett was not only kept within the fold but was promoted from valet to consultant responsible for organizing functions – which, to give the man his due, he does extremely well and in precisely the way the Prince likes.

Stung by such a sustained assault on the reputation of his household, the Prince of Wales announced the very day after the *Mail on Sunday* story appeared that he was setting up an inquiry – led by Sir Michael Peat, assisted by Edmund Lawson QC – to look into four areas that had been raised in the press following the Burrell trial.

1. Was there an improper cover-up of the rape allegation made by Mr George Smith in 1996?
2. Was there anything improper or remiss in the conduct of the Prince of Wales's household with respect to the termination of the Burrell trial?
3. Have official gifts given to the Prince of Wales been sold?
4. Have any staff in the Prince of Wales's household received improper payments or other benefits?

Four months later, in March 2003, Peat held a press conference – the first time a Private Secretary to the Prince of Wales

351

had spoken other than through a Press Secretary – to announce the results of his inquiry, which some saw as instantly flawed because of the author's position in the royal household. Had the pecking order been reversed, had Peat been assisting Edmund Lawson, the results might have been more convincing. Nevertheless, Peat found plenty of faults under the Prince's roof and admitted that there was work to be done in creating systems and tightening those already in existence.

Essentially, however, he found there had been no improper cover-up of the rape allegation but that 'A serious allegation of this sort should not, in our opinion, have been treated so dismissively, even though there was universal disbelief as to its veracity, without full and documented consideration of the decision not to investigate.' He found that, although the Prince of Wales had serious concerns about the implications of Burrell being tried and the information and revelations that would come out and be picked up by the media, 'there was no improper conduct by or on behalf of the Prince of Wales in respect of the termination of the Burrell trial'. He found that the whole area of official gifts being sold or given to staff was murky and promised that guidance and procedures had already been put in place. And he found that there was no evidence of staff selling, without authorization, gifts given to the Prince of Wales or of staff taking a slice of the proceeds if authorization had been given. Discounts from suppliers, he admitted, were received, but that was not unusual in a number of organizations and there was no evidence of such gifts having influenced decisions.

And as for Mr Fawcett:

Insofar as the press comments and allegations have been directed at Mr Fawcett, our investigation has not produced any evidence of financial impropriety on his part. He did infringe the internal rules relating to gifts from suppliers, but opprobrium cannot attach to this because the rules were not enforced and he made no secret of such gifts. Press suspicions were understandably aroused by his involvement in the sale of gifts (which, unknown to the media, were all authorized by the Prince of Wales) and by it being widely known that he received valuable benefits from third parties. His robust approach to dealing with some people combined, perhaps, with his having been promoted from a relatively junior position within the household, undoubtedly caused jealousy and friction in some quarters. This has encouraged some to voice rumours as to his financial probity; but they are just that, rumours. There is no evidence to justify a finding by us that he has been guilty of the alleged financial misconduct.

The same morning it was announced that Michael Fawcett had resigned. His settlement from the Prince of Wales was reported to be in the region of £1 million; he was allowed to buy from the Duchy the £400,000 grace and favour house that he and his wife and two sons had been living in and he was guaranteed freelance earnings from the Prince of £100,000 a year. Peat had achieved more than most; he had managed to get Fawcett out of the house but not entirely out of harm's way.

But there was another, more sinister strand to George Smith's story, which was said also to have been on the missing 'rape tape' and which began dribbling out over the next year and more. He claimed to have taken breakfast on a tray to a principal member of the family and witnessed an 'incident' between a member of the Royal Family and a Palace servant. Once again, the story had been circulating in Fleet Street and among people in the know for a long time; the implication was that it was a homosexual incident. Some people thought it referred to the Prince of Wales, others that it might have been the Duke of York or Prince Edward. Either way it seemed unlikely the story would ever see the light of day. George Smith was a likeable and honourable character, no doubt, who had had a rotten time of it, but, with his history of alcohol, post-traumatic stress and depression, he was not a reliable witness and it was widely accepted that there was no evidence at all for the allegation. As a money-spinner this story was irresistible and in November 2003 the *Mail on Sunday*, which had been looking after Smith, now out of work, divorced and a broken man, prepared to publish a second interview with him in which he told the story of what he had seen, naming both the servant and the member of the Royal Family. It was a gamble – the evidence was insubstantial and they knew it – but it was one that paid off. On the Saturday night in advance of publication, an injunction was obtained to stop the story appearing in all its detail, giving the *Mail on Sunday* the best of all possible outcomes – a banner headline that couldn't have been more tantalizing, 'Royal Servant Gags *Mail On Sunday* In Court Drama'.

But the injunction was not enforceable in Scotland and, although they were not seen south of the border, the *Sunday Herald* published the allegations. Meanwhile, the same royal servant tried to stop the *Guardian* from naming him, but the newspaper, which had been intrigued by the curious nature of the injunction, successfully mounted a challenge in the High Court and won the right to name the man who had sought the injunction to gag the *Mail on Sunday* – but not to specify the allegation.

It was becoming a farce. Those people who knew what it was all about were greatly amused; those who didn't were simply bemused. And to add to their confusion, four days later Sir Michael Peat issued a statement from Clarence House which said:

> In recent days, there have been media reports concerning an allegation that a former royal household employee witnessed an incident some years ago involving a senior member of the Royal Family.
>
> The speculation needs to be brought to an end.
>
> The allegation was that the Prince of Wales was involved in the incident.
>
> This allegation is untrue. The incident which the former employee claims to have witnessed did not take place.

Many thought Peat's statement was lunacy – to be denying an unnamed accusation, to be involving the Prince in tawdry tabloid tat – but the story had already appeared in an Italian newspaper, it was floating around the internet and was the subject of much sniggering in saloon bars. I happened to think it was rather a good idea; confronting the issue head-on did take the sting out of it.

No one knows exactly why the Prince of Wales is so reckless in his determination to keep Michael Fawcett. The press has repeatedly tried to assassinate his character – this is the man, it was revealed, whose job had been to put toothpaste on the royal toothbrush during his years as a valet. One answer is that he is very good at what he does. He is a brilliant fixer and he has very good taste. Parties he organizes – and I have been to several – run like clockwork; the decor is rich and flamboyant – as is he – the parking arrangements perfect, the food delicious, the wine excellent, the service good and everyone feels that they have been somewhere special – as they should if they have been entertained by the heir to the throne.

The Prince entertains on a grand scale – nearly nine thousand people a year. Every Christmas he gives a couple of parties at Highgrove, which is a goodwill exercise for neighbours and locals; but most of the people he entertains are big-time donors to his charities, or stars and show-business personalities who have donated their time and talent to the Prince's Trust. Either that or they are experts and advisers from any one of his fields of interest who have volunteered time and expertise in some way, and it is important that these people should leave Highgrove or Clarence House feeling their generosity has been appreciated and having had a very good party. Fawcett organizes the Prince's shooting weekends at Sandringham, and any private or charitable entertaining in any of the other royal residences he may use. He also organizes the Prince's family events. Shortly after moving into Clarence House (where Fawcett had been involved in the refurbishment), the Prince held a dinner for his parents and other members of the family (to which Camilla was invited) to mark the 50th anniversary of the Queen's coronation. It was just weeks after the Peat Report, just weeks after Michael Fawcett's resignation, and yet he organized it. He also organized Prince William's twenty-first birthday party at Windsor Castle, which was overshadowed by a gate-crasher dressed as Osama bin Laden in a pink frock. Aaron Barschak called himself a 'comedy terrorist'; not only did he manage to get into the castle grounds without being stopped, it wasn't until he was on stage with microphone in hand, before the entire Royal Family, that anyone realized he was not part of the cabaret.

Charles knows that if Fawcett is in charge, barring the odd intruder everything will be perfect. After so many years in close proximity, both as the Prince's valet and his party organizer, Fawcett knows, probably more than anyone else alive, the Prince's likes and dislikes. And Camilla likes him and leans on him, as she once did on Mark Bolland. She has known him for nearly twenty years and he was a friend to her when the press were camped outside her door and the hate mail was at its height. The Prince sent him and Bolland to look after her on her first trip to New York in 2000; he helped her refurbish Birkhall, the house in Scotland that Charles inherited from his grandmother; he helped with her house in Wiltshire and he helps her when she entertains.

So that is one explanation as to why he keeps him; he knows he can trust Fawcett to provide what he wants and it's easier to stick with the devil he knows. His advisers will also say it's because the Prince is fiercely loyal and he is rewarding the loyalty that Fawcett has shown him over the years. I find that one hard to swallow. The Prince *can* be fiercely loyal – and has been with Camilla – but there are plenty of people to whom the Prince has not been terribly loyal, including some in the early days of his marriage who went quite unjustly because Diana didn't want them around. Another explanation is that Fawcett was with the Prince during the Wars of the Waleses and for all the years since; he knows every last detail of the Prince's life down to his brand of toothpaste. His memories, were he to commit them to paper, would make every other treacherous ex-royal servant's book read like Enid Blyton.

'He has a very forceful personality,' says a key figure at Clarence House, who has watched the relationship for years, 'and he hasn't been managed at all well.'

Fawcett is unusually able – he came from the bottom of the pile – and he's very poor at reading and writing. I've never seen anything on paper from him, but he has the real talent of a salesman and has flair, brings style to a party – and he manages to get people to cough up money. He's also known

357

the Prince a very long time. The Prince knows he's a bully – a delegation from the staff went and told him so – but the Prince did nothing about it, I think out of a mixture of naivety and niceness. Until Peat came along he had far too much influence.

Peat is a different calibre of person from previous private secretaries. He is intensely serious, very clever and he's tough. He's not the greatest manager; but he's very tough, and much more systematic than any of the others. I'd give him six marks out of ten as a manager; Stephen Lamport, three or four out of ten. He was a nice guy but he didn't have much of a system; he was such a gent you never knew what went on in his head. Mark Bolland was a very clever operator but there was a total absence of management or systems with him; it rather felt as though he was being managed by the *Daily Mail*. Peat is respected – not universally liked – but he has brought order, increased income – he has an accountant's pen – he's concentrated on performances and he's incorruptible. He's more deferential than I would have anticipated – does a lot of Your Royal Highnessing and bowing, but he is very tough minded, stealthy, determined and he is certainly not a man who says 'Yes, sir, no, sir, three bags full, sir' – and in that environment it's quite hard not to be. Red-carpet fever is a very serious disease; it gets in the way and a lot of people suffer from it.

But for all Peat's virtues, Michael Fawcett still seems to have far too much influence. Someone running an event at Windsor Castle recently, for a charity of which the Prince of Wales is patron, was astonished by the tone and authority that Fawcett displayed in the planning process. He appeared to speak categorically on behalf of the Prince. This man was also less than chuffed to learn that the money raised at the event would be shared between his charity and the Prince's Trust (a common complaint, but nothing to do with Fawcett, more with the Prince's private secretaries who decide which charities will benefit.) The organizers of other charities have been similarly dismayed by Fawcett's high-handedness – if nothing more, he is a bad ambassador for the Prince of Wales.

And although he is self-employed and no longer the responsibility of the Prince's household, and technically, therefore, no longer a liability, his influence is as great as ever. At the beginning of 2004 he was back in the driving seat – albeit temporarily – at the shop at Highgrove. After his resignation in March 2003, much to the relief of everyone who has to deal with the shop, the business was run by Duchy Originals. The new buyer of all non-Duchy products worked closely with the shop manager and built up a good relationship with suppliers, many of whom are small local businesses who had found Fawcett's manner tough to take. Last January they were informed that Duchy Originals were no longer responsible for buying and branding – and phone calls to the friendly Duchy buyer to ask what was going on were met with ignorance. 'If you find out would you let us know, please?' Fawcett had moved back and immediately requested meetings with all the suppliers. He announced that he was changing the branding, the packaging and point-of-sale material and, although supposedly only assisting the acting managing director, Nigel Price (from the cutlery company Arthur Price of England), he has already put backs up. Two shop managers have gone in less than a year. Fawcett and Price have been hopelessly inefficient and introduced some highly questionable supply contracts which seem to go against everything that the Prince of Wales, as a supporter of small businesses, ought to stand for. Ownership of the goods goes to the shop on delivery (as opposed to on payment, which is more usual); invoices are to be raised by the supplier no more frequently than quarterly and will be paid within sixty days from the date of the invoice. So a supplier delivering on 4 January could have to wait until the end of May for payment, which could cause severe enough cash-flow problems to put a small company out of business. Highly advantageous for the Prince of Wales's Charitable Foundation but not the best way of raising money for charity.

I would be very surprised if the Prince was aware of what was being done in his name, but if there is just one lesson for him to have learned from the Peat Report it is that, before putting the rest of the world in order, he needs to take a closer look at what is happening under his own roof.

FORTY

Bear Traps

On Mike Gretton's second day in the job as director of the Duke of Edinburgh's Award he was asked to go to London to see Sophie Rhys-Jones, who, a year later, was to become the Countess of Wessex. Sophie, who at the time was working as a consultant for the Award as well as running her own public relations company, was writing a feature on the new director. After more than an hour's grilling about his past career, which he admits he found very agreeable, Gretton went back to his office in Windsor. The next day the phone rang and his PA said she had 'Sophie' on the line. 'Hello, darling,' said Gretton, thinking it was his daughter Sophy, who was in the middle of exams at medical school. 'How really good to hear from you.' There was a pause and a bit of a hush. 'Michael,' said the voice, 'I didn't know we knew each other quite so well, and quite so quickly.' 'Oh God, Sophie,' he said, to peals of laughter in his ear, realizing his mistake. 'I told you yesterday I had a daughter called Sophy. I thought it was her.' Later that day he was in a meeting in his office when a head suddenly appeared around the open door and said, 'Hello, darling.' It was the Queen's future daughter-in-law.

Mike Gretton is not the only person who thinks Sophie is fantastic or that she has been fantastically good for Prince

361

Edward. She has a lot of fans within the handful of charities she has taken on, such as Brainwave, in Somerset, which offers hope to brain-damaged children, and Chase Children's Hospice in Guildford. They all say she is warm, relaxed, interested, easy and very good for fundraising. She also has fans at Buckingham Palace, where staff love her because she is courteous and friendly. And Edward is considerably less pompous than he once was, more relaxed, infinitely more mature and also friendlier.

But Sophie was not born to the position she now holds, and for a while it looked as if she might turn out to be the third daughter-in-law who looked so promising at the start but turned into an embarrassing liability. Sophie was a middle-class girl with a career that, quite commendably, she wanted to keep going. But she failed to see the pitfalls and the bear traps that awaited her, and there was no one at Buckingham Palace capable of reining in an HRH. They couldn't do it with the Princess of Wales and they couldn't control the Duchess of York either; and because each member of the family has its own household and its own set of advisers and staff there is no mechanism for central control. Lord Luce, the Lord Chamberlain, spent three months looking into the subject, but only as an afterthought once the damage had been done.

In April 2001, Mazher Mahmood, an investigative journalist from the *News of the World*, dressed up as an Arab sheik, hired an expensive suite at the Dorchester Hotel in London and invited the Countess and her business partner for a working lunch to discuss the possibility of giving her company R-JH a contract worth £20,000 per month. The room was bugged and, despite knowing nothing about the stranger she had only just met, Sophie chatted confidently, and very indiscreetly, about members of the Royal Family and figures in British politics and government. She referred to the Queen as 'the old dear', described Prince Charles and Camilla as 'number one on the unpopular list', only likely to marry once the Queen Mother, 'the old lady', was dead; she called Tony Blair too 'presidential', William Hague, then leader of the Tory Party, 'deformed', and Cherie Blair 'absolutely horrid, horrid, horrid'. Worse, she made it clear that her royal connections were 'an unspoken benefit' to her clients.

First she denied she had said any such things, then she issued grovelling apologies to those public figures about whom she had been rude, and then, to make matters worse, she made a pact with the *News of the World*. To prevent them using the tape recording, she agreed to give the paper an exclusive personal interview. It couldn't have been more personal or more bizarre. She talked about her life and marriage, the rumours about her husband's sexuality (a constant feature of his adult life) and their determination to have a baby, saying they were even contemplating in vitro fertilization – all of which the newspaper published with great glee under the headline 'My Edward's Not Gay'. But Sophie had been 'had' a second time. The tapes didn't appear in the *News of the World* – the tapes were tame compared to what they had in exchange – but they found their way to other newspapers which gave maximum exposure to edited highlights of the secretly recorded conversation.

But the sting was not the first of Sophie's faux pas. She was in trouble for appearing in a photograph with a Rover car – a royal endorsing a commercial brand was clearly not on. She then took on the Miele electrical appliances account whose closest competitor in the vacuum cleaner market was the British firm Dyson – not clever, when her PR material, with her name on the letterhead, effectively tried to rubbish the firm. One of the company's directors went to see Robert Fellowes about it. 'He didn't think it was on either but there's a limit to what the Queen can do. I know Sophie must have got a frightful ticking off because a friend we have in common was staying somewhere and the Wessexes were also guests. My name came up and Sophie spat blood. But there's a problem; there's no command and control system within the family other than Prince Philip, so that tends to put people into camps.'

Prince Edward was doing no better. He had been much criticized for trading on the family name and using his connections to make films. He made a string of royal documentaries that no other television company would have been given the access to make. His films were criticized, his company, Ardent, was losing money – almost £2 million over ten years – and he was getting flak for doing too little to support the Family Firm. In August 2001 he and Sophie announced that they were intending to concentrate on their careers and would only carry out one public engagement in the following four months. The *Daily Mail* noted that during that same period Princess Anne had undertaken to do 166, the Duke and Duchess of Gloucester 39 and Prince Andrew 27 – and a Labour MP called it 'scandalous' that they were being paid £141,000 by the taxpayer to do so little. (In fact they were not being paid by the taxpayer – since 1993 all money paid to the Queen's children, apart from Charles, is paid by the Queen out of her income from the Duchy of Lancaster, although newspapers, like MPs, continue to inflame us all by suggesting we are paying for them.) Then there was the St Andrews fiasco, with an Ardent film crew staying on in the university town after every other journalist and film crew had left at the request of the Prince of Wales's office, which incensed the Prince of Wales and led to a rather public and unfortunate family falling-out.

The experiment of mixing royal work with a business career had been a disaster, and in 2002 Edward and Sophie gave up the unequal struggle and, with the Queen's Golden Jubilee celebrations providing a dignified excuse, retired from the business world to spend more time with the Family Firm. The decision must have damaged their pride and it certainly didn't help their bank account. The Queen was said to have paid them £250,000 to compensate them for loss of earnings but that was pure speculation; in fact, she paid nothing. They now live on the £141,000 a year that Edward was awarded in 1990, plus the £45,000 increase he got when he married. It's a hefty amount by most standards, but it does have to cover their office and household expenses plus the cost of official duties, plus the upkeep of Bagshot Park, their absurdly over-sized fifty-six-room house in Surrey. At least with a baby, Lady Louise, born in November 2003, not quite so many of the rooms are empty now.

Marrying into the Royal Family after a normal life imposes other difficulties, too. When Sophie Rhys-Jones walked up the aisle she was known to everyone as Sophie. When she walked down with Prince Edward on her arm and a ring on her finger, she was Your Royal Highness; and whether she liked it or not, or insisted upon it or not, people's attitudes towards her changed. And as a working member of the Royal Family that change was imperative.

Paul Arengo-Jones, who until his recent retirement ran the Duke of Edinburgh's Award International Association, has known Sophie for many years – they were trustees of a breast cancer charity together. He has known Edward for many years too; they have worked together, travelled together and spoken regularly and often for more than ten years. An avuncular figure, I asked if he ever saw them socially.

I see them a bit socially but with members of the Royal Family there is always going to be a line beyond which you do not cross, and that's one of those things that is not so easy for the younger generations. Within the Organization here it's a very interesting debate. If you want to have a focal point for an association – or a nation – you want someone on a pedestal; someone with an aura about them. They have a title, they have certain rights you don't have, they've got a certain situation that is not yours to have, because they are something for you to look forward to meeting, somebody who can be of great value, they can open buildings, fundraise, be an attraction.

If you're going to do that, you have to say that they are 'Their Royal Highnesses, the Earl and Countess of Wessex' and when you meet them you call them that, and you sit them in a car – you don't clasp them round the shoulders and say, 'Hey, Early, come with me'. Before the Countess was allowed to do things on her own I got her involved in the Haven Trust as a trustee, I wanted her to get involved in something which in the long term she could make a contribution to, and she comes to trustees' meetings and makes a contribution and is a valued member of the team, and is very good with people, very confident, very photogenic. To begin with she was known as Sophie Wessex because she wasn't being used in a formal capacity; but when we started using her in her royal role for fundraising, I had to say to the staff there I thought it was inappropriate for them to carry on calling her Sophie. Because if you're going to ask someone to pay £200 to sit down and eat a meal attended by Her Royal Highness, you've got to put her on a pedestal whether she likes it or not; and if you do that, you have to surround them with an aura. It's the same with the President of the United States. You don't say, 'Hi, George'; you call him Mr President, you give him an aura and he's God. You put a line round them too, beyond which

366

you don't cross – and that, I think, is the loneliness of being in that position, as well as a fact of life. For someone like the Earl and other members of the Royal Family, they were born into it and have to accept it, but for someone like the Countess it's quite a tough line to step across, but if you want her to be HRH you have to put her in a glass case. We need people in glass cases. And, yes, she's become grand; grand enough for us to be able to sell her. It would be an embarrassment if you put her in a glass case and she kept trying to climb out of it, if she didn't turn up suitably dressed or say the right things to people, but she's not grander than she ought to be. Some people say she has become too grand but I say, for goodness sake, she's a princess, she's HRH. You can't have it both ways, you put them up there and that's the role you want them to play. She does it very well, she's very relaxed.

Arengo-Jones feels sorry for the Wessexes.

The Earl of Wessex works hugely hard. He had a rocky start being the youngest and, like all of them, he didn't have a job. He legitimately thought he'd better go out and try and get one, and didn't much like being tea boy to Andrew Lloyd Webber, has always had an interest in the arts and the theatre, then when he did eventually get some backers and do the thing he was interested in, he wasn't allowed to do it, essentially, and neither was she, and so they have been left with no option but to go out and be members of the Royal Family, that's the only thing the general public will let them do. I feel very sorry for them in a way. They don't have great estates to fall back on, they can't just go and hide and disappear, they're not allowed to get a job, and so they have no choice. Yes, they made errors, but there but for the grace of God go all of us, but we do it and come back another way; they can't. They are never allowed to forget it.

Another chapter in his life which Edward has never been allowed to forget – apart from *It's A Royal Knockout* – was his sudden and premature departure from the Royal Marines in 1987. Life in the Armed Forces was always going to be a safer option than business but Edward couldn't hack it, and Paul Arengo-Jones, who was a Marine himself for three years and did the same course as Edward, has always admired his courage for that decision.

It is much harder to say you want to leave the course than stay on. It is such a tough course you cannot pass it unless you give 110 per cent. It is physically extremely demanding and if you're not able to give 110 per cent you're not going to pass it, and 99 per cent of people haven't got the courage at that point to say they want to leave, because the peer pressure is so great; so they stay in and fail. He said no, my heart's not in it. He knew what would happen and I thought, how brave; and it was so unfair because people don't know what that course is like. Most Marines thought it was a very strong decision.

Mike Gretton agrees. 'Why he went into the Royal Marines I'll never know. Maybe out of loyalty to his dad who is Commandant General of the Corps. Edward is aesthetic; he's much more interested in things like personal development of young people, the disadvantaged and music. He loves music.'

But once the press has it in for you it is very hard to alter the public perception. Yet Edward does some sensitive things and nice stories abound. Just before he went into the Marines he went to a National Youth Music Theatre performance of *The Ragged Child* at the Edinburgh Festival. 'A whole crowd of people were in the foyer,' recalls Jeremy James Taylor, director of the company, 'and one of our young front-of-house staff had some peanuts. She offered one to Edward who said no; then she backed into someone and all the peanuts went flying and were all over the floor, and, poor love, she bent down to pick them up, and Edward – I shall never forget this – said, "Perhaps I will have one after all", and bent down and ate one off the floor, then helped her pick them up. I thought, that's wonderful.'

Shortly afterwards, Edward became the NYMT's president. 'He has been everything we could have wished for,' says James Taylor.

We were doing *The Beggar's Opera* at the Lyric Hammersmith in September 1997; Edward was coming on the Tuesday to the opening night and on the Sunday Diana died. All royal engagements were off. I got instructions on the Tuesday to have the whole cast on stage at 6.45, and Edward came along, wished everyone good luck, said, 'I'm sorry I can't stay but have a wonderful evening, I'll be thinking of you.' It was a wonderful gesture; he was worried that with all the hype of a royal opening the kids would be upset if he didn't turn up.

Prince Harry is in grave danger of being branded as Edward was, and as the second son – the 'spare' as his mother called him – he has no clear vision of his own future. Prince William does. He has inherited a sense of responsibility, a sense of destiny and gravitas, that are entirely lacking in his younger brother, and also a sense of humility that seems to run in the blood. Harry is not likely to feel out of place in the Army –

he is a much more rugged type than his uncle and, if he can cope with the discipline, it will probably be the making of him – but he is seen as the wild child, the irresponsible one, the volatile one, the rogue, the womanizer, the good-time boy who will always find trouble. He is utterly charming and far more sensitive than he is ever given credit for but he has not been disciplined and the chances are he will find trouble. Princess Margaret, the Queen's younger sister, was also rebellious and her behaviour was quite shocking when seen alongside the Queen's. She was vivacious, colourful – in language as well as personality – she fell in love with the wrong people, had affairs, had a divorce and managed, despite all of that, to bring up two very level-headed, charming children. Her friends speak very warmly of her; she had compassion and she was deeply religious. But she never lost the 'spoilt and difficult' label from her youth.

Princess Anne is the one member of the family who has managed to turn around her publicity. She was once the most unpopular member of The Firm; she was rude and ungracious, uncooperative and surly. And I would say, from my experience of her and that of several people I know, still is today. But that's not how she is regarded. She is seen as hardworking and thoroughly admirable. And there's no doubt that she is. And like her father and her older brother she has made a real difference to the world. Through the Princess Royal Trust for Carers which she founded in 1991 (having thought of the idea while sitting round a kitchen table with friends in Scotland) she was the first person to recognize and address the isolation and needs of that army of unpaid people in this country – more than 6 million and some of them as young as four – who care for friends and relatives with long-term illness. 'One in ten of us are carers and the figure's going up because of the ageing population,' says Alison Ryan who is the charity's chief executive. 'Two out of three of us will be carers within the next ten years and some of them are very young, children looking after disabled parents, and if there are mental health or drug or alcohol problems they tend to go underground. The person who identified that these people needed support was the Princess Royal. She saw it as an absolute consequence of community care. If you're a princess you tend to open things, so she was opening day centres and replacement facilities when they closed the long-term hospitals and she was the one who asked the question, "What happens at the weekends, in the evenings, what happens in the summer when you're closed?" And on the whole there was a lot of shuffling feet and no very good answers. So she thought there might be a gap there.' The first Carer Centre opened in Banbury in 1992 and there are now 143 nationwide.

'It's a huge issue, the amount of money saved by carers doing the work they do has been evaluated by the Institute of Actuaries and it is £57 billion, exactly the same cost as it takes to run the NHS, so there's a parallel unpaid-for NHS. It's a huge issue all over the world, even in the undeveloped world, and the first country to have a thorough-going comprehensive support system for carers is the UK and that organization is the Princess Royal Trust for Carers. We are in demand now all over the world to tell people how to do it and it was her idea, she identified it.'

Anne went through a divorce and married again and, a few years ago, there were rumours that her second marriage was in trouble. Adam Helliker reported in his diary column in the *Mail on Sunday* that she was leaning heavily on Andrew Parker Bowles at this difficult time. Andrew, who is Camilla's ex-husband (now married to Rosie Pitman) was a boyfriend from Anne's youth, and is Zara's godfather. There were a couple of follow-up stories elsewhere at the time but nothing since. Friends say the rumours are nonsense, that she and Tim Lawrence are happily married and that is the end of it, and I don't doubt it. Anything similar about her brothers, however, whether true or not, would never have passed with such little coverage; but just a look from Anne is enough to wither the boldest reporter. She went hunting in December 2004, just after the ban was announced, something she hasn't done for years, and was out again in 2005 just weeks before the ban came into force to make a point presumably. The publicity was negligible. Who would cross someone who looked as terrifyingly humourless as Anne – particularly on a horse?

A High Court judge of my acquaintance was seated on Anne's left at dinner one evening. For the first two courses she ignored him and spoke to the person on her right. As the pudding was served she turned to my acquaintance. 'And what do you do?' she asked. 'I'm a judge,' he replied. 'Oh really? Dogs or horses?'

Anne has a very good sense of humour and can be good fun – and when she smiles she can be very pretty, too. Her friends adore her and say she is deeply loyal and not remotely grand; there are no butlers or footmen at Gatcombe Park, her house in Gloucestershire, simply a housekeeper; it feels like a family home and Anne sometimes does her own cooking. However, the teenage daughter of a friend of mine was once invited there by Peter Phillips, her son, and Anne was so rude to the girl she rang her father and asked to be taken home. And I confess to having been faintly appalled one day at the Savoy Hotel in London when the Princess Royal was presenting awards to Women of Achievement to mark the 75th anniversary of her old school, Benenden. She gave the most perfect speech from the podium, turned to put her speaking notes on the chair behind her, picked up a pair of gloves and put them on before shaking hands with some of the most remarkable and able women in the country.

Anne doesn't go out of her way to be friendly or even polite. I was at Benenden with her. I was a year older but it was not a vast school, and, although we were not friends because we were in different boarding houses, we knew one another, had friends in common and overlapped for four years of our teenage lives incarcerated in the depths of Kent. When I saw her in Uzbekistan thirty-odd years later I expected there to be some acknowledgement – as there is with every other Senior (as old Benenden girls are called) I meet. During the course of two or three full days Anne, known as PA at school, didn't even catch my eye. Though we stood, at times, no more than four feet from each other looking at archaeological marvels, she studiously avoided eye contact. I had joined an unusually small group of journalists and photographers – five in all, if I remember correctly – on the last leg of her trip. Most of the rat pack had followed the Princess of Wales to Africa and Princess Anne, on her first foreign tour with her new husband, was a secondary attraction, but I had been asked to write about it and, having made arrangements through her Press Secretary at Buckingham Palace, arrived to join the party in Tashkent. My fellow journalists had been with the royal pair for over a week and yet, in all that time, in all the bizarre and uncomfortable situations they had experienced – the desert storm, the sheep's eyes – she had not addressed one word to any of them and had not once smiled in the direction of their cameras. Having only ever previously been anywhere with the Prince and Princess of Wales, both of whom invariably said good morning to the press, I was stunned.

When I followed Anne on a day out in Kent a couple of weeks later, visiting some of her charities, where I was the only journalist, she was exactly the same. A hatred of journalists,

I thought to myself, until we happened to arrive at our local railway station one evening and found our cars parked so closely together that I had to hold my door closed to enable her to open hers. This time I thought she was bound to say something – if only 'thank you', as one would to any stranger who did the same. But no. It was a hatred of me, I decided. I wondered whether I had written something rude about her in the past but had no memory of it, and the piece about her visit to Uzbekistan – including the cerebral palsy hospital (which she might have found rude) – had not been published. Maybe she was still smarting from what I have just discovered my father had written about her in the *Sunday Express* in November 1978 . . .

It must have been tough for Princess Anne to find herself publicly pilloried because she failed to show warmth to a small boy in hospital who was demanding to be cuddled and to have, as a result, angry Norwegians demanding that she go back to Britain.

I saw the incident on TV and I do not believe for one minute that the Princess acted with deliberate coldness. All she showed was her natural shyness and reserve.

Even so, and to prevent international incidents in future, might it not be wise when she goes on goodwill tours abroad if instead of visiting sick children in hospitals she contents herself with administering sugar lumps in stables?

No one is ever likely then to mistake the look of genuine love and compassion in her eyes.

Baroness Chalker, the former Tory minister, has known Anne for years and is very fond of her. She admits she can be tricky but is impressed by how effective she is.

We share a number of charities together and she is clearly far more on the ball than I realized. I was at a function the other night and her husband Tim Lawrence was there. I've known Tim since before he started courting her and he came over to see me and he asked about one of our charities and I said, 'Bit of sticky weather at the moment', and he said, 'Yes, I think you and my wife are of the same opinion.' I said, 'What could that be, Tim?' And what he came out with was a hundred per cent right. I hadn't told her; how she's picked it up I don't know but she's picked up the thing I'm having a battle about. It's nothing drastic; it's a management thing, which is why it's all the more interesting that she knows what's going on. She has her finger much more closely on the pulse of her NGOs than others have and that's partly because she will not employ somebody to do it. She sees me as president and chairman of the board herself, and she sees the chief executive every few months.

Prince Charles leaves his private secretaries to keep in touch with the chairmen and chief executives of his charities – except for the few key ones. He has five private secretaries in all: Michael Peat; his deputy, Elizabeth Buchanan; and three assistants, Paul Kefford, James Kidner and Mark Leishman, and they each have responsibility for different aspects of the Prince's life. Princess Anne has one Private Secretary, a jolly ex-naval officer called Nick Wright who, on the day I met him, wore a tie with elephants on it and paperclip cuff links. I mentioned Starbucks and he said he'd never been into one. 'What are people doing in there?' he said. 'Why aren't they at their desks?' 'You can see who he works for,' said Ailsa Anderson, laughing. She is the one in the Buckingham Palace Press Office who handles the Princess Royal.

The Press Office at Buckingham Palace has changed a lot since I first met Michael Shea there in 1981. Penny Russell-Smith is the Queen's Press Secretary and she has ten people plus a PA in the department, with different titles and grades and all but four of them assigned to a particular member of the family; the other four run the website or deal with ceremonial and court circular type of things. Penny Russell-Smith is rather like a kindly schoolmistress: constantly preparing for Speech Day, slightly harassed and anxious, a little earnest, always immaculately dressed and made up. She is not the promptest at answering emails, however – in common with some of her colleagues both in the Press Office and in other departments in Buckingham Palace – and entirely failed to show up at one of our first meetings. She was due to be my guest for lunch in a restaurant; after waiting for forty minutes I rang to discover from her colleague that a meeting had overrun. She wouldn't be coming. If I hadn't rung I might still be waiting there now – she never rang, never apologized, never mentioned it. But she has been very helpful – as has her team – and there is no longer the feeling that their sole job is to keep the press at bay. The regular royal photographers and cameramen all love the girls in the office – who currently seem to be in the middle of a baby epidemic but they are good fun and totally unaffected and matter of fact about the people they work for. They share a smart hat that lives in the office for formal engagements and go out of their way to get the press the shots they want.

Robin Janvrin (also bad at responding to emails), to whom they all ultimately report, is well aware that the monarchy stands or falls on its media coverage. The day the phones are silent and no emails arrive – the day when no one wants to read about the Queen or look at pictures of the Royal Family – is the day the monarchy dies. As one of the Prince of Wales's former private secretaries says, 'I think even adultery may be a better thing than boredom.'

Mark Bolland's brief as Deputy Private Secretary to the Prince of Wales was to make his relationship with Mrs Parker Bowles acceptable to the British public. Sir Michael Peat's has been to get adultery off the front page and promote the Prince's work which had been largely obscured by the media frenzy over his private life. Peat felt that the Bolland approach – pandering to people's craving for celebrity news – was dangerous, an effective way of boosting the Prince's image in the short term but not wise in the long term, which is what the Royal Family is here for, because celebrities have a limited shelf life. He doesn't deny that people are much more interested in sex and money than good works, and accepts that a certain amount of the Prince's private life – and that of his sons – will filter out, but feels it has to go hand in hand with some knowledge about what they do in the course of their jobs.

'We were having Beckham without the football,' says a former colleague.

I think Michael was also dubious about Bolland's methods, of spinning and trading stories with favoured newspapers, which, although effective, did not earn the institution respect – and caused huge divisions between St James's Palace and Buckingham Palace, which was extremely damaging. It worked in the short term but in the longer term it was helping to undermine people's respect for the institution; it put the Prince of Wales and Mrs Parker Bowles into the celebrity category and it damaged people's view of the honesty of the institution. The prime ingredient of any leader is trust, and the Queen and the Prince of Wales are in leadership roles. People must be able to trust them, and if they employ people who go about using techniques that don't display trust then you're in trouble because it's very corrosive.

Michael Peat has worked with Robin Janvrin for more than fifteen years and if anyone can heal the rift between the two Palaces and repair some of the damage that has been done, not just during Bolland's years at St James's Palace, but ever since the Prince set up his own show, then it will be him. He came to the job with an overall view of monarchy. His predecessors were concerned – as most private secretaries are – with their principal, their boss. And that is the weakness of the current system. Robin Janvrin, or even Lord Luce, the Lord Chamberlain, has no jurisdiction over the Prince of Wales, and Penny Russell-Smith no influence in Clarence House. They are two separate organizations both theoretically working for a common cause – The Firm – but not always giving out vibrations of unity. Even within Buckingham Palace there are a series of separate fiefdoms, each member of the family having their own household and their own private office. Although there are regular meetings between private secretaries and regular communication within the Press Office, outsiders who have to deal with more than one member of the family find it intensely frustrating. 'It's interesting how compartmentalized the household is,' says one chief executive. 'If I tell a Private Secretary something there's no guarantee it will reach the others. I have to tell each one. They do seem to look after their own person. If I want to be certain I will tell them both. What they need is a decent director of communications at the Palace – they need Alastair Campbell over there. The problem is no one has set up an office to look after the Royal Family; every office is private.'

FORTY-ONE

In the Genes

One evening last summer I had a call from Paddy Harverson, the Prince of Wales's new Communications Secretary. He was in Gloucestershire. Knowing I lived nearby, he asked me to join him in the Hare and Hounds at Westonbirt for a drink at about 9.00 p.m. I had rung him earlier to say I was writing a piece about Prince William: could he help me with some background information? We had met a couple of times. On one occasion we had had lunch – and he was there bang on time. Every time I had emailed him or phoned him since he had come back to me within hours if not minutes. It gives a very good impression of the man he is working for. (Mark, dearly love him though I do, was completely hopeless in that respect.) 'I hope Prince William is going to join us in the pub,' said Harverson that night. The Hare and Hounds is less than a mile from Highgrove. When I arrived, the saloon bar was filled with journalists and photographers – about fifteen in all – some familiar to me, some not. They had all come down to Gloucestershire in preparation for the following morning's informal photocall – the latest series in the St Andrews Agreement – when Prince William was going to perform in front of the cameras and answer a few questions about life at university. As a change, he had decided to do it on the Home Farm

379

at Highgrove. Paddy was also there, dressed in jeans and a jumper, as was his deputy, Patrick Harrison. Both men looked distinctly off-duty. And as I talked to my media colleagues I realized that none of them knew who was about to walk through the door. Paddy had simply invited them to join him for a drink in a friendly kind of way.

At about 9.25 the door opened and in walked William with Mark Dyer, the ex-Welsh Guards officer who travelled with him on his gap year. He was wearing jeans and a sweatshirt and, but for the familiar face, could have been any tall, slim, tousle-headed twenty-one-year-old walking into the pub. Paddy immediately sprang up to greet him and introduced him to the people standing round, even the most hardened of whom were looking flushed – and I don't think it was the beer. Having shaken each and every hand and looked us all in the eye as he did so, the second in line to the throne of England said he would like a pint of cider and sat down on a bench with his back against the wall. Those who could find chairs sat in a circle around him; others stood and for nearly an hour, while he drank his pint and we drank ours, we all chatted. Seldom have I seen such a self-possessed, confident yet self-deprecating, skilful, thoughtful and charming young man – nor such a group of seasoned hacks (myself included) leaning forward so intently to catch and savour every word. Questions he didn't want to answer he simply bounced back or laughed knowingly at, as if to say he wasn't going to fall into that trap, but it was done with such charm that there was no offence. He asked the *News of the World* journalist whether he came here often, did he know the area? 'Oh, yes,' he said, 'I've been here quite a lot but I can't say I've ever been invited.'

The photocall had been arranged on the farm quite simply because William was down from university for the summer holidays and the Prince's staff who organized it thought it might provide some interesting shots – feeding pigs, driving a tractor, that sort of thing. Little did they know when they set it up six weeks earlier that that very week one of the tabloids would announce that, according to 'senior courtiers', William was planning to turn his back on the Army after university to pursue a career in farming. Suddenly an innocuously pastoral photocall looked like a major statement about the future intentions of the future king of England.

But as William made clear that night, and again in an interview he gave to the BBC and Press Association in November 2004, the first term of his final year at St Andrews, he is not planning a career in farming, any more than he is planning a future at the Lewa Game Reserve in Kenya, where he spent another part of his gap year. Nor is he planning to go into the City to work for Coutts, the royal bankers. All of which had been authoritatively put forward as plans for the future by unnamed sources.

Another common assumption frequently put forward by the media is that Prince William is a reluctant royal. If he is, all I can say is he is a remarkable actor. The impression I came away with that night was that he may not enjoy the attention and the lack of privacy that goes with the role, but that he has *Ich Dien* (I serve) stamped on his forehead just as indelibly as his father had before him – a product, I suspect, of nature as much as nurture. A senior courtier at Clarence House agrees. 'I think it's the hereditary system. You get bred for the job and you do what you've got to do. If you apply for a job, you can turn it down; if you don't apply for it it's a lot more difficult to hand it over or retire, because it's not really a job: it's a vocation, a duty, you're called to do it and that's the strength of it. William knows that, it's his duty to do it and he will do it very well.'

William certainly does seem to have an indefinable quality

– a presence – that sets him apart. He kids around but deep down has maturity beyond his years – not surprising given his childhood experiences – and a beguiling mixture of confidence and humility that suggests he has never once questioned the certainty of the job that awaits and the significance of the family motto. Because, although the Princess of Wales introduced him to baseball caps, hamburgers and big dippers, and taught him how to have fun – and thank God she did – she also made absolutely certain that William understood what lay ahead and the importance and seriousness of his position. Since her death he has been particularly close to his grandparents, the Queen and the Duke of Edinburgh. Speaking about the relationships in his December interview William said of the Queen, 'She's been brilliant. She's a real role model. She's just very helpful on any sort of difficulties or problems I might be having', adding, 'but I'm quite a private person as well so I don't really talk that much about what I sort of feel or think.' As for the Duke of Edinburgh, he admired his bluntness. 'I'm very close to my grandfather. He makes me laugh. He's very funny. He's also someone who will tell me something that maybe I don't want to hear and he won't care if I get upset about it. He knows it's the right thing to say and I'm glad he tells me that because the last thing I want is lots of people telling me what I want to hear.'

He is a most enchanting young man, with very definite star quality, who could easily become an icon just as his mother did. The difficulty for her, though, was that stardom was thrust upon her at the age of nineteen, having had a life before that of virtual anonymity. William was born to it. As he says, 'Being in the centre of the spotlight is kind of awkward but it's something I've got to do and something I can adapt to. I've spent twenty-two years being in the spotlight. You don't really know much different but I value the normality I can get, doing simple things, doing normal things, more than anything, rather than getting things done for me which I'm not a big fan of.' He seems to have inherited the best attributes of both of his parents and none of the worst. He has his mother's gift for talking to people and putting them at their ease – something his great-grandmother also had – and his mother's relaxed, easy style; also her sense of humour. He has her steely determination too, but, as far as one can see, none of her insecurity. He has his father's charm and sensitivity and his way of looking people in the eye while he speaks to them, with, it seems, none of Charles's tendency to whinge and feel sorry for himself. He also has his father's love of the countryside and interest in people as well as wildlife. But he seems to be less grand than his father, having inherited more from his grandparents, perhaps, and less spoilt.

When the Duke of Edinburgh goes to an Award conference in Barbados he takes a police protection officer – because he's not allowed to go further than the lavatory without a police protection officer. When the Prince of Wales went to Chatsworth one weekend in the days when the Duke of Devonshire was still alive, as well as his police protection officer he took two valets, one helicopter and enough luggage to fill a medium-sized living room. He was staying for two days – and Chatsworth is one of the last remaining grand houses in England to have enough valets for twenty guests. He needed to take nothing.

The Prince enjoys his luxuries and lives far more grandly than his siblings or his mother ever has. The Queen is comparatively modest. 'There wasn't a clear distinction between the Queen's personal staff and the staff of Buckingham Palace who are there to receive diplomats or to serve at state banquets or assist at garden parties,' says a former Private Secretary to the Queen.

My impression is if you made that separation, the number of staff there to look after the Queen and Duke personally is quite tiny, and that a large part of the manpower is to do with official activities. But the same group of people is used for both and therefore looks quite large.

Is there an argument for separating the two? There may be, but then you would lose the economies of scale. You'd have people who had a bit of spare time on their hands. The Queen's dresser, for example; a lot of her work is getting the Queen's clothes ready for official occasions. The staff she needs for a country weekend in Windsor or Sandringham is pretty tiny but once you do have personal staff you have to have people to replace them when they have weekends off and that sort of thing, so inevitably you have to have a certain number around. All the Queen has is someone to be there if needed, not to do absolutely everything for her. At Christmas, when she and Duke are at Sandringham, they stay in Wood Farm, which is really quite a modest farmhouse, which has a bit built on for the security staff to stay in – the inevitable appendage, which I am quite sure they would rather not have to have – but the actual living area is very modest, and there is certainly not a maid living in the room next door waiting on them hand and foot. There will be somebody within call but not someone there to be summoned every moment of the day.

The Prince of Wales is much more like his grandmother in this respect: she also lived in style – and at vast expense. There is no reason why the Prince shouldn't – he can afford it. As Prince of Wales he has income from the Duchy of Cornwall of £11.9 million, which amply funds both his official and his private life. He has no money from the Civil List and, since Peat's reforms of 1993, pays tax at 40 per cent on all his income, just like anybody else. But a lifestyle that involves valets, chefs, house managers and housekeepers, butlers, chauffeurs, secretaries, high performance cars, a string of horses and three large houses – Highgrove, Clarence House (refurbished at a cost of £4.5 million) and Birkhall – doesn't sit entirely comfortably alongside a man who spends so much of his life worrying about the environment, inner-city deprivation, poverty and giving a leg-up to those at the bottom of the pile.

Lynda Chalker doesn't entirely agree.

In his thinking he's so advanced but in his lifestyle he's from a different age. When we've been flying places he's said, 'I'm bored with my own company, come and sit and talk to me', and I've sat whilst he's had dinner, and he's eaten the food he has brought with him from Highgrove – goodness knows how many thousands of feet above sea level and across two continents. I said to him once, 'You know, British Airways food isn't all that bad', and he said 'It might upset me'. It's being a system apart. Okay if you've got to have separate food for safety reasons, but actually not to be seen to eat what other people eat it gives entirely the wrong impression. I think it was coping with circumstances like that that Diana found totally and utterly impossible.

And, yes, Prince Philip is frugal but there are a huge number of jobs in the household. Who keeps that going? It's down to the Comptroller of the Household and to Janvrin and Luce. But the Queen is now seventy-eight; it's very hard for her to change her ways, but one ought to be able to give her the same service without this unbelievable number of people. Okay, she pays for it so you could argue she has every right to have it that way. Highgrove is much smaller, it's very simple by comparison, probably two house staff certainly in the public rooms, couple of extra maids, most people are on the farm, but even so, preparing Charles's food . . . he's very precise and it has an element of the four moves of the marmalade [A. A. Milne again] about it.

I just wish that the Royal Family, excellent as they are, could be a little more like the rest of us.

Thanks to his relatively normal education, Prince William's world is much closer to the one the rest of us inhabit. Eton may be privileged – although no more privileged than most public schools – but life at St Andrews was more or less the same for him as for any other student. He lived his first year in a hall of residence, where there were people to cook and clean, as at school, but he has been sharing flats and houses ever since, and queuing for his shopping, his fish supper and his pint in the pub along with everyone else. Washing up, he admits, was a major sticking point in the house he was sharing in his last year (with three others) until they found a solution.

Thankfully we've just got a dishwasher but before it was a complete disaster. There would be piles and piles left in the sink and one of us would come back in and immediately walk out when they saw it. It would just get bigger and bigger. It would never get done. The amount of arguments about washing up and cleaning or whatever . . . It still goes on but it's better now. Again it's the dynamics of living with people. When you all live together you've got to muck in and help out.

The fortunate thing is I have had such a normal childhood in certain extents [sic] and it would be very hard to see that slip away. But I always hope that, no matter what, I'll keep that side going. Keeping your feet firmly on the ground is the most important thing.

My meeting with Prince William in the pub was entirely off the record. Paddy Harverson was taking a chance. He hoped that if the royal writers could sit down with Prince William, chat over a pint, look him in the eye and see him as the likeable, vulnerable human being that he is, they would feel less inclined when things went wrong to kick him in the teeth in print. It had worked with Man United stars, but it was a brave departure from anything that has ever been done before with the royals, and only time will tell how successful it was. Only one paper used the story – despite being told not to – and the reporter apologized at once; luckily no harm was done and William was happy to meet journalists a second time before the interview and photo sessions in November.

Lord Salisbury, who, as Viscount Cranborne, was a minister in John Major's government, believes that dialogue with the media can be hugely beneficial. Just over ten years ago the then Prime Minister asked him to organize the 50th anniversary of the end of the Second World War.

I just spent an awful lot of time talking to people, thinking and taking advice, seeing what the veterans themselves wanted, what the monarch wanted, talking to the reptiles [the press] and saying, 'You can make a complete fool of me, it's not very difficult, but I'll do a deal with you. I'll tell you everything, but I will expect you to support me in return; not for my sake, but we've got to make a good show of it for the veterans and if you've got any suggestions they're very welcome.' And we got along fine and when things went wrong, they covered it up for me. And I think in a sort of way that's the relationship the monarchy needs to develop with the public as a whole, so that they have a feel for trends and the way people are thinking.

Of course you have to include the press. They are the villains of the piece; they are the people who are causing the trouble. You're not going to get anywhere by saying how ghastly they are and keeping them out. The only hope you've got is gradually, gradually, to see whether you can't make them part of the conspiracy.

Who is my friend at the *Sun*? Trevor Kavanagh, the political editor. He and I have lunch together, have done for years, and because we're quite good friends, he's kind enough to waste his time with me, and we still keep talking. He works for Rupert Murdoch, which is very helpful to me because Rupert and I agree about Europe, and he was very helpful over the 'No campaign'. What matters is not the fact that his boss is anti-monarchist, but the fact that you have a personal relationship with a key person, and I have always found it extraordinary how much sympathy springs up, even though you disagree. You're not going to change Rupert's views about the monarchy but you're going to make it much more difficult for the people who are his servants to be gratuitously rude about people who have become their friend.

If members of the Royal Family don't meet journalists face to face and nurture friendships then they are all the more dependent upon the quality of the people who work for them. Guy Black believes direct contact is not the way to go. 'Part of the magic of the Royal Family,' he says, 'is the mystery, and if you cease to have that mystery, what makes them special? On their own they're not particularly remarkable people; one's a pensioner, one's a dotty middle-aged man, one's a quite nice lad who's at university and goes shopping at Tesco, and we see pictures of him with his shopping bag. What makes them remarkable if they're not mysterious? You destroy the mystery if they have a direct relationship with the media.'

But doesn't the Tesco carrier bag detract from the mystery?

I don't think they've yet got to grips with problem of William wanting to appear like any other human being. I was part of that in a way; there was a clear view that he had to lead a normal life at university which meant doing what everyone else does and that photo was part of the price to pay for giving him a normal life. From his point of view it was the right decision to take. But it has the danger of persuading the public that there's nothing special about him, and if you go too far down that route – that he's just one of us – then you get into all sorts of difficulties. But I don't think we're there yet. People know he's different; but if he went out and got a nine to five job in the City and wandered around with sandwiches at lunchtime that would soon begin seriously to erode the mystery.

Prince William hasn't yet decided what he is going to do when he leaves St Andrews. The City is not a likely contender. He has been reading Geography and has neither the qualifications nor the interest. The Army seems the most likely place, which he spoke about that night in the pub and again during his television interview. He has been mulling over a few ideas with his father and various friends and relations, but it is clear that whatever he does do with the next stage of his life, it will be largely his decision and not a plan devised by a council of wise men. Times have changed since the Queen called for advice on what the Prince of Wales should do with his life; and the dynamics were different. Charles was heir to the throne; William is second in line so he has more leeway. But his decision is likely to give an indication of what path the monarchy is likely to take in the future – whether it will go down the route of becoming ordinary or whether they will try to keep some of the mystery.

Says Guy Black:

The Army retains the mystery and it is an established pattern of royal life, but it won't play into the hands of the people who think they must make him popular and ordinary, and it's not an institution which will necessarily endear him to his peer group and he's anxious to be liked by people of his age. Anyone below the age of forty wouldn't begin to understand why he'd be going into the Army and he's very sensitive to that, and his advisers will be sensitive to that. But if he's allowed to do something he wants to do he risks getting into Prince Edward territory and maybe doing something he's not terribly good at. With Edward it didn't matter at the end of the day, but when was the last time a Prince of Wales or heir to the throne went out and did something ordinary? If he goes down the path of the ordinary it will be the first time and they cannot be clear about the consequences; they may be letting a genie out of the bottle that would be very difficult to put back in.

The way William spoke about the Army seemed to suggest that a mixture of nature and nurture had moulded his decision – with some youthful idealism – and an awareness of how he might be able to use his position to do something useful. The Armed Forces nominally fight in the sovereign's name – at that moment they were putting their lives at risk while the government was disbanding age-old squadrons. Prince William made it clear he knew that by joining their ranks he could demonstrate to those men and women how much their service and sacrifice was appreciated.

On 11 November 2004 he joined the rest of the Royal Family for the annual Remembrance Sunday service at the Cenotaph in Whitehall. He particularly wanted to be there, believing that, by his presence, he could speak for young people.

> I just thought what with the Iraq war and troops being abroad and particularly the Black Watch going through a very tough time – I thought it was just the right time for me probably to make an entrance and be there for the youth and make a point that the young still haven't forgotten and still very much appreciate what's been done for everyone.
>
> The Army is obviously a lot more in the spotlight at the moment . . . The Remembrance service really does bring it home when you're there and there's actually a war going on somewhere at the time and the guys are fighting their hearts out.

The difficulty he will face in the Army is whether he would be allowed to fight, something he has agonized over.

> The last thing I want to do is be mollycoddled or wrapped up in cotton wool, because if I was to join the Army I'd want to go where my men went and I'd want to do what they did. I would not want to be kept back for being precious or whatever, that's the last thing I'd want. It's the most humiliating thing and it would be something I'd find very awkward to live with, being told I couldn't go out there when these guys have got to go out there and do a bad job.

Remembrance Sunday, when the sovereign leads the nation in paying tribute to Britain's war dead and those of the Commonwealth who fell fighting for King or Queen and country, is one of the most important dates in the royal calendar. Up until 1956 it was held on the eleventh hour of the eleventh day of the eleventh month, to coincide with the end of the First World War on 11 November 1918, but it was moved, for greater convenience, to the second Sunday in November. More than a million men and women from the United Kingdom and the Commonwealth died in the First World War and nearly half a million in the Second, and they are remembered – along with the many thousands more who have died in lesser conflicts since 1914 – by a two-minute silence. Since the end of the Second World War there has been a seamless sacrifice of young lives – only one year has passed when not a single British serviceman has been killed on active service. The toll of those lost in Iraq up to the Remembrance service that November was twenty-one.

Prince William said how proud he had felt to be British as he watched the ceremony which never fails to be profoundly moving. Whitehall is filled each year with detachments from the Royal Navy, the Royal Marines, the Army, the Territorial Army, the Royal Air Force, the Royal Auxiliary Air Force, the Royal Fleet Auxiliary, the Merchant Navy and Fishing Fleets, the Coastguard, the Merchant Air Services, the Civilian Services and thousands of veterans, some in wheelchairs, polished medals proudly pinned to their chests. Just before 11.00 the Queen, dressed in black, and senior members of the Royal Family, dressed in military uniform, emerge from the old Home Office building and stand to attention facing the Cenotaph. Other members of the Royal Family traditionally stand and watch from the Home Office balcony – as William did last year. At the first stroke of Big Ben at 11.00 a.m. a single round is fired from a gun of the King's Troop, Royal Horse Artillery, in Horse Guards Parade. And the silence that follows is not solely an act of remembrance; it is also a moment of dedication when all those who still live undertake to be worthy of those who died. And with the leaders of the different political parties standing side by side, and the leaders of the country's many denominations and faiths standing side by side, along with men, women and children of every colour, creed, class, community and country, it is an affirmation of unusual national unity.

Two minutes later a second round of gunfire breaks the silence and the Last Post is sounded by buglers of the Royal Marines. The Queen then steps forward to lay the first wreath of poppies at the foot of the Cenotaph, followed by members of the Royal Family, the Prime Minister and leaders of all the political parties and other organizations present. One wreath alone is different. The Foreign Secretary's wreath is made up of flowers from the UK Overseas Territories and he lays it on their behalf. A short religious service follows – mirrored in churches all over the country and the Commonwealth – led by the Bishop of London, with the same hymns every year, 'Oh God, Our Help in Ages Past' sung by the Gentlemen and Children of the Chapel Royal, wearing their scarlet and gold coats. Then it's reveille sounded by the trumpeters of the Royal Air Force, the National Anthem and possibly the most moving sight of all, thousands of veterans slowly marching past the Cenotaph – led last November by the Normandy veterans and, close on their heels, members of the Black Watch Association, wearing desert camouflage armbands in recognition of their boys serving at that point in the most dangerous area of Iraq.

A senior civil servant at the Home Office, now retired, used to be part of the royal reception committee on Remembrance Sunday and had the same conversation with the Queen Mother every year as he escorted her up the stairs to the balcony. She had seen the high commissioners forming and used to ask who was the one wearing the carpet – 'It was rather naughty but she wanted to see my reaction. There was a woman in the Home Office who was ready to escort them to the loo in case they wanted it; they never did. While the Queen Mother was talking to me she would find a way of looking and acknowledging this woman's curtsey. There must be thousands of people who can give you reminiscence of a little encounter like this and they remember it.'

In addition to the Cenotaph service, the Queen Mother used to visit the Garden of Remembrance outside Westminster Abbey every year, where ex-servicemen laid more poppies. 'It was always a cold November day,' recalls Michael Mayne, the former Dean of Westminster,

> ... and we were always told she would be there for half an hour and she would never stay less than an hour, sometimes longer. She used to end up in St Margaret's to sign the visitors' book, and when she got there she sometimes could hardly hold a pen her hands were so cold. In the Garden of Remembrance she had wanted to speak to every single person she could. You saw the effect and it was quite remarkable. Like all of us she had her failings, but she had that extraordinary quality, that charisma, which you saw reflected in people's faces.

That is the star quality the monarchy needs. As a Privy Councillor and member of the House of Lords points out, the Royal Family is not the only one that lives in multiple houses with servants and security.

> Squillionaires live at least as unreal a life. If the Royal Family had connected in other ways I don't think people would mind so much. The Queen of Denmark is good fun, smokes like a chimney, she's totally natural, highly intelligent, a

good egg, strong views, but everybody likes her and would never let on what her strong views are, no one would ever let her down. The Danes love her, she's got flair. All this Way Ahead Group seems to me to be completely hopeless. What you really need to do is ask yourself 'How am I going to produce a spark?' A very good case in point – Queen Elizabeth: we all loved her dearly but she was a tough old bag, she really was. Did people give a damn about her overdraft? One smile and she had them, and it's that one smile that they've lost. Overdraft and extravagance; she liked to drink and was very funny, quick as quick, and she made people feel a million dollars. She had star quality; just that.

Diana was a complete disaster. Johnny Spencer's family solicitor was staying the weekend with us when the engagement between Charles and Diana was announced, and I said, 'I don't know this one.' 'Well,' he said, 'you know Sarah. This one's got a quarter of the brains and twice the determination and I smell trouble.' But she had star quality. Even from the grave she is doing damage to Charles and will continue to do so. Charles hasn't got that star quality and self-indulgence is not good. You've got to say, 'If I really want the monarchy to survive and prosper, it can only do so if I'm a success and I've got to be a king.' Then you've got to deny yourself certain things to achieve that, you just can't bloody well have it every which way.

Camilla. I didn't think it was right to install your mistress in Clarence House, even in 2003. Henry VIII might have done it but our monarchy can't. Marriage is a problem, but it's one solution. I think he should have been rather Victorian about it and keep her hidden away. Okay, the paparazzi, yes, but if you're doing a good job elsewhere, people will say, 'Oh, poor chap, he needs a girl. That's his girl' and people come to accept that. What I find difficult is this in-your-face stuff, 'I want it every way and I expect to be treated as monarch' without any sense of propriety or self-sacrifice for doing so. We all behave frightfully badly, I'm sure, but he's got to keep the show on the road and he's taking risks that are not paying off. Do they have a duty to be exemplary? No. They have a duty to do an exemplary job. Nobody's perfect, and people are very understanding. If the Prince of Wales has a mistress I think the country would have been perfectly happy about that; it's just that he seemed to want to keep her as his wife while not actually being his wife and that does violence to the institution.

I'm not one of those who thinks hypocrisy is a bad thing, none of us can get by without a little bit of white lying and hypocrisy; it's how you manage it that matters. All you have is process. You can't define it, it's feel; and if he had Queen Elizabeth's touch and clear dedication without self-indulgence, and Camilla Parker Bowles had lived in even a grand house in London, but he hadn't rammed her down our throats, I think we'd all have been perfectly happy.

And there's the history, the Diana factor. The more you push Camilla the more you reinforce what people think. The more the public believes there were three in the marriage, the less sensible it is to confirm their prejudices by ramming Camilla down our throats. Maybe if he had concentrated on the job and doing it with flair and building relationships and being sensitive – as well as all the great things we admire him for – we're not asking much of the poor chap, are we? – then maybe everybody, including the paparazzi, might not have minded too much about Camilla and got used to her being in the background.

FORTY-TWO

Conclusions

'I think it is a complete misconception,' the Duke of Edinburgh once said, 'to imagine that the monarchy exists in the interests of the monarch. It doesn't. It exists in the interests of the people.'

And at the moment the polls show that between 70 and 80 per cent of the British people are very pleased that it does; furthermore, that they expect the monarchy to last at least another fifty years. Of the remainder, some couldn't care one way or another and the rest want to see the Queen and her family pack their bags and install some suitable democratically elected president in her place. Doing that would involve unravelling hundreds of years of history – the monarchy is woven into every strand of our national life. Not impossible – although deeply divisive, given that between 70 and 80 per cent of the population would be against it. But even if 100 per cent of the British public was in favour of abolishing the monarchy, there would never be unanimous agreement on a replacement. Whether selected or elected, the position would be politicized and would split the country as violently as the election of a government does. And once installed, could any figure plucked from politics, business, academia, showbiz or even football be an improvement? Could they command the

397

respect worldwide that the monarch does? Would they be as effective? Would they have the long-term interests of the country at heart or would they look no further than their own term of office or the next election to fight?

Tony Benn, the former Old Labour minister and life-long republican who renounced his hereditary peerage in 1963, believes that our entire system of government is danger-ously undemocratic and would like to dismantle everything, including the honours system: 'It takes forty-three million electors to elect 651 MPs, but took only ten Prime Ministers, from Attlee to Major, to make 840 peers – and introduce a written constitution.' In his book *Common Sense*, pub-lished in 1993, he puts forward a compelling argument that 'the mythology and magic surrounding the Crown and the Royal Family have always been used . . . to veil a whole range of undemocratic powers protected by the concept of "royal prerogatives". . .'

> Certain executive powers are always vested in the Head of State, as such powers normally derive either from the written constitution of a country or from a statute passed by Parliament.
>
> Not so the British Crown, which can in law dissolve Parliament, ask an individual to form a government, declare war, sign treaties, make ministers, create peers, appoint archbishops, bishops and judges, grant pardons or issue commissions without consulting Parliament at all. All but the first two powers are actually exercised by and with the advice of the Prime Minister, and, in theory any Prime Minister could be brought down in the Commons if the powers were grossly abused. One important prerogative is the right to go to war without consulting Parliament. The House of Commons has no legal right to be consulted. The

Falklands and Gulf wars were never put to the vote for decision.

Writing in the *Guardian* last November, Benn described his Utopia:

> Britain is gravely handicapped by this medieval system of government which gives us a president without any checks and balances, and keeps the serfs firmly in their place. Any serious democratic reform of our constitution would give an elected parliament control of all executive powers, firmly cap the fount of honour, and arrange for the election of a small senate to act as a revising chamber, whose speaker could occasionally act as head of state for ceremonial purposes.
>
> This would have the advantage of liberating the Royal Family, leaving them free, as citizens, to live their own lives, say what they like, and take part in elections like the rest of us. They could then safely vote for King Tony and his neoconservative courtiers, at No. 10, knowing that New Labour could be trusted to preserve privilege in Britain.

It is the prospect of King – or more probably President – Tony, or President Thatcher or Hattersley, that sends shudders down many a spine and makes many people who might intellectually think the monarchy has had its day opt for maintaining the *status quo*. And for many of the people who want the Windsors booted out of Buckingham Palace it is a straightforward question of class and envy. The constitution is a red herring, just as cruelty to the fox was a red herring in the hunting debate. The opulence and the privilege is what sticks in the craw, particularly when members of the Family Firm are seen to abuse it. That and the belief that we pay huge amounts of money for them to enjoy a life of luxury, while we in our humdrum lives struggle. In the year to June 2004 the Head of State cost £36.8 million – effectively paid for, not by us, but out of revenue from the Crown Estates that were surrendered in exchange for the Civil List. It amounts to 61p per person per year, or less than the price of two pints of milk. And in comparison with other institutions funded by the taxpayer, the monarchy is a positive bargain.

The difficulty is that no matter how often you do the sums, make the comparisons or even cut the cost, the impression lodged in the national psyche is that the House of Windsor is a bastion of privilege. Its incumbents are seen – even by monarchists, who admire the job they do – as people who have next to nothing in common with the majority of their fellow countrymen. Prince Andrew, an unlikely role model, is far closer to ordinary people with his passion for golf than any other member of the family. Golf is a good egalitarian sport, enjoyed by millions all over the world, and he raises a lot of money for charity while he's playing it. Hunting, shoot-ing, polo and carriage driving are not. They are sports tra-ditionally associated with the landed aristocracy and alien to great swathes of the population. Prince Edward plays real tennis, which he took up at Cambridge, a great game but not a populist one; there are only a handful of courts in the land. As John Major says, 'The most important thing for the mon-archy is that they aren't seen to be curious creatures drafted in from Planet Windsor that have nothing in common with and no relevance to the way most people live their lives.'

'One of the most difficult things is the fact that for historical and all sorts of reasons, the monarchy has been identified, and still is, with the aristocracy and the equivalent, the upper classes now,' says a senior Anglican.

I think it was a great pity that people like Charles and William hunted because there was a huge popular desire that that should be ended and it wasn't whether it was right or wrong, it was that they were identified immediately with a continuation of large houses, lots of servants, mixing with certain sorts of people. I know that day by day they meet all kinds of people but for choice, when they are on their own, inevitably they meet with their friends who are of a certain kind, as are the courtiers and the officers of state. That somehow has got to change. Charles had a fairly normal education, and William has had Eton but also St Andrews which should have enabled him to make lots of friends of a more general type. This constant kind of identity with just that particular class is not going to work any longer because Britain has changed. The trouble is you can't overnight de-friend your friends and make changes. So maybe it will be William. They are aware of the need to make changes, I know, but I don't know how aware of that side of it they are. I would expect most Palace officials are quite far on the right politically and that inevitably has an impact on how you view things. £4.5 million spent on Clarence House improvements? I don't think anyone is telling him. It's a pretty ritzy life even for the Queen; but how do you do this other than by bringing in trustworthy, radical new thinkers? And who do you trust? That's the difficult thing about the monarchy.

The Queen is in her late seventies and she is a product of her generation. She has a number of close friends who have been friends for years and are people she met either when she was growing up or who are related in some way or who she has got to know through horseracing. They are aristocratic, titled, and moneyed – some are ladies-in-waiting, and their young teenage sons serve as pages of honour, carrying the Queen's train on ceremonial occasions. Having been educated by governesses and never having had the opportunity to meet people outside her social circle, it is hardly surprising.

Prince Charles, however, went to boarding schools and university and was in the Navy; in theory he could have acquired a wider circle of friends but he didn't. His closest friends tend to share his love of country sports and see life from a privileged perspective. There's no reason why the Prince shouldn't mix with the people he enjoys being with but there is a danger that too many with both double-barrelled names and shotguns give him a limited view of life and a false sense of security. Past advisers have found they were in competition with his friends; his private secretaries would advise one course of action, friends would talk him out of it, either telling him what he wanted to hear or pushing their own agendas. His decision to carry on hunting, for example, and to let his sons continue to hunt during the run-up to the controversial Bill last autumn, was a massive coup for the pro-hunting lobby but in PR terms a mistake. It placed him fairly and squarely in one camp and reinforced the impression of a Prince who lives in a different world from the majority of his future subjects. The facts about hunting were irrelevant; it had become a Them and Us situation, and by siding with Them he alienated Us.

The hope is that Prince William, whose exposure to real life has been far greater and, with luck, will continue for longer than his father's did, will make his friends from a wider constituency and not fall back on the rich, privileged and rather unimaginative hunting and polo-playing Gloucestershire set of his youth. It will be on his style that the long-term future of the monarchy will rest, and the way he lives and behaves and the people with whom he surrounds himself which will be all important.

When the HIV/AIDS epidemic hit London in the eighties, Michael Mayne, then Dean of Westminster Abbey, did a great deal of fundraising for the AIDS charities. In addition, three or four times a year he invited up to sixty people, many of whom had full-blown AIDS, to a buffet supper in a room adjoining the Abbey. Afterwards they would sit down informally and say a few words about themselves before going on a night tour of the Abbey, ending up with a prayer and a blessing in one of the little chapels. The year before she died, he wrote to Diana, Princess of Wales, and invited her to join them. She said she would love to but asked for it to be kept quiet. She arrived half an hour after everyone else when they were in the midst of supper. 'I met her in the Deanery,' he remembers, 'and took her through.'

They had no idea she was coming and I shall never forget their faces when they saw her, nor will I forget the way she was with them. She knew – she had a marvellous intuition – exactly what to say, who to hug, whose hand to hold, who to sit with, she was quite remarkable, then we had the circle, then she came with us on the tour and the prayers; and they were on a high when they left that night. It was a remarkable gift to be able to do this. I know she did some very silly things but she was in an impossible position, and I didn't like some of the effects of what happened after her death, I felt it was a bit odd, unhealthy, but one could understand it. Here was someone from the monarchy who was relating to people in a new way, and in doing that she had transformed people's expectations of the monarchy but she also made it much more difficult for the monarchy to fulfil them.

I think with care, and if the media don't destroy him, William could combine the best of both approaches. He is

403

likely to be impatient with some of the court ritual – for example how you behave in the royal presence. Those who go and see the Queen are instructed to walk six paces in and bow; and on leaving to walk back for six paces and bow again. There are other ways of showing respect for a person – by how you treat them. So that will go I imagine, but he will respect the tradition and bring a real humanity to his relating to people in a different age and in a different culture.

The Queen's style of monarchy has been hugely successful, largely because of her personality, her total dedication, but also because she saw the need to modernize and to allow the institution to evolve. It will go further with the Prince of Wales; his style will be and should be markedly different – for a younger generation, a changed society. The difference will begin with his coronation, whenever it happens. There will be plenty of trumpets, a lot of gold, a lot of music, the coronation chair and crowds in the streets, but there will be Church and Faith leaders from every major tradition. The Queen is Supreme Governor of the Church of England, which automatically falls to the sovereign; but Charles expressed a desire many years ago to become Defender of Faith and unofficially a group has been discussing a coronation which could encompass both the new and the old. Part of it is certain to be in Westminster Abbey because of the history – coronations have been held there for the last nine hundred years and that is where the religious part of the ceremony would be held – but it is more than likely that afterwards there would be a multi-faith gathering in St Edward's Hall in Parliament.

There is no doubt that to have a Head of State in the twenty-first century who is selected by an accident of birth is anachronistic and entirely out of keeping with modern society, but we are not alone. There are no fewer than seven hereditary monarchies in Europe – Norway, Sweden, Denmark, Spain, Belgium, Luxembourg and the Netherlands – all, with the possible exception of Denmark, much younger than our own, all more pared down, none with the Commonwealth or the history of Britain's; but those with proportional representation, like Sweden – the bicycling monarchy – with more power. 'It is noticeable that the countries in Europe in which monarchy has survived are amongst the most stable and the most prosperous in the world,' says Vernon Bogdanor in his book *The Monarchy and the Constitution*. 'One cannot, of course, draw the conclusion that they are stable *because* they are monarchies. It is, rather, more likely that certain countries have retained their monarchies because, enjoying a stable and continuous evolution towards parliamentary democracy, they found no need to alter the form of the state.'

Before the First World War monarchy was the predominant form of government in Europe. After it, 'the world witnessed the disappearance of five Emperors, eight Kings and eighteen more dynasties'. But this had more to do with military defeats and revolutionary upheavals than the spread of republican doctrines. 'Republics do not generally come about through adherence to republican doctrines,' says Bogdanor.

> Republicanism in practice is adopted less because it seems an ideal system than because it is all that is left after monarchy has been rendered unsustainable . . . A constitutional monarchy settles beyond argument the crucial question of who is to be the head of state, and it places the position of head of state beyond political competition.

The Queen from early days hasn't a party history; she has been trained to be neutral and in that way can represent the country to itself. That is in some ways more important now than it was because the prestige of politicians has fallen because somehow we've become more partisan as a country. That began with Margaret Thatcher who tended to take the view that there was no such thing as a non-political person; you were either for her or against her, and the idea of the great and the good above the battle has gone, the classical mandarins have disappeared. The Queen is a fixed point in a changing world and a world in which people are more sceptical of party politicians.

And I think it's for that reason that the Australian referendum showed a majority for the monarchy. It wasn't so much that people wanted a non-resident head of state as much as that people didn't like the alternative and that was a professional politician. I think John Major once said, 'If the answer's more politicians, you're asking the wrong question.' There's a lot of truth in that.

Lord Hurd, the former Foreign Secretary, agrees.

The country needs someone to represent it, and in terms of government there's an election process that produces somebody, but that's all very controversial, bound to be, should be; the subject of endless arguments and endless change. And there's a great deal to be said for somebody who's outside that, who's not subject to those changes, that rides above them, and that is the case for the monarchy in a world of nation states. You then run the risk of heredity unless you do like the Arabs and gather together in a little cluster and choose one of you; but we don't do that, so you run the risk. On the whole I think that's better than the alternatives which are either to have a hugely controversial figure, changing all the time, subject to endless political criticism and debate, or some nonentity who is elected precisely because he or she is nobody. One thing I think is important; an old country does need a link with its past. After decades of the tabloids yammering away, the misfortunes and huge mistakes, you get events like the Queen Mother dying, or the Golden Jubilee and 80 per cent of the people see the point again; they go out in the streets, they walk round the catafalque and if you ask why, the point about the link with the past comes out, the link with their parents and grandparents; going through what they went through. One of the advantages of being an old country is you have that strength and it is a great strength and the monarchy embodies that more effectively than anything else.

John Major, who was born with no privileges and lived in a slum in Brixton for the best part of his childhood, believes the justification for the hereditary system is that it works and we'd be poorer without it.

If you look at the hereditary system in the twenty-first century purely on intellectual merits you'd find it hard to make a case for it, but if you ask 'Does this work and is it of value to the country and would we be the poorer without it?' the answer in every way is 'Yes' – and it does add value to our country. The chattering circles of Whitehall and Westminster, who question its value, don't represent the vast majority of the British people and if you ask those questions around the country you'd come back with a resounding answer in favour of the monarchy. The justification is a) that it works, b) that it contributes to the country, and c) that it is a unique selling point for Britain in the eyes of the rest of the world.

'Almost everyone who has strong views about the monarchy has them for the wrong reasons,' says Lord Garel-Jones.

407

The traditional people on the Right like it for all the ceremony and toffery that goes on; the traditional Left hate it because they think it's a symbol of privilege and all that sort of nonsense. We just all have to get it into our heads that the monarch is Head of State, and in this country she acts on advice, therefore within certain sensible limits will do what the government and Prime Minister advise her to do. Our Head of State is known all over the world; no one knows who the president of the Federal Republic of Germany is – the largest country in the European Union, the richest country, and no one knows his name.

Robert Davies, CEO of International Business Leaders' Forum, encounters every kind of system and says that very few of them have the dignity and sense of continuity that some of the monarchies have. Politicians rarely take a long-term view or commit themselves to prolonged support; and they come and go. He can't think of anyone who has been in the same position for the last twenty years. The Prince of Wales has; he brings a sense of history – he knows where he has come from and where he is going and has the stamina for the long run. He's not just in it for an election campaign or to publicize a movie; and he's not an egomaniac. 'He's not an egomaniac at all; zero, compared with most politicians and many other leaders, yet at the same time he has got unshakeable views on the continuity of life.'

Vernon Bogdanor believes that the position of the monarchy today has to be considered in the light of the very strong anti-political mood that is spreading in Britain and other democracies. Only 58 per cent of the population voted in the last general election and politicians no longer command the respect they once did. Prime Ministers like Churchill and Attlee were regarded as leaders of the nation and there was tremendous deference towards them. That has gone and the monarch's role, therefore, as someone who can speak for the country as a whole, rather than one small section of it, has become more significant. On key occasions it is important to have someone well known who can represent the whole of the nation to itself – as the Queen did on the anniversary of VE Day when she appeared on the balcony of Buckingham Palace. A politician could never have done that; neither could a retired politician acting as president. That's what happened in Germany and Italy and most people have great difficulty in remembering their names. They don't have the same resonance with the public as the sovereign.

Elizabeth II has been a very remarkable sovereign. She has not put a foot wrong in more than fifty years and, while she may not be the most exciting of figures or the most inspirational of speakers, she is utterly genuine, totally dedicated and entirely professional and is as constant and predictable as the British weather. Privately she is much less predictable. 'You suddenly find yourself having conversations with the Queen that you can't believe you're hearing,' says a former minister. 'She's extraordinarily indiscreet and very funny – not all that often, but you realize there's another person there who is fascinating and enchanting and girlish. Every now and again I have to pinch myself to believe what she's saying and the questions she's asking me.' Her public persona is very different, very narrow and almost devoid of personality, which perhaps accounts for her universal appeal. She is loved and respected not just in Britain but in the countries she visits all over the world – even republicans tend to have a grudging admiration for her. There has never been a whiff of scandal surrounding her life – and attempts over the years to suggest that Prince Andrew was not Prince Philip's child have never gained much currency. There was criticism over her intervention in the Burrell trial, but that was transitory.

Prince Philip has attracted more controversy. Quite apart from his gaffes, for most of his married life there have been stories and rumours about extracurricular activities. I don't know whether they are true or not, although I certainly know that a number of people who have worked inside Buckingham Palace believe they are true, as do some of the families who have played host to the Prince while he has been taking part in his carriage-driving competitions. It could all be malicious gossip. I don't think it matters one way or the other – at least not to anyone outside the marriage. What matters is whether Philip has been a supportive consort and it is demonstrable that he has. Rude and bad-tempered though he may be, he has put duty before pleasure, worked tirelessly to advance his charities and organizations and made a major contribution to the success of the Queen's reign.

Having known him for years, one former Foreign Secretary believes Prince Philip is the least understood member of the family and that 'his roughnesses', as he calls them, come from the fact that the Prince leads an extremely boring life and every now and then feels compelled to stir the waters. He is a radical within a very traditional cast of mind, and he may not be politically correct, but he's a very good consort. He always notices if the Queen has forgotten to talk to someone or if the conversation has been cut short or doesn't go quite right and is always there to take care of it. And he's right. I saw it myself. During their visit to the Surrey town of Dorking in March 2004, I watched him pick up a disconsolate child with a single daffodil clutched in her hand, who had been desperate to attract the Queen's attention and failed. He went across to the barrier, lifted the little mite over it and told her to go and give the Queen her flower.

*   *   *

Australia has been toying with republicanism for years and, with a sovereign thousands of miles away, there are very strong arguments for changing its constitutional make-up. No one was fooled by the results of the recent referendum and there are many who think that when the Queen dies there is no question that the country will become a republic. It is the affection and regard for the Queen as an individual that many believe has prolonged the *status quo* and made her such a powerful force within the Commonwealth. But that affection and regard does not extend to the Prince of Wales. 'If Charles were to come to the throne either now or in twenty years' time, the British political system would be quite worried,' says a former diplomat, 'whichever political party was in power because of his position vis-à-vis the fifteen or sixteen countries in which the Queen is Head of State, whether they would simply take over Prince Charles. I very much doubt they would given the past – the marriage, the adultery – and given public opinion in those countries. Also any suggestion that he would automatically take over the Commonwealth is very questionable. That is my judgement of public and political opinion in these countries.'

John Major is convinced that the Queen has played a vital role in those countries.

I do not believe the British Commonwealth would be a single entity if we did not have a monarch as the focus for it. Unity is better than disunity and you have some of the richest nations of the world, like ourselves, to some of the very poorest, facing terrible problems and the Commonwealth Conference brings them all together. It is in the nature of life that often there are squabbles, but there is a sense of real comradeship and from time to time these diverse countries act in a spirit of unity which is quite remarkable. When Ken Saro-Wiwa [the writer and political dissident] was murdered by the then Nigerian government during a meeting of Commonwealth Conference, I proposed action against Nigeria and received immediate support not only from Australia and New Zealand but from Nelson Mandela and, surprisingly, Robert Mugabe. Action was taken, because Nigeria's behaviour was outside the principles agreed in the Harare Declaration. Immediately after the Gulf War [of 1993] the Kurds were being murdered in very large quantities. I went to a European summit and proposed pretty much off the top of my head a policy we called Safe Havens for the Kurds; we needed to get it approved by the American government, crucially, and the United Nations. I proposed it at the European Union Heads of Government meeting, got the support of Mitterrand and Kohl and then got in touch with the whole of the Commonwealth. With them and the European Union, I had huge support at the UN, there was a great weight of opinion behind it and the Americans rode in. Whether they would have done without all that support I don't know, but the united Commonwealth meant the UN were immediately on our side and the overwhelming amount of world opinion was behind the concept that we had to do something to help the Kurds. As a result, tens, maybe hundreds of thousands of lives were saved.

I do not believe our relationship with the Commonwealth would be so powerful if we didn't have the focus of the Queen. She is often the point of unity when the Commonwealth is divided. If ever there is a big row about something it is put aside while the Queen is there. There's a genuine and universal affection for her.

The Queen attaches great importance to her role in the Commonwealth and is held in great affection by its member states. But those who have worked with Prince Charles feel that he has never shown quite the same interest. The historic link with Britain will not end with the Queen, but will inevitably loosen a bit. In Britain there is every confidence Charles will succeed his mother and be a very good king – provided he doesn't turn people off by being controversial on political issues. His decision to marry Camilla will never please everyone but the majority of people in Britain are supportive and the announcement has been welcomed by the Commonwealth. In many of those countries Prince Charles is popular and well-accepted, but at the end of the Queen's reign I think the Commonwealth might well think, 'We're an organization in our own right, Britain holds a pivotal position, it was right for the Queen to be head, but is it right in the twenty-first century that it's automatic? It's a group of fifty-three independent nations; it shouldn't automatically be the British sovereign who heads it.' There is bound to be an internal debate about this in the Commonwealth in due course.

The Queen has been exceptional but there is no reason to suppose Charles will not match up. 'Monarchy is better in wartime,' says my senior civil servant, 'having someone to die for.' Would they be prepared to die for the Prince of Wales? 'Yes,' he insists. 'He will change overnight when he becomes king, both himself and people's perception of him. People in this country are very short term in their recollections. Previous controversies will fade overnight. Dignify it with the word "pragmatic" or else "short-term memory" but it's one of the great strengths of this country; but you do need the institutions there as vessels in which you can put these thoughts. Democracy needs institutions; it can't rest on the media.'

The media is probably the biggest question mark hanging over the future of the monarchy. Photographs of the Queen and the Prince of Wales may not be so compelling any more but there is always a market for scandal and will always be one for sex – and with the Royal Family there is usually a means of linking the two. And with a character like Prince Harry on the loose there is potential for disaster. HRH is a very heady title and opens all sorts of doors; and there is no one, with the possible exception of his grandparents, who can say no to him. He is a nice boy but he has no sense of responsibility and no self-discipline – and since his mother died he has had no real discipline from outside either. Loving though the Prince of Wales is as a father, he has never put in the necessary time with his sons and by the time he woke up to the fact that Harry was keeping bad company and running wild it was too late to do anything about it.

It is not his fault that his Zimbabwean girlfriend Chelsy Davy had a chatty uncle only too ready to tell the world that his niece and the Prince had discussed marriage. But if Harry had been more controlled we might not have had to know that he and the buxom blonde enjoyed their first romp in a lavatory cubicle in a nightclub. 'What an awful job,' says Sir Richard Needham, who almost wrote to the Prince of Wales once to say, 'If I were you I'd tell your sons to give it all in; the Brits don't deserve a monarchy.' 'What a monstrous life those two boys have to live. It's all very well saying, "Well, they've got all this money", but that's irrelevant. Why can't they live their own lives? It's really, really awful. They are the only people in this country born into something from which they have absolutely no escape and in which they are hounded, absolutely hounded. The press will get Harry sooner or later – even as an ex-royal he'd be hounded. But the Prince of Wales has got such an incredible sense of public duty he wouldn't understand what I was talking about.'

FORTY-THREE

The Way Ahead

Shortly before 8.30 on the morning of 10 February 2005 I was driving to London when my mobile phone rang – the first of about 58 calls from the media that day. It was the *Sun* newspaper with the news that Charles and Camilla were about to announce their engagement. Could I write something for Friday's paper? A moment later it was GMTV, the programme was just about to end, could I comment before they went off air? Radio 5 Live had an outraged Anglican with whom I suddenly found myself in a heated exchange, and so it went on – Radio Gloucester, Cornwall, Wales etc. – all the way down the M4. The announcement had taken everyone by surprise – even Clarence House – which to Sir Michael Peat's irritation had been bounced into making it public earlier than planned after the news leaked to the London *Evening Standard* (shortly after Tony Blair's weekly Audience with the Queen).

The Prince had first cleared it with the Queen, his sons and the rest of his family at Sandringham over Christmas. He had then popped the question when he and Camilla were at Birkhall over New Year. As soon as she had said 'Yes', Sir Michael Peat set all the formal wheels in motion.

Within less than an hour of the news breaking on that Thursday morning, the world's media had descended on the

Mall, and Canada Gate had turned into a mass of satellite dishes, television trucks and radio cars; and freezing presenters picked their way carefully over a snake-pit of communication cables to stand with their backs to Buckingham Palace and fill-in their viewers on when, where and how the couple would be married and the implications for the future. And on hand were royal watchers, historians, politicians, experts and commentators of every kind to give their reactions.

Most people seemed to be very pleased for the couple, and felt about time too, but my angry Anglican was not alone in his disgust. Talking to ITN outside Clarence House a little later I met a woman who was so appalled by the news she had come all the way across London to express it. 'If Charles is going to marry that woman,' she said spitting out the words, her face twisted, 'he should never be king.' Phone-in programmes called it an insult to Diana's memory, and on BBC *Breakfast* the next morning there were emails from viewers that were so terrible they couldn't be read out. 'The adulterer should not be allowed to marry his whore' was one of the more extreme I happened to see.

But the anger passed and by the weekend there were other matters on the front pages of the newspapers and opinion polls were beginning to suggest that the country was not going to be split so violently down the middle as at first seemed likely. The romantic element was creeping in. Camilla had revealed that Charles went down on bended knee to her, her diamond engagement ring was a family heirloom that the Queen had given them, the Archbishop of Canterbury, Dr Rowan Williams, was pleased they had decided to 'take this important step', the Queen and the Duke of Edinburgh were 'very happy' and had given the couple their 'warmest wishes', William and Harry were '100 per cent' behind their father, and 'very happy for him', and Tony Blair sent congratulations on behalf of the whole government. And photographs of the Prince and Camilla – both utterly radiant – at Windsor Castle on the night of the announcement were enough to thaw even the coldest heart.

A not insignificant part of the reason why they had waited until 2005 to announce their engagement was a sensitivity towards the boys. They didn't want to foist a step-mother on William and Harry before they had fully grown up. Accepting Camilla as a fixture in their father's life has been difficult for them and although they have been genuinely pleased to see him so happy, and genuinely like Camilla – and her children – the issue is complicated. The notion that their mother was a sacrificial extra in a long-standing love story between Charles and Camilla – a line most of the newspapers ran after their engagement – is hurtful. They loved their mother and are fiercely loyal to her memory – and know that Camilla was the cause of her terrifying unhappiness.

Harry has been particularly affected. Whether or not any of this is related to his behaviour is a matter for the psycho-analysts. In the meantime, it is important that a solution be found, before he, like his mother, self-destructs. The answer perhaps is to cut Harry free from the Family Firm. The concept of a Royal Family, of an idealized, closely knit unit that sets a shining example to the country, has had its day. We don't expect our prime ministers' families to be on parade. We certainly don't expect them to play any part in national life, work in government – heaven forbid – or to press the flesh on away days on his or her behalf; and if we elected a president as head of state we wouldn't expect it of his or her family either. If, as Tristan Garel-Jones would have us do, we think of the Queen as Head of State, then a consort and an heir are as many as should be expected to put up with the demands we make of them. The Lord-Lieutenants would be enormously disappointed – they would like more rather than fewer royals – and the charities would miss out. Celebrities and politicians don't have the same impact – even as minor royals – and they seldom have the commitment or the staying power. But there are thousands of charities that don't have royal patronages and they manage perfectly well.

The late Princess Margaret's two children, Viscount Linley and Lady Sarah Chatto, don't feature in public life. Their names come up occasionally in gossip and society columns but they live normal lives, have married normal people and are not held up to public scrutiny. Princess Anne's two children, Peter and Zara Phillips, live normal lives. Not many people would even recognize Peter, he is so seldom seen. Zara is instantly recognizable but that's her choice. She invited *Hello!* magazine into her living room – and bedroom; she wears daringly skimpy outfits to Ascot, parades her boyfriends at public venues and clearly enjoys her celebrity status. And nobody minds. Her antics may upset her family but they do not reflect badly on the monarchy because she is not part it; she doesn't work for the Family Firm. But so long as Harry is expected to, he will attract attention and, because he has already got off on the wrong foot, the media is watching and waiting for the next incident which will come as surely as a London bus.

I can see no purpose in making him knuckle down, forcing him into a mould that doesn't fit. He is never likely to be king so why make him spend his life shadowed by security, visiting factories, opening hospitals, shaking hands and doing good works, knowing that the slightest indiscretion is going to embarrass his grandmother or his father or, in time, his brother? Why not let him step back from it all and do what he wants with his life? His father found it hard enough to carve out a role for himself and he is heir to the throne; the

Army won't keep him for ever; and the Wessexes have already demonstrated how difficult it is to combine royal life with a career. So let him go out and earn a living free from all encumbrances. If his heart is really set, as he said it was, on following in his mother's footsteps and carrying on with her work, he could do it as a private citizen. He will always be a name that any charity would want on its notepaper. And if the time ever came when he was needed to take up royal duties, then he could be brought back into the fold.

Which brings us neatly to the subject of the fold – or The Firm. Lord Airlie and Sir Michael Peat revolutionized life at Buckingham Palace in the eighties when they implemented so many of Peat's recommendations but they didn't alter the basic structure. Every member of the Royal Family who carries out public engagements has their own household with private secretaries and other staff, and although there are channels of communication in place they don't always seem to work. According to Mark Goyder, who is director of Tomorrow's Company, an independent think tank that promotes good governance in business, 'the structure in management terms is three decades out of date. It's not a firm, it's more like a number of tribes, a federation of tribes, and although there is a titular head, corporately it's quite inefficient.

'If you were in General Motors in the 1950s or British Rail in the 1980s you saw exactly those things. Then modern management came along and said this is crazy, we must have a structure that reflects function, must have an organization that is effective with compartments, but united towards a common goal.'

A former Press Officer to the Prince of Wales believes doing away with the households is imperative.

It's divisive. Why have we had this punch-up between St James's Palace and Buckingham Palace? Because they were working for the individuals and not the institution. It creates tensions. The difficulty for ordinary human beings to understand – and I didn't understand until I got closer – is you are not selling a product, or a service or a commodity, you're supporting that individual's psyche and what they are and do every day of their lives; and they can't walk away from it, and we the public owe a sense of responsibility which I don't think we're acknowledging at the moment, in terms of what price they have to pay and what price we should insist that the media should pay to allow them more privacy than they are allowed at the moment.

I am not suggesting a state department to look after the Royal Family but having people who have responsibility for the institution rather than the individuals and who have a code of practice and standards, not dissimilar to the civil service in terms of how they work, so they do the right thing for the institution. In the civil service we had a change of administration; the machinery kept going and was more important than the individual.

One solution, proposed by Tristan Garel-Jones, would be for the Head of State to have a private office that mirrors the Prime Minister's. At No. 10 a series of bright young stars from various government departments work in the Prime Minister's outer office for two or three years as part of the career path. This means they go back to their department with some knowledge of how the Prime Minister's office and No. 10 function. This could be reproduced at Buckingham Palace at the push of a button. It is already moving in that direction but he would institutionalize the practice. The advantage is it would feed back into Whitehall a whole raft of up-and-coming civil servants who, having been doing the briefing notes and writing the speeches, would have an understanding of the Head of

State's functions and an appreciation of how important and difficult it can be at times. He would also do away with the separate households – even the Prince of Wales's, and would route everything through the Head of State's office. 'So if you're a minor member of the Royal Family and you're invited to go and open a hospital in Nottingham, you get on to the Head of State's office and say "I've been invited, should I do it?" And they would say, "Yes, we'll send you a briefing note and a speech." Nothing can do more, in my view, to strengthen the institution than if we all got used to referring to the Queen as the Head of State and that she was provided with the sort of administrative back-up that the Head of State in a country like ours ought to have.'

Another good idea, suggested by a former press secretary, would be to find ways of engaging the public, giving them a feeling of ownership and involvement in the business of monarchy, so that they too understand what the institution is for. She would like to get schoolchildren to do projects for Trooping the Colour, for instance, and let the best ones go into the programme and have the winners meet the Queen; she would like to see ordinary children at the State Opening of Parliament – have them carrying the Queen's train perhaps; and she would like to see people from the Palace go out into the community to explain to people what monarchy is all about. She once asked why the media were not allowed into investitures, given that the Queen was presenting medals on behalf of the country, and was told it would destroy the mystery. 'I was made to feel as though I'd grown two heads,' she says. 'You won't ever get the mystique back but I'm not sure you need it. It's partly the mystique that has produced this lack of relevance.'

There is also a section of the community that the monarchy needs to reach out to. People at the top of the tree are rewarded with gongs and garden parties and people at the bottom of the heap are catered for by the charities with which the Royal Family are involved. Their problems are well understood. But there is very little contact and therefore little understanding of the people in the middle. 'What they have no feel for,' says an equerry to the Prince of Wales, 'is the middle-manager of a building company, who has a £100,000 mortgage on his house and has been told his job is redundant. Monarchy has a lot of support from the working class and the upper class. It's the ones in the middle who feel it's not relevant to them. That's where the issue is. You go to a housing estate on a Wednesday afternoon in November and you know who you're going to meet. Somehow you need to include those others.'

What monarchy needs, like any modern business or organization, is a regular health check; it needs to ask itself why it is there, what it is aiming to achieve, and whether it is being successful. According to Mark Goyder

> a well-led company is one where there's a very clear sense of purpose, of who and what you are and where you come from, clear values and a very clear understanding of all the relationships that are critical to your future success. The other idea we talk about is the licence to operate, the implicit permission that any business has – not granted by a regulator but by reputation, by trust, by the legitimacy in which you're held. In the sense of clear purpose, I wonder if the question has ever been asked of the Queen, what are you here for? Or is that what it means to be the Establishment; that you're so established you never have to ask that question? That might be the answer. In a world in which everyone else questions who they are and what they're for, this is the one institution that doesn't have to answer that question and maybe that is what defines them.

'The Queen appeals to those things which are beyond controversy; the basic values, she enunciates them, she points to
that realm where we are still united despite all the political
shenanigans and argy-bargy. You may feel, sitting in London,'
says Richard Chartres, the Bishop of London, 'that the appeal
of these things ebbs, is ebbing, has ebbed.'

I am wondering whether the monarchy still has the capacity
to overcome the differences of education and community
disintegration. I think the death of the Queen Mother was
an astonishing revelation of the world outside the chattering
classes of the Westminster village, where there is huge cynicism about all of this. Mind you, there's huge cynicism
about everything. It isn't that the monarchy is regarded
as decrepit; it is that we have, astonishingly, an Establishment that seems to want to liberate us from any sense of
constraint or universal value and fundamental meaning.
That's obviously an enormous challenge for an institution
like the monarchy whose whole *raison d'être* is social cohesion pointing beyond the argy-bargy of politics to some
of the deep laws, the abiding themes of all human life, love
and loss, values that we all basically share.

'The Queen didn't choose to be Queen,' he says.

She hasn't competed for her place on the greasy pole. Anyone who knows anything about it realizes what a heavy
sentence it is in some ways and the institution therefore
speaks also about Call, Acceptance of Call, Doing your
Duty, Service, and that is real. Also there's no escape clause,
it's a contract. In all those ways it's a very remarkable institution. However, England is changing so that we may not for
ever be worthy of it. If there is no principled, philosophical

423

support for monarchy then the whole thing depends much more on what, in a celebrity culture, is made of the individuals, how they are used. The Queen is a canvas on whom people project, as well as someone who stands for things. There is such confusion and shame about the British story that it hasn't been taught and communicated for the last twenty, twenty-five years. We feel very sorry for individuals who have lost their story – their memory – they've lost part of their identity, they live an impaired life – but if the community has no sense of its story, if you exalt diversity as the only virtue then you find that you have a giddy, rootless population which can easily be swayed by gusts of indignation and emotion.

As Lord Salisbury says,

By its nature the monarchy is a long-term institution and perhaps the greatest thing in its favour is that it endures while fashion doesn't, politicians come and go and editors come and go. So the fact that it is always there, like the papacy, is a huge strength. It occupies a position no one else does and by occupying it they prevent anyone else from doing so. It's very difficult, not impossible, to have a military coup when the officers are loyal not to the Prime Minister and government but to the monarch. It's very difficult, although much easier now with the European Court of Human Rights legislation and supremacy of EU law, but still difficult so long as judges owe their oath of fealty to the monarch rather than the government, for the law to lose its independence entirely – a keystone of the way our free society operates. It's also very important that people should recognize the monarchy in this context that the Queen is part of Parliament. There are not two parts of Parliament;

there are three: Monarch, Lords and Commons, and ultimately one of the great restraints of being in government is
the feeling that you don't want to drag the monarchy down
into the pit of parliamentary and political dispute although
that is becoming more difficult with the question of the
monarchy's existence being in play. So long as senior politicians of all parties owe a genuine allegiance to the Crown,
always before you do anything, you have to ask yourself,
does this breach the club rules? That is a great guarantee;
but as soon as that consensus breaks down you're in trouble.

Tristan Garel-Jones again concurs.

It's true that power corrupts, absolute power corrupts absolutely; when you're a minister, even if a junior minister of
state, it's quite easy to end up thinking you're quite important, because you have lots of people laughing at your jokes
and telling you how clever you are and writing clever
speeches for you, and you could end up thinking you're
quite somebody; and the beauty in Britain for me is there
are certain positions that no politician can hold, ever. No
politician can ever be Head of State. The Armed Forces in
Britain do not swear an oath of loyalty either to Parliament
or the Conservative or Labour Party or anyone else. Every
officer in Britain is commissioned by the Queen. You can
argue it's all mirrors, but it removes all positions, albeit
symbolic, from the hands of politicians, which is not a bad
thing at all. Even in my case, if ever when I was a whip it
passed through my mind that I was quite important, I had
to sit down at the end of every day and write an eight-
hundred-word letter to the Queen. Another thing that went
with this position, you were a kind of messenger, you carry
the messages from the Queen to Parliament, bits of paper

425

she had to sign, and there were certain moments when I had to put on a morning coat, get into a motor car, go round to the Head of State's office, stand to attention, present the Head of State with certain papers, and go back. It reminds politicians that there is something up there that is the Nation – the national interest – that is going to go on and on and on long after they're dead and buried.

The beauty of all this is because I held these positions [Vice Chamberlain, Comptroller of the Household and Treasurer – all of which go with the whip's job] for quite a long time, all three, one after the other, I had quite a lot of contact with Buckingham Palace and with the Head of State. And audiences – you go in with your bits of paper, and whilst I can honestly say the audiences were perfectly courteous and even amusing sometimes, never once by hint or gesture did the Head of State imply to me that I was some kind of friend, that she was rather pleased I was a Conservative and not a Labour member, ever. I regard this as wonderful. I used to go in there regularly, write her letters regularly, and at the end of the day I have no doubt whatsoever, if instead of me standing in front of her it had been my opposite number, the Labour member for Jarrow, it wouldn't have made a scrap of difference and I think that's something the country needs to know. Certainly a lot of Conservatives think she secretly likes us. That's bollocks. I am a person representing a function which is part of her duty and she does it with courtesy and humour and wit but never, ever, ever on any single occasion did I feel that I was in some way special or my party was in some way special.

The Queen's will be a very tough act to follow but the Prince of Wales has great strengths and rightly has many fans – but he has more detractors. His determination to cling on to Camilla

Parker Bowles at all costs has damaged him and inevitably, therefore, damaged the monarchy. A stronger man would have put the greater good of the institution before his own personal happiness – as his mother, in the same situation, almost certainly would have done.

But he was doing even greater damage by failing for so long to put a ring on Camilla's finger when the majority of the public had so obviously come to accept the situation. It left the way open for so much debate, so much criticism. Shortly before the engagement was announced in February, a powerful group of MPs, led by Alan Williams, a known republican, grilled the Prince's accountants about how he spent his income from the Duchy of Cornwall and how much Charles was paying to support his mistress. In recent years he had begun to look like a victim and victims attract bullies.

And the situation left so much uncertainty about the future. The Queen will be eighty in 2006 and although she is in the best of health – and if she lives as long as her mother, might have another twenty years or more to go – the prospect of Charles being crowned with Mrs Parker Bowles sitting four rows back in Westminster Abbey – or even, on his insistence, at the front – would have caused constitutional mayhem.

Their marriage at the Guildhall in Windsor on 8 April 2005, with a blessing afterward at Windsor Castle, settles all that. It may take time after all the blunders that followed their engagement but I think it will heal a great many wounds that have been festering for years and tie up a host of uncomfortable loose ends. Charles had insisted that he wanted Camilla to be seen as a legitimate part of his life. Now she finally is, and the arguments of whether it was right or wrong for the country, good or bad for the boys, what kind of service it should have been, whether she should have been called HRH The Duchess of Cornwall or something more low-key, and what the Princess of Wales would have thought, disappear. The public didn't want her to be Queen and she won't be. She will be The Princess Consort and have much the same role as the Duke of Edinburgh has in relation to the Queen. There may be opinion polls on whether she should, in fact, be Queen rather than Consort when Prince Charles ascends the throne, and more opinion polls on whether now he is married to a divorcee he should still be King, but there is nothing new in that debate.

And with Camilla finally, officially and legitimately by his side and the divisions and the controversy over, he is a changed character. But he must stop feeling so sorry for himself, stop whinging about everything, stop blaming others for his troubles and start letting people see the enthusiastic, excitable, unstoppable and compassionate Prince that those who know him love and admire. MPs and others might then stop questioning how much he spends and start marvelling at how much he raises for charity, how hard he works and what hope he has brought to so many hopeless lives.

'You can't say to the Prince of Wales, "Why aren't you more like Queen Elizabeth" because he's not,' says someone who knows the family well. He believes that Charles's self-indulgence gets in the way of getting the job done properly. And that, in turn, gives him very little leeway in terms of public tolerance. 'If you're failing in convincing the world you're doing the job properly, then all your personal failings weigh in against you as well, but if you are clearly doing a terrific job, you've got flair and people love working for you, they see that the monarchy has a point. You've got much more capital with the public, and you can afford the inevitable drawing on capital. Charles has been running an overdraft.'

I am sure the Prince of Wales, with Camilla to cherish and

support him, will turn public opinion around, but in the long term it is the institution more than the individuals that matters. It is a continuity act – things go on through thick and thin. Throughout history there have been good monarchs and bad, strong monarchs and weak ones. Charles will be judged by history, when all the facts (those that were not shredded after his wife's death) are revealed and his son is on the throne. William is the great white hope for the future. He said in his interview in November 2004 that the important thing was to keep his feet firmly on the ground.

For a twenty-first-century monarch, that is precisely where they need to be.

Bibliography

I am very grateful to the authors and publishers of the following works:

Allison, Ronald and Riddell, Sarah, editors, *The Royal Encyclopaedia* (Macmillan Press, 1991)

Benn, Tony, *Common Sense* (Hutchinson, 1993)

Bentley, Tom and Wilsdon, James, editors, *Monarchies* (Demos, 2002)

Bogdanor, Vernon, *The Monarchy and the Constitution* (Oxford, 1995)

Brandreth, Gyles, *Philip and Elizabeth* (Century, 2004)

Burrell, Paul, *A Royal Duty* (Michael Joseph, 2003)

Dimbleby, Jonathan, *The Prince of Wales: A Biography* (Little, Brown, 1994)

Healey, Edna, *The Queen's House* (Michael Joseph, 1997)

Hutton, Will, *The State We're In* (Vintage, 1995)

Junor, John, *The Best of JJ* (Sidgwick and Jackson, 1981)

Major, John, *John Major: The Autobiography* (HarperCollins, 1999)

Lacey, Robert, *Royal: Her Majesty Queen Elizabeth II* (Little, Brown, 2002)

Morton, Andrew, *Diana: Her True Story* (Michael O'Mara Books, 1992/1997)

431

Pimlott, Ben, *The Queen* (HarperCollins, 2001)
Sampson, Anthony, *Who Runs This Place?* (John Murray, 2004)

Index

433

Index